THE GUN DIGEST® BOOK

GLOCK

2nd Edition

Patrick Sweeney

Published by

Gun Digest®Books

An imprint of F+W Publications
700 East State Street • Iola, WI 54990-0001
715-445-2214 • 888-457-2873
www.gundigestbooks.com

Our toll-free number to place an order or obtain
a free catalog is (800) 258-0929.

Library of Congress Control Number: 2007942609

ISBN-13: 978-0-89689-642-0
ISBN-10: 0-89689-642-0

Designed by Patsy Howell
Edited by Dan Shideler

Printed in the United States

Contents

Acknowledgments

I'd like to thank the manufacturers who sent me items for this book and who were so generous with their time and knowledge, especially Irv Stone III of Bar-Sto. I would also like to thank Al Allan of Double Action Indoor Range and Chris Eders of Chris' Northwest Gun & Ammo Supply for the loan of pistols, parts, books, knowledge and experience.

And for Felicia, without whom I would not be so accomplished, known or happy.

Dedication

I'd like to thank Jeff Hoffman and the crew at Black Hills ammunition for the supply of ammo they sent. Also, Mike Shovel and Peter Pi of Corbon, and Erik Leslie of Magtech. A new supplier of ammo was the grand old Italian firm of Fiocchi, who sent me some of their new .357 Sig ammo to test. If you have a Glock in .357, you really want to be feeding it Fiocchi.

Memory can be a tricky thing. When I wrote the first edition of Glock I was walking our then poodle Baxter. I tested various parts of the book while walking him, reciting parts out load. It was easy, as he could jump vertically to my head height, and would do so for miles.

As I read through re-wrote and updated the book, I could at times see him jumping alongside me, even though he died in-between the first and second editions.

Felicia and I had to fill that hole in our hearts, and our new poodles, while as smart and good looking, don't jump.

So, for Baxter partly, and Felicia mostly I give you this book.

Introduction

ere we are again, covering things Glock.

So why an updated book on the Glock? I could give you all sorts of good reasons, such as lots of loaner pistols to play with, free ammo, an afternoon with the Glock G-18 and its selector switch, free t-shirts and the fact that my publisher is paying me.

Humor aside, there are good and valid reasons why so many police departments have switched to Glocks – why so many shooters in the marketplace have exercised their right and paid their own money to own a polymer wonder – why Glocks are found on every range in the United States. And there have been changes since the first issue of this book, not the least of which is the change in magazine capacity law, something you should all keep track of when in the voting booth. These things matter.

The Glock pistol has been turned into an icon of violence or manhood. If you want to get a roomful of politicians into an instant slathering frenzy of do-goodism, don't throw out a bundle of campaign contribution checks, flash a photo of a Glock. If you want to be sure your photograph or airbrush artwork ends up on the cover of a rap album, include a Glock. The Glock design exudes a businesslike air unlike any other firearm. Yes, it is irrational to attach an emotional state to an object, but as emotional creatures that is what we humans do. A Colt single action revolver and a Colt 1911 pistol both evoke different responses from what a Glock does, even though they can be just as businesslike and lethal. (And they all show up on x-rays.) The only firearm I know of that has a greater iconic status is the AK-47.

Introduced in the United States in 1986, in short order the Glock went from a curiosity, to the eye of the political storm, to the accepted standard of many shooters and a staple in Hollywood. The radical design and material, the no-nonsense looks, the utter reliability

This time around, Glock came through with loaner guns. No questions answered, but loaner guns.

all combined to make it both controversial and common.

And just to make sure you know where I stand on the issue (firmly in the middle) it is my personal feeling that a Glock has all of the warmth, charm, personality and character of an industrial tool. It also has a standard of reliability, durability and function that I'm not sure other pistols can achieve, even the 1911.

I have to admit, having spent more time with them, and learning more since the first book that I'm starting to warm up to Glocks. Just don't say that so loudly, will you? The rest of the guns in the safe might feel neglected. Glocks are legendary for working right out of the box, every time and without fail. If you were to say to me, "We expect you to put this warehouse full of ammo downrange as quickly as possible, with as few malfunctions as possible," I'd have to go with a Glock as the tool for the job. If you allowed me a lot of enjoyment at the possible cost of a very small margin of reliability, I'd much rather do it with a 1911.

As far as accuracy is concerned, it's hands down for the 1911, but the margin isn't as large as you'd think. For the jobs we ask of a handgun, anything better than three inches or so at 25 yards is gilding the lily.

The fact that some competitions require more accuracy than three inches at longer distances than 25 yards should not distract us from the Glock's reliable performance. Yes, more is better, but just because a Bullseye target has an X-ring that is less than a couple of inches at 50 yards doesn't mean a pistol that can't deliver to that standard is a failure (except as a Bullseye pistol, which explains why you don't see many Glocks at Camp Perry). Glocks deliver as much accuracy as we need and more than many can take advantage of. So much accuracy, in fact, that practical shooting competitors often

don't bother to change the factory barrel for a better one.

When I'm writing about firearms, I try not to say too much about the bad ones. Not that I'm sucking up to the manufacturers (no one who knows me would believe you if you were to assert that idea) – I just don't have the time or room. In most writing projects, I have a specified and limited amount of space, and if I spend it thrashing a bad product I can't get that space back in order to talk about a good one.

But there is no avoiding things here. This is a book about the Glock. If I leave something out, my editor will be the first one wanting to know why, and the readers would be the second. So, you'll get the straight skinny from me. Good, bad, indifferent and downright strange, it's all here. Or at least as much as I could get my hands on. In the world of firearms, you'd think pages of essentially free advertising (while running the risk of falling into the clutches of a cranky gun writer) would call for lots of free and loaned "stuff." Guns and ammo, and parts, and accessories. T-shirts, posters, key rings, etc. Guess again. I wrote about what I could get. If I couldn't get it, I wasn't going to speculate, at least not much. I have to get my hands on stuff to write about it. What I got, is in here.

I'd like to regale you with tales of how Glock flew me down to Smyrna, put me in the Presidential Suite and let me shoot to my heart's content on the test-fire range. I'd like to be able to tell you all that and more, but it wouldn't be true. Every request of Glock USA was met with the same answer: "We have to ask Austria." In the first book and the second, not a single question could be answered without approval from above. If I wanted a repeat of the answer, I had to call them and ask, as no one in Smyrna knows how to dial a phone and return a call.

Apparently I was not being singled out in this regard, as getting anything out of Glock is apparently a quixotic quest best left to those with more time, patience and a better calling plan than I have. And a longer deadline. I did, however, make use of my position in the gun world to actually lay hands on loaner guns. Apparently I am among a few dozen in the writing field who actually get loaner guns from Glock. However, no questions were answered.

I did manage to talk to some representatives of Glock, people who had been through the Glock armorer's school (which I've done, not once but twice) and people "in the know." Some were more helpful than others, but the reaction was always the same. "Don't quote me." "Don't name me." "No photographs of the G-18."

Why? I don't know. I was able to glean a great deal of useful information from the contacts I was able to make. I was also left scratching my head when otherwise reliable sources offered contradictory information. And me with no way to ferret out the truth about the conflict by asking the head office. (There were times while talking to recent graduates of the armorer's school in my attempts at gathering information that I felt more like an interrogator than a writer. I also got some very suspicious looks, too.)

I can only surmise that the media savaging Glock received when they first showed up in the United States has made everyone in the chain of command a little shy about releasing any info. Did any of the treatment hurt my feelings? As I've said before, no one who knows me would believe that my feelings were hurt.

Glocks. I don't love 'em, and I don't hate 'em. I guess that makes me the only one. I really do respect the engineering that goes into them, and I sure did have a lot of fun writing about them, even without help. ♦

CHAPTER 1

History of the Glock

A long time ago, in a galaxy far away, there was a time when blue steel and hardwood ruled the earth. That time, remembered so fondly by the denizens who strode the planet (referred to as "old farts" by some), is also known as "PG", or Pre-Glock. And how some of us do like to prattle on about it.

The pre-Glock world would seem strange to many who have grown up knowing the Glock. There was a time when plastic was viewed as a cheap substitute for real substances (i.e. wood, metal, leather, and for those really stuck in the nineteenth century, stag grips) and not something to depend on. Oh, you might have plastic plates and forks for eating with and on at a picnic, and you certainly didn't object to plastic being used in crappy Japanese trinkets, but you wouldn't depend on it for anything important. Japanese camera makers had by the 1960s finally carved a niche for themselves, one viewed with respect if not actual

warmth. No longer did you have to depend on hideously expensive German optics to get a good photograph. But except for cameras, manufactured goods from Japan were viewed as junk. (Little did anyone know about the cars to come, but I digress.) Modern digital devices are all plastic. Indeed, if someone were to come out with a cell phone made if metal, we would all look at it with a bit of wonder, a lot of astonishment, and perhaps even a bit of fear.

American handguns for many decades of the twentieth century consisted of a few staples: the Colt 1911, the Colt Single Action Army and copies of it, double action revolvers from Colt and Smith & Wesson, and an ever-shifting cast of niche manufacturers usually trying to carve off a portion of the existing market, like Dan Wesson in the double action revolver market segment. In the early 1950s Smith & Wesson had designed and begun production of a double-action pistol, the Model 39.

They did it primarily because the Army had expressed interest in replacing the 1911 as a sidearm. The thought went something like this: "The .45 kicks too much, sidearms aren't really useful in winning fights, and we are having too many accidents with the single-action 1911. What we need is something simpler, lighter, with less recoil and a safer action." S&W gave them the M-39. Colt offered the lightweight commander, or the option of converting existing 1911s and 1911A1s to 9mm (pre-dating the IDPA division by half a century.) But due to the large inventory of 1911's still on hand the Army decided to keep the .45, and S&W was left trying to convince the buying public of the 39's value. By the late '60s they hadn't had many takers with the public at large, but had convinced a few police departments. The big news of the 1970's came from three events: the design bureau of S&W, when they came up with the Model 59, a high-capacity DA pistol; Bill Ruger's jumping into the DA revolver market;

and high velocity lightweight hollowpoint handgun bullets.

One big problem the S&W M-39 had had with gaining acceptance was its limited capacity. Who wanted eight or nine shots of 9mm when for the same size you could have eight shots of .45 in the Colt 1911 or Lightweight Commander? But when the M-59 came out, with its 15-round magazine, the game shifted. Suddenly, a police officer could have 16 rounds in the gun, and 30 extra shots on his belt. Compared to a revolver, with six rounds loaded and 12 or maybe 18 extra shots in "dump pouches," the 59 started to look a whole lot more attractive. And the development in the early '70s of "reliably" expanding softpoint and hollowpoint

bullets added more fuel to the fire. What fire, you ask? Why, that fire was the police market, and the police market could do a lot for a manufacturer who was intent on garnering the rest of the market for handguns.

Up until 1976, it seemed that Bill Ruger had it in for Colt. He made single action revolvers, revolvers that were as modern as the Colts were not, rugged as the Colts were not, and chambered for cartridges that the Colts were not. And none of those shortcomings could be overcome by Colt simply by improving the alloys they used or improving the heat treatment of their SAA. Ruger also made the most-excellent Mk I rimfire pistol, such a durable, accurate, reliable

and economical to produce pistol that it killed the Colt Woodsman. The Woodman was a Browning design, rugged and durable, but expensive to produce. No, Colt needed new designs, new tooling and a new plant. It wasn't going to get any of those as a wholly-owned subsidiary of a giant conglomerate that viewed it as a cash cow.

In 1976 Bill Ruger unveiled his double action revolver design, and the executives at S&W had to know they were in for a struggle. S&W fought back in the DA revolver market, but also prepared to lure police departments into converting to their pistol. And why not? Their pistol (and any hi-cap pistol) offered more shots, faster reloading and what one old-time shooter of the period I knew referred to as an "on-off switch." Revolvers don't have safeties. Then and now, a too-high percentage of police officers are killed with their own sidearms. The safety on the S&W offered an additional incentive to convert.

What about Europe? After all, wasn't it the German firm of Walther that devised the first reliable double action pistol design? Didn't German firms make reliable pistols? Yes, and yes. But the P-38 pistol wasn't something American shooters wanted except as a souvenir from The War. It was a single-stack 9mm with an annoying tendency: the top cover over the loaded chamber indicator would occasionally

In addition to pistols and magazines, Glock makes holsters and mag holders.

fly off under recoil. It held not enough rounds, and those rounds weren't big enough for American shooters. Other DA designs were too small: fine as backup guns, but not as a primary sidearm. And the big stumbling block was cost. I was working retail in a gun shop in the early 1980s when I bought my first 1911 for $175. At the time, a Heckler and Koch P-7 went for nearly $600. German pistols were too expensive and too "fiddly." (Translated from crusty-oldtimer-gunspeak to read: too many control levers.) Other European designs were either curiosities like the French Mab or war souvenirs like the French, German,

Italian, Czech and Hungarian pistols I often picked up for a song as they drifted through the shop.

But all the designs involved steel or aluminum, no plastic. Well, plastic was used in some small things, like magazine basepads, the backstrap or grips on some models, things like that. Despite the advice of the father in "The Graduate," by the early 1980s plastic had not yet taken over the world. It was a curious situation for modern shooters to contemplate. After all, standing on a streetcorner today so many of us are simply dripping plastic, even if we aren't carrying a pistol.

The cell phone, pager, Palm Pilot or personal organizer, even shoes, belt and some clothing, are synthetic or plastic. For those of us who avail ourselves of the right to carry a concealed weapon, add a holster, spare magazine pouch and perhaps even (this is after all a book about the Glock) a pistol.

What changed all this? The Austrian Army and Gaston Glock. In the late 1970's the Austrian Army decided it needed a new sidearm. Actually, most of the various armies of Europe needed new sidearms. They had been too busy since the war replacing obsolete rifles and machineguns, mortars,

The old style frame (right) and the third generation.

In the old days, parkerizing was the toughest finish going. Glock's Tenifer finish laughs off treatment that would make this old S&W cry. And no one uses revolvers in the military anymore, anyway.

tanks and artillery, with modern designs to pay too much attention to pistols. And truth be told, as far as most armies are concerned, pistols are dangerous oddities that soldiers insist on having. Left up to the choice of many commanding officers, pistols wouldn't be allowed. Except for officers, of course. Handguns are dangerous, prone to malfunction, easily concealed, rarely used and ineffective in combat. Just ask the commanding officers who have to explain accidental discharges, injuries or even deaths to Senate Sub-Committees. And yet the soldiers who actually got shot at all seemed to insist on having one. (My father served in Europe in WWII, and he said once the men in his unit had gotten their

first experience of being shot at, everyone laid hands on and carried a pistol just as quickly as they could. You'd find more pistols than decks of cards in the pockets of the soldiers in your average WWII combat infantry company.)

Having spent the time since WWII improving rifles, machineguns, mortars and other "proper" military weapons, the Austrians, like so many others, had simply been too busy to do more than use what handguns were available from the old days. Well, by 1980 the war had been over for 35 years. Those pistols were wearing out. So, the word went out that the Austrian Army would be conducting pistol trials, and all who were interested could show up and have their designs tested.

Enter Gaston Glock. His company had been making plastic objects for a few years and had recently won contracts to make utility knives (another thing the frontline troops insisted on, to the concern of higher command), entrenching tools and a grenade casing. The knife was not just a success with the government (150,000 units delivered in the first contract) but also on the civilian market, too. I have been told that contrary to perceived wisdom, the guys downrange do not carry expensive, custom knives. As one decorated vet has commented to me, "If you drop a $400 custom knife off the boat, you feel compelled to go in after it. If you drop a Glock, you just buy another." The grenade is a plastic casing with the fragments incorporated into the plastic, which only required a bursting charge and fuse assembly. And no, Glock did not provide any grenades for testing for the book. Nor would I have been all that eager to test some.

Gaston Glock figured that a pistol is a manufactured product, right? So why *not* enter a design? However, not being a firearms manufacturer presented him with a slight problem: he didn't have a pistol to enter. Hmm. Well, with bright engineers, drafting supplies and a grasp of the manufacturing process, designing one shouldn't be a problem, right? Tell that to the Japanese. Not to pick on them, but they had spent decades before WWII trying to come up with a suitable sidearm, and failed. Have you ever tried to shoot a Nambu Type 14? I have. Or keep it or a Type 94 running? Or perhaps ask the Italians, who came up with a durable pistol in the M-1934, but not one destined for much of a future. The French had been at the repeating sidearm design business for a century at that point, and still didn't have much to show for their efforts. And as for competition, there was the German juggernaut of Heckler & Koch. H-K had lots of designs, and if local manufacture was a requirement, then building a plant wasn't much of a problem, right? So how was it that Gaston Glock was able to get it right? One would argue he got it right because he hadn't done it before. One of the largest problems in getting a new design accepted by an established manufacturer is not just the "not invented here" syndrome, but also the "we don't have the tooling" syndrome. Why invent something new when you can simply modify what you have? So once a design is implemented, it evolves (or not) into future products. The history of manufacturing is replete with "evolved" designs. When the US Army in WWI wanted a high-volume weapon for individual soldiers, did they draw up something from a clean sheet of paper? No, they tried to fit the Pederson Device

to the existing Springfield rifle. When they wanted to produce a better rifle after WWII, did they start over? No, they modified the Garand. When many armies were first handed machineguns, they mounted them on wheeled carriages and gave them to the cavalry. Or artillery. Why? The cavalry was the premier arm of many armies, so give the new guns to them. Or, "it's mounted on wheels, so give it to the artillery."

But before he could go on to make history, first Gaston Glock had to meet the requirements of the Austrian Army.

The Request for Proposal

Anytime a governmental agency wants to buy something, they have to specify just what the item is. Have you ever seen the printed requirements for providing chocolate chip cookies to the United States

Armed Forces? I have. Pages of description detailing size, weight, ingredients, packaging, and so on. The number of chocolate chips, and the ingredients that go into them, is specified. The packaging is specified. The acceptable shelf-life is specified. All of this for cookies.

A slight digression: some wonder why the Army doesn't improve the M-16. After all, "we all know" what the better parts are, right? The inertia of the mil-spec system is what keeps it from happening. Nothing can be done until 17 different committees sign off on it. And they all demand proof, proof that the change is warranted. Otherwise, they won't do a thing, as they do not want to be on the hook for squandering government money.

The Austrian Army was no different, but since what they wanted was a bit less known a property (and they were looking for new designs, too) they had to be a bit less

An early (and bulged) Glock barrel from a G-19. Made in November of 1989, according to the date code.

dogmatic. For their pistol trials, the new pistol (known as the P-80, as testing began in 1980) was not a known quantity. It wasn't as if they had a particular one in mind and simply wanted to write up a set of rules that it, and it alone, could satisfy. I encountered the requirements when the Glock was new, and hung onto my copy as what the Austrians wanted seemed quite rational and focused (if you overlooked the beauracracy-specific items). Rather than subject you to a literal translation of the technical German, I've taken the liberty of listing them in their plain English equivalents, followed by my personal observations of each.

The Seventeen Requirements

1 The firearm must be a self-loading pistol.

And who in the latter half of the Twentieth Century would entertain the idea of a revolver? While the American law enforcement community was still greatly enamored of revolvers in 1980, the military organizations of the world had long since given them up. Revolvers simply aren't as durable as well-made pistols, at least not in the military environment.

2 The pistol must fire the 9mm Parabellum round.

Before and during WWII, the Armies of Europe had used many .32 and .380

The contract said the pistol must not require a magazine loader, but a loader sure makes life easier. And it's easily moulded, too.

pistols. Many European police departments still did as late as 1980. Austria wanted to make sure they had something up to the task of military use, and also wanted to make sure they could use NATO ammo stocks. Why not .45? Besides being viewed as an American affectation, the .45 was not a NATO-spec round. 9mm Parabellum was and is. Disparage it all you want as a "europellet" launcher, but a 9mm handgun is a lot better than the .32 or .380 options.

3 Filling the magazine must be possible without the use of tools or assistance.

Many 9mm submachinegun magazines require the use of a magazine loader to get them past the half-full mark. If you lose the loader, you can't physically load the magazines past a dozen or so rounds. Austria didn't want their pistol to be saddled with an extra (and essential) piece of gear.

4 The magazine must have a minimum capacity of eight rounds.

You may be a a good machinist, but that doesn't mean you're good at design. The Nambu Type 94 on the left is simply awful as a pistol although the machining on this example is pretty good.

The Austrian army didn't want to have to depend on magazine loading gizmos like this subgun loader for an Uzi.

And why not? Their current pistol, the P-38, held eight. Why should their new one hold any less? Notice that they did not specify a higher number or require a large capacity. Austria did not view the handgun as a fighting tool. It was simply an emergency tool. If you needed more than the eight, 10 or 12 rounds a pistol holds, you needed more than a pistol, and too bad about not having more ammo in the pistol. Only we crazy Americans view the handgun as more than simply a badge of office or emergency tool, and require more.

5 *All manipulations for preparing to fire, firing, and manipulation after firing must be single-handed capable, right-handed and left-handed.*

Smart. No extra safeties that required two hands to work. No safety mechanism that made it impossible to work left-handed or couldn't be manipulated by an injured soldier. In an emergency, you never know what you're going to have to do, and making the pistol simple and easy to operate improves the soldier's odds of surviving his exciting job. The then-issued P-38 is a good example. The safety works only for right-handed shooters. If you pick it up with your left hand, pushing the safety off is nearly impossible. To remove the magazine you have to use both hands, as the magazine catch is a latch on the bottom-rear of the frame. A pistol such as the Beretta M-92 also fills this requirement, with its ambidextrous decocking lever. (The magazine button can be used one-handed right or left handed even without being switched from one side to the other.) The 1911, as standard issue, didn't. To meet the requirement it would have to have an ambidextrous safety, and in 1980 ambi safeties were a custom gunsmithing option. If you want an example of the worst possible pistol in this category, look at a Nambu Type 14. Yes, the magazine button looks like it is a "one push" affair, but not so. The leaf spring on the front of the frame traps the mag, and you have to pull it out with your left hand. (I guess there were no left-handed Japanese officers.) But far worse is the safety. Unless you have thumbs like an orangutan, you cannot push the safety to Fire with your shooting hand.

6 *The pistol must continue to function after being subjected to shocks and strikes, and dropping onto a steel plate from two meters.*

Again, a smart requirement. What use is a pistol if it stops working after being dropped? After all, the one thing you can count on is that if it is issued to a soldier, it will be dropped. If falling on it, dropping it, or having it struck by some other piece of equipment renders it inoperative, what good is it? The "two meters onto a steel plate" part is another smart idea. It is the greatest height you'd expect a soldier to be dropping a pistol and retrieving it. Steel is easy to duplicate, so you don't have to add pages of description about just what the impact surface is.

7 *Dismantling of the main parts for cleaning, and reassembly, must be possible without any tools.*

Just like the loading tool for submachinegun magazines, the Austrian Army didn't want to have to issue a specialized cleaning kit with their pistol. At most, they wanted to simply have to issue 9mm bore brushes and patches. And those brushes and patch holders could be designed to work with the already-issued rifle cleaning kits. Soldiers are notorious for "losing" unessential gear. A pistol is essential, but if it requires a kit (however compact and light) holding the specialized screwdriver, tool and other gear simply to maintain said pistol, well, that kit will end up in a ditch somewhere. Better to adopt a pistol that doesn't require a kit. You don't think so? Again, ask my father. Apparently the GIs of WWII who were actually shooting at people stripped the bipod and carry handle off the BAR. At most, it saved a pound. But they wanted that pound gone. A specialized cleaning kit? You'd find that in the ditch.

8 *Maintaining and cleaning of the pistol must be possible without any tools.*

I think they went a little overboard on this one, but perhaps they were influenced by the legendary ability of the AK-47. You can literally disassemble an AK with your bare hands, and slosh it around in a reasonably clean puddle to clean it, and it will still work. Expecting a pistol to be able to do the same is asking for the stars. However, if this requirement was intended to weed out pistols such as the HK P7 (as one example) that might need a specialized hollow brush to clean the gas piston rod, then I can understand it.

9 *The total number of parts must not exceed 58.*

Why 58? The P-38 has 58 parts, and the Austrians didn't want to have more than that. Again, why 58? Hey, they had to pick a number. The pistol they had at the time held 58, so it seemed like as good a number as any. Would 57 have been a better figure? Fewer parts does not necessarily mean a more robust firearm, nor more parts a less robust one. You can get too hung up on things like this. They had to pick a number, so the

Austrian Army went with what they already had. That Gaston Glock was able to cut that number almost in half, to 33 parts in the G-17, was amazing.

10 *Gages, measuring and testing devices must not be necessary for long-term maintenance.*

In any military organization, the holy grail of small arms is parts interchangeability. If a soldier or armorer has to use a dial caliper to measure a part and see if it has worn beyond a certain measurement before changing it, forget it. That design will not be accepted unless the weapon system is so important, or so effective, that the Army can justify the hassle. Handguns don't fall into either category. The test of "will it work?" should be manipulation of the part or weapon in question. While the unit soldiers must be able to repair broken small arms by scavenging parts from other inoperative weapons, at higher levels the armorers would have gages and tools to measure parts.

11 *The manufacturer has to provide the Armed Forces at the time of supplying the pistol with a complete set of drawings and exploded views. The drawings must show measurements, tolerances, specify materials, surface treatment and all necessary details for the production of the pistol.*

The Austrian Army didn't want to be buying a pig in a poke. If the maker wasn't willing to tell them just what things were made of, or what the tolerances were, the Austrians weren't interested. After all, unless you know what the dimensions are supposed to be for a part, how can you check to see that you're getting what you wanted in each delivery? How can you tell if the manufacturer is actually fulfilling the contract? For many years after the US Armed Forces were buying M-16s, the US government didn't really know what dimensions Colt was making those rifles to. It wasn't until

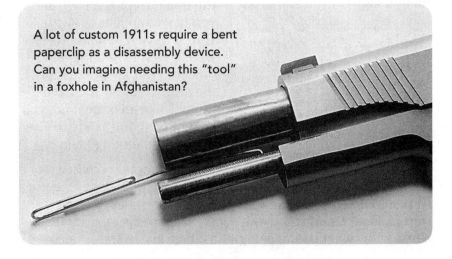

A lot of custom 1911s require a bent paperclip as a disassembly device. Can you imagine needing this "tool" in a foxhole in Afghanistan?

the "A2" upgrade that Colt had to specify and reveal to the Army, Navy, Marine Corps and Air Force just what the manufacturing dimensions were. (I suspect that so much of the manufacturing and assembly of the M-16 was handwork that even Colt didn't know for a long time.)

12 *All component parts must be interchangeable without any adjustment.*

The Austrian Army did not want to be saddled with the need for files, hammers, fixtures, etc. As an example, with proper design, and rigid dimensional controls at the manufacturing level, every extractor can fit in, and work properly in, any Glock. Assuming you're using the correct caliber, of course. After all, expecting a .40 or .45 extractor to work in a G-17 is expecting too much of the design. Using the proper caliber, no filing or tension adjustments are required to install a new extractor in a Glock. As the best example of the situation the Austrians wished to avoid, the 1911 pistol is notorious for requiring hand-fitting of new parts.

13 *In firing the first 10,000 rounds, no more than 20 malfunctions are permitted, even if the malfunction does not require tools to correct. [The requirement also specified the type and source of the ammo, hardly germane to our discussion.]*

The Austrians weren't going to be sold an unreliable pistol simply because most of the malfunctions could be corrected "with a push of the thumb there" or a "slight tap here." They wanted something reliable. Twenty malfunctions in 10,000 rounds was a stiff standard in 1980. The then-new sport/tactical training of IPSC refused competitors a re-shoot because of malfunctions. In 1980, a standard of "one malfunction in a thousand" was a high (or low, depending on how you looked at it) but achievable goal. Austria wanted nearly that standard for issue guns

> **Twenty malfunctions in 10,000 rounds was a stiff standard in 1980.**

and ammo, and not just clean and tuned competition guns using tested competition ammunition. In the early 1980s, self-loading pistols were still trying to escape their unreliable reputation. Yes, in 1910 the Colt pistol had fired 6,000 rounds without a malfunction. But in the minds of many shooters, something had gone wrong since then. It would take a lot of convincing to get them to accept a pistol over their revolvers.

14 *After firing fifteen thousand rounds of standard ammunition, all parts must be secure and intact. Then a*

Proof load will be fired, and all parts must still be secure and intact.

What use is a Service Pistol with a short service life? Fifteen thousand rounds may seem like a lot to some shooters (it seemed like a real lot back in 1980) but for a military organization, it isn't. And back then, things were a lot different. A unit might have a dozen pistols on the range for qualification and practice. The rest would be locked up in the armory. Every one of those dozen pistols would be used to fire all the ammunition used for practice and qualification for the unit. The range guns might see thousands of rounds a year while the armory guns were never fired. Despite the average soldier not firing more than 100 rounds a year through a handgun, those range guns would be beaten to death. Today, you can probably go to your local gun club (you *do* have a gun club you belong to, don't you?) and find a whole host of shooters who shoot 15,000 rounds a year. Some of them might actually shoot that much, but the average at your club is likely to be a couple of thousand rounds.

We expect more today, and we've been getting it since 1986.

15 *The firer must not be endangered by case ejection.*

Simple enough. I've had occasion to fire pistols that

threw their empty brass right in the shooters face. Some Soviet submachineguns eject brass straight up, and will fall back on the shooter if he stands still. The brass must go in a safe (to the shooter) direction.

16 *The muzzle energy must meet a certain minimum when firing a specified round.*

Nothing underhanded about this requirement; they wanted the energy the round had to go downrange. No ultra-short barrels, no tricky gas systems that bled off energy, just standard performance from a standard round.

17 *Pistols achieving less than seventy percent of the maximum points will not be released for military use.*

The highest-scoring pistol on the trials wasn't going to be adopted unless it achieved at least 70 percent. Nothing new in this either, as the US Army told Colt and John Browning (along with the rest of the entrants in the pre-1910 trials) to go back and work on their pistols several times. The whole process for the 1911 took ten years. That Austria did it in a lesser timeframe, nearly a century later, is cause for congratulations.

In order to design and produce a manufactured product, you need to know what exists in the marketplace. Otherwise, you may be in the embarrassing position of bringing to fruition a brand-new AMC Pacer or

Yugo. Gaston Glock set about studying what existed, and what had been built. He also looked to the component parts from the viewpoint of "how to make them" with known technology, rather than simply copy existing designs. One example is the slide. Why are slides machined from bar stock or forgings? Because in many cases that is the way many of them were initially made when they were first designed. John Moses Browning designed his firearms to be made from machined forgings because that was the state of the art in manufacturing when he was working. I can well imagine his delight and design efforts if someone had dropped the manufacturing specs of a

heavy-gauge steel pressing plant onto his workbench.

You can do a lot with castings and with sheet-steel stampings. But the learning curve is steep and expensive. Also, those approaches and their products, castings and heavy-gauge steel pressings, can and do have their own drawbacks, and in the end Glock decided to go with a slide machined from bar stock. The square cross-section of the design makes machining easy, especially with modern CNC machining centers.

Since the firm of Glock made many things from moulded polymer, the idea of making a frame for a pistol was a natural. Including a pressed steel skeleton for the

A Glock G-19 with factory holster.

slide rails was an obvious enough idea, and the striker-fired mechanism required only a suitable method of making it safe to be utilized. The firing pin safety, drop safety and trigger safety covered those bases.

At the conclusion of the Austrian trials (basically, measure and weigh everything, count the parts, then shoot the pistols until they are all broken or the ammo is gone) Glock won. The Austrian Defense Ministry placed an order for 25,000 pistols. Not bad for a company that hadn't made any pistols (or any firearm at all) before the trials.

The American Market

Meanwhile, back at the ranch, things were getting interesting. Police departments across the country were starting to want more than what revolvers could deliver. Crime was up. The accepted .38 Special had been given a boost with lighter bullets, jacketed hollowpoints and higher velocities, but it still only held six shots. Shooting fast double action shots was not a skill easily acquired. It didn't help that the customary police training and competition course, the PPC course, required a relatively slow firing rate and rewarded inconsequentially-measured levels of accuracy. And getting six more rounds into action with a revolver was not quick or easy. Even with the relatively new speedloaders, reloading a revolver was such a difficult job under stress that many officers simply carried another loaded gun. Called the "New York Reload" after the department where the practice was most common, adding six more shots meant packing the weight of another revolver.

Bigger calibers for greater-than-.38 Special power meant even larger revolvers. There had to be a way to get more. There was, and Smith & Wesson had been working for decades cultivating it. The high-capacity 9mm pistol was their answer. Instead of six shots, then six more later, the S&W M-59 carried 14 shots. And 14 more in a couple of seconds.

The 9mm cartridge wasn't any better than the .38 Special in stopping power (by whatever measure you cared to use) but at least an officer could have as many as he needed at the time he needed them. And the .357 Magnum, while offering more stopping power, wasn't something every officer could qualify with. Too much noise, too much recoil, too much practice required to stay good with it.

In the early 1980s, you had the choice of S&W, or their competitors H-K and Sig. Since the imported pistols cost at least twice what the S&Ws cost, that wasn't much of a choice. And in the midst of all this, the FBI got the kind of headlines neither they nor any other law enforcement agency wanted: Agents Killed in Shootout. Eight FBI agents stopped two men wanted for robbing armored cars. The ensuing shootout was messy and costly, and it was a high-

The third generation frame, with light rail and finger grooves.

shooting-volume affair. Both suspects were killed, two Agents were killed and five of the six others were wounded. In the few minutes of the shootout, there were 119 rounds fired for sure, and perhaps more than 130.

If their regular shift experience and knowledge of their own precinct wasn't enough to convince officers they needed more ammunition on call, the FBI Miami shootout certainly woke them up. All of a sudden gunshops couldn't keep high-capacity 9mm pistols in stock. Departments that had hung onto their revolvers through years of study and "paralysis through analysis" suddenly had to switch, and switch right now. The WonderNine Wars were on. Making the market even more exciting was the recent introduction of the Ruger P-85. It was large, it was a little clunky, but it was $50 to a $100 less than an S&W, and almost two thirds less than the cost of the aforementioned German pistols. Since 1982 Glock had been courted by many US importers who wanted to be able to sell a durable, reliable and inexpensive pistol in a hot market. Instead, Glock formed its own importing corporation and brought the pistols in themselves. The first Glocks were imported in January 1986, and in less than 10 years there were a million in the US.

Getting permission to import was not as easy as

you'd think. Did you know that there is a scoring chart for imported pistols? Yes, and if your pistol doesn't score well enough (74 points) you can't get permission to import it. A sample pistol gets points for things like safety mechanisms, length, weight as well as points for target fripperies like a thumb rest and adjustable sights. The G-17 fell short of 74 points, mostly due to its light weight. At one point per ounce, the 25 ounce M-17 couldn't rack up enough points. (All contestants are weighed with an empty magazine.) To remedy that problem, Gaston Glock came

> ## Did you know that there is a scoring chart for importing pistols?

up with an adjustable sight. It was the cheapest, flimsiest and most useless part you might ever have seen on a production pistol. (Although I've seen some US-made pistols that would give the Glock adjustable sight a run for that title.) Could Glock have modified the G-17 in some other way? Probably, but every potential solution would create other problems. First, of cost. To change the frame design meant altering a mould or moulds. Changing the slide to add weight meant changing the tooling and re-springing it for a heavier

slide, and then the new pistol wouldn't fit the old holsters. And would the current users accept the changes? Could Glock have simply added some otherwise extraneous part that was heavier? Perhaps, but when you're dealing with bureaucrats who can nix your whole corporate investment in a fit of pique, do you want to test them by adding something superfluous like a steel grip frame filler?

No, Glock took the smart way out and made a disposable adjustable sight. Once the pistols came into the US with the adjustable sights, it was perfectly kosher to remove them when customers declined that option and asked for the fixed sight instead. (Glock later changed the frame moulds, but that story is related in the Importation chapter.)

Then there was the matter of the serial number. Federal Law was quite clear: a serial number had to be permanently stamped into the frame. Good idea, but how to stamp polymer? In an amazing display of common sense, Glock was allowed to incorporate a steel plate with the serial number on it into each cast frame. The way I said that makes it sound like Glocks didn't have steel serial number plates before. No, the Customs and State Departments simply accepted the existing design. That's the amazing part. With the import hurdles out of the way, Glock was free to ship pistols and parts from Austria to Georgia, where they had set up their American headquarters.

At first, the Glock product line was simple. One pistol, the G-17. When it came out there was all kinds of outrage and controversy. On the gun owners' side it was simple stuff like the designation G-17. No, not because it held 17 rounds, or the Austrian Army had some secret code with their seventeen requirements, but because it was the seventeenth product Glock had made. On the part of Glocks competitors, the question of the durability of the polymer frame came into question. (The frame proved quite durable enough, thank you, although the front sight has always been a question mark.)

On the legislative front, things were not so easily settled. More than one journalist tried to raise a stink about the polymer frame and its near-magical ability to evade metal detectors. In an x-ray machine a Glock looks just like what it is: a pistol. If a metal detector is properly adjusted to detect more than the fillings in your teeth, it will beep plaintively when you attempt to pass a Glock through it. But when you're up against those who don't like you (and buy ink by the barrel) even the truth is not much of a defense.

But the truth did prevail (mostly, although you'll still find people who think a Glock is something that is invisible to modern

technology) and the Glock has stayed with us. Mostly what happened was the Glock was bought in large numbers by police departments. Its one thing for journalists and politicians to kick around gun manufacturers, but when the Chief is going out and buying the vilified object it becomes difficult to persist. The first big departments to buy Glocks were St. Paul, Minnesota, and Miami, Florida. Soon everyone was looking at Glocks, and the resulting media frenzy quickly had everyone aware of the new kid from Austria.

The Glock and DoD

In the early 1980s, the United States was also going through pistol trials. The idea was to finally follow through on the early 1950s program of finding a "more reliable, less recoiling, safer pistol" to arm the troops with. The program was a model of efficient scientific endeavor. The subject pistols were treated to hot and cold, wet and dry, thousands of rounds of ammunition, and even the infamous mud test. The mud was not just a bucket of dirt from the range, but a specified mixture of graded components. So much sand of a specified average diameter, dirt of a particular composition, etc. Pages of specs just for mud. (That's our procurement buearacracy!)

And I can't help but think the tests were rigged. Oh, don't get me wrong, I don't think the fix was in for any particular pistol, I just think

they were making sure the 1911 wasn't going to make it. After all, if you're testing state-of-the-art 9mm pistols fresh off the assembly line, and comparing them to high-mileage 1911s left over from WWII, Korea, and Vietnam, who do you think will win? Which pistol or pistols will be more accurate, reliable and durable? But then we all have our own personal conspiracy theories, don't we? I just have to wonder what kind of a 1911 has an average service life of fewer than 5,000 rounds? As an example of rigging the results, the testers found that the test 9mm pistols were either less accurate than, or only marginally more accurate than, the comparison 1911s. The result was a crash program to improve the accuracy of the 9mm cartridge. They developed a "new" service load for the 9mm, which was a bullet as accurate as they could make it. And then they compared it to the old .45 round. (The technical term for this is "comparing apples to cinderblocks.") Applying the same improvements to the .45 bullets would have restored the relative accuracy levels.

In all this testing, the Glock was conspicuous by its absence. Why? I don't know. It's a mystery that Glock has yet to reveal to me.

Today's Glock

At the moment, Glock offers pistols in all the major calibers considered as serious competition, defense and hunting calibers. When I wrote the first edition of this book I predicted that there would not be any new calibers forthcoming in the Glock lineup. Boy, was I wrong. Not only did Glock add a caliber to the lineup, they invented their own in the process. Can they do it again? Well, at the risk of eating yet more crow in this Third Edition, I'll say "no." If they did, where would they put it? Smaller than 9mm? The .380s already cover that. A Glock in .25 Auto? To steal a quote from a movie mogul of decades ago, "they'd stay away in droves." Bigger than .45? I can't see making a frame we could hold.

But, I'm willing to be wrong if it means more Glock stuff to play with, test and write about

A decade ago, there were some thoughts of a Glock carbine, but the market for a carbine proved too small to warrant the development and tooling costs. After all, why go to the trouble of making a Glock carbine, only to try and shove the HK MP-5 off its pedestal. Since the first book, the MP5 has been shoved off its pedestal, but not by a Glock carbine. The AR-15 has emerged as the new police patrol carbine. Given the now-established base of AR users, and the ongoing efforts to replace it with a piston

variant, the field would be crowded indeed for a Glock carbine. The market has moved on, and I do not expect to ever see a Glock carbine.

A prediction from the First Edition was that at the moment, the future of Glock looks to be a matter of refinement. If the desires of shooters shifts, then more products will be developed, but for now Glock is concentrating on making their current lineup better. Personally, I'd be very interested in a single-stack .45 ACP that is sized to match a Government 1911. With the Safe Action trigger, Glock reliability, and a frame whittled down from the huge

A Beretta M-93: three-shot bursts and not as much fun as it looks.

double-stack grip of the M-20/21, I think Glock would sell a bunch in the US. Especially if they use a .45 proportioned slide for this model, and not the slightly-lightened 10mm slide they use on the G-21. But then, they're selling bunches of stuff in the United States without my input. And a new mould is so very expensive.

So I said in the previous edition of this book. And then Glock went and introduced not only the 37, 38 & 39, in .45 G.A.P., but they modified the 21 with the 21SF, or Short Frame. My prediction record is starting to look pretty tattered. (Not that that will stop me.)

History in the Making - the Glock in Florida

One of the first big departments to adopt the Glock, the Miami PD as a customer was a big coup for Glock. Buying 1,300 pistols beginning in the Fall of 1987, Miami got the ball rolling for Glock.

At the 2002 USPSA Factory Gun Nationals I had the opportunity to watch Armando Valdes shoot his Glock and to talk to him about the adoption of the Glock by the Miami Police Department, where he is a Training Supervisor and Sergeant. Back in the late 1980s and early 1990s Armando was quite an up and coming IPSC shooter and was all the more noted for using a box-stock Glock. At the time, the 1911 ruled the roost, and

there were no categories for the pistols that police departments used. If you wanted to shoot with a Glock you had to shoot it against expensive custom 1911s or Springfield P9s (an early EAA/CZ-75 import), and they all had compensators on them. Now there is a Production Division, and if you want to do well there you almost certainly need to be using a Glock. Or you can do as Dave Sevigny has done and shoot a Glock in Limited. Many others shoot Glocks in Limited Ten. IDPA is aswarm with Glocks.

Armando had been exposed to firearms as a kid, going to a range in the Everglades with his dad, but wasn't exposed to a formal training program and competition until he joined the Miami PD in 1982. As with all the other officers, using an S&W M-64 on duty almost always meant the competition to enter was PPC. There, you shoot revolvers double-action, within generous

time limits at a tiny X and 10 ring. When the Glock was introduced, one of the reasons it had been adopted was the perceived need for a double-action handgun for law enforcement use. Many police administrators felt that handguns had to have as many "safety" features as possible, to preclude accidental discharges. (Whole books can and have been written on this subject alone.) The Glock not only fit the description but was a high-capacity pistol to boot. But Glocks aren't particularly suited to PPC, so to get practice with it, Armando tried his hand at IPSC. And found he was good at it.

In the course of testing the G-17, Miami PD threw it, dropped it, submerged it and tried everything that might be encountered in police work in Florida on it. Salt water didn't faze it. Sand was no problem. Sweat? Get real. In the course of testing the pistol, Armando put a lot of ammo through

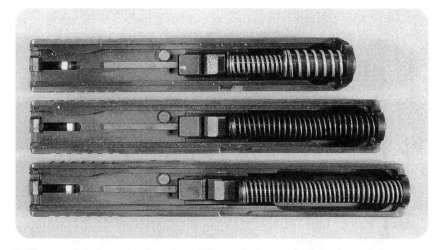

Different slide lengths, but they differ only forward of the breech face. Everything in back of the breech face is the same, which simplifies manufacturing.

So many of the things 1911 gunsmiths (and shooters) love to do, like lowering an ejection port, don't apply to Glocks.

his. Then, during teaching and annual qualifications (and match use) it got more. He finally shelved his G-17 at the 67,000 round level when the department went with the G-22. By the mid-1980s, 67,000 rounds wasn't a lot of ammo for IPSC shooters. But it was a ton of ammo for the average police officer, even those who taught or competed.

The adoption of the 40 came in a roundabout way, unlike other departments. Officers were carrying their G-17s and G-19s on and off duty. Some had requested to be able to use the new Glocks in 40 as off-duty weapons. The big advantage was the increase in caliber without needing to change holsters, magazine pouches and the like. And the grip was the same size, so if you could handle one you could handle the other. So Armando looked

into the situation, wrote up a proposal, and was rejected. The comment from the brass was, "If it's so good, why adopt it as an alternate off-duty weapon? Why not adopt it as the departmental duty weapon?" So, he re-submitted the proposal as a change of duty weapons, and Miami started the whole process over again. Durability, accuracy and reliability testing proceeded with several competitive products included in the program, and you know what? Glock 40s sailed right through. (As an aside, when the new Glocks showed up, they had a special prefix: "MIA." The Chief got MIA 0001 and Armando got MIA 0002.) They now issue G-22s to uniformed personnel, G-23s to detectives and G-27s for undercover use.

In the course of testing, they went through truckloads

of ammo and couldn't break the guns. In the course of issuing them for use on duty, some started breaking. But not how you'd expect. Departmental practice and qualification for Miami PD consumes about 300,000 rounds of ammo annually. Where they found pistols breaking was in the magazines. (In all of them: 9mm & .40, G-17 and G-22.) It seems that when it came time to make magazine changes, officers would rip them out of the gun and throw them to the ground. "I saw officers actually take extra time and effort to throw the magazine down, rather than simply let go and let it fall," said Armando. "The follower hold-open tab would break off under the abuse, and the pistols would start failing to lock open when empty."

The solution was simple: teach them not to hurl the magazines, and check and replace the followers as needed.

After suffering a devastating knee injury on duty, Armando had to go through surgery and physical rehabilitation. He spent a year in restricted duty, hobbling around the station, and was gone from practical shooting competition for several years until his knee was strong enough to take the running, jumping and crouching. Back in the saddle again, he's cutting a new swath through the competition, with an utterly stock G-22.

And the Glock just keeps on gobbling up market share. ♦

CHAPTER 2

How the Glock Functions

To paraphrase *A Tale of Two Cities*: "It is like any other pistol, and it is unlike any other pistol." In many regards, the Glock is just like any other pistol. It is a modified Browning, tilt-unlock locked breech pistol that is actuated by recoil. It feeds from a magazine inserted through the grip, it fires one round per pull of the trigger (except for the extremely entertaining G-18) and it locks open when empty.

Of the eight steps to function for a self-loading pistol (feed, chamber, lock, fire, unlock, extract, eject, cock) it does seven of them. Well, seven and a half of them.

The ubiquity of the Browning tilt-barrel locking system is such that pistols that use some other system are notable by their rarity. One such is the H-K P7, or "Squeezcocker" pistol. It bleeds gas through a port just in front of the chamber, and the bled-off gas impinges against a piston that keeps the slide closed – at least long enough for the chamber

pressure to fall to normal levels before the inertia of the slide overcomes the falling pressure against the piston. Then the slide simply blows back like any pocket pistol would. The extremely rare Auto Mag used a gas port to unlock and cycle a rotary bolt, like a rifle bolt as found on the AR-15. The immense Desert Eagle uses much the same type of system.

But non-Browning locking styles are rarities in handguns. Why is the Browning (and variants of it) tilt-barrel system used so much? For the size of the cartridge, the mechanism can be very compact. The Browning method uses fewer moving parts than others, and it does not depend on specific rates of gas flow or chamber pressure to work properly.

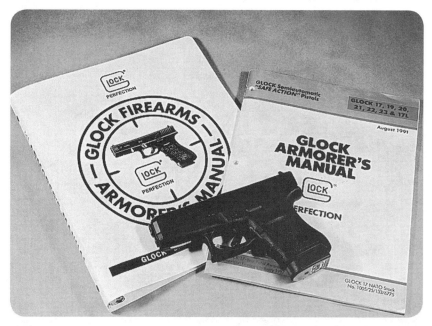

There have been several different versions of the Glock armorer's manual, and they're all slender volumes. It isn't hard to learn how to keep a Glock running.

The Glock's design makes Glock barrels much easier to manufacture. The hardness of the Tenifer finish prevents the kind of peening visible on this 1911 barrel.

The Browning system is very forgiving of powder burn rates. From the fastest to the slowest, the system really doesn't care much. But anything that uses a gas port has a relatively narrow range of port pressures within which it will work properly. Get too far out of that range and you'll have an unhappy gun. A friend of mine purchased the P7 when it was first available. He and his buddies (a bunch of them bought their own) basically killed their P7s by reloading ammo with the "wrong" powders. The ammo they loaded would work just fine in their Hi Powers, but not in the P7s.

One big drawback to the gas-port system (HK P7 or Automag) is its inability to work with cast bullets. While this is a concern mostly of American shooters, it still is a drawback that the Browning tilt-barrel system does not have at all. The gas-port acceptable range of gas pressures to work limits reloaders to a handful of powders. If the pressure is too high the system is worked too hard. If the gas port pressure is too low, the system doesn't work at all. (Except for the H-K P7, where things work in the opposite: a too-high port pressure reduces function, and a too-low port pressure leads to excessive function.) The Browning system depends on the momentum of the bullet and powder overcoming the inertia of the moving parts. Within a very broad range, much broader than other systems, the Browning tilt-barrel system will function with 100 percent reliability.

Having set upon a crash course in pistol design at the beginning of the story, Gaston Glock knew that he had to use one of the variations of the Browning tilt-barrel locking system. What he settled upon was quite simple. Instead of locking lugs machined into the inside upper surface of the slide, as on the 1911, he used the ejection port itself as the locking lug area. The top of a Glock barrel is rectangular in shape, corresponding to the ejection port of the slide. The barrel locks into place in the opening, and the simplicity

The Glock's barrel locks to the slide using the ejection port shoulders as engagement surfaces.

of the arrangement makes manufacturing much easier. Rather than the elaborate machining setup of the 1911, the Glock is very simple. Unlike the tall barrel/locking block system of the Beretta M-92, the Glock's is compact and low.

On the bottom, the unlocking occurs via the cam. Instead of the separate link and pin, as found on the 1911, the Glock design uses a cam surface, similar to the P-35 or Browning Hi-Power. Like some variations of the P-35, and unlike the CZ-75 variations, the Glock's cam is not an oval. It is an angled cam surface underneath the chamber. Again, the design allows for a simpler manufacturing process and a simpler job for an armorer or gunsmith replacing a barrel.

Let's pick up the process halfway through your firing a Glock.

The Easy Seven

You've just fired a round out of your Glock. As the slide

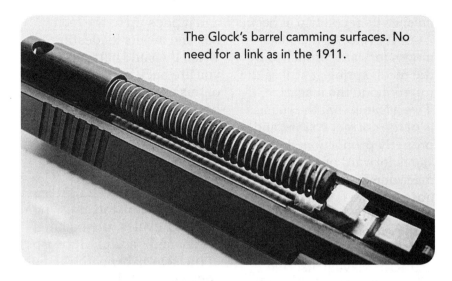

The Glock's barrel camming surfaces. No need for a link as in the 1911.

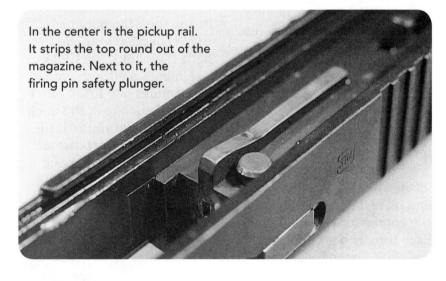

In the center is the pickup rail. It strips the top round out of the magazine. Next to it, the firing pin safety plunger.

The Glock's extractor on the rim of a testing dummy, shown in a Glock cutaway model.

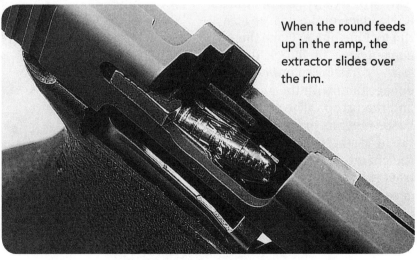

When the round feeds up in the ramp, the extractor slides over the rim.

finishes its recoil trip, it begins its next cycle. As the slide moves forward, propelled by the recoil spring, it strikes the top round in the magazine. If we assume that the round is of the correct caliber, and properly proportioned, it slides forward out of the magazine feed lips until its nose hits the barrel ramp. There it tilts up, camming out of the magazine, up the ramp, and its rim slides under the extractor. Having inserted the round in the chamber, the slide then pushes the barrel forward. The barrel cam rides up the locking block until the locking surfaces on the top have fully engaged the slide. The last bit of travel covers (and re-establishes) the locked dwell time, and once the slide has completed its forward travel it is ready.

You pull the trigger again, and the chambered cartridge fires. The force of the combustion through the case thrusts backwards on the slide. Locked together, the slide and barrel travel together for a short distance (the "dwell time") before the angled face of the cam strikes the locking block. Once the cam engages the block, the barrel cams down out of engagement with the slide and then stops. The slide keeps moving, extracting the now-empty case from the chamber. When the slide travels far enough, the empty case strikes the ejector and is propelled out of the pistol. The slide in its travel uncovers the next cartridge,

and it pops up to the feed lips and awaits its destiny. When the slide bottoms out, you are back at the beginning of this exercise. What we have missed is the entirety of "Cock" and part of "Fire."

How the Glock Cocks

Simple, it doesn't. At least not as other pistols do. When the 1911 cycles, the hammer is cammed back until the tip of the sear is beneath the full-cock notch of the hammer. When the slide goes forward, the hammer impacts the sear tip and then the hammer stays cocked. (Or at least that's the plan.) The Glock design uses a striker instead of a hammer and firing pin. I can see someone in the back getting a bit nervous. "If the Glock uses one part instead of two, and it doesn't cock when it cycles, then is the striker resting against the primer each time?" Every time this question comes

up, the class squirms. No one wants to be handling, let alone carrying, a pistol where the striker or firing pin rests directly against a live primer. The answer is no, it doesn't rest against the primer.

The Glock design has two internal safeties and one external safety, and the striker has two positions besides striking the primer when fired.

The internal safeties are the passive firing pin safety and the drop safety. The external safety is the trigger safety. The striker positions are full-cock just before release, and the disconnector position.

The five-sentence summary of the Glock trigger operation is like this: When you pull the trigger, you cock the striker from its resting (but not contacting the primer) position until it reaches full cock, where the trigger bar is cammed downwards out of engagement. When the trigger cams down, the striker

The firing pin tail in its normal at-rest position.

No external safeties on the Glock. If you don't want to fire, don't press the trigger,

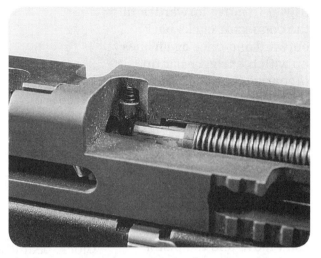

The firing pin resting against the firing pin safety plunger.

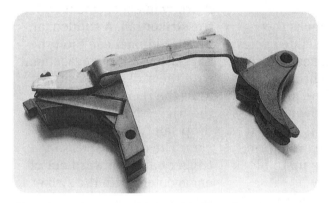

The trigger bar assembly, attached to the ejector block.

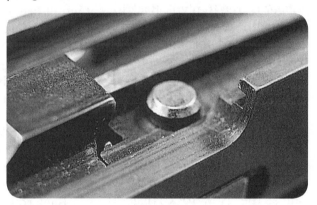

The firing pin safety as it appears on the bottom of the slide.

goes forward and fires. When the slide cycles, it flexes the connector inwards away from the trigger bar, allowing the trigger bar to pop back up into the striker path. When the slide closes, the striker is held back by the rear of the cruciform (i.e., the back end of the trigger bar). When you release the trigger you re-set the mechanism, allowing the

The firing pin and its safety at full cock, moments before firing.

The firing pin safety plunger at the moment the firing pin strikes the primer.

trigger to move forward until the connector clicks back outward and once again lines up with the trigger bar tip, preparing the Glock for firing. Let's take these one at a time and look at them in detail.

Trigger, Trigger Bar, Passive Safety and Cam

The external safety is on the trigger. If you don't depress the safety, the trigger can't move and the pistol won't fire. When your finger depresses the safety, the trigger is free to pivot. Back in the ejector block, the trigger reset spring determines the feel of the initial trigger pull, or "slack" as it is called. A light spring means a light slack. A heavier, or early-engaging spring, means a heavier initial pull, similar to a revolver trigger pull. Most shooters know this kind of pull as the "New York Trigger" after the New York Police Department, who wanted a trigger pull that as completely as possible replicated the pull of a double-action revolver. There are now two New York Trigger springs, an olive-colored one (the lighter of the two) and an orange one.

On the top forward part of the trigger bar is the passive safety arm. Up in the slide there is a spring-loaded plunger that blocks the striker. The safety arm pushes the striker safety plunger out of the striker's path when you pull the trigger. If you don't pull the trigger, the plunger blocks the striker and prevents firing. Drop the

The trigger bar tip and the connector just before the trigger stroke.

Glock, beat it with hammer, or drag it along behind your car (I've seen all three) and it won't fire, because the passive safety blocks the striker. When the slide cycles, the trigger bar loses contact with the passive firing pin safety plunger. The plunger is free to press downwards. When the striker is stopped by the rear of the cruciform, the plunger snaps up to block the striker path.

Back to the pre-firing sequence. As you pull the trigger, the trigger bar is cocking the striker. As it is moving, the trigger bar is sliding along the shelf of the drop safety. The drop

safety prevents premature downward movement on the part of the trigger bar, keeping it firmly in engagement with the striker tail. A sudden jar, drop or impact can't jolt the trigger bar out of engagement with the striker, releasing it. At the rear of its travel, the trigger bar clears the drop safety and strikes the cam. The cam pushes the trigger bar downward out of engagement with the striker, releasing the striker.

The angle of the cam determines the force needed to disengage the trigger bar from the striker, and thus the felt trigger pull. It is possible to fine tune the Glock trigger

The trigger bar contacting the connector.

The trigger bar cammed down out of contact with the firing pin, releasing it to strike the primer.

pull into many variations by changing the cam and the trigger return spring. You can have a light and clean trigger pull very much like that of the 1911, with no apparent force needed in the slack, or you can have a long and persistent trigger pull very much like that of a double action revolver. We'll go into that more in later chapters, but keep one thing in mind until you get there: you can't just swap parts willy-nilly. Some combinations of springs and cam will create inoperative Glocks. Some will have trigger pulls so heavy you can't fire them, and other won't re-set.

The Suite of Safeties

The trigger safety blocks the movement of the trigger simply by bearing against the frame. Until it pivots out of the way, nothing is going to happen. Some criticize the Glock for this feature, posing the possibility of something getting into the trigger guard and depressing the safety. True, but the Glock isn't

unique in that regard. On almost every other handgun made, if you let something get in the way of the trigger while holstering (the most common object being a finger…I'm not kidding),they will fire. To be fair, the Glock does not have a slide-mounted or frame-mounted safety. So if you <u>do</u> allow your shirt, jacket, keys or something else to get into the triggerguard when holstering, you'll have a loud noise as a result.

The trigger safety came about from the extreme drop tests Glock performed. Apparently, if you dropped an original-design Glock from enough height, and it landed on the back of the slide, the mass of the trigger was enough to cock the striker and release it, firing the pistol. One might call it poetic justice, as the pistol would be pointed at the person who dropped it. One might also call it an aspect crying out for another mechanical block, which is what Glock did.

The passive safety blocks the striker until the trigger has been pulled. In

operation it is similar to the firing pin safety found on Colt Series 80 pistols and the firing pin safety of a host of other pistols. Unlike the Colt, the Glock passive safety doesn't interfere with a good trigger pull, or cause firing malfunctions, and it shouldn't be altered or "tuned." Make sure it is clean, very lightly oiled and properly assembled, and leave it alone. The Colt passive safety is over-rated as a detriment to good trigger pull. Many are just fine as-is, and a good gunsmith can easily make a Series 80 trigger pull feel just like a Series 70. The smart gunsmith doesn't bother working on the Glock passive safety; it doesn't need any work.

The drop safety is the simplest, as it doesn't even move. Its purpose is to block the trigger bar and prevent its inadvertent disengagement from the striker until the trigger bar has been pulled fully to the rear. With the drop safety in place, the striker is tightly locked from ever reaching the primer until you pull the trigger.

The drop safety at rest.

The drop safety, with the pistol ready to fire.

The drop safety in the fired position.

The Disconnector

On many pistols, the disconnector is a separate part. The disconnector acts as a link between the trigger and the sear. On the Glock, the disconnector is a raised portion of the slide track. The raised portion flexes the connector inwards, out of the path of the trigger bar, letting the trigger bar overtravel the connector cam surface. When you release the trigger, the trigger bar moves forward, and before it comes to rest the connector can flex outwards so as to once again line up with the trigger bar cam tip.

A pull of the trigger fires the Glock again.

Disassembly

For complete disassembly the early Glock ads pushed the fact that all you needed was the famous Glock Armorers Tool Kit: a single 3/32" punch. Well, that's all you'll need unless you plan to go swapping sights and such. To change sights you'll need more. But not much. A small

The rear of the slide, with the firing pin tail, disconnector shoulder and the anti-seize compound Glock daubs on. (Don't clean off the compound – let it work in.)

screwdriver like those used to fix eyeglasses, a dental pick and a small needlenose pliers are all the extras you'll need for most work. A sight pusher is a definite asset when it comes time to change or adjust your rear sight. And in any case you'll need safety glasses. The Glock is typical in that it has parts that are worked by springs. When you go to take some of those assemblies apart, you release them from their compression.

There is the distinct possibility of parts being launched across the room. It is depressing to have to patch drywall. It is expensive to have to replace glass or china. It is a tragedy to have to go to the emergency room and have a Glock part removed from your face. Trust me, outside of romance novels women do not find eye patches appealing.

To disassemble your Glock, first make sure is it unloaded. No, I mean make sure! Unlike other pistols, an essential step of disassembly of the Glock is to dry-fire it. If you get casual in checking, sooner or later you're going sit down to disassemble your Glock and in short order put a hole through something. Save yourself the razzing from your shooting buddies and the frosty looks from your wife, and check. I make light of it, but it is possible to put a hole through more than just your TV or bookshelf. Check it, and check it again.

A note that may not be out of place here: At the last couple of classes I

Unload and dry-fire to disassemble...

...then retract the slide a short distance.

attended at Gunsite, they had dealt with the problem of accidental discharges in the hotel rooms with two approaches. For those of you who don't know, Gunsite is in Arizona, which is an Open Carry State. If you want to carry a handgun, just don't let your coat cover it, and you're fine. As a result, many of the students at Gunsite drive to their hotel at the end of the class wearing a loaded pistol. It has to be unloaded in order to clean it, and to do draw and dry-fire practice.

With hundreds of people in a year's time practicing tens of thousands of draw and dry-fire strokes, you can bet one will be a live-fire stroke. Heck, one of the guys in my party did it. Noisy and nerve-wracking? Sure is. Dangerous? You bet.

So, Gunsite did two things: they made special pistol cases, and they told the students that anyone who has an "ND in Quarters" (a negligent discharge in the hotel room) that they'd be dismissed from class. The pistol case? A hard-plastic single pistol case with a carpet-covered slab of steel cemented in it and a target stenciled on the carpet. For draw and dry-fire practice, open the case, stand it on a desk, unload and show clear, and commence. In the event of an AD/ND, the steel will stop and fragment the bullet.

I thought it was such a neat deal that I have ever since used a piece of steel with a target on it as my dry-fire and Glock disassembly

While holding the slide back, press the disassembly lever down on both sides at once and let the slide go forward.

target. If the firearm is loaded (shame on me!), yes, I will lose a bit of my hearing, but at least I won't put a hole through the wall.

A few years ago I ran into Steve Camp of Safe Direction, LLC. He makes pistol cases that are built of Kevlar. You use the case both as a transport case, and as a safe direction (thus the name) in which to point when loading or unloading. With so many States now issuing carry permits on a regular basis, a lot more people are carrying, and thus loading and unloading on a daily basis. I now use a Safe Direction case or wall target,

instead of the steel plate. The biggest advantage of the Safe Direction method is that if I do have an AD, the bullet will be contained in the case, and not splattered and launched by a steel plate.

To return to disassembly: with your unloaded and magazine-less Glock in your hands, dry fire it. Now, keeping your firing hand thumb where it is, pivot your fingers up over the slide, and pinch the slide back a fraction of an inch. (The manual suggests 2.5 millimeters, or a tenth of an inch.) If you pull too far you'll reset the mechanism and have to dry-fire again. Hold the slide back.

With a little imagination, you turn turn your Glock into just about anything, including a competition Open gun.

With your other hand, pull the disassembly lever down on both sides at once. Holding it down, ease the slide assembly off the frame. You now have two assemblies, slide and frame. Once you get a feel for the gyrations of Glock disassembly, you can do it so quickly and smoothly that someone who isn't familiar with the process won't see what you did. Not that Glock disassembly is a parlor trick or magician's sleight of hand, but it can go quickly.

Slide Disassembly

Turn the slide over and look at the recoil spring. It should be a contained assembly. Glock upgraded recoil spring assemblies in 1991 to a captured system, where the spring is held to the guide rod even after it comes off the slide assembly. If yours isn't a captured system, Glock will change it for you. Upgrade it when you get the chance. (One good way is to go to a GSSF match. The on-site armorer will upgrade anything on your pistol that is out of date.)

The rear of the recoil spring assembly rests in a circular cutout on the bottom of the barrel. Press the base of the guide rod forward, and lift it out of the barrel seat. Set it aside. Now press the rear of the barrel up (you're holding the slide upside down) from the ejection port, and pull the barrel out of the slide. Unless you need to get into the striker assembly, you're done taking the slide apart.

To clean, wipe the crud off the rails and breechface. Get the small end of your brush under the extractor to get the grunge out of that area.

If your Glock is brand-new, you'll notice a copper-colored goo on the underside of the slide, to the side of the cartridge rail. It is a special anti-seize compound and lubricant that Glock intends to be burnished into the surface of the steel. Leave it alone. It will gradually disappear over time, as the cycling wears it in. Once it is worn away or obscured by firing residue, feel free to scrub the underside of the slide. Swab the barrel out and lightly oil it, and reassemble in the reverse order.

What if you have a comped barrel, like those found on Open Division guns in USPSA/IPSC competition, and the barrel won't come out? Lift the chamber end out of the ejection port and run the barrel forward. You'll now have clearance to swab the barrel and wipe the slide and breechface clean.

Striker and Extractor

At the rear of the slide you'll see a cover plate. Underneath the slide is the clearance slot for the striker tail. At the forward end of the slot you'll see a second, polymer shoulder. Stand the slide on its muzzle on a hard surface. With your disassembly punch, press the striker sleeve shoulder toward the muzzle. The slide of the Glock is thin at this point,

and you may, if you are over-enthusiastic, chip the slide. Not to worry, your Glock will work just fine with this small "ding" on it.

The striker sleeve bears against the rear plate. Once you've pressed the sleeve forward, you can prepare to slide the rear plate down out of the slide. The striker assembly is under a good deal of spring tension. If you simply slide the cover plate off and pull the punch out you can launch the assembly across the room or into your face. Slide the plate partway down until you can see the edge of the striker assembly. Then get your thumb over the assembly and slide the cover plate the rest of the way off.

The factory says to slide the "slide cover plate" down with your thumb. They must have people with really strong thumbs in Austria. Here is where your little screwdriver comes in handy. Use it to

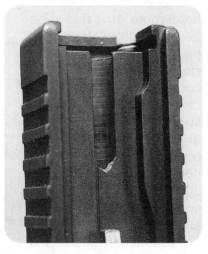

If you aren't careful in pressing the striker sleeve on disassembly, you'll chip the slide. (It'll still work fine, though.)

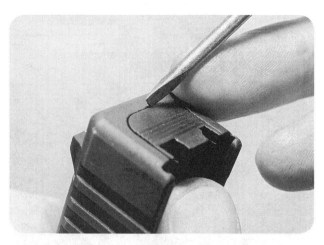

A small screwdriver is useful in prying open a tight rear plate during disassembly.

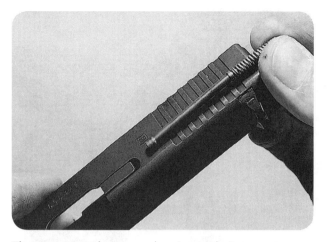

The extractor plunger and spring in their correct orientation.

pry the plate down a bit, enough that you can get some leverage with your fingertips to pull it free. When you have the slide cover plate out, turn it over. You'll note a recess moulded into its face, a recess that fits the rear of the striker spacer sleeve. The spacer sleeve rides in that recess and prevents the plate from dropping down when you reassemble.

Pull the striker assembly out, and then pull the extractor spring and plunger assembly out. They are one piece, and you needn't pry them apart. Turn the slide onto its side, with your hand under the ejection port. Depress the firing pin safety plunger and the extractor will fall out of the slide into your hand. Then lift the firing pin safety and its spring out.

At this point you have a slide with only the sights attached to it, and the channel sleeve or striker liner installed. You don't need to remove the striker liner unless you are going to

replace it. And you only need to replace it if you've been shooting in a very sandy and or dusty environment and need to replace it because it has gotten chewed up – or because you haven't paid attention to the owner's manual, which told you not to oil the striker liner or any part of the striker assembly. Oil attracts grit, which chews up the plastic of the striker liner, the striker cups and the spacer sleeve. Once the sleeve, liner or cups get chewed up, you start getting light firing pin hits due to the added friction on the striker as it travels forward on its merry trip to the primer. (The typical need to replace the striker sleeve comes from two groups: one law enforcement and one military. The law enforcement group are marine officers, who spend a lot of time on boats, near beaches and in the salt air. The military group are those who have to swim to shore and or wade ashore. The result for either group is a pistol with lots of

salt and/or sand in it, and a premature demise of the channel liner.)

What to do if you've got a chewed up sleeve on your hands? Replace it. I must say that in the nearly 15 years after the introduction of the Glock that I spent gunsmithing, I never had to replace one. The subject is covered so quickly in the armorer's class that I have no recollection of the process from the class. How to remove it? Rather than spend large amounts of money for the custom Glock tool (if it exists) go to the hardware store. Buy a three and a half inch long 5/6" lag bolt, and a section of 3/8" dowel. Turn the lag bolt into the channel liner and once it has enough bite, pull the bolt and liner out.

This is obviously a destructive removal. However, you should not remove the liner except to replace it. Since it has to come out anyway, and you are replacing it, who cares that it gets chewed up? If you find that

Once the plunger is out, press the firing pin safety.

The firing pin tail in the slide stop.

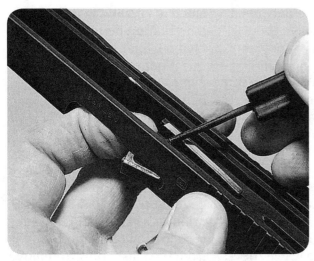

Pivot the extractor out while holding down the firing pin safety.

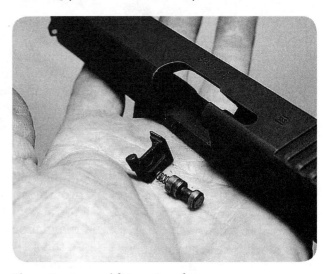

The extractor and firing pin safety.

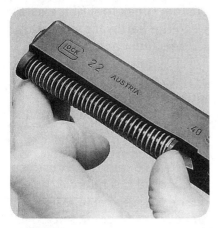

The recoil spring is a captured unit, at least on guns made since the early 1990s.

the bolt can't get a bite on the liner, use a fine cut file to cut the end of the bolt like a tapered tap. (Those who have one can simply use a 5/16" tap.) Scrub the striker channel out and use the dowel to press the new liner in. The new liner goes in beveled end towards the breech.

Striker Assembly

The striker assembly itself sometimes needs cleaning, either from large amounts of ammunition leaving powder deposits behind, or from getting dirty or muddy. Usually, hosing it with a cleaner and letting it dry before reassembly is quite sufficient. Sometimes, however, you need to take it apart due to the extreme amount of crud that has built up. You can disassemble it with your bare hands, but a disassembly fixture makes it much easier. Luckily, you have a disassembly fixture lying on the table in front of you: the slide.

Turn the assembly around and insert it backward into the slide. Rotate it slightly so the tail of the striker stops on the outside of the channel. Now gently compress the striker spring and remove the retaining cups from the front of the striker. Ease the spring forward. Lift it off the striker, then pull the striker and spacer sleeve out of the slide. Remove the striker from the sleeve. You're done except for the cleaning.

All told, an experienced Glock Armorer can have the slide off and detail-stripped in less than a minute flat.

One curiosity that you'll probably never see are the amphibious spring cups. The regular striker assembly fills the channel liner so well that if the striker tunnel is filled with water it may not fire. Glock developed the amphibious cups so that they provide gaps for water flow. The cups are so strictly controlled that Glock will not release them to regular armorers. They only go to law enforcement agencies and military organizations, when requested on letterhead. (One Glock rep told me they are a "factory install" item only. You want amphibious cups, send your Glocks in and they'll swap them for you.) Are they dangerous? Will using them out of water make your Glock malfunction? Explode? No. It is simply another demonstration of the European firearms manufacturing mindset. The

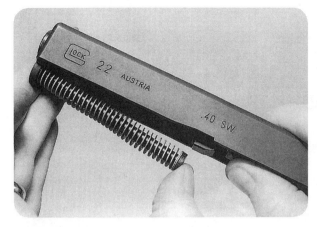

Hook your thumb on the recoil spring rod, press toward the muzzle, and lift it away from the barrel.

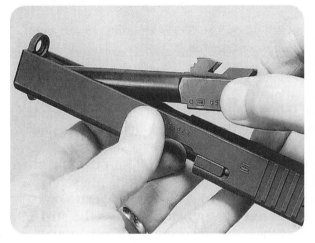

The barrel lifts out and away from the muzzle. It's a convenient way to make pistols, but it's tough on gunsmiths when they're trying to install competition compensators.

cups were developed for a secret, special operations military organization, and as a result they must forever remain a controlled item.

Reassembly

Yep, it's the infamous "reverse the above," with a few additional instructions along the way. To reassemble the striker, push the striker through the sleeve until the tail of the striker bottoms out in the slot on the sleeve. Put the sleeve and striker back into the slide (backward) as you did when taking it apart. Put the spring over them and compress it. Wrestle the tiny and lightweight spring cups

into place and ease the spring forward to capture them. Then set the striker assembly aside.

Install the firing pin safety and its spring. Depress the firing pin safety then press the extractor into its slot. Release the pressure on the firing pin safety. The extractor should be flush with the slide and stay in place even as you handle the slide. Slide the extractor depressor plunger assembly into the slide, long end first and plastic end to the rear. Slide the assembled striker into the tunnel. Start the slide cover into its rails, recessed side towards the striker assembly. Compress the striker spacer, and then the extractor depressor, as

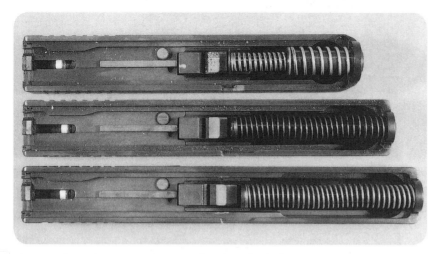

The recoil springs on current-production Glocks are captured and length-specific. The early ones were not captured.

the plate bumps up against each in turn. Once in place, you should not be able to pull or press the plate down off the slide.

When you are done, none of the parts should fall off. Turn the slide over onto its sights. Look at the breechface and press the striker tail forward. If the striker protrudes, either the firing pin safety is not correctly assembled or the striker rode past it in assembly. Pull the striker tail back until the firing pin

safety clicks in place, and try pushing forward again. The striker should not protrude. If it does, disassemble and start over again. If there is no firing pin tip protruding, then press the firing pin safety down with a fingertip or punch and press the striker forward. It now should protrude. When you pull the striker back to its original position, the firing pin safety should audibly snap back up. Flex the extractor slightly. It should return to its original location. If it falls out, the

firing pin safety isn't locking it in the slide.

Once you're done, install the barrel. Slide the muzzle into the front of the slide, and then press the breech end of the barrel back and down until it locks into place in the ejection port. Press the front of the recoil spring assembly into the front of the slide, and compress the spring enough to get the end cup of the guide rod into its recess on the bottom of the barrel. Once in place, the recoil spring assembly should be centered between the rails of the slide, and parallel to them. There should be a gap between the recoil spring guide rod and the bottom corner of the barrel lug. If there is no gap, the recoil spring guide rod is resting in the disassembly notch, and you won't be able to reassemble the slide to the frame.

To reinstall the slide on the frame, line the rails of the slide up with the front rails of the frame. Slide the slide back until it the rear frame rails ride into the slide

The beginning of slide disassembly.

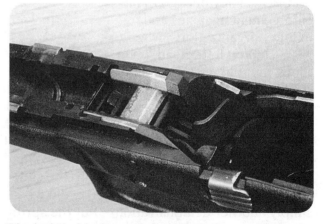

The locking block, nestled snugly in the moulded frame.

rails. Once you have all four rails encompassed in the slide, run the slide all the way back. Release it forward and it sill snap into the locked closed position.

Frame Disassembly

The frame can be a puzzle to the uninitiated. No screws, no obvious levers, no knobs to grab and pull. What to do? First, notice the metal rails sticking up above the polymer of the frame? Those are the slide rails, and they don't come out. They don't need the sharp edges rounded, and they don't need to be fitted to the slide rails. All the rail technology that gunsmiths

Glock compacts do not have light rails, not even in the third generation pistols. But for compact and durable power, it's hard to beat a compact Glock in a big caliber.

love (or hate) to fuss over on the 1911 is as useful as a compression gauge is to a computer mechanic.

Look at the frame above the trigger. On early G-17s (pre-2000) you'll see a single cross pin. On other models

and post-2000 G-17s you'll see two. The pin/pins hold the locking block in place. The larger pin passes through the slide stop lever and trigger, and the slide stop rides in a notch turned in the pin. The slide stop lever spring acts

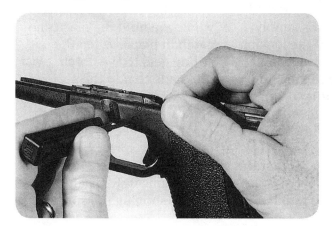

Hold the slide stop lever and press the front pins out.

Lift the slide stop clear.

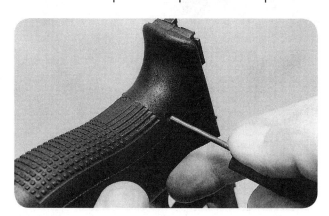

Press the rear pin out.

Pry the locking block out.

to keep the slide stop lever riding in that notch. If you simply try to pound it out, the pin will become damaged. Push out the small pin, relieving pressure on the slide stop lever. Grab the lever with one hand and lift it and push it forward. Press the second pin to the side with your punch pin, and wiggle the slide stop lever. When the hole in the lever lines up to clear the pin, the pin will push out to the side. Pull out the pin, and then the lever.

The locking block is now free to slide up. If you use a punch or screwdriver as a lever, avoid resting it on the trigger bar as you might bend it. Lever the locking block up and lift it out.

At the rear of the frame you'll see another cross pin. It holds in the ejector assembly. Press it out. (None of the pins in a Glock are "sided," that is, it doesn't matter which direction you push them out. Glock says to push them out from left to right. I've measured the pins and can't see a difference, and I've

disassembled hundreds of Glocks in each direction and haven't seen a difference.) Notice that while the other pins are steel and have sections turned out of them, the rear pin is polymer and smooth.

Hook your punch pin under the ejector and lever the ejector block up out of the frame. You can now lift the entire trigger bar/ejector assembly out of the frame as one assembled section. Keep them together until you have had a chance to observe the relationships between them.

There are two things left on the frame to take apart. (Refreshing, isn't it, not having to deal with grips and screws, grip screw bushings, and all the rest?) The disassembly latch is in front of the locking block and is worked by a flat spring. To remove the latch, press the flat spring down. While holding it down, turn the frame on its side and let the latch fall out. Note that the latch is "sided" in that the rear face has a slight groove milled or stamped into it. The

groove catches the tiny ledge on the front of the barrel lug and prevents the latch from being depressed until the slide is slightly retracted. As for the spring, it is pressed into place. It can be replaced, but I've never seen or heard of one needing replacement. (Heck, I've never heard of latches breaking or wearing out. Only getting lost from disassembly.)

The magazine catch is held in by a section of wire spring. Hold the frame up toward a light, with the rails toward you and the magazine opening toward the light. You'll be able to see the spring, and the assembly notch in the magazine catch. With your screwdriver, press the spring toward the notch while you hold the magazine catch in place. When the spring gets to the notch, twist the blade to pop the spring up. When the spring clears, you can slide the mag catch out. If you need to, you can remove the spring by reaching in with your needlenose pliers and pulling it. Replacing is simply shoving the spring

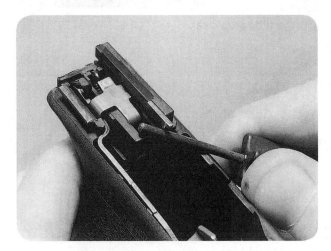

Cam the ejector out. . .

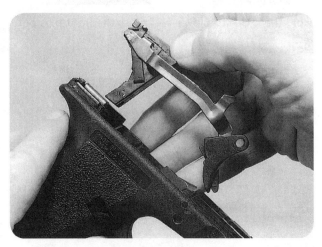

. . .and the whole trigger assembly comes out.

The rear of the frame, with the trigger bar cruciform and trigger view in plain sight.

The assembly latch rests in a slot moulded into the frame just forward of the locking block.

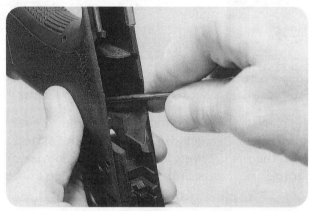

The magazine catch spring is down in the frame. Use a strong light to see when working on it.

The magazine catch spring is the simplest spring in a Glock – just a rod of spring steel.

back into its seat, prying it to clear the magazine catch, and pushing the magazine catch into the frame until you can line up spring with notch.

You now have the heart of the firearm itself, the serial-numbered part that the government is so interested in keeping track of. All the rest are just parts, but this is the controlled piece. When I went through the armorers course lo, these many years ago, the parts list they supplied us with (yes, the same one that listed magazines at $10.50 each) showed a replacement frame listing at just over $20. That price alone showed the beauty of the Glock. After all, once the moulding machine was paid for, all it cost to produce a frame was a few cents worth of polymer, a stamped tab with the serial number, and a precision-blanked set of slide rails. At twenty bucks each they were probably making a killing.

The interesting part is the trigger assembly. Take a moment to study it. Actually, take a few.

The Trigger Bar and Ejector Assembly

At the front is the trigger, a plastic part with the trigger safety in it. The trigger safety acts by pivoting under the pressure of its spring to stop against the frame. When your finger rests on the trigger it pivots the safety out of the way and allows the trigger to move. On top of the trigger bar is the firing pin safety cam. The nose of the cam rests in front of the firing pin safety plunger when the system is at rest. As you pull the trigger, the bar moves back and the cam pushes the plunger up into the slide and out of the path of the firing pin. When the firing pin is released at the end of the trigger stroke, the cam holds the plunger up out of the way.

The disassembly catch spring hardly ever breaks, and it usually breaks only if someone has tried to remove it.

A plain stamped piece of flat stock. You can't get much simpler than that.

What keeps the cam from holding the path open to the firing pin when the slide closes after firing?

Nothing. But the striker never gets that far. When the slide goes forward, the striker is stopped by the rear face of the cruciform and held back from the breechface. There is no way for the striker to ride over the cruciform, as there simply isn't enough space available. It has no other choice.

At the rear of the trigger bar you see the cruciform section and the trigger bar nose. On the right side of the ejector block, the trigger bar nose runs up against the connector. On the top, the rear end of the cruciform section rides against the tip of the firing pin. As you press the trigger back, the trigger bar compresses the firing pin against its spring. When the trigger bar contacts the connector, the angle of the connector presses the trigger bar down until it releases the firing pin. The trigger bar has already pushed the firing pin safety plunger up out of the way, so the firing pin is free to snap forward and set off the primer.

So far, so good. Remember that section of

WHY WON'T MY GLOCK FIRE WHEN DROPPED?

Despite all the descriptions, I still found when describing the Glock system that I needed a quick mental picture that would convey the situation to students and prospective buyers. Here it is:

The firing pin is trapped until you pull the trigger. The firing pin safety keeps it from going forward. Pressing the trigger clears the firing pin safety from the path. The firing pin can't go backwards, as the striker spring is pushing it forward. Until you push the trigger, it can't compress the spring that will launch it. The cruciform tip holds the firing pin tail in place. The cruciform can't move down out of the way because the drop safety ledge keeps it up, blocking the firing pin.

And as the final safety, the trigger can't move because the trigger safety spring keeps it pivoted out, blocking the trigger movement.

Just banging around, the Glock can't fire. Something (like your finger) has to press the trigger safety and then the trigger.

the slide that had the copper-colored goo on it? When the slide cycles to the rear, that machined shoulder pushes the connector out of the path of the trigger bar. The trigger bar is thus freed to snap upwards and back, propelled by your trigger finger, back into the path of the firing pin tail, and past the cam surface of the connector. Upon slide return the cruciform section catches the tail and holds the firing pin back. When you release the trigger, its return spring pushes it back out in front of the angled section of the connector, starting the whole cycle over again.

Turn the assembly over. On the other side you'll see the lefthand side of the cruciform section, the drop safety. Since the assembly is out of the frame, the spring has it contracted, so the cruciform is in the rear, or fire, position. In the Glock, it rests in the front of the slot, where the shoulder prevents it from moving out of the path of the firing pin tail. This is what allows the Glock to be abused and not fire. The cruciform can't move down, so it can't release the firing pin. (Even if it did, the firing pin safety would prevent its going very far.)

Trigger Assembly Parts

The trigger assembly has to come apart for cleaning and to replace the trigger spring to change trigger pull. Hold the trigger in your right hand and the ejector block

To strip the striker assembly, stick it backward in the slide, with the tail to the side.

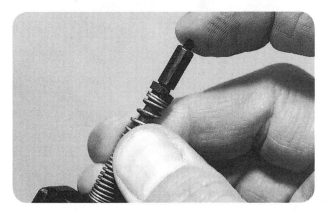

Compress the spring and let the cups fall free. (Catch them – don't let them get lost!)

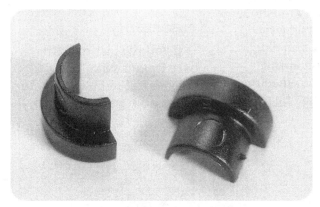

The cups are small, plastic and easily lost. It makes sense to have spares.

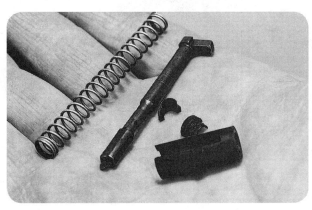

The striker, spring, cups and sleeve.

The stripped Glock frame with all of its parts.

in your left. Twist the trigger to push its rear towards you and out of the ejector block. Disassembly finished, for cleaning. For trigger spring swapping, you'll need to remove the coil spring, and that and the connector are covered in the Trigger chapter. To reassemble, twist the trigger bar back into the ejector block.

Reassembly

If you're starting with a bare frame, install the magazine catch first. Then the disassembly lever. If that is out, press the spring back in place. Be careful to press where you won't bend it, or grasp it on the sides with a needlenose pliers to hold it. Take the trigger assembly and press the rear down into the frame. Insert the rear cross pin and press it flush.

Press the locking block down over the front of the trigger assembly. Press the locking block pin (the upper one) through and flush. Now, start the trigger pin in from the right side, and capture the trigger with it. Once you have the trigger held, grasp the frame in your left hand with a fingertip over the end of the trigger pin. Insert the slide stop with your right hand. Line the slide stop hole up with the trigger pin and press the pin through. Release the slide stop. It should snap down to the frame. The frame is done.

If you do the trigger pin first, you will find that you have to catch and compress

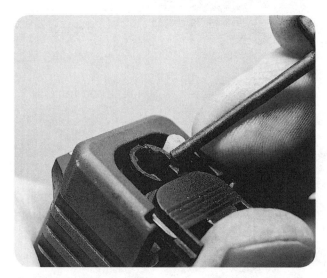

On reassembly, press the striker sleeve in and slide the plate part way up.

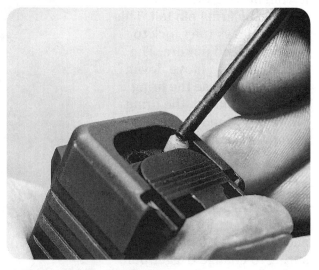

Then press the extractor plunger and slide the plate the rest of the way on.

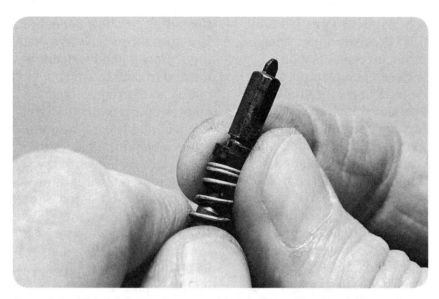

One of the "fiddly" parts of reassembly is getting the tiny plastic cups back in place on the firing pin. Practice makes it easier.

the slide stop spring in order to get the locking block pin through. It is easier to do it the way I have described.

Manufacturing

If you haven't seen a modern manufacturing plant, you will be amazed.

Glocks differ between models in slide and frame length, but many internal parts are interchangeable nevertheless.

If, like me, you're a student of tools and manufacturing, you'll recall film clips of the dawn of mass production: Huge forges, stamping machines and row upon row of lathes, mills, surface grinders and assembly benches nearly to the horizon. Each machine performing a single operation, and its operator grabbing a part out of a rack, performing that single operation and returning the part to the rack. Once the rack was completed, it was wheeled to the next line of machines. Dawn to dusk, hundreds or thousands of trained machinists performing the same task over and over and over.

Not any more.

The modern plant features rows of computer-controlled machines, each one referred to as a "machining station." A row of machining stations is also called a gold mine, at least if they are all working. The most modern stations are known as five-axis machines. If you grew up thinking of the three axes, up and down, right to left and forward and back, add turning the part over and swapping it end for end and you'll have the modern five. The result is a machine that can pluck the parts out of the rack itself, insert or swap its own cutting tool, make many cutting operations with that one or swapping to other cutting tools, then putting the part back in the rack. It is possible, but not always efficient, to have a single machine perform every machining operation necessary to a part.

The newer a machine, the greater the number of cutting tools it can have in its "package." That is, early machines would have five, 10 or more cutting tools. The newest (and more expensive) ones now can hold up to 128 tools. That is 128 different-diameter cutters, or special-radius cutting tools, or rough and finish-cut tools – so many tools a part need not come out of the machine until it has to be turned over to do the other side.

As if all this wasn't enough, the machine remembers how many times it has used each cutter (each of which has its own bar code or microchip for easy identification) so they can be resharpened on a regular

schedule. How precise is all this? Precise enough that parts interchangeability between manufactured items is taken for granted. Precise enough that the really high-tech machines require temperature and humidity controls so the finished dimensions aren't out of spec. So precise that modern firearms parts are a dream compared to the rough parts we used to have to deal with in the old days.

The modern machining plant is not all peaches and cream for the owner. There are downsides. You as the manufacturer must have people known as programmers. The programmers write the software that dictates the cutting, or cutter paths as they are called. Where does

the cutter cut, how deep, how fast does it travel, where does it lift? How much lubricant is needed to cool the part being cut? A good programmer creates cutter paths that are efficient and leave a smooth surface behind. A bad one busts cutters, leaves parts that require polishing, and costs you tools, wasted parts and slows your output.

You also have to pay for the machines as well as feed them electricity, metal and lubricant. Since a single machine can easily run hundreds of thousands of dollars (and the really big and new ones over a million) each, you have a heck of a lease note to cover. Yes, lease. The dictates of modern economics hardly ever include actually buying these things. Long before they're paid for, the latest models are so much better that sticking with the old one will give your accountants an attack of the vapors.

All of this explains what everyone who has a better idea of how to make anything runs smack into: it costs a whole heck of a lot of money to start up a new widget factory, let alone a firearms factory.

Glock slides are machined from bar stock. The alloy, heat treatment and actual cutting operations are all closely-held secrets. After all, it took a while to figure out the most efficient method, and there's no point in simply announcing it to the world. One tidbit I have learned is that it takes eight hours of machine time

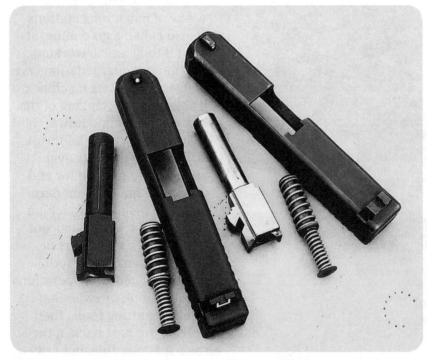

The precision of modern manufacturing means these Glocks can have any part exchanged and still work.

for a slide to be done. Now, I was not able to pry the details from my source, as he either didn't know them for sure or had taken a blood oath not to reveal them. So I don't know if "eight hours" is the total time from raw steel in, to finished parts out, including time to be bolted into trays, unbolted, walked from machine to machine, etc., or if "eight hours" is the total of just the machine-tool-cutting-steel time. (I kind of doubt that, as that would be a whole lot of cutting time.)

Once machined, gauged, inspected and serial number stamped, the slides go to the Tenifer section. There they receive the surface treatment that Glock is so well known for, the one that turns out tough slides. Once the Tenifer treatment is finished, the slides then get their black oxide coating. The black is not the Tenifer. The black is simply the coating required to make the surface dark and non-reflective. If you were to buff off the black oxide (not an easy thing to do unless you get sandpaper or power tools involved) the slide would still be protected by the Tenifer treatment, which provides the real hardness and rustproofing protection.

You may see the occasional Glock where the owner has had the black oxide stripped off and then hard chromed the gun. If it's for looks, fine. But any additional protection is hardly worth the cost, as the hard chrome isn't much harder than the Tenifer-

treated steel it covers. As for rust protection paint would work as well, compared to what the Tenifer offers.

Frames are a different matter. The skeleton of the frame is the steel stamping that forms the slide rails. Modern fine-blanking and sheet metal forming technology allows the manufacturing engineer to produce a product that is as precise as a machined object.

The stamped and formed skeletons are heat-treated and fed to the moulding machine. Feeding in from the other side of the machine are the serial number plates. In between is the mould itself, with moveable parts of the mould and power feed tubes to pump the polymer mix in. The complete assembly requires three steel parts: the front and rear rails, and the serial number plate.

Each frame is formed when the rails and a serial number plate are placed in the mould, the mould closed and the polymer fed into it. As with the machining stations, the details on temperature, feed rate, production rate

and curing are closely-held production secrets. I do know that each one spends something just over a minute in the mould. Everyone I talk to keeps repeating the same figure: 80 seconds. Color me cynical, but when everyone has such a precise and consistent number, I have to wonder if it really is "80 seconds" or if the number was selected for some reason and once it was uttered by a single source has been repeated ever since.

Anyway, we can think of frames coming out of a moulding machine at one every two minutes. That sounds fair.

Glock has a Quality Assurance staff and program. Each part is inspected, and selected production samples are measured to minute tolerances.

The striker falls off of an automated lathe, the rotational equivalent of the machining stations that made the slide. Other parts, like the trigger bar and cruciform, are fine-blanked and folded before heat treatment and nickel plating. They all end up

While the Glock's durability has been proven by dragging the pistol behind a truck, I'll leave that test to the factory.

on the assemblers' benches. There, experienced factory assemblers install each part in turn and check them against the list. After a day or two, you'd think the list could be dispensed with, but memory can fail. Then it's off to the test-fire room. There each Glock is test-fired before it is boxed with its owners manual, brush and other accessories.

Are they assembled in Austria, disassembled, then shipped to the United States? Are they made in Austria, then shipped as parts and assembled here? I had conflicting reports, but the latter seems to be the answer.

We do have one update on the manufacturing process since the first edition: the E-series recall. As it turns out, there were three individual

machines stamping rail sections, hidden deep within caves in the Austrian mountains. Apparently, one of those machines was suddenly not punching rails to spec. Rebuilt? Overhauled and set up incorrectly? Mountain trolls creating mischief? No one would say, but I have to suspect there is someone now working in the Sales Department in a very un-choice location. The problem was quickly caught, the machine corrected, and the offending frames replaced.

The information did come with an extra tidbit that was even more interesting: there are apparently people who work in Glock's Smyrna, Georgia, location and who have been with the company for years, who have not

set foot inside the Austrian plant. It is apparently entirely possible to work for Glock until retirement and never see the inside of the plant, never see Glocks being made.

Durability: The Torture Tests

When Glock began offering their G-17 here in the United States, they were very aggressive about proclaiming its superiority. It didn't take long for tales to be told at matches and clubs, tales of Glocks being towed behind the rep's car as he drove into the parking lot of the range where he would demonstrate the new G-17. Of Glocks thrown into running cement mixers (sans cement, of course) tossed over walls, thrown out of speeding vehicles and dropped from helicopters. Even of Glocks being fired underwater. And, it would be hard to find such a tale that was indeed a tale and not the truth. For the then-new and subsequent Glocks have gone through all that and more.

And Glock still extolls the abuse. The question is, could other pistols do the same? Let's go through the biggest ones, and see how they'd stack up. As it just so happens, I replicated the Glock tests in my own book *Gun Digest Book of the 1911, Volume 2*.

First, let's look at the single greatest advantage the Glock has over all others that came before it, and those still

Banging on a Glock with a hammer proves what we all know: plastic flexes more easily than steel. But Glock was the first to apply that knowledge to a workable pistol design.

There is a 1911 underneath that truck tire.

based on earlier designs: the flexibility of a polymer frame. A steel or aluminum frame, when struck hard enough, will bend and deform, where the Glock frame will bend and flex back. The physical resistance to deformation is known as the modulus of elasticity, where any material has a distance within which it can be flexed without remaining permanently altered. A piece of glass doesn't flex much before it breaks. Steel, depending on the alloy, flexes more, but finally bends and remains bent. Plastics bend a great deal before they finally crack.

So, impacts that would bend our 1911 will be shrugged off by the polymer frame of the Glock. How much of a problem is this? Good question. In nearly 20 years of gunsmithing next to a town known for lots of carry guns, lots of shootouts and lots of people who carried guns for a living, I recall exactly one pistol that had been dropped and was inoperative as a result. It was a S&W 9mm. The magazine was trapped in the frame. However, while you couldn't get the magazine out, the pistol still worked. By locking the slide open and driving the magazine down far enough, I could remove the slide. I loaded the magazine, reinstalled the slide, pounded the magazine back up, and the pistol shot fine.

The customer didn't want me bending it back, or filing the frame to clear the magazine, so it was sent back to the factory, where they replaced the frame for a reasonable fee. Now, it is entirely possible that bent frames are a more common problem that I realize, and that those who drop theirs simply turn them back into the departmental armorer for repair or replacement. I cannot say.

The following is just a sampling of the kind of reliability testing Glock has performed on its own pistols. How does the Colt 1911 compare?

1911s can take it, too. Under that mud and silt there is a ferociously expensive 1911 being abused. And it worked afterwards, too.

1911s can take winter weather, too.

Glock Torture Test #1

A G-17 was frozen into a block of ice and left that way for two months. The ice was broken away (I would have been more impressed if they got it free by throwing the block onto the pavement) and the thawed pistol fired 100 rounds without fail.

A 1911? Sure thing. I've fired frozen pistols, and all manner of firearms left in the cold for long periods of time. A tie.

Glock Torture Test #2

The G-17 (I assume all the test were done to the same pistol) was buried in five different types of soil, and then fired for 100 rounds after each soil test. No failures.

Again, a proper 1911 (not a super-tight Match pistol) would do the same thing. And did. I buried the test 1911s (I used four of them) and found they would still work just fine after being buried and then dug up. My only question is, who got to fire the wet and muddy G-17 after each time it got buried? Nothing like needing a face shield as a piece of range equipment. I sure did when conducting the experiment. A tie.

Glock Torture Test #3

Mud. As if the soil wasn't enough, thick, runny river mud was used. Hmm.

I used mud of several consistencies. I tried sandy mud, silty mud and clay-ey

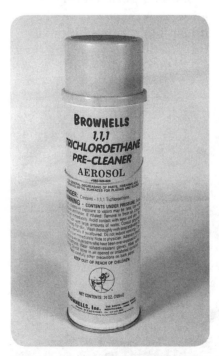

While it lasts, my dwindling supply of TriChlor strips oil off parts quickly. (It's banned now, of course, but other stuff works equally well.)

mud. Whjle some of the 1911s had trigger pulls that got a lot heavier, they all worked just fine. The Glock didn't show the trigger pull variances that the 1911s did, so I have to reluctantly give the nod to the Austrians. Advantage: Glock, barely.

Glock Torture Test #4

Water. Left submerged to three feet for one hour, then retrieved and fired for ten rounds. Repeated ten times for 100 rounds.

The only problems with this test are boredom and getting wet. Sloshing pistols around in a bucket and then shooting them splashes water all over the place. A tie. The worry for some (and I was a bit concerned myself) is trapped water bulging the barrel. You need not worry. The water will begin to drain out as soon as you lift the pistol from the bucket. While I can't suggest you try this, it isn't dangerous. Instead, learn from my tests and save yourself the soaking. If you don't clean properly and thoroughly afterwards, you'll let rust get started, which can be worse than the experience of shooting it while wet. Another tie.

Glock Torture Test #5

Chemical degreaser. Detail stripped, the parts were hosed with a chemical degreaser until they were bone dry. Then they were reassembled without lubricant and fired 100 rounds without fail.

In the first edition, I gave this one to Glocks, and I should not have. My own test showed that dry 1911s work fine, at least up to 100 rounds. I didn't try to extend that past the 100 rounds specified, what's the point? In the first edition, advantage Glock, again marginally. Now, I'd have to call it a tie.

Glock Torture Test #6

The truck tire. Left lying on a gravel parking lot, the G-17 was run over from every direction by a "large SUV." That could mean as much as four or five tons. Once it was run over, then the truck was parked on it for an hour. The Glock went through its apportioned 100 rounds without fail.

A 1911? With four manufacturers 1911s on hand, I was willing to try this one. My gun club's parking lot was gravel a long time ago. It now has enough grass and weeds growing in it that it requires mowing. It is still a gravel surface under the green stuff. I placed 1911s on the range and drove over them, and then parked on them and took photos. The unspectacular end result was four 1911-shaped depressions in the parking lot. No cracked grips, no bent frames, no inoperative pistols. It would take a truck a lot heavier than my fully-loaded Ford Ranger to stress pistols. Certainly more than the 3,000 pounds or so it was able to muster. A tie.

Score in the first edition: Glock two, Tie four, 1911, none.

Score in the Second Edition: Five ties, one for Glock (barely), 1911 none.

What of the legendary tests? Dragging the pistol, dropping it, etc.? All fall into the category of "How much does it take to bend this frame?" Dropping a pistol several stories out of a building, or throwing it out of a moving vehicle while racing down a deserted airstrip, are simply testing the deformation limits of steel. I'm sure if we went to the trouble of subjecting a 1911 frame and slide to being built of tougher alloys and better heat-treatment, we could improve its performance. But we'd still fall short of the ability of polymer to shrug off impact.

The better question is: how useful is it to us? Viewed from some perspectives, very. Lets say you're a SWAT member, and while rappelling down a building to crash in through the window, your sidearm falls out of the holster (not possible if you'd bought the right holster) onto the sidewalk. First of all, no one except fellow team members will be endangered, as they are the only ones it might fall on. No Glock pistol will discharge. A 1911 without a firing pin safety might, if it fell directly onto its muzzle from a great enough height. (How high? From personal testing, I can tell you eight feet isn't enough.)

Will you go down and get it? Heck, no. If you weren't carrying a shoulder weapon, you aren't going through the window now. If you were, you're going regardless of

On the second go-round, I ran over my guns. Glocks and 1911s both passed the test.

where your pistol ended up. Later on you can retrieve it. As to whether it works or not, that ends up being an economic problem. Will you, personally, have to buy a new one? Will the department replace it, or require you buy another? All questions that are unrelated to the mechanical integrity of the firearm being abused.

It might be a bit different if your pistol falls out during a vehicle chase. But unless your vehicle stops close enough, (like, less than 50 feet away) again, you aren't going to go running after it.

OK, so there you are, a highly-trained operator, going into an area of operations in a helicopter, and your sidearm goes overboard. I think you know where this is going. Unless you are right over the landing zone, you'll never find

In a rough-and-tumble environment, a lanyard makes sense.

it again. And until you have the time to go looking, you've got a plethora of weapons to use against the enemy du jour.

Dropping pistols is something we personal users, not employees of law enforcement agencies or military organizations, have to think about. Thinking of it from the viewpoint and question of "How expensive is this gonna be?" as we watch our pistol sailing through the air should put it in perspective. For an administrator, the ruggedness of the Glock system is very comforting. After all, he (or she) won't have to spend nearly as much of the budget replacing dropped and damaged pistols, if they are Glocks. Dropping is expensive to personal owners and administrators. To the guys on the sharp end, dropping

is a matter of personal image and paperwork. Having dropped firearms more times than I care to recount, I can tell you from personal experience that various 1911s, having traveled up to seventeen feet, still work.

When I was waiting for the arrival of my personal Gunsite ATP, (a 1911, as you'd imagine) the shop manager of the Gunsmithy told me of the experience of one of their customers: He had been chasing a suspect across a city street when his pistol fell out of its holster and into the gutter. A passing streetsweeper sucked it up, and rattled it around the containment tank an unknown number of times before the owner could climb on board, show his badge and get the driver to stop the vehicle. As you could imagine, it looked horrible, but it still worked.

Yes, Glocks are better, there is no getting around that, but how much should we expect a pistol to take? And if it can take more than we can, what would we look like, falling out of a moving vehicle, or falling from a helicopter? I hope none of you ever need find the answers to those questions.

Durability: Ammunition Consumption

Now we're getting somewhere. After all, "everyone knows" that a Glock simply gobbles ammunition and never quits, right? Much more so than any other pistol, right? The question of "how much ammo does it take" has been an evergreen for gun writers for as long as I can remember. And probably before. I recall one article that the late Skeeter Skelton wrote about the 1911 in .45 in the early or mid-1970s. He had heard that a particular military competition team was in the habit of replacing the barrels on their pistols every year. Since each pistol was fired about 5,000 rounds in a season, it then (of course) became gospel that barrels were worn out after 5,000 rounds. This is hardly logical. In fact, the Latin term for this logical fallacy is "post hoc, ergo propter hoc." Translated: "After that, therefore because of that." In other words, "Y happened after X; therefore Y happened because of X." Not necessarily.

Skeeter set out to find out if the number was true. He managed to talk several ammunition companies into donating a total of just over 15,000 rounds of ammunition to his project.

(As a gun writer, I was then and still am, in awe of him. 15,000 rounds, for a magazine article? Wow. I managed to talk a dozen ammunition companies into donating approximately 40,000 rounds of ammunition and components for reloading for my book "*The Gun Digest Book of the 1911*" and that was work. If I were to ask for 15,000 rounds for a single magazine article, I'd be deaf after hearing so many phones being slammed.)

A large part of the resulting article was devoted to just how much work all this was. Skeeter had two assistants to help him, and they spent months shooting "all that ammo" in the Herculean labors that resulted. By todays standards, not that much work or shooting. 15,000 rounds today would be a good couple of months' work for an aspiring IPSC Grand Master, or one who wanted to move up from the middle of the ranks. A good shooting school will get you through 1,000+ in a week's time, and you'll spend more time getting lunch, lectures and feedback than you will actual on the line trigger time. I would often end up doing a significant fraction of Skeeter's number in my annual spring warmups before the Second Chance match.

At the end of it, Skeeter couldn't see where the pistol was any worse for the experience. In the interests of science, he sectioned the barrel and even viewed it under a magnifier. He couldn't see much wear at all.

So what can we expect from any good pistol? I have some high-mileage 1911s that I've put close to 100,000 rounds through. I know from talking to Jerry Barnhart that he owns a 1911 that he's put over 300,000 rounds through. Still not enough. Glock has a rental program, and as part of the rental agreement the range has to keep track of how many rounds each pistol goes through. How about 350,000 rounds and up? And still counting.

I talked to Al Allen, co-owner of Double Action, an indoor range in the Detroit area. (Madison Heights, to be specific.) He has been running rental Glocks for many years and had had some very high-mileage ones back before the rental program changed. In the old days, range owners bought rental guns from Glock and then were responsible for maintenance and returning them for upgrades and factory service. His record Glock was a G-17 that had a total of 465,000 known rounds through it. When he returned it at the change in the Glock rental program, he says, "Glock wasn't impressed with that figure. They'd seen some with lots more rounds through them." Now, Glock retains ownership of the rental guns, and they are returned each year for factory service and inspection. As such, the most Al sees going through an individual pistol is "only" 250,000 rounds.

In the decade since the change, one pistol at Double Action has had to be significantly serviced. (The old G-17 went through two or three trigger return springs in its 465K run.) That one was a G-22C, which cracked a slide. A minor crack, but Glock replaced it.

So, unless you win the lotto I wouldn't worry about putting enough ammo through your Glock to wear it out. ◆

CHAPTER 3

Calibers of the Glock

Glock's first model, the G-17, came out in 9mm Parabellum. Why? Because that was what the Austrian Army wanted. The 10mm and .40 hadn't been invented yet (unless you counted a crazy experimenter working for a particular gun magazine out of Southern California) and only Americans wanted a cannon like the .45. The 9mm was and is a near-universal police and military caliber, so much so that in some countries possession of the ammunition or a firearm chambered for the ammunition is forbidden. If you needed to, I'm not sure there is a country on the face of the planet (perhaps save for Vatican City) where you couldn't lay hands on at least some small supply of 9x19.

The Nine had to be first, and as a result the limitations of the 9mm created the limitations of some of the Glock models. But the basic design of the Glock is scalable, that is, you can adjust the dimensions to create a slightly new product. Let us use the

1911 pistol as an example, since so many seem to view it and the Glock as competitors. Starting out at a .45, the 1911 probably could be scaled down as a 9mm. However, Colt didn't do that when they developed the 9.8mm pistol for the Rumanian pistol trials of 1910. They shortened the slide and barrel but didn't scale the design down. They also didn't do that when they

made the 9mm Lightweight Commander for the US Army in the early 1950s. All 1911 pistols, regardless of caliber, have the same basic exterior dimensions, those of a .45. However, the Glock 9mm (G-17, etc) and the Glock 45 (G-21, etc) have different exterior dimensions.

Another example of a scaled product would be the S&W revolver line. The .44 and

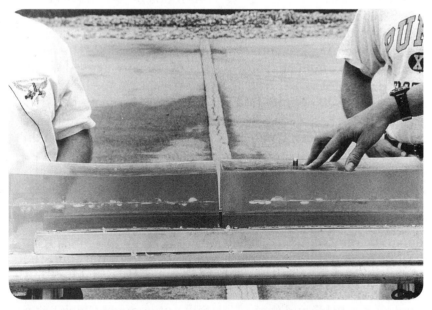

Ballistic testing can tell you many things about the caliber you've selected and the ammunition available for it. This factory 180-grain FMJ load in .40 S&W penetrated 36 inches of ballistic gelatin. Not a good police load for crowded streets.

Smith & Wesson went with different frame sizes for different uses. From top to bottom: a .45, a .357, and a .38.

.45 revolvers are larger in all dimensions than the .38 and .357 revolvers. Making the .38s the same size as the .44s makes no sense. (S&W did make the .357 at first only in the .44 frame. But they wanted to make sure the gun was up to the power and pressure of the .357 Magnum and to make

sure the gun was large enough it didn't beat up the customers from excessive recoil. It was, after all, the mid-1930s.)

Why, then, wasn't the Colt scaled down for a 9mm model? Because no one wanted one. The 1911 was in .45, and anyone who wanted a lesser caliber could damn well go and find someone else to make it for them. Besides, Colt was making it for the government, who only wanted .45s, and any extra R&D work on other calibers would come straight out of Colt's pocket. As a result, the 9mm and .38 Super are for all purposes a .45 caliber 1911 with the "wrong size" hole drilled down the barrel.

Colt did, later, scale down the 1911 when they created their Colt Government .380 pistol. It had some manufacturing differences (to the detriment of the pistol) from the 1911, but it was a scaled-down 1911 in most regards. The neat trick would have been to have made a pistol that small in 9mm Parabellum. Now *that* would have been a pistol that would have sold by the truckload.

There are limits to scalability, however. The Glock models manufactured in .380 Auto, the G-25 and G-28, are simply the 9mm G-19 and G-26 modified to be blowback and .380 Auto. I'm sure Gaston Glock is fully capable of designing them from scratch as .380 pistols, but for the size of the market (basically, places that don't allow military or

The 1911 can be scaled, and it has been. The pistol in the middle is Colt's attempt to scale it. The one at the bottom is John Browning's pre-1911 .380 pocket pistol, the Model M.

You can make a .30 Luger barrel for your Glock as I did, just for kicks. You can't get one from Glock.

The calibers you can have in your Glock are not limited by the availability of the brass but by the unavailability of barrels. Left to right: 9mm Parabellum, 9x21, .38 Super, 9x23, .357 SIG (*barrels now available*), .400 CorBon, .40 Super, .460 Rowland.

police caliber pistols) why go to the expense? We run once again into evolutionary vs. revolutionary design.

An example of a non-scalable design is the Beretta M-92. You could increase the size of everything on or in it to make it a .45 instead of a 9mm. but the grip would end up being so large no one could hold it and shoot it. The most that could be done was to replace the 9mm barrel with one in .40, which Beretta has done. The marriage is not always a happy one, as many report the Beretta in .40 to be a real beast to shoot. At least, a beast compared to other .40 pistols, not "a beast" as compared to, say, an S&W in .500 S&W Magnum.

Following up on the revolution of the Glock, American experimenters evolved new models and new calibers. New models, you ask? I'd call a pistol with compensated barrel, red dot sight, replacement trigger parts and high capacity magazine a different

model from what the Glock factory produced. And since there are tens of thousands of gunsmiths, armorers, machinists and tinkerers who are fully capable of fitting a new barrel, the Glock you can have does not necessarily have to be just the Glock that came in the box.

In many of these calibers, the mechanical difficulty of

changing to a new barrel is non-existent. For example, changing a G-17 from 9mm to 9x21, or .30 Luger, is simply a matter of the appropriate spring and a new barrel. However, finding a barrel is not an easy thing. So, while a caliber may be possible, finding the barrel may be unlikely. The dimensions of the Glock barrel are not so complex that you couldn't find a machinist capable of re-creating a Glock barrel from a

The .30 Luger (*left and right*) is used in some places where the 9mm Parabellum (*center*) is prohibited.

CARTRIDGE POWER & PRESSURE

The traditional method of measuring external ballistic power is by calculating kinetic energy. Kinetic energy is mass times velocity squared. (The headaches come in converting all the numbers to the proper units.) The big problem many shooters have with kinetic energy (besides the need for a calculator to figure it) is that it gives too much emphasis to velocity. Increasing a bullet's speed by, say, 10 percent has the effect of increasing its kinetic energy figure by 21 percent. Too much, some say.

In the early days of practical shooting, the "computer" used to calculate stage and match results was a four-function battery-powered desktop calculator. (I still have the desktop calculator our club bought in 1981 to speed up tabulating the match results.) To speed up calculating whose ammunition made Major or Minor, Jeff Cooper, the originator of practical shooting, came up with a simple formula: Bullet weight in grains times velocity in feet per second. To save writing, we then simply dropped the last three digits of the resulting six-digit number. Thus, a 230 grain bullet from a .45 (that's about all anyone shot back then) going 825 feet per second posted a raw factor of 189,750. Rounding it off got a Power Factor of 190. Back in the early days, you had to post a 185 to make Major.

We quickly found out two things: most factory ammo didn't make Major, and it was not fun to shoot ammunition that really made the 190 Major power factor. I had a precious stash of RA 69 ammo I hoarded in the late 1970s. It was factory ammo, with the 230-grain bullets traveling a sedate 730 fps. In those days, factory ammo was exempt from requiring proof of Major. It gave me an advantage in a bunch of matches, before the advantage went away when it was all used up. In IPSC shot in the United States, the Power Factor, or PF, needed to make Major has been coming down. From that initial 185, it slipped to 180 for a short time, then to 175 for a long time, and is now 165. To shoot Minor, you need only meet or exceed 125. Many factory loads in 9mm make Minor with room to spare.

Other shootings competitions have differing limits, and some don't have mathematical limits so much as they have equipment that limits leaning out your loads.

Power depends on pressure. If you want to push a particular bullet faster, you can do one of two things: increase the maximum pressure, or stretch the time the expanding gases push in the bullet. (Or both, if you're really eager to increase performance.) Since the maximum pressure is set by SAAMI, the Sporting Arms and Ammunition Manufacturing Institute, and all firearms are designed with the particular caliber limit in mind, exceeding the pressure limit isn't a good idea. To get a longer push, you need a slower-burning powder. But the short barrels of handguns limit how much you can do. Basically, if you want more power you need to go to a larger caliber.

suitable-bore barrel blank. If you really, really had to have a G-17 in .30 Luger, you could have one. It would just cost money. That said, I present the calibers of the Glock, factory and otherwise.

.380 Auto

John Moses Browning was not just a brilliant firearms designer; he came up with a number of cartridge designs. The .380 is one of his longest-lived. What it amounts to is the largest case that can be wrestled into a pistol originally designed for the .32 Auto (another Browning design). A straight-walled case using a 9mm bullet, it is called the 9mm Corto, 9mm Kurz, 9X17, and 9mm Browning Short as well as .380 Auto. Despite both being 9mms, bullet weights of the .380 and the 9mm Parabellum do not overlap. The low operating pressure of the .380 cartridge and the blowback design of pistols chambered for it don't allow for more than bullets heavier than 90 to 95 grains, launched at just under a thousand feet per second. (At best. Some loadings are more like 90 grains at 900 fps.) Light bullets at modest velocity doesn't seem to add up to much, but the .380 is still a step up from the .32, which features 72-grain bullets at much the same velocities. The .380 has been heavily favored as a defensive round for over a century not because it is a powerhouse, but because it has been chambered in the

sleekest and most compact pistols for all that time. And when it comes to flat and compact, you can't beat the champion pistol of the Pre-Glock era, the Colt Model M.

You can load heavier bullets than 90 to 95 grains if you want, but since the overall length of the cartridge has to remain the same, the heavier bullet uses even more of the small cases available capacity. Heavier than normal bullets thus end up being launched at much-reduced velocities. Since there is nothing to be gained, no one bothers. And since in the Glock you can have the same-size package in 9mm Parabellum, who would want the .380? Collectors, for one group, but they can't have them. More on that in the chapter on the G-25 and G-28. As for .380 Glocks, if Gaston could come out with a Glock system pistol proportioned like the old Colt Model M, he'd sell even more pistols than he does now.

9mm Parabellum

The first, and the most popular. The 9mm came

about over a century ago for much the same reason the .380 was invented at much the same time: more bullet. The German Army liked the then-new Luger pistol. But they weren't too enthusiastic about the .30 Luger cartridge. It was and is a bottlenecked round that features an 86- to 93-grain .30-caliber bullet at around 1150 fps. What Georg Luger did to satisfy the German Army was neck the case up as much as he could, resulting in a 9mm bullet, basically a .35 caliber. The result was a 115-grain bullet at 1150 fps. A big step up at the time, and one that has found favor ever since. And similar to the .380, it wasn't because it was such a thunderbolt. The 9mm has found favor for many shooters for almost a century because it represents a reasonable amount of power for a handgun, at the cost of a controllable amount of recoil, and one that can be had in robust and durable designs that are not too large. A handgun as a sidearm has to be portable, or what's the point? If you make a handgun too bulky, you might just as

Left to right: 9x18 Makarov, .32 ACP, .380 ACP and 9mm Parabellum. Glock makes pistols in .380 and 9mm Parabellum, but only the 9mm is available to us – a situation that's not likely to change.

well carry a rifle, and then also get the power of a rifle, too.

Remember, we aren't talking of handguns as hunting or target competition tools, even though they are eminently suitable for those tasks. The first and foremost thought that follows the question of needing a handgun is that of defense.

For a machinegun crew, having rifles as well as the machinegun is just too much gear. But a pistol in a holster is always handy and often enough of a tool to solve an emergency. For a police officer, carrying a rifle around would be a real drag. Not that there aren't lots of places where they do. But not because the rifle is handier. As a backup to a rifle, not much beats a handgun on your belt, unless it is your buddy standing next to you with another rifle ready to go.

For the question of defense with a handgun, many consider the answer to be something in 9mm.

9x21

The 9x21 is not only a rule-beater caliber, it has the distinction of being a rule-beater on two continents for two different reasons. The cartridge was designed and first loaded in Italy, where those fine, upstanding citizens are forbidden possession of military-caliber pistols. In particular, the 9x19. If you had guessed that the 9x21 was simply the 9x19 case lengthened by a whopping two millimeters, you'd be correct. However, to make a reasonable manufacturing process possible, the overall lengths of the 9x19 and 9x21 cartridges are identical, as

Which 9mm is best? It depends. For which game? For what purpose? By whom?

are their standard operating pressures. Therefore, any pistol that can be made for the 9x19 can be made for the 9x21. Does it make sense? Only if you are an irrational, firearms-fearing politician, but again I digress. If the operating pressure or overall length of the 9x21 had been altered from that of the 9x19, it would not be possible for manufacturers to offer pistols at a reasonable cost. To keep cost reasonable, the 9x21 is the barest possible disguise of the 9x19.

Here in the United States (where we also have firearms-fearing politicians) the 9x21 existed for a different reason. When the competitors in the sport of IPSC shifted to high-capacity pistols in the early 1990s, many shooters looked longingly on the 9x19 cartridge. Cheap, plentiful brass made reloading an extremely inexpensive proposition. Compact (in girth) high-capacity frames and magazines of 9x19 pistols were common and inexpensive. The only fly in the ointment was operating pressure. To get the 9x19 boosted up to Major scoring levels, the standard pressure had to be exceeded by a wide margin. The resulting loads back then were in the pressure range of Proof loads, the loads fired when a pistol is first manufactured to make sure it can withstand excessive pressures.

The Board of Directors of the United States Practical Shooting Association were worried about 9mm proof-

Left to right: 5.7 from FN, 9mm Parabellum, .40 S&W and .45 ACP. NATO's search for a Personal Defense Weapon (PDW) centers on something like the 5.7 and not the good old calibers that have always worked.

load level ammunition being used on a regular basis in competition, and so forbade 9mm Major ammunition. (There had been years of precedent of 9mm proof loads being hard on guns, from the use of the British 2-Zed load in certain UK military organizations. The pistols they used lasted only a short time before being worn out, and they were not shot as much as IPSC pistols.) Since there were no loading specifications on the 9x21 cartridge and no published pressure ceiling, some competitors

The difference between a 9x19 barrel and a 9x21 barrel is the chamber. Many barrels – not Glocks, however – can be converted with a reamer such as this one from Loon Lake Precision (Manson Reamers).

You should gauge every round you load to make sure it will function properly and not jam.

began loading those cases to Major to get around the 9x19 prohibition.

As it has a habit of doing, physics took care of the problem for a while. The majority of the 9mm Major loads were so hot they had a tendency to break parts on the guns they were being fired in. Progress in powder design has brought the pressure ceilings of 9mm Major loads down to an acceptable level, while gunsmiths found ways to make parts fit better and made them stronger. Then, 9mm Major was allowed as a competitive caliber in late 2002, but only in Open Division pistols. It is not allowed in the other Divisions with the exception of Revolver. Just like that, the 9x21 died in the US. Since then 9mm Major has had a small but dedicated following.

Other 9s

The "other" nine in the United States is the .38 Super.

As a competition cartridge, the Super reigns supreme. Accurate, reliable, able to handle the pressure needed to make Major, it unfortunately can't fit in a G-17 sized Glock. It is too long to fit in the 17-22 (9mm and .40) frame. The 20-21 (10mm and .45) frame is big enough, but the breechface on those slides don't accommodate the .38 Super rim size. And the 9mm slide on Glocks won't fit the frame of a 10mm/.45. If we want a .38 Super, we'll have to wait for Glock to make a specific model of it. (Not much of a chance there, but you never know.)

Or you could pester Caspian for a Glock slide to fit a G-20 or G-21 frame, one with a .38 super breechface. But please don't call them until after you've solved the magazine problem. Where are you going to get a G-20 or G-21

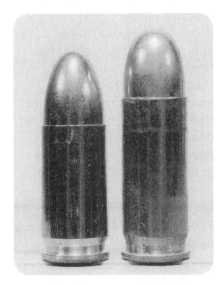

The 9mm Parabellum (*left*) and the .38 Super. Though it offers extra case capacity, the Super can't fit into the magazines or frames of the many 9mm pistols.

magazine tube with .38 Super feed lips?

10mm

The 10mm Glock is not as popular as the 40, so why list it first? Because the 10mm is the father of the .40, and the .357 SIG and others. In the 1970s, experimenters writing for *Guns & Ammo* magazine were trying to break the "9mm vs. 45" argument by finding a third path. For the technically-oriented, they took .30-30 brass and turned it on a lathe to remove the rim. (.30 Remington would do the same, and not require rim removal.) They shortened it and reamed the resulting pistol case to take bullets from the old .38-40 WCF cartridge, a true .40 caliber. (I read the article and tried making a case for myself. It is even more work than it sounds like.) With a round to use, they modified (and heavily so) a Browning P-35 to take their new invention. Why the Browning? One of the arguments in favor of 9mm was capacity. Rather than develop a new round and plug it into the same platform (1911) for the same number of rounds (then only seven per magazine) they went with the Browning. They could stuff 10 or 11 rounds into a Browning mag, splitting the difference between .45 capacity and 9mm capacity. The result was a cartridge that split the difference in power, capacity and recoil but was no larger than the standard service-pistol samples of either. The overall length of the .40 G&A cartridge was deliberately designed and made such as to fit into a Browning 9mm magazine. Keep that interesting data in mind for later.

Did it work? Yes. Was anyone interested? Aside from a bunch of other inveterate experimenters, not really.

The next step was another dead end in itself, but one that advanced this most-excellent caliber. Two fellows formed a company called "Dornhaus & Dixon." They designed and made a pistol to beat the band. It had a trigger system that could be either single action like the 1911, or double action like the wondernines. The trigger mechanism and grip shape were both inspired by the Czech CZ-75. The safety could be switched from one side to the other. It had high-capacity magazines, a comfortable grip shape even for being hi-cap, and the whole enterprise was cheered on by none other than Jeff Cooper himself. Oh, yes, this new pistol, called the "Bren Ten," was chambered in a new cartridge, the 10mm. In overall length, the 10mm matched that of the .45 ACP, not the shorter .40 G&A that fit into the rebuilt Browning Hi-Powers. Loaded by Norma, the 10mm ammunition promised, and delivered, a 200-grain bullet at 1200 fps. It was one hot load, and it looked like it would be the new hammer of Thor.

Except for one thing. The subcontractor making the magazines couldn't do

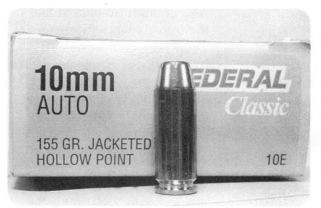

The 10mm is factory-available with bullet weights from 155 to 180 grains and can be reloaded in a range of 135 to 220 grains.

it. Early purchasers got their pistol with a magazine or magazines. Those not in the very first bunch of buyers got pistols lacking magazines. The guns weren't common, but the magazines were downright scarce. Magazines became a hot property, and prices quickly skyrocketed. Some other source quickly stepped in and offered magazines for $125 per! Today, paying $125 for a brand-new high-capacity magazine doesn't seem too painful. At least not for those worked over by a specialist and gunsmith like Dave Dawson, who tunes magazines for top IPSC competitors. Imagine paying that much in 1985, when you could buy a bushel basket full of 1911 military surplus magazines for $5 each. The gunsmith who taught me, Dan McDonald, had a Bren Ten, and glory be, his even came with magazines. He had a steady stream of potential buyers, all wanting the gun "and the magazines." He even had offers for just the magazines.

The Bren Ten even had the ultimate 1980's product

placement, in that it (for some reason) was selected as the sidearm of the main character on *Miami Vice*. Now a syndicated show on late-night cable, in the 1980s *Miami Vice* was the hottest thing on television. And Sonny carried a Bren Ten, at least for a couple of seasons. What with its being flashed on the tube each week it was the gun to have!

Without magazines, the Bren Ten was quickly a historical curiosity, and the 10mm was going to die an agonizing death. But then Colt saved it. (I can't imagine how such a serendipitous event came out of Colt back then, but as one of the fellows who taught me a great deal about selling guns once said: "Even a blind squirrel finds a nut now

Colt rescued the 10mm from oblivion.

and then.") Colt came out with the 1911 in 10mm, and called it the Delta. And in stainless, too! Smith & Wesson soon followed suit with their model 1006, and 10mm fans were in hog heaven. Then in 1986, a rolling stakeout squad of FBI agents attempted to arrest two armed bank robbers in Miami, Florida. The perpetrators objected, and when the smoke cleared the robbers were dead, two FBI agents were also dead, and most of the others were wounded. The FBI was not at all happy with the performance of the 9mm cartridge they had depended on, and soon instituted changes. The big one was caliber, and from then on, the 10mm was going to be the FBI cartridge. Unfortunately for all involved, reality soon reared its ugly head.

Smith and Wesson offered the only 10mm double action pistol on the market. The FBI decided (for reasons only they know) they wanted "improvements" to the trigger, in the design S&W had been fine-tuning for what was then over 30 years. While S&W made the required design changes, the FBI started training agents in the new 10mm. Even with an all-steel gun, the 10mm was too much of a handful. Agents who had been qualifying for years now found they couldn't manage the new gun using the hot new ammo. (I briefly owned a couple of S&W M-1026's, and I can't imagine trying to get the average law enforcement officer qualified on Norma ammo with one of them. "Not easily" is the answer.) Even backing off the load wasn't enough, as 180-grainers at 1150 were still too much. You see, just a few years before, the FBI had gotten itself in trouble in court because the firearms training program had been deemed behind the times and disproportionately unsuited for women. Backing off on the load didn't help much, as going from 200 grains at 1200 fps (a 240 PF) to 180 grains at 1050 fps (189 PF) is still a far cry from what the 9mm load had been: 115 grains at 1150 fps (132 PF).

On top of all that, how could those who did qualify carry the thing? An all-steel 10mm pistol is a big and heavy thing. Compared to the much lighter 9mms and revolvers agents had been carrying, it was far too big and heavy a gun for daily carry. S&W, worried about durability, refused to make an alloy-framed 10mm if the Bureau was going to insist on using full-power 10mm ammunition.

Oh, and the modifications the FBI wanted on the S&W pistol, the M-1076? Didn't work. The guns trigger mechanism locked up at random intervals, and the two sides ended up wrangling it out to no one's satisfaction.

In an attempt at making the load manageable, the FBI asked the ammunition makers to come up with yet another new load: 180 grain bullets at 950 fps (171 PF). The engineers at S&W and Winchester took one look at those specs, considered the dead air space that the resulting powder charge would leave in the case, and immediately thought of shortening the whole thing to fit a 9mm magazine tube. The result was the .40 S&W. Remember the .40 G&A that would fit into a Browning Hi-Power (9mm) magazine? Yes, the whole enterprise had come full circle. And the 10mm? It is the best pistol cartridge that most people don't shoot. It can be anything from a soft target load to a full-house hunting load. But because it requires a big gun, it gets neglected.

Left to right: standard .40 S&W cartridge; .40 loaded long for ISPC competition (too long for any Glock); 10mm.

40 S&W

So what is the attraction of the .40, if it isn't as powerful as the 10mm? Simple: It fits in a 9mm-sized pistol. Remember we were talking about pistol size when discussing the 9mm? The final package you have, once you fit all the needed parts around a 9mm cartridge, ends up as a compact and often ergonomic one. If you get much bigger in cartridge size, you can easily end up with a pistol that is too big to be convenient. When the ballisticians took the dead air space out of the "FBI Lite 10" and shortened the cartridge, they ended up with a round that would just barely fit in a 9mm pistol.

In 1990, the year the .40 was introduced, police departments across the country were in the midst of switching to 9mm pistols. While the 9mm offered more rounds than the traditional

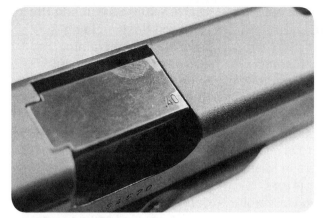

Glock barrels are plainly marked as to caliber, but they don't mention other manufacturers (like S&W) by name.

38 Special revolvers, it didn't offer much if any increase in stopping power. The .40, with heavier bullets, did.

When the 40 S&W was introduced, everyone involved had their fingers crossed. The introduction of any new cartridge is an uneasy time for the manufacturers. It takes a lot of money to do the R&D, set up the tooling, advertise and ship ammo to dealers. If the cartridge doesn't gain acceptance, they don't make money and may well lose a lot of cash. They needn't have

worried. Police departments that had just spent years analyzing and agonizing over switching to 9mm pistols couldn't dump the nines fast enough. They had to get their hands on 40s. Not all managed to do so as quickly as they might have desired. It took most of the 1990s to complete the transition, as some departments lagged behind.

The .40 is not the most forgiving cartridge to reload. It runs at roughly the same pressure as the 9mm and 10mm, but it lives in 9mm-framed pistols. To fit the .40 in a 9mm pistol, you have to have thinner chamber walls and thinner barrel walls. As an object feeding up the frame or barrel ramp, a .40 is a fat, stubby object compared to a 9mm. Vary the overall length too much, and you won't get a .40 to feed. Too long and it won't fit the magazine. Too short and it tips down when the slide tries to push it, and it ends up stubbed against the feed ramp.

The .40 runs at such a high pressure, with such a small combustion chamber (the space in the case left

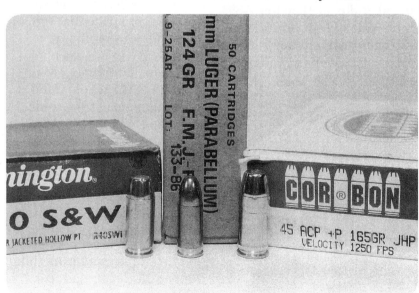

The .40 S&W compares favorably to the 9mm and .45, just in different ways. As a compromise, it's quite popular.

New calibers require new brass, and Starline makes plenty.

over once the bullet is seated in place), that any change becomes disproportionate compared to other cartridges. One problem new reloaders run into is bullet setback. A fat, stubby .40 has to be rudely shoved against the feed ramp and shouldered up into the chamber in order to feed at all. If the neck tension or crimp aren't up to the task, the bullet can get shoved back against the powder charge. What with the high operating pressure and the short case, a .40's pressure is going to be disproportionately increased by bullet setback compared to a 9mm. Add to that the thinner (in the .40) chamber walls, and you can bust a gun with ham-handed reloading faster with a .40 than with any other caliber.

But as a factory load, the .40 offers performance that does indeed bridge the gap between 9mm and .45, thus fulfilling the design objectives of those experimenters back in the 1970s.

.357 SIG

When stopping power was finally looked into with a little scientific rigor (there is still a large amount of contentious debate on the subject) one of the cartridges that stood out was the .357 Magnum. In particular, the .357 Magnum loaded with 125-grain jacketed hollowpoint bullets to the upper ends of velocity. In the "three fifty seven" those bullets could reach 1450 fps. Not orbital escape velocity by any means, but a lot more than the 9mm could manage. Not that the 9mm manufacturers didn't try. But not even special Law Enforcement

Only (LEO) loads, marked "9mm+P+" and loaded so hot the manufacturers wouldn't warranty them, could do it.

And without that velocity, the 9mm couldn't offer comparable stopping power. When IPSC competitors were hot on the trail of efficient compensators, one approach to getting enough slow burning powder into a case to feed the comp was the 9x25 Dillon. The short-lived Dillon is simply a 10mm case necked down to 9mm, and it is and was too much of a good thing. The noise, harsh recoil and abrasive effect on barrels and comps wasn't worth the marginal improvement in combatting muzzle rise that the comp offered during recoil. But what it did do was show how to get .357 Magnum velocities in a 9mm-sized pistol.

While the .357 SIG is essentially a .40 case necked down to 9mm, you can't make your ammo by necking down .40 cases. If you try, the neck won't come out the correct length; it will be too short. (And the .357 SIG case neck is

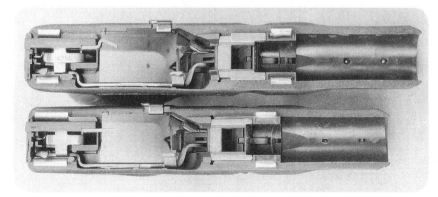

Converting from one caliber to another requires a correct-caliber frame, and you must know the frame length to select the correct barrel.

The .357 SIG fits any magazine (and thus any pistol) chambered for the .40 S&W.

already as short as it can be and still work. Make it shorter still and it becomes unsuitable for loading.)

The .357 SIG equals the .357 Magnum in velocity. If you worship at the altar of "velocity for stopping power" the SIG is for you. And it fits in the same size pistol that the 9s and .40s do.

The 9x25 Dillon? Dead as a competitive caliber for many years now. Does it have a use? Probably, but I can't think of one.

.45 ACP

It was only a matter of time. When Glocks first appeared, legions of American buyers looked at it and said "Neat! When will it be available in .45?" The word then, and for a long time, was "Never." After all, Glock was selling every single one they made in 9mm, so why make a new Glock? And since it would require a new design (or the old one re-proportioned) and thus new moulds and new tooling, why do it unless you're going to sell more pistols? But the American market insisted on a Glock in .45 and eventually got it.

As a cartridge, the .45 reflects the design imperatives of the era in which it was born. It is big and over-built, it operates at a low pressure and it is unbelievably forgiving. You can reload it with almost any powder made and come up with something useable. (Not that I would recommend using anything but published

The 9x25 Dillon was all the rage for a few years. Now, any pistol chambered for it is a curiosity, if it hasn't been converted back to 10mm.

powders and loading data.) You can load it with anything from roundballs or skinny 152-grain semiwadcutters to 300-grain bullets. (The 300's were experimented with for curiosity only; nothing useful came of it.)

.45 cases last forever, and I'm not sure you could wear out a .45 Glock by shooting ammo through it even if you won the lottery and ammo cost never entered your mind.

What the .45 didn't offer for a long time was a compact pistol. Oh, the shortened version of the G-30 was easier to carry and hide, but just as big around the grip. You can't

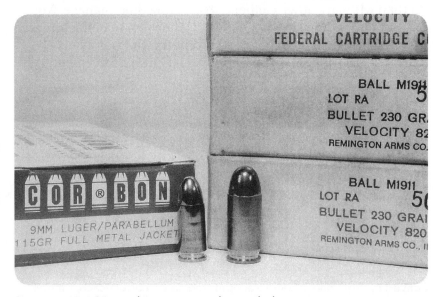

9mm vs. .45 ACP: a subject never to be settled.

have a double-stack magazine full of fat .45 cartridges and have a grip everyone can wrap their fingers around.

.45 GAP

Just when it looked as if things would proceed normally, Glock had to go and throw a wrench into the machinery: the .45 GAP. The .45 GAP is simple: a .45 ACP (more or less) shortened enough to fit into a 9mm magazine tube. Now, that thumbnail description glosses over a whole lot of engineering changes that had to be made, but it sums it up nicely.

Why? Again, the G-20/21 were and are just too big. Most people found them too large to handle, some found it simply too large, and even those who could manage it found the 9/40 frames a lot more manageable.

The .45 GAP has found quick acceptance with law enforcement, and a number of agencies have jumped on it right from the start. It has everything its advocates say it does: all the power of the .45 ACP, with as many bullet choices in weight and style,

and accuracy comparable to any other Glock. Just be aware that you can't get something for nothing: the 9mm/.40 sized Glocks, chambered in .45 GAP, are going to have stout recoil. Get used to it, because it is worth the price in recoil.

.45 HP

Along with 9mm being prohibited, the military caliber of .45 ACP is also prohibited in Italy. The .45 HP is simply a .45 ACP differing in length from the original. I haven't heard of Glock making any pistols in it, and there is no reason to do so here in the US. It does not differ in any way in bullet diameter or weight, velocity or loading data. If you are an oh-so-lucky collector who comes across a factory-marked G-21 in .45 HP, why would you shoot such a rare prize anyway?

.400 CorBon

The CorBon is cartridge with a long, and simple, heritage. I first saw its predecessor, the .41 Avenger, a .45 case necked down to .41, before the 10mm was invented.

As soon as 10s came about, the .41 Avenger lost favor due to most .410" bullets being designed for the .41 Magnum and therefore too long.

The .400 CorBon is the .45 case necked down to 10mm. Running at slightly elevated pressures (in the +P range for .45ACP), the .400 can push light 10mm bullets at impressive velocities. But the advantage is for light bullets only, for by the time you get to 180-grain bullets the .400 has lost its velocity edge over the .45. For someone wanting to run a comped pistol, the .400 has some allure. For example, I could see using .400 CorBon in a bowling pin gun, if you wanted 10mm (or slightly better) performance without buying a 10mm pistol. As a .45 ACP-based cartridge, it is obviously available only in .45 ACP-chambered pistols. If you can find barrels, you'll find them just for the full-sized G-21.

.45 Super

Instead of limiting things to .45ACP+P pressures, the .45 Super creeps up towards the 9mm/.40/10mm pressure ceiling. As a result, you can have velocity and power gains over the .45 even with full-weight bullets. The cost is simple: Different brass, increased powder consumption and increased muzzle blast and recoil. The standard .45 ACP brass is designed for an operating ceiling of 17,000 psi. To get .45 Super performance, you need

The .40 CorBon can be made from necked-down .45 ACP brass. It's also available from CorBon.

to be going up close to, or even edging beyond, the 30K range.

.45 Super brass is made tougher (and supposedly heavier, but I've weighed it and it isn't the heaviest stuff out there) to take the higher pressure. (.45 Super brass is the same size as regular .45 brass, so you must be very careful not to get Super powered ammo into a regular .45.) To boost bullets faster you need more powder, which increases reloading cost. And the higher pressure and slower-burning powders you're using increase recoil and muzzle blast. If you need the power, fine. If you don't, what's the point?

And you can do it all with a 10mm. Considering the cost of converting your pistol to the .45 Super (the originators insist it is more than simply installing a heavier recoil spring) you could simply buy a G-20 10mm Glock.

.460 Rowland

The Rowland is even hotter than the 45 Super. It uses cases that are longer than .45, so you can't get Rowland ammo to fit into a standard .45. The operating pressure is right up with the top loads in 10mm, and you get honest .44 Magnum ballistics: 230-grain bullets at 1350 fps! However, you simply must use a compensated barrel to keep the gun from beating itself to death. You'll have .44 Magnum recoil and muzzle blast.

But if you have to have .44 Magnum power and you want

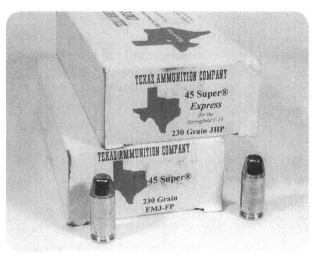

.45 Super brass is specially made for that cartridge. Don't use .45 ACP brass for .45 Super loads!

it in a self-loading pistol, the Rowland does the trick.

.38 Casull

The Casull is the winner and still champion of high velocity. The idea is simple. Make the biggest case (.45ACP) in the toughest manner (thick walls, tough brass, small primer pocket) and pump it up to the top

The .460 Rowland (*right*) uses longer brass than the .45 ACP to keep it from being chambered in .45 ACP pistols.

pressure the mechanism can stand. Then neck it down to take 9mm bullets and see just how fast you can squirt them out. In the .38 Casull, it means 124-grain bullets at 1825 fps. Are barrels in .38 Casull available for the Glock? I haven't seen any, but they are available in the 1911. Do you need one? Who said anything about need?

.22LR

I've saved the smallest for last, and because strictly speaking it isn't a caliber you can get as a Glock. What you have to do is obtain the conversion upper assembly to turn your Glock into a .22 rimfire. Rimfire conversions are an economical way to get practice, and a low-recoil way to introduce new shooters to the game. To convert a pistol to rimfire, you need not just a new barrel, but an entire upper assembly of barrel, slide and striker assembly. The slide for modern conversions is made of aluminum. The rimfire cartridge only has so

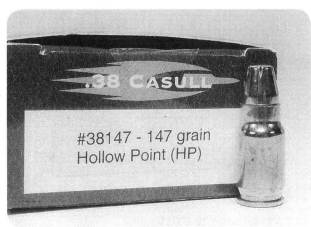

The .38 Casull comes loaded with 124- and 147-grain bullets. You can load others if you wish.

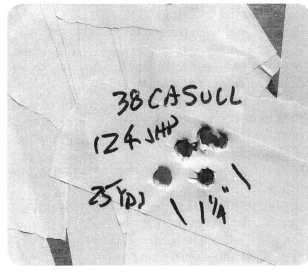

The .38 Casull is hot-hot-hot and plenty accurate.

If you want to shoot rimfire ammo out of your Glock, you'll have to get a conversion unit such as the one available from Advantage Arms.

much power, and can't cycle the weight of a steel slide. By making the new upper aluminum, and a blowback, the rimfire can cycle the slide. Conversions may seem a bit pricey, but the savings in ammo costs can recoup the investment in a few thousand practice rounds. Also, if you cannot lay hands on one of the Glock training guns, the .22 LR conversion is your lowest-cost firing practice pistol available.

The Really Odd Cartridges

The Glock is also available in two other versions, a training paint marker and rubber bullet version, and the "no-caliber Glock." The G-17T is available in a blue-framed version for Law Enforcement only, and can fire (depending on the barrel) either the 9x19FX cartridge or the 8x21AC. (The 9x19FX will not chamber a 9x19 Parabellum round.) They are used for two widely different applications. The paint marking rounds are used for force-on-force training. With proper face protection and additional padding, Police Officers can train against role-playing opponents, and the paint left by the impact of the rounds determines the outcome of a scenario.

The rubber-bullet rounds are not meant for use on live opponents. Instead, they are used for training where the use of live ammo would be unsuitable or dangerous. The rubber bullets could cause injury. Where they are useful would be for a SWAT team practicing room entry against cardboard targets, where the police range isn't set up for 360 degree firing. With rubber bullets, an old house, office building or abandoned warehouse could be pressed into service, and there would be no danger from live fire.

The "no-caliber Glock" is the red-frame G-17T. While the slide cycles, and the trigger works as expected, the barrel does not have a chamber or bore, and the striker tunnel does not have an opening in the breechface. A red-frame 17T can be used to demonstrate to a class, practice draw and dry-fire, and be handled in a crowd of students, without worry about pointing an actual firearm at anyone.

Unfortunately and as with so many other things, all the really neat toys are reserved for Law Enforcement only.

Calibers You'll Never See

Well, first, all the rimmed revolver cartridges. While I'm sure with a bit of work and ingenuity you could convert a Glock of some kind to feed .38 Special wadcutters, or .32 S&W Longs, what's the point? If you need them, you can get them already. The odd calibers that never made it are also goners. The .40 Action Express, a .41 bullet and case with a 9mm rim, never made much of a splash (and for good reason). With

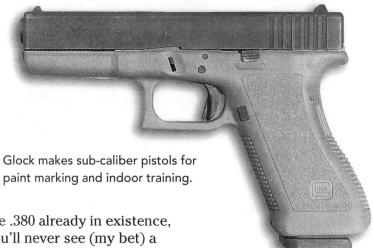

Glock makes sub-caliber pistols for paint marking and indoor training.

the .380 already in existence, you'll never see (my bet) a Glock in 9x18 Ultra or 9x18 Makarov. And with the fall of the Soviet Union and many of the technical standards it had, I don't think you can count on drawings of a 7.63 Tokarev Glock being on anyone's drafting table.

According to manufacturing economics, the purpose of a factory is to make saleable products. Unless there is a market somewhere for a lot of Glocks in a particular caliber, you won't see any. And that goes for all the other firearms makers, too. Unless 9x18 Makarov ammunition is cheaper than dirt because the Chinese are giving cases of it away with every set of chopsticks purchased, you won't see Glock, S&W, Ruger or anyone else making pistols for it. After all, if they're giving away the ammo, it's to prop up sales of their own (Chinese) pistols, not ours. You want a Glock in the weird ones, you'll have to make it yourself.

Caliber Conversions

In the 1911 world, it is common to convert a pistol

from one caliber to another, or build a pistol that has multiple barrels or upper assemblies, to shoot other calibers. Two factors work to make 1911 combo guns more common: there is a large pool of parts to be had, and the cost of buying a new pistol can be significant. Adding to the initial cost of a new pistol would be the duplication of any custom features the first one has. Thus, if you start with a basic .45 1911, and you add a few custom tricks like a beavertail, adjustable sights, hard

You'll never see a Glock in .38 Special. No need for it, with accurate 9mm models available.

chrome, etc., you can quickly come close to the $2000 figure. Doing all that again in 10mm is hard to justify when with a little careful planning you can build a new 10mm upper assembly for your .45 for $500 to $600.

Why not do this with a Glock? First of all, buying a new 10mm Glock would cost about as much as the built upper assembly for the 1911. And since you wouldn't need the beavertail and hard chrome job, you could have four or five Glock for the cost of the custom 1911 and its new-caliber upper assembly.

1911 owners rebuild old guns and build new assemblies for them to get more use out of an existing frame. Glock owners just buy another Glock. But some conversions make sense. If all you need is a new barrel and recoil spring, they will certainly cost less than a new Glock. And if you happen to live in some god-forsaken jurisdiction where getting another pistol is a major hassle, converting an existing pistol also makes a lot of sense.

Where it starts to break down is when you need to add a slide to the cost. While Caspian makes excellent slides, it is hard to justify buying one when you can buy a new Glock for the conversion cost when converting involves a new slide, except for something like a Racegun. Let's say you have a G-17, and you want to shoot in Open competition in USPSA/IPSC. You need

to install a compensated barrel. The barrel on a Glock is removed from the slide to the rear during disassembly. A comp, to work best, must be securely fastened, usually by using epoxy or Loctite on the threads. Once locked in place, the comped barrel won't come out of the slide. You can't go back to Stock configuration easily.

If you have an additional slide, you can build a new top end and go from Open to Stock by switching assemblies. In Open you'll need a red-dot sight, but you can easily get a clamp-on mount, and re-zero your pistol when you change from one to the other.

Another example would be in making a 9-pin 9mm Glock for bowling pin shooting. Again, you'd need a comped barrel. Yes, you could buy another 9mm Glock (most likely a G-17) and then add an extended, threaded barrel and comp. Either way, you'll be buying a barrel and comp. So, which costs less, another whole Glock, or a slide and its internals?

The cost comparisons are simple, but figuring out what you want, and how much extra work and effort you're willing to go to in order to get it is something you'll have to decide for yourself.

Ammo and Reloading

Given the recent increase in ammunition prices, many shooters who have not reloaded in the recent era are now eyeing the prospect.

The Glock's distinctive firing pin hit is clearly visible on the right. The impression on the left is from a non-Glock pistol.

For a few years until the war, ammo costs were so low that in some calibers shooters simply didn't bother to reload. (9mm is the big one there, as you could buy 9mm FMJ ammunition so cheaply for many years that it really didn't pay to reload.

Glock pistols are designed to be reliable in function. You will have to search long and hard to find a pistol more reliable than the G-17 or any of its stablemates. But you can choke them. If you expect your Glock (or any pistol for that matter) to be reliable, you have to feed it proper ammo. By proper, I mean the correct caliber, within accepted pressure levels, and dimensionally correct. You will be hard-pressed to find factory ammo that is off the mark, but you can. Ditto commercial reloads. (If you're curious, a little cruising of the more popular forums on the internet will get you the names of the prime suspects.)

If you want to use commercial reloads in your Glock, ask around. The other shooters at your gun club can tell you who they've had good and bad experiences with. Take the recommendations with a grain of salt. Some shooters have bad luck with everything they try. Others don't. If you get three or four guys at your club telling you they've had bad luck with a particular brand, then you should listen.

I had an instructional experience recently on just this subject. I was at a National SWAT conference and ran into a commercial reloader I had known of for years. I had known of them because I'd had a number of customers arrive a the shop with busted guns, and that brand of reload featured frequently in the bulged barrels, blown mags, etc. I figured I had nothing to lose, so I asked the owner about the problem. He asked. "Did the problems ever stop?" I thought for a moment, and mentioned that after a certain year I stopped seeing guns come in with bulged

barrels. He said "Yes, I fired my brother-in-law about that time, and took things over myself." See, companies can learn, improve, and change the perceptions of their customers.

Personal reloads are another matter. First things first: Using reloaded ammunition voids the warranty on your Glock. Nothing new there, as using reloads voids the warranty on every other firearm you could buy, too. And why not? Glock (and all the other firearms manufacturers) have no control over the quality of the ammunition you produce. If you produce good ammunition, your Glock will perk along famously. As will every other pistol or revolver you put your ammo in. If you produce shoddy ammunition, why would you expect Glock to make right the result of your poor workmanship? End of soapbox.

Use correct brass for your loads. Don't go converting it from something else just to save a few bucks. In the case of .40 Super, conversion will be more expensive than buying factory brass.

If you are using factory-new or commercially-reloaded ammunition, then you can expect years of satisfying shooting. If you are going to reload your own, then you'll need to know a few things about what self-loading pistols in general, and Glocks in particular, demand. And then you too can produce flawless ammo for years to come.

Sizing

Your brass must be sized down to minimum factory or book dimensions. There is no such thing as "neck sizing" in handgun reloading, as there is in rifle reloading. Each and every case must be sized fully. You can't expect cases that have bulged over the feed ramp to work unless you iron the bulge out. And if you iron the bulge too many times, the case may be work-hardened and brittle. If your 9mm brass is cheap because it comes from the local police department SWAT team and

If you're going to load ammo, get current manuals and pay attention to the advice they offer.

their submachineguns, sort out and toss the bulged ones. (Yes, you can go to extra effort and size the bulge down, but if the brass is free, why bother?)

If you try to exceed the velocities in the reloading manuals, you may do some brass bulging yourself. There are good and valid reasons for the upper limits in published data. Believe them. I've known reloaders who quite heatedly argue that the upper limits are there just so the ammo makers can charge extra money for +P and +P+ ammo. (One in particular told me with a straight face that he could exceed .357 Magnum velocities in his 9mm Parabellum: "The brass is built extra tough for use in subguns. Handguns can use the extra margin built into the brass." Rather than argue the point, I just made sure I wasn't standing nearby whenever he was shooting.) Bulged brass in your reloads is a sign you have greatly exceeded proper pressures. Buy a reloading manual and pay attention to the upper limits they publish. Inspect your brass and stop using loading data that produces bulged brass.

Primer Seating

The primers must be seated flush or below flush with the case head surface. In the feeding process, the base of the cartridge must slide along the breechface, and slip under the extractor. A high primer acts as if the case had a too-thick of a rim, preventing good feeding. Oh, you can get away with it sometimes, but sooner or later the high primer is going to cause the round to hesitate just a bit in feeding, throw off the feed timing, and stop your Glock.

And high primers create another problem: failure to fire. A high primer that still feeds and chambers can fail to fire. The high primer isn't fully seated, and some of the impact of the striker goes to bottoming the primer into its pocket. If the final primer seating takes too much energy from the striker, there won't be enough left to set off the primer. When you extract the

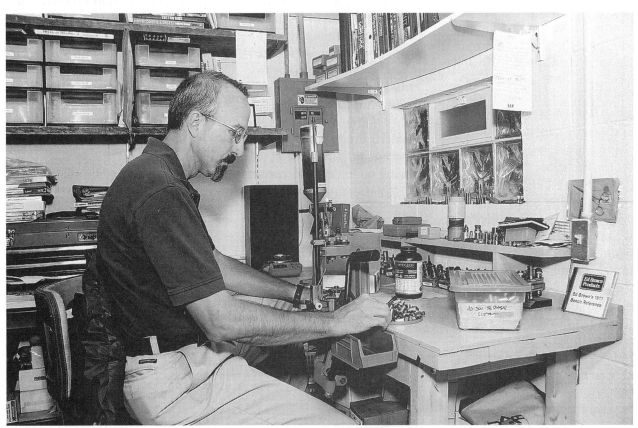

Reloading can save money. Keep your reloading bench clean and keep good records.

round, you'll see a smaller than usual dimple in the primer. New shooters often assume it is due to a hard primer or a light strike. Not so. If failure to fire happens with your reloads, look to a high primer as the cause. If factory, then look to a grubby pistol that wasn't fully closed as the problem.

Case Neck Diameter

Guy Neill, in the September/October 2002 issue of *Front Sight* (the publication of the United States Practical Shooting Association), reported finding a .40 cartridge with the bullet set back in the case. Luckily, it had been one chambered but not fired, as it had set back .060"! Experiments by the NRA some decades earlier had shown that a setback amount of only .030" could cause a doubling of the chamber pressure of the 9mm Parabellum. As the 9mm and 40 run with a pressure ceiling of 34,000 PSI, even moderate reloads can be a problem when the bullet sets back. Let's say your conservative and moderate reloaded ammunition only runs at 26,000 PSI. If the bullet goes back .030" and thus doubles pressure, you now have a 52,000 PSI round. As a Proof Load in .40 S&W would only be about 44,000 PSI, you can see what the new pressure is: a busted case ready to happen.

Guy sat down and measured the neck wall thickness of the cases he had

Primed cases are expensive. When you seat your primers, make them flush.

on hand, and found that the wall thickness varied by .0012" from thickest to thinnest. That might not seem like much, but it is.

A set-back bullet, with greatly increased chamber pressure as a result, could lead to a blown case or damaged gun. I had been loading my .40 ammo using a .397" diameter expanding bell. (The expander opens up the case after the sizing die has squeezed it down, making room for the bullet.) A .397" bell, with thin walls, could cause a setback. That I had not seen any could be attributed to most of my loading and shooting of .40 having been done in various 1911 platforms. I went down to

the loading room and started measuring my .40 brass. Sure enough, I found a few that had thin neck walls. I loaded those up with my standard load and proceeded to test case setback by pressing them against the bench. They all held.

Feeling just a bit silly from rampant paranoia, I then proceeded to hand-feed them through my G-22 several times. Measuring them afterwards I felt just a bit self-conscious. Until I measured the last one. It had set back .015" in overall length! Not as much as Guy's had, not enough to be instantly obvious from looking, but set back.

What to do? I took my expander and chucked it in

Thin case necks and lack of neck tension can cause bullet setback, resulting in a kB! (ka-boom!).

my drill press and polished it down with an india stone until it was just over .395" in diameter. I then finished polishing with 600-grit emery cloth to .3950" diameter. Is it enough? With a heavy sigh I sat back down and fished through the .40 brass to find some more thin-walled brass. After an hour I'd found another couple dozen, so I loaded them with the new diameter belling stem and tested them. This time there were no setbacks, either bench-test or fed through the G-22.

My future .40 loads will have a tighter grip on the bullet. They all will also be working the brass harder, but the end result will be a fractional increase in the rate of neck cracking with repeated use. Neck cracks are not a problem, as they act to decrease chamber pressure if not discovered. My dies for .400 CorBon and .40 Super have belling stem diameters of .389" and .390" respectively. Both cases have short necks and thus a need for tight neck tension. Using those as examples, my .40 S&W die can be tightened even more without causing loading problems, should I wish to polish down that belling stem even more.

Crimp

You have to have enough crimp to securely hold the bullet. If you don't, the bullet may set back into the case when it hits the feed ramp. (See above.) A bullet set back in the case increases (sometimes greatly) the chamber pressure when fired. And insufficient crimp leads to inconsistent ignition, too, leading to velocities varying a great deal, and accuracy suffering. However, too much crimp is bad. In particular, the 9mm can be quite touchy about the proper crimp. Too little, and you get wildly varying velocities. Too much, and you get tumbling bullets, especially with lead or plated bullets.

Generally, you want your crimp (tapered, always, for a pistol) three thousandths under the standard case plus bullet diameter. As an example, if you're loading .45 ACP, you take the bullet at .451", and the case mouth with a wall thickness of .010". Double the case wall thickness (both sides, remember?) and add to the bullet diameter to get .471". Subtract .003" and your taper crimp figure comes to .468". Since many .45 shooters load lead bullets, which measure .452", the common taper crimp you'll hear 1911 shooters talking about is .469".

Use the same process for the other calibers. Then check accuracy over sandbags, or in the hands of the best shooter at your club.

Overall Length

How long? As long as will reliably fit and feed through the magazine. No great secret here. If you're going to load 115-grain bullets for your 9mm, save a few 115-grain factory loads and set them in a drawer or box. Measure and record their lengths. Load your ammunition to match the average of those lengths. How short? No shorter than the shortest factory cartridge of that bullet weight. Since you have to have at least some of the bullet in the case, you won't be loading many

Neck tension and crimp are important on loads for every pistol, not just for Glocks.

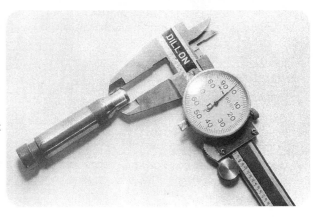

Measure your belling expander diameter and make sure it's tight enough.

88-grain jacketed hollowpoint bullets. No loss. Short bullets nosedive, and the changed angle of the cartridge in feeding makes it tough for the slide to wrestle the stubby thing up the ramp and into the chamber. If you want to try, go ahead. But if it turns out your pistol won't feed extremely short ammunition, give up. No point in making yourself crazy for no advantage gained in a match.

Bullet Weight

Stick with weights in the normal range as loaded by the various manufacturers. There is a reason you don't see 115-grain jacketed hollowpoints in .40 or 10mm or 147-grain hollowpoints in .45. Not only are they tough to fabricate and load into cases, the bullet weight and size don't couple well with the case volume. (There is also that overall length problem, too.) You don't see many 180-grain bullets wrestled into 9mm cases or 300-grain .45ACP loads. The cases don't have enough volume to hold the bullet and have any room left over for powder. I tried both in the interests of scientific inquiry, and they traveled so slowly I could easily see them in flight.

Powder Selection

Powders are made for different burn rates and density. Within the loading limits they are designed for, they work fine. Take a powder too far outside of its "comfort zone" and you'll be surprised at what you get. Stick with published data, and resist the impulse to "get a little more" out of a powder. If you really need more velocity, and you're at the maximum listed powder charge, then start all over again with a slower-burning powder.

A fast powder pushed past its upper limit can become very touchy. As an example, if you were to load a fast-burning powder to the maximum, and then forget and leave a box of it in the sun, you might find pressures have exceeded your expectations. A blown case can be the result.

If you need a soft load, but only have magnum powders, invest in a pound of fast-burning stuff intended for soft target loads. A slow powder loaded below its efficient ignition pressure becomes a very dirty load indeed. I've seen shooters loading small charges of slow-burning powders that left so much unburnt powder behind that the residue gummed up their handgun in short order.

And if the slowest powder for that caliber still doesn't deliver the power you need, get a bigger gun. Don't try to turn a .40 into a 10mm. Buy a 10mm. It's a Glock; it isn't expensive.

If you are going to load your own ammunition for use in competition where there is a threshold, or power factor minimum, you must own a chronograph. You cannot depend on known data for accurate velocities. There is just enough difference in barrels, powder charges, bullet weights, diameters and hardnesses, that what looks in the book to "Make Minor" might in your gun be

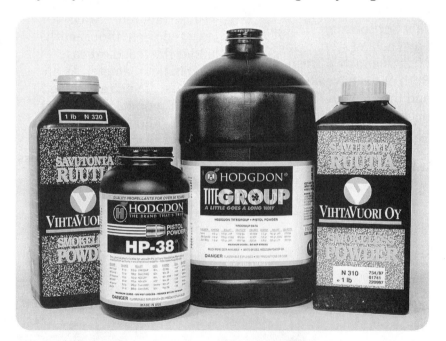

Powder selection depends on the caliber and the intended use. Most of the time, if what you want is more power, you should have started with a bigger caliber.

quite a bit under. It would be a disadvantage to think you were loading your ammo to 130 PF, only to find at the match that you are actually shooting a 151 PF load and putting up with the extra recoil for naught. Or worse, if you thought you were loading a 130 PF load and arrived at the match only to find at the chrono station that you were actually loading to a 123 PF, you didn't make Minor, and your "score" for the match was now zero.

I have recently switched to a CED chronograph (the one used as the official chronograph in USDPSA competition) and have found it very convenient, easy to use and portable. My old system with all its paraphernalia took up a case the size of a steamer trunk. The new one is smaller than my camera bag.

Lead

Ah, the big question. Lead and Glocks. Lead is a dense, soft metal with a low melting point and one that readily alloys with a number of different hardening elements. Atomic symbol Pb, from the Latin *plumbum*, which is also the root of "plumbing." The Romans used to use it for water pipes and seals in aqueducts. They also cast it into balls for their slingers to hurl in support of the Legions, complete with the legion's name, number or motto cast in them.

Lead has mild to moderate medical hazards. Listen to the EPA and anti-

gunners and you'd think lead was as toxic as plutonium. It isn't, with few exceptions.

Lead bullets and Glocks don't get along. Generally speaking, the factory barrels on Glocks lead quickly, causing a decrease in accuracy and an increase in chamber pressure. The use of lead bullets in .40 caliber Glocks has been implicated in the "ballistic disassembly" of a number of those pistols. Why? No one is quite sure. There is a great deal of speculation. Some focus on the polygonal rifling, surmising that the better seal it offers increases leading. I'm not too hot on that idea for two reasons. One, H-K uses polygonal rifling, and they don't seem to suffer from leading like Glocks. And two, past experience with cast bullets has shown that it is a poor seal that leads to gas-cutting and really severe leading, not a tight one.

Another line of speculation is that the Tenifer treatment makes the surface of the bore "too hard" and thus increases friction. Again,

I'm not buying it. A harder surface, all other things being equal, has less friction, not more. And proper bullet lube should protect a bore regardless of its hardness.

One promising line of inquiry is the matter of bullet lube. The black powder shooters among us have found that lubricant is critical to accuracy, preventing leading, and reducing fouling. It's my bet that some enterprising caster could make a killing by tracking down just what lubricants reduce or eliminate leading in Glocks. Properly marketed, such a lube or line of bullets could prove very popular. After all, if it won't lead a Glock, it can't be bad in other pistols, right?

My own theory on the matter is that a number of small variables have to stack up against the Glock in order for the problem to surface. After all, the observation of leaded Glock bores is not universal. So if the bore diameter or the bullet diameter vary, or if the bullet's hardness vs. its

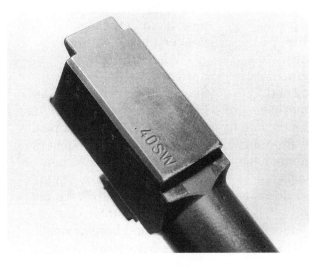

Glock used to mark their .40 barrels with ".40SW" but they're now marked only "40." If you want to use lead bullets in your Glock, swap out the factory barrel for a cut-rifling match barrel.

velocity and pressure limits are incompatible, or if the lubricant is too hard or too soft, or if the powder is too fast or too abrasive, you'll get leading. And whereas in other pistols where you'd need all of these causes to get leading, in the Glock you only need two or three of them.

In the midst of all my speculation, Robin Taylor sent forth his Second Edition of *The Glock in Competition*. In it he has a chapter by Mark Passamaneck that gives the best technical explanation of Glocks and lead bullets I have read. Basically, the bore is tighter than a cut-rifling bore is, swaging the bullet and thus increasing leading. There's a bit more to it than that. However, as I am not one to simply appropriate research data, if you're really curious about all the gory details, get Robin's book. (Taylor Freelance is the publisher.)

If leading is such a problem, why doesn't the factory solve it? Let's see. The rest of the world hardly lets anyone reload ammo at all, and those that do use jacketed bullets. Factory ammo is almost exclusively produced with jacketed bullets. With jacketed bullets the pistols work just fine, offering reliability, accuracy and durability. Only Americans are in the position of being able to afford to do lots of shooting, load their own, and are cheap enough to use unjacketed bullets. Austria just doesn't see it as a problem.

What to do if you want to use lead? The simple solution

is to switch barrels. Get a replacement barrel from a barrel maker who is familiar with the unique American insistence on lead bullets, and be happy.

And if you are going to be cheap and obstinate, and refuse to swap barrels? First, use hard-cast bullets with a good lube. A little experimentation could find that a particular brand works better in your Glock than others. Second, brush your bore regularly during a shooting session. (Unloaded, of course!) One of the Glock shooters in our club brushes his G-19 out between stages. Brushed every 30-50 rounds, his accuracy and reliability don't suffer. The Boresnake is a very useful tool for this: you can go to a Safe Area between each stage of a match and run the Boresnake through your Glock a couple of times, and keep the leading under control. Third, never, and I mean NEVER use lead bullets in a .40-caliber Glock. We may not know the exact mechanism by which leading and pressure spikes occur, but we do know one thing: they primarily are a problem in the 40s. Why? A convergence of variables.

When the .40 was designed, the intent was to make it fit a 9mm size pistol. Pistol makers soon found that it took more than just opening the breechface, changing the barrel and installing a heavier recoil spring to turn a 9mm into a .40. The Glock 40s are 9mm-sized pistols. A larger chamber and bore means a thinner barrel wall. To make

the pistols feed reliably, the chambers are on the larger side of the specifications. Brass fired in a .40 Glock gets worked harder that it would in another .40, and it won't last as long. When the tired brass lets go, the thinner walls aren't able to contain it like other pistols would. And the polymer frame can't take the gaff.

I've seen several other pistols blow cases, and I was on one occasion shooting a 10mm Colt Delta that blew a case. In all the instances I've seen, the damage was limited by the rigidity of the steel frame. In the steel-frame guns, the magazine was blown out of the gun and damaged beyond repair. Curiously, the 10mm didn't even damage the magazine when it blew. I think it was because the magazine came apart as it was designed to for cleaning and assembly. Once I found all the magazine parts, I reassembled it and it worked fine. I still have it. It still works fine. I don't use that load any more.

I've seen the aftermath of one aluminum-framed gun that had a blown case. The frame bulged, the magazine was damaged, and the slide was cracked.

Now, imagine the ability of polymer to resist impact. That's why a Glock that gets a blown case ends up as such a spectacle. The problem isn't that the Glocks in .40 are so "fragile" but that .40s are more likely to let go. It is a rare 10mm, and not even a common .45 that blows. (Haven't seen a 9mm yet.)

The Ka-Boom! Phenomenon

So, how to explain all those Glocks that have blown up? First of all, we have to define "all those" as a figure. Let's assume for the moment that there are only one million .40-caliber Glocks in the US. (A conservative number. Glock passed the one million total mark in less than nine years, and the .40 was only a couple of years old at that time.) Now let's assume that each of those Glocks has 100 rounds put through it each year, another conservative number. Yes, we all know of pistols that have been bought but never fired, but they aren't Glocks. Glock owners love to shoot. Police Departments that issue Glocks can plan on each pistol getting a bunch more than a hundred rounds a year through them.

That's one hundred million firing events a year. Now, assume we have 10 ka-booms a year. (A higher number than I know of.) Wow, assuming the events are totally at random, your chances are one in 10 million of experiencing a ka-boom the next time you pull the trigger on your Glock. But we all know that every one of those occurrences will be splashed across the internet and find their way onto tens of thousands of web pages. That's why it seems like a bigger problem than it is.

Let's make it even better. We know that of the 10

This 1911 didn't survive a double charge of powder. Glocks aren't the only handguns that occasionally suffer a ka-boom! problem.

blowups, one will be a truly mysterious random event, and the other nine will be reloaded ammunition, probably using lead bullets. If you use jacketed bullets in your reloads, your odds now drop to one in a hundred million. If you're still worried at this point, I'd suggest offsetting your worries about the cost of a new Glock by investing in lottery tickets as a retirement plan. Your odds are actually better at hitting the lottery than they are at experiencing a ka-boom in your Glock if you take even the most rudimentary precautions.

Of those nine, they will almost all be lead bullets, and probably seven or eight of them will be 40s. So, the lead-fed .40 Glock starts to get leading in the bore. As the lead builds up, it reduces the space in the front of the chamber for the round. The round is kept from fully chambering, and if it happens to almost-but-not-quite close and still fire, there can be a problem. The case is in this instance even less supported than usual. The case wall exposed is even thinner than

the thicker base and lets go.

Now, let us add one more insult to the problem. The reloader perhaps hasn't paid attention to his loading, and on this particular round, the bullet has set back into the case. The setback has happened before, but the bore had been clean then. The grubby bore holding the action almost-but-not-quite closed has happened before, but not with setback. In both earlier instances, the gun survived. Not this time.

The violently jetting gases from the blown case hammer into plastic and gain additional leverage on steel that wouldn't otherwise have to stand the pressure. The result is a trashed gun And since there are so many people predisposed to dislike Glocks, the results get published.

The solution is simple, and not at all expensive. If you really, really, don't want to run the (astronomically small) risk, use factory 9mm ammo. Or, change your barrel to a cut-rifling barrel designed for lead, and stop worrying about it.   ◆

CHAPTER 4

The Advantages of the Glock

Besides its cool looks (although some argue that traditional blued steel and wood are what "real men" carry), just what are the advantages of the Glock? There must be some reason police departments across the country, and hordes of individual owners have plunked down their money to own a Glock.

few egregious designs that should have never seen the light of day, like the Nambu Type 94) what the Glock had going for it to start with was timing. When the Glock was designed and manufactured in the early 1980s, every other design it was facing had been on the market for decades. In those preceding years, the

other pistols had in many cases been manufactured to a less demanding standard. They had been made when precision meant hand fitting, and everyone expected pistols to be somewhat less reliable than revolvers. Soon the "hand-fit vs. reliability" debate would sputter out, but until then, Glock was first.

Reliability

While the Glock design is not inherently more reliable than any other design (with the exception of a

A good 1911 gunsmith carefully adjusts the extractor tension. The Glock doesn't need it.

Unlike 1911 extractors, Glock extractors drop right in without requiring careful polishing and adjustment.

The changes came about for two reasons: competition and law enforcement. Competition shooters had been making a change in perception ever since IPSC burst on the scene back in 1976. In Bullseye shooting, a malfunction afforded you the opportunity to re-shoot a string of fire. Called an "alibi," it was expressly forbidden in IPSC shooting. Many malfunctions that an IPSC competitor encountered in the course of shooting in a match were viewed as problems he had to solve – and solve while the clock was ticking. As a result, IPSC competitors demanded both reliability and accuracy. When police departments started really looking to switch to pistols from revolvers, they demanded reliability. There is nothing mysterious about a reliable pistol; it is simply a matter of correct dimensions in design and manufacturing.

For a long time, one of the obstacles (real or imagined) to police departments adopting pistols and leaving their revolvers behind was

Will a Glock frame crack? Yes, occasionally. But if it does, Glock will replace it.

reliability. "Revolvers always work" was a statement made to me by a big-city police officer back in those days. As a gunsmith I knew better, but there was no way I was going to convince him otherwise. A few departments had tried, switched to or allowed pistols to be carried before the early 1980s. The Indiana State Police used S&W M-39s. The Bakersfield PD used 1911 pistols. The Detroit PD allowed double action pistols, used with full metal jacketed ammunition. But if an officer in DPD couldn't get his pistol through the qualification course without a malfunction, it wouldn't be allowed on the street.

Meanwhile, the county that I lived in then issued 4" .38 Special revolvers and allowed personally-owned revolvers of certain brands as back-up. A sergeant who ran the PPC league was known to carry his department .38 on his belt and a S&W .44 Magnum in a shoulder holster in the wintertime as his "backup." Revolvers had worked for them for decades, and they, and many other police departments, had not seen any point in changing.

And then Glock showed up with their "indestructible pistols," as one officer remarked to me. The Glocks in the cement mixer and dragged behind the car were certainly showy, but when they were quickly followed with thousands of rounds of reliable shooting, the sale was made. Once Glock had shown the hesitant purchasers of police

departments that reliability could be taken for granted, other manufacturers had to prove as good, or fail in sales.

Glock was just "fustest with the mostest" as a certain Civil War General was known to remark. (He was talking about what wins battles, while Glock was going for market share.) The level of reliability that Glocks demonstrate can be approached and matched by other pistols, but there is a definite advantage in being first.

Durability

Here Glock has a definite advantage. The polymer frame shrugs off impacts that would dent or crack other frames made of aluminum or steel. Unless you're willing to make your handgun excessively bulky (and thus solid) it won't be as durable. And that heavy, who'd want it?

When the Miami Police Department was testing the Glock to see if it would be suitable for issue, the officer tasked with the test, Armando Valdes, came up with a brutal test: He would stand at some location in a precinct house and ask everyone who walked by to throw the test Glock. Some simply dropped it. Others took advantage of the opportunity and hurled it as far and hard as they could. It survived. When the thrill of that test wore off, he took it to a parking structure and dropped it off the fifth floor onto the concrete driveway. It continued to work fine.

I shudder to think what a 1911 would look like after all that. As for its working, I wouldn't bet on it.

Weight

The Glock's big Glock advantage is its weight. Or lack thereof, really. The standard G-17 tips the scales empty at a feathery 22 ounces. Comparable pistols come in 25 to 30 percent heavier, and revolvers must be quite compact to beat the Glock. Big revolvers can't do it; small or airweight can; but they all lack capacity. The following list of handgun weights will give you some idea of the differences:

1911 Government Model: **36 to 40 oz.**
1911 Commander, steel: **29 to 33 oz.**
1911 LW Commander: **22 to 24 oz.**
Beretta M-92: **30 to 31 oz.**
S&W M-59: **35 to 38 oz.**
S&W M-65 .357 Mag 3": **33 to 34 oz.**

There is not a single precise weight for a given model for the simple reason that changing things like sights, grips, guide rods safeties and magazine funnels can alter the weight. The ones listed are for relatively bare models. You can easily add several ounces with something like a magazine funnel, and a few more with a replacement recoil spring guide rod.

It isn't unheard of for a competition 1911 built for Open IPSC shooting to weigh 48 ounces, empty. I've hefted some Limited class guns (no compensator, no red-dot scope) that came really

Glock's Tenifer finish shrugs off the rust that can attack ordinary blued-steel handguns.

close to that three pound figure. In researching weights of handguns for the book, I recorded the weights of every pistol I own, plus every pistol that had come through the shop for the last few years for various articles and testing for other books. How many weighed less than an empty G-17? Twelve of the 132 pistols I have recorded weights for

beat the Glock G-17. And of those 12, two were .38 Special revolvers, one was a five-shot S&W stainless, and one a Colt six-shot airweight. The rest were various .380s, .32s .25s and .22 rimfires.

As an interesting note, there are some .32s and .380s I weighed that were actually heavier than the G-17. Two in particular, a Colt model M

If you're going to shoot in Open, you'll need more than a box-stock Glock.

in 380, at 23.7 ounces and a Hungarian M-37 in .32, at 26.4 ounces, were eye-openers. At a measly seven shots each, and in only .380 or .32, they would have been perfect examples of acceptable European police sidearms for decades prior to the development of the Glock. Comparing them to a G-17 gives you an idea of just what a revolution the Glocks were in Europe, even before they started turning American heads.

One theoretical disadvantage of the light weight is the change of balance due to ammo. The weight of a loaded magazine can noticeably alter a pistol's balance, and some have latched onto the idea that as the ammo supply changes while you're firing, the balance can also change. Nice theory, but it doesn't seem to change enough to keep shooters from shooting excellent scores.

to manufacturing. The sides are flat, the front is rounded to match the contour of the magazine (which is shaped to accommodate the jacketed round nose ammunition first used in it) and the rear of the grip is designed to house the mechanics of the hammer spring, strut and the grip safety. The grips bring the frame to a shape that is comfortable to grasp. But the design requires 10 extra parts just in the grips and their attachment hardware.

The S&W is made to house the magazine, with the rear left open as a simple structural frame. The grip is a plastic moulding that gives you a place to grab and to shoot with. The grips are one piece and held in place by the cross pin. The disadvantage to the S&W method is the structural framework of the rear of the frame. While plenty sturdy

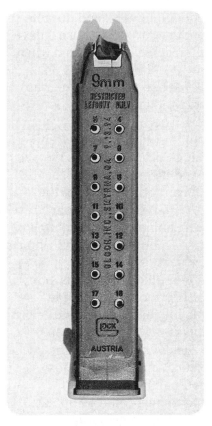

Restricted, "Law Enforcement Only" markings are now just collectors' curiosities – in most states, anyway.

Grip Shape

The advantageous shape of the Glock grip stems from two things; the polymer design and the European search for a "natural pointing angle" between grip and bore.

The polymer design of the Glock frame means that there is no need for grips. And the deletion of grips also means no grip screws, no bushings for same and no need to worry about them coming loose. Two examples of the earlier design efforts in pistols are the 1911 and the S&W M-59 series. The 1911 has a frame shape conducive

The Glock with a couple of earlier-era defense pistols: a Hungarian M-37 *(top)* and a Colt Model M *(bottom)*.

enough to work and durable enough for most abuse, I have seen some that cracked when dropped and one bent on impact so the magazine was trapped in place.

The Glock's grip angle comes from Gaston Glock's design study. He used measurements from the shooting hands of the Austrian Cadet Corps to determine the proper angle of grip to bore. While the whole subject of "pointability" in my opinion is just this side of voodoo, many people place great stock in it. (I guess my indoctrination to reflexively use the sights at every opportunity is just too much of a hurdle for me to overcome.) And if a pistol has a grip that falls within the useable range, then many will find it quite comfortable to use. Hey, if I'm wrong and Gaston Glock was on to something, then that would go a long way toward explaining why so many find Glocks so easy and comfortable to shoot.

The Glock's grip is shaped well to the hand, the angle is certainly within the allowable range, and the lack of sharp edges definitely aids shooting. On the last subject, I've seen pistols right out of the box that had sharp edges or corners that made shooting painful. Glocks certainly don't have sharp edges. Indeed, for many custom gunsmiths, the search for a "dehorned" pistol, one that feels like a bar of used soap and won't abrade the hand, consumes much

of their time. Glocks have rounded edges and corners and no sharp parts to gouge you on firing.

Low Bore

Most pistols pose mechanical problems if you try to get the bore low to the hand. Once you've machined the rails (in the design stage) in the slide and frame, then wrestled a barrel in there and provided room for it to move up and down in the lock and unlock cycle, you've got a tall stack of parts. Three examples that many would be familiar with are the 1911, the S&W M-59 series and the Beretta M-92. In all three examples, the hammer pivot hole has to be below the slide rails. Otherwise, there wouldn't be sufficient support for the hammer pivot pin. Could you move the pivot pin up? Sure, but then you'd have to do something about the linkage to the trigger. On the 1911 and the S&W, the barrel locks into the slide with locking lugs machined into each. The slide has to be taller as a result. (It doesn't directly affect hand to bore distance, but it does result in more weight higher in the pistol.)

The Beretta doesn't use locking lugs between the barrel and slide as the 1911 and S&W do, and is the worse for it. The Beretta uses a locking block that rides under the barrel. Once you build the locking block seat into the frame, place the barrel on top and provide for slide rails, you're getting tall. The Beretta

reduces the top-heavy mass of the 1911's slide by scalloping the slide out on top, but it doesn't do anything for the height to bore.

The Glock? The rails are so small they hardly add anything to the parts stack height up to the bore. There is no hammer, so the hammer pivot isn't in the way of lowering the bore. The barrel locks into the ejection port of the slide, so the thickness of steel above the barrel is no more than that needed for structural integrity. And the firing pin height is only what is needed for the tail to reach down to the cruciform of the trigger bar.

The idea of measuring the height of the bore above

The Glock's frame curve is relatively high, positioning your hand higher behind the gun and lessening its leverage during recoil.

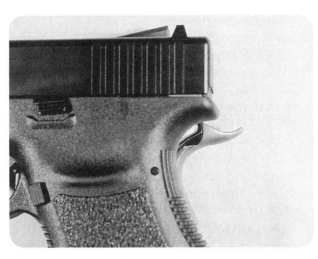

The backstrap curve of a custom 1911 still isn't as high as a Glock's.

someone's hand and using that as a benchmark is not very scientific. I for one have a grip that makes measuring quite tough. Rather than try to eyeball some distance between a vaguely defined part of the hand, and the bore, I measured a slightly different path. I compared the distance from the center of the trigger to the bottom of the frame rails. I then measured the distance from the frame rails up to the firing pin hole in the breechface.

The idea is to see what the difference is in these two: how high is the frame above the trigger, and then how high above the frame is the barrel? The Glock was the definite winner here.

Low Felt Recoil

Low felt recoil results from the combination of the flex of the polymer frame, the grip angle and the hand-filling grip that doesn't have joints where the (non-existent) grips meet the frame, and the low bore line. The low bore aids low felt recoil, as the cycling parts do not have as much leverage when they bottom out against the frame. Also, the flex of the polymer frame changes the nature of the impact between slide and frame.

On other pistols, the slide smacks to a halt when it hits the frame. The steel Glock slide striking the polymer frame doesn't produce anywhere near the jarring recoil and vibration of the metal-on-metal impact of other pistols. For all of its light weight, the 9mm Glocks have the impression of being softer in recoil than other 9mm pistols are. The effect is less so with the larger calibers, due to the greater amount of force they must dispose of.

Maintainability

The amount of hand fitting and training needed for function check of new parts installed on other pistols makes it tough for the do-it-yourselfer. If you have the proper instruction, fitting a new extractor to a 1911 can be a relatively painless operation but it can still take files and stones and some way to adjust and measure tension on the new part. An extractor on a S&W or a Beretta requires less training but can require more tools. The pinned-in-place extractor on those can sometimes require three hands for reassembly. On a Glock, you can practically teach your dog to swap extractors.

For a quick clean, the Glock's ease of disassembly beats all comers.

More parts a Glock lacks: bushing and spring retainer.

And more involved work, like adjusting the trigger pull or fitting a new safety, takes training, practice and a supply of sacrificial practice parts on other semiauto designs. If you want to change the trigger pull on your Glock, all you need are the new parts and a diagram of how they fit. Pull out the old, put in the new, and check function.

So much of the custom work beloved by 1911 aficionados is meaningless in the Glock universe. Checkering the frame? Fitting a new grip safety? Peening or swaging the frame rails and lapping the slide to a perfect fit? Suggesting any of those to a Glock owner is likely to get you stared at. They have no meaning because the Glock design eliminated the need for them.

You can swap parts yourself, once you've had about 10 minutes of coaching. You can replace worn or broken ones, or replace lost ones that you dropped on the last cleaning. About the only things that might require extra tools or some training would be installing new sights or fitting a new, non-Glock-made barrel.

The polymer frame won't rust. You don't have to worry about the "finish" coming off the frame, as it can't. The slide and barrel are protected with a process called "Tenifer." The black finish you see is simply a black oxide and not the actual Tenifer treatment. The Tenifer process penetrates the surface of the steel, and even after the black oxide has been worn away the Tenifer keeps doing its job. Indeed, getting your slide or barrel hard chromed or nickel plated doesn't add protection, as the coating you're putting on is less durable than the original Tenifer.

Capacity

For its size, the Glock holds more rounds than any

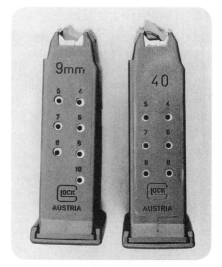

Subcompact Glocks still hold enough rounds to make them viable concealed carry guns.

other pistol. For a brief time during the Assault Weapons Ban of 1994, all pistols held a maximum of 10 rounds, at least those with magazines made at the time. Since the sunsetting of that egregious law we are back to full-capacity magazines. When the G-17 came to be, the top capacity pistols were the traditional Browning Hi-Power at 13 rounds and the S&W M-59 at 15.

The Browning loses a few rounds from being a bit smaller; the S&W comes close but is actually a bit bigger

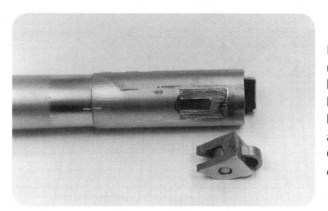

I haven't seen many 1911 barrels quit like this, but I haven't seen any comparable Glock examples. I doubt that I will.

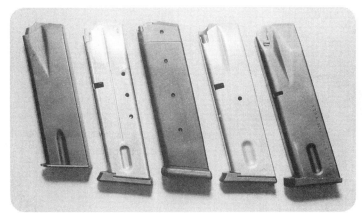

Magazines and their capacities. Left to right: Browning/13; S&W .40/11; Glock/17; S&W/14; and Beretta/15.

The Glock subcompact is actually smaller than a S&W J-frame revolver, has a longer barrel and holds more rounds.

and much heavier. Later Glocks like the G-19 and the G-26 are even tougher on the competition. The G-19 is slightly smaller than a Lightweight Commander and holds 15 rounds of 9mm to the LWC's nine or 10 rounds of 9mm/.38 Super and eight of .45. Browning never made a compact Hi Power, but S&W made compacts of their pistols. The results were even more in favor of Glocks.

The G-26 is the size of a six-shot snubnose revolver or an Officers Model 1911. Compared to the Officers Model with eight 9mms or seven .45s, the G-26 holds 12 9mm's and the G-27 holds 11 .40s. The compact G-27 holds as many .40 cartridges as the full-sized S&W 4046 and weighs less as well.

We may yet see another magazine limit but for the moment we are in a period of high-capacity magazines for all hands. Except for those living in a few states, of course.

Simplicity of Use

Part of the learning process in getting comfortable with other handguns is figuring out where all the controls are and what they do. Learning the location of the safeties is not always an academic exercise. I learned first on single action revolvers, then switched to the 1911. I shot 1911s for a decade before I started branching out to other pistols, so many of my habits are deeply ingrained

Which would you rather have: six shots of .38 Special or 10 shots of 9mm Parabellum +P?

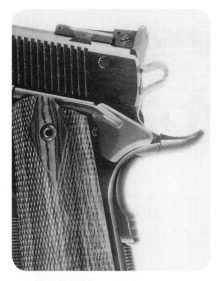

Here are two 1911 parts you won't find on the Glock (except for the fabled G-17S): the thumb safety and grip safety.

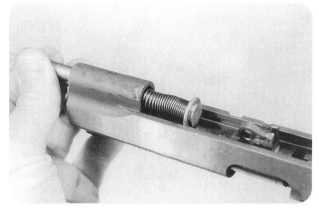

While many 1911s now come with full-length guide rods, none is captured like the Glock's is.

to the 1911 system. At one point I was going through a class dedicated to SIG pistols. I quickly found out that no SIG was ever going to lock open for me when empty. The slide stop lever on the SIG 226s we were using was in the exact location of the thumb safety of the 1911. Since I shot with my thumb riding on the 1911 safety, I was always pressing down on the SIG's slide stop. No amount of trying to remember that afternoon had any effect. The buzzer would go off, and I'd draw to a thumb-high hold and shoot until the gun went click instead of bang.

The Glock doesn't have that problem. First, the slide stop is up front and out of the way. Second, the "controls" are a choice of one: the trigger. If you want a Glock to shoot, you press the trigger. If you don't want it to shoot, then don't press the trigger.

The safeties are built-in, and there are no safety levers to press up or down, depending on your need of the moment.

Indeed, part of the initial attraction for law enforcement was that they could view the Glock as a "magazine fed revolver." The decades of revolver training could be easily shifted to the Glock. (That didn't keep some police administrators from being irrational, almost to the point of schizophrenia. Some would castigate the Glock for its lack of external safeties, while wearing a revolver that had even fewer safeties. And publicly, too.)

For training, less time spent learning the "knobs and buttons" meant that more time could be spent learning sight alignment and trigger control. Students issued Glocks posted higher qualification scores with less time and shooting than those issued revolvers or other pistols.

Less time spent learning the "knobs and buttons" means new shooters are put under less stress in the early stages of learning to shoot. It is hard enough to line up the sights and press the

trigger consistently, without having to keep track of other controls, too.

The Safe Action mechanism of the Glock also aids in learning marksmanship. Many pistols considered suitable for military or police duty are what's called Double Action pistols. The initial trigger pull is long and heavy, as the hammer is being cocked for the first time. Subsequent shots are fired with the hammer already cocked and are lighter in pull and shorter in distance. Transitioning from the first shot to the second can be difficult for many shooters. (The 1911 doesn't have that problem, but some shooters have an attack of the willies whenever they see a cocked hammer.) The Glock's Safe Action is the same every time. It is also shorter to reach than other high-capacity 9mm pistols (speaking of the G-17 as the comparator) and thus easier to handle for shooters with small hands.

In all, it's easy to see why so many have switched. Heck, even I own more than one Glock. ◆

CHAPTER 5

Which Caliber for You?

The prospect of a caliber choice usually breaks down to a simple one for many shooters: 9mm vs. .45. While that isn't the only consideration, we'll start with that one, as many of the variables come into play with the other calibers, too.

Both the 9mm and the .45 are closing in on a century of service. Indeed, by the time you read this the 9mm Luger will have passed the century mark and be into the triple digits. The 9mm was finalized for the German army acceptance trials and specified for the Pistole 08, aka the Luger. The German army wanted more caliber than the .30 Luger cartridge provided. The 9mm size was the biggest the case design and pistol could be adapted to. If the German Army then had wanted something even larger, Georg Luger would have had to scale-up the whole pistol, something he had tried and failed to do for the US Army during its pistol trials.

The .45 was finalized for the American Army acceptance trials, going through a few minor variations until the specs were set down in 1910. The initial cartridge featured a 234-grain bullet, then a 200-grain bullet, before becoming a 230-grain jacketed round-nose bullet. Why so big? The usual tale spun at this point concerns the Moros on the islands of the Philippines. After America trounced the Spanish and took possession of the Philippine Archipelago, the American Army had to deal with the fierce combat offered by the Moros. The US Army had just a few years earlier adopted a double action revolver in .38 to replace the single action revolvers in .45 they'd been issuing. The new caliber failed in its task often enough that a hue and cry went up to re-issue the old revolvers – and to never go down to such a puny handgun cartridge again.

As a powerful, compact and handy package, the Colt 1911 Lightweight Commander is a good choice. . .

. . .but the Glock G-19 is lighter, more compact and holds more rounds.

That's the legend, but I'm not buying it. The American army, unlike the British, did not have a history and tradition of dealing with fierce native infantry in colonial settings. A British officer buying his sidearm would purchase one with the prospect in mind of having to stop a charging, spear or sword-wielding opponent at close range. The American army was for the most part a cavalry service. (Yes, I know there were many other units, and my grandfather served in some. But the Cavalry ran the show.)

The US Army had spent decades riding the plains, dealing with the finest light cavalry the world had ever seen: Native American Plains Indians. Any pistol, and pistol cartridge, selected would be thought of in terms of "can this stop a charging mount?" It would not surprise me in the slightest to find that Cavalry officers were the most vocal about the inadequacies of the new cartridge and

Even in the smaller models, Glocks hold plenty of ammo.

advocated a return to the .45 in any new sidearm. I recently came across some training manuals concerning the use of pistols, dismounted, at long range. Apparently it was not unknown for cavalry troopers to use their mounts (willing or dead, it didn't matter much to the troopers) as cover and also firing support with rifles, carbines and revolvers. As anyone who has tried it knows, you can actually make life interesting for an opponent at medium rifle ranges, using a handgun. The Colt SAA is quite capable of dealing a lethal blow at 300 yards. However, you need to see your bullet impacts at range to "walk in" your aim. A .45 not only hits the opponent harder, but kicks up more dust. So, in the first decade of the twentieth century, .45 it was.

Run the tape forward 60 years to the disco decade, and the argument was the same: capacity vs. size. But the advent of high velocity hollowpoint bullets that actually expanded started changing shooters' minds favorably toward the 9mm. There had been softpoint and hollowpoint handgun bullets before, but they never expanded much. By the 1970s, reliably-expanding designs began to become the norm.

For almost 15 years the advocates of high velocity held sway. A standard 9mm round of 1970 would have featured a 125-grain full metal jacket bullet at around 1050 or 1075 fps. By 1985, the

"standard" (there were many, many choices) 9mm cartridge would have been a 115-grain jacketed hollowpoint at 1200 fps. It would have been easy to obtain the same 115s at nearly 1300 fps. Velocity promoted expansion, and expansion was good because it stopped fights and also prevented excess penetration.

Then came the infamous Miami shootout, and the score after the FBI attempted to apprehend two bank robbers was two robbers dead, two FBI agents dead, and five of the six other agents wounded.. The FBI was not too happy when the autopsy found that one of the bad guys had sustained a center hit from a 9mm hollowpoint bullet that, while it did a very good job, failed by not having penetrated a couple more inches. Those inches could have stopped the fight a whole lot sooner. The FBI wanted more penetration, and the then-current 9mms didn't offer it.

Meanwhile, advocates of bigger calibers and more penetration had been doing studies of ballistic gelatin. They found that the highest-velocity and therefore most aggressively-expanding bullets couldn't always be counted on to penetrate to vital organs.

The stopping power statistics and arguments can be summed up in a nutshell: The 9mm/high velocity crowd argues from "street statistics" showing real-world performance and downplays the theoretical aspects of

With a good hollowpoint in at least 9mm caliber, you're well-armed for self-defense.

predicting performance from gelatin. The .45/penetration crowd feels that the "street statistics" are cooked and that the choice of bullet shouldn't be made from a handful of shooting incidents with messy and uncontrolled variables. Use gelatin instead.

One thing lost in the argument is the fact that current ammunition in all calibers features higher velocities than it used to (expanding now beyond the simple 9mm vs. 45 debate) and high-tech hollowpoint bullets.

Both sides, when they are reminded, will tell you that a handgun cartridge, any handgun cartridge, is a very poor tool with which to stop violent acts being committed by violent people. Even the most powerful defensive calibers or loadings pale in comparison to rifle cartridges that would be viewed as poor choices for deer hunting.

Which for You to Carry?

That depends. For many of you, carrying a pistol larger than a 9mm is too difficult. A larger pistol is harder to carry and keep concealed, and too tempting to leave at home. Smaller is better, but a small gun in a large caliber is easy to carry and hard to shoot. I would not feel defenseless packing a 9mm, provided I was using the hottest ammo I could lay hands on. For the 9mm, that means +P ammo. A 9mm +P load will push a 115-grain bullet out of a G-17 at over 1300 fps. While you might be able to lay hands on some +P+ ammo (It is sold to law enforcement agencies only, not for retail sale) I don't feel the extra 25-50 fps is worth the noise, recoil and wear and tear.

For many shooters, a .40 is a bigger caliber but not a bigger gun than a 9mm. (For a lot of uses/loadings, it is simply a big nine.) The advantage of the .40 is a bonus when you consider that it fits into a 9mm frame. One of the reasons so many police departments went with the .40 (Miami among them, trading in their G-17s for G-22s) is that they could get a bigger caliber without having

Ballistic testing is hard work and takes lots of time and money. But you don't have to do it to benefit from it. Just buy good ammo.

Which Caliber for You? | **89**

to go to a bigger frame. A bigger frame means not only would the department have a problem getting smaller-statured officers to carry and qualify, but all the holsters, mag pouches and other leather or web gear would have to be changed.

The bigger guns, in 10mm and .45, are harder to carry and shoot. For many carry applications they would be the best choice. My friend Mas Ayoob was one of the first to point out that in cold weather, the .45 is king. Indeed, clothing can matter so much in measuring "stopping power" that the FBI protocol for ballistic gelatin testing includes a section called "Heavy Clothing" where the bullet must first penetrate multiple layers of heavy cloth before striking the gelatin block. Heavy, layered clothing can defeat the expansion potential of hollowpoint bullets.

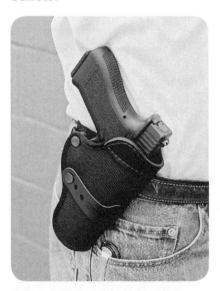

With a good holster (like this one from Shooting Systems), your Glock can be an easy burden to bear.

If there is no expansion, bigger is almost always better. After all, a 9mm might expand up to .45, but a .45 is never going to shrink down to 9mm. In cold weather, concealing a big gun is easier. The big disadvantage to choosing a .45 is gun size. Not just in carrying and concealing it, but handling it. The .45 Glocks can be too large for some shooters hands.

However, in the end the choice comes down to this: which can you shoot well? If the big caliber and the big gun are just too much, then you'll have to learn to use the smaller one to best advantage.

As for ammunition selection, the choices available in 9mm and .45 alone would be enough to crush some gun dealers' shelves. Any manufacturer who makes handgun ammunition offers something in 9mm and .45. It could be a career just in testing all the available loads. And if a dealer has any ammunition for sale at all, at least some of it will be 9mm or .45 (or both). For choices and availability, these two and .40 are the only ones you should consider.

Which for Competition?

Here the choice is simpler. Unless you need the power, go with the 9mm. Bowling pin shooters will go with the .45. For events with a full three foot setting (not on the back edge of the table) the 9mm won't be able to clear the pins off.

Which caliber for you? That depends on what you're comfortable shooting. Some might find a .40 in a G-27 a handful; others might not.

The 9mm will be softer to shoot (if you don't need the power) and plenty accurate. Ammunition will be cheaper than .45, and for those who reload, just as reloadable.

The rules of some competitions almost require a 9mm. If you are to shoot in USPSA Production Division, you will gain no additional score for using a cartridge more powerful than 9mm. So competition shooters there do not subject themselves to the greater recoil of full-power 40, 10mm or .45. The same imperative applies in IDPA, where you gain no advantage using a bigger than 9mm cartridge in Stock Service Pistol.

Matches like the Steel Challenge or the American Handgunner Shootoff offer no advantage for more power. So again, 9mm is king.

Other Calibers?

The main one to consider is the .40. It came about from the brief FBI experiment with the 10mm. What advantages does the .40 offer over the

Don't confuse what wins matches with what is comfortable and useful for daily carry.

9mm/.45 choices? Capacity, power and pistol size in varying mixes. The .40 has been around only since 1990 but is now so common that some commercial reloaders accept .40 brass only as exchange for other ammo purchased. (9mm is often taken only at its brass scrap weight value.) The .40 fits into a frame built for a 9mm, so you don't have to go to a bigger pistol to get the bigger cartridge. The magazine/frame size that holds 17 rounds of 9mm in a Glock G-17 holds 15 .40's in a Glock G-22.

For some competitions, the .40 can be loaded up to equal the power requirements of the .45. (IPSC/USPSA competition recognize the .40 as being equal to the .45.) Once you meet or exceed the threshold power level for making Major (currently 165,000) a .40 is scored the same as a .45. As any given magazine size holds more 40s than 45s, the choice is easy: go with the .40. For other competitions, the .40 isn't the equal of the .45. Again, those pesky bowling pins prove the lie. You simply can't pump a .40 cartridge up to the power levels needed for pin shooting and stay within safety margins.

As an example, a 200-grain bullet going about 975 fps is considered a suitable load for pins. That is, it delivers a Power Factor of 195,000. A .45 can do a 195 PF without breaking into a sweat. In fact, many bowling pin shooters commonly shoot .45 loads that post a 210 to 215 PF. If you want to try and match that 195 PF load in a .40, I want to be standing someplace else. It isn't a smart thing to do. And making the 210-215 load? An even worse idea. Some factory loads come close to the 195 PF, but in bowling pin shooting, "close" isn't close enough.

The drawback to the use of the .40 in a 9mm sized package is felt recoil. You can't get something for nothing, and going from a G-17 to a G-22 is proof of that. The G-22 is going to thump you harder, which is the price you pay for more power.

Is the .40 enough better as a carry caliber that it is worth the extra recoil? Perhaps, depending on your own personal ability to deal with recoil. Some find the .40 is no big deal, while others find it is just over the line in what they can stand, or like to stand, in recoil. It is, however, enough smaller than the .45 pistols that it is worth considering just to make your job of staying concealed easier.

The 10mm

A big gun, with big recoil, the G-20 is suitable for a lot of things, but daily

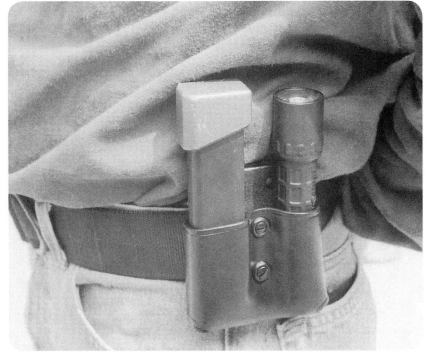

With your Glock, you need spare ammo or a spare magazine in case your first one malfunctions. A Sure Fire light is nice to have, too.

The right-sized Glock is easy to handle. For this shooter, moving up from a .40 to a .45 would be too big a frame.

The Ten has plenty of power to dispose of bowling pins (indeed, many who use the caliber load down from factory levels just to aid control and fast shooting) and even hunting. The Ten is a good choice for hunting both because it has power and accuracy, but also because some state's deer hunting regulations require a straight-wall case. (They don't want T/C Contenders in .30-30, .30 Herrett, *et al* being used in the handgun-only zones, and I can't say as I blame them.)

The drawback to the Ten is also shared by the .45, in that the frame is large – so large, that there are custom gunsmiths who experimented with epoxy formulas until they found ones to match or be compatible with the Glock polymer. They'll fill the hollow backstrap of your Glock and then carve it down until it is nearly the size of the 9mm/40 frames.

You won't have the choices in ammunition

concealed carry probably isn't one of them. (If you can handle the recoil, the G-29 might be concealable. But boy, what recoil.) The Big Ten-Mil is a wilderness gun. With hot factory loads, or handloads with full metal jacketed bullets, the 10mm can handle most any problem you can expect to solve with

a handgun out in the woods. If we understand right from the beginning that any handgun is a poor tool for dealing with bears, the 10mm ranks well in that job slot. A 180- or 200-grain bullet at 1200 fps is going to penetrate well. (I've put a 180-grainer at 900 fps through 36 inches of ballistic gelatin and have no doubts about its ability to continue well through another block were it there, as much as 54 inches of penetration.)

Glocks work on pins, too. For the Main Event, I'd rather be running a .45, like the custom Bar-Sto longslide, than a .40.

Use the correct magazine, not something that's a "bargain."

selection with the Ten that you'd have with 9mm, 40 & 45, but there are several good loads. And the Ten is easy to reload.

.357 SIG

Neither fish nor fowl, the SIG is a carry-only caliber. It isn't big enough to be a hunting caliber. For competition, it can't be loaded to equal the .40 or .45 in power (at least not as the rules currently read). And if you wanted to use it in an Open gun, where the excess power could be used to feed a comp, you'd lose magazine capacity. In Open competition, shooters use a variant of the .38 Super, and you can fit 28 of them in a competition-kosher high capacity magazine. The same mag would "only" hold 22 rounds of .357 SIG. When a few Match points can determine the difference between winning and not winning, no one is willing to forego the extra rounds.

For carry, the velocity of the SIG offers extra stopping power, at least by the calculations of the "velocity is all" advocates. Some departments have adopted it, but it is not taking the law enforcement community by storm as the .40 did a decade ago. It does, however, have some adherents. The Chicago Transit Police use it, as the hollowpoints will not only expand (big surprise there, at nearly 1,400 fps) but also penetrate windows and car seats. Also, the Border Patrol uses the .357 SIG. Many of the agents work in the great outdoors, and if you're on the wrong end of a handgun vs. rifle fight, the best handgun round to have is a flat-shooting one. Nothing shoots flatter than a .357 SIG.

.45 G.A.P.

The Glock .45 came out after the first edition was well-established on the book-store shelves. The idea is simple, and perhaps you've heard it before: shorten an otherwise too-long bigger cartridge until it fits into the magazine of a 9m pistol. Exactly what had been done for the creation of the .40, Glock did for the .45 GAP. (I'm leaving out the extra periods from now on. I'm going to be writing about this cartridge a lot, and it makes things a lot easier for both of us. Just mentally inert the periods every time you see "GAP" and we'll both be fine.)

You can't get something for nothing. If you could, the world would be an entirely different place. So, what did it "cost" Glock to fit a .45 into a 9mm? In cartridge terms (we'll discuss the pistols themselves in their own chapter.) it costs pressure. It also apparently cost some rim alterations. To make the .45 GAP deliver muzzle velocities as good as those of the .45 ACP, the GAP has to run in the low end of the .45 ACP+P pressures. As the standard and +P pressures are quite low, that isn't a big deal. A point of comparison: the 9mm and the .40 both run at 34,000 PSI. You can't make the .40 do more by running the pressure up, there isn't much room left. Standard .45 ACP pressures have a maximum ceiling of 17,000 PSI. .45 ACP+P has a max of 21,000. So for the .45 GAP to be running at 21,000 PSI is no big deal.

The .45 GAP case is not simply a shortened .45 ACP case. The rim is smaller in diameter. Despite the assistance of Glock in the Second Edition, there were some things they were not willing to discuss. The exact reason for the rebated rim is one of those subjects. Why is it a matter of concern? If the rim is rebated (smaller in diameter than the case body itself) then the stripper rail, the part of the slide that pushes the top round out of the magazine, has a smaller target. Previous pistols using a rebated-rim case were found to be marginally reliable. Not so with .45 GAP pistols from Glock, probably because the rebated rim is smaller than the case body by such a small margin that it doesn't matter to feeding. If it is so small it doesn't matter, why is it smaller and not the same size? Sigh. The questions just add up.

All the fussing over the "rebated" or rebated rim of the .45 GAP amounts to no big deal: the gun works, the rounds work, and if you want a compact, reliable big-bore pistol that isn't a big pistol, you will have to search long and heard to beat the G-37, G-38 or G-39. ♦

CHAPTER **6**

Importation

When overseas manufacturers (or Canadian or Mexican, for that matter) want to bring a firearm into the United States, they have big a job ahead of them. You see, in order for a firearm to come in, it has to meet all the requirements of a veritable thicket of laws. As one example, you can't bring in military firearms for general sale. You can't even re-import US military arms that were used by foreign military units, just those sold for civilian or law enforcement. (Ergo,

scads of M1 Garands and M1 Carbines are prohibited from reimportation, since we gave them to the governments who then owned them.)

Firearms brought into the USA have to be "generally accepted for sporting purposes," which leaves out a lot of fun toys. Even if what you make meets the previous qualifications, you still have to score enough points. You see, the determination of what is "sporting" was left to a bunch of bureaucrats and lawyers. What they came up with was a list of desired features, desired by them

and not necessarily by the shooting public. The list looks suspiciously like a collection of all the common features found on the big, expensive target pistols. I have reproduced the scoring chart for you, so you can see how the Glock models stack up.

When Glock went to bring the G-17 into the country, they had a problem. Because their frame was polymer and not steel or an aluminum alloy, they were giving up 15 or 20 points right away just on overall weight. The lack of a grip safety or magazine safety meant they gave up another eight. The minimum to pass is 74, and the Glock design gave away 28 of those points right at the start.

With the G-17 in its original trim, the points total came up to 65. What to do? As mentioned in Chapter One, you come up with a cheap click adjustable target sight, getting you 10 more points; and *voila!* The score now stands at 75! Once the gun was brought in, the sights could be removed and for all I know shipped back to Austria

If it was issued to a military unit, like these carbines, it can't be re-imported, even if it makes the necessary import points.

for installation on the next batch. In the armorer's class, we were instructed that the sights, once removed, are not to be re-used. Apparently the little steel plate in the bottom of the polymer sights is deformed on insertion and removal, and can't be used again. Gee, I wish I'd known that before I started working on Glocks. I spent some eight years working on them before going to an armorer's class, and I'd removed and re-installed a bunch of sights. I suppose I could have charged more for the replacement sights I was supposed to have used. But I digress.

None of this matters if the firearm is made in the USA. That's right, a domestic manufacturer's score is immaterial, because they don't have pass the test. So why not make Glocks here in the US? Tenifer. The Tenifer process is a nitriding surface hardening process that also oxygenates the surface to prevent further oxidation (rust). Part of the process uses (and produces in the waste stream) cyanide. If you think jumping the importation hurdles is hard, you obviously haven't uttered the word "cyanide" in the presence of an EPA official. So Glocks are made in Austria, then imported and assembled in Smyrna, Georgia. Glock tells us that manufacturing here in the USA is commencing, but as far as I know at the moment of writing this, all guns are still coming in from Austria. They are assembled

in Smyrna and shipped to us. Once the US manufacturing facility is up and running we'll see "Made in USA" Glocks, but not for a while.

What's Tenifer? Beats me. What I can tell you is what anyone with a degree in the field can figure out. The process does what Glock says it does. Surface-hardening is an old process, and patents for various methods (including those using cyanide) of surface-hardening go back into the nineteenth century. We know that Tenifer removes oxygen from the surface so the steel doesn't rust. That is another old trick, used by mechanical engineers with stainless steel, called "passivation." By either stripping out or otherwise locking up the oxygen in the surface of a steel, you remove those locations where oxidation could commence. No oxygen, no oxidation, no rust.

Ever wonder about the second and third generation Glock frames, and the presence of the vestigial thumbrests? Again,

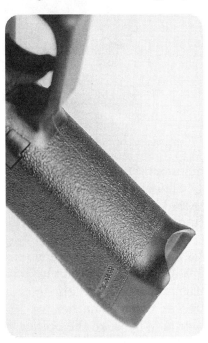

The original G-17 frame. The pebble finish is good enough for gripping, but it doesn't score many points on the import scale.

The finger grooves and thumb rest add import points. On this training Glock, the blowback action deducts points.

The new adjustable sight that doesn't have to be thrown away. An adjustable sight adds import points.

You can clearly see the "thumbrest" on the Glock at the left. Hey, it's good enough to score import points.

importation is the answer. The small swells on the sides of the frame count as a "target grip" and gain Glock models five more points for importation. By adding grooves to the trigger, the trigger becomes a "target" trigger, gaining another two points. Why go to the bother?

Because the subcompact Glocks lose points due to their small size, that's why. The G-26 loses four points in the size line entry, and three more in the weight category. By changing the mould and adding the thumbswells, Glock gains five of those points back. By changing the trigger to a grooved "target" trigger they gain another two. By importing the pistols with target sights and then taking them off before shipping within the US, they gain a grand total of 10, getting back to the magical 75 points. Since one mould has to be changed for that model, all the other might as well be too, (after all, product uniformity requires it, and moulds do have to be replaced periodically) and the

third generation G-17 gains another five points, to 80. Glock could put the "target" trigger on G-17s, but they don't need it, so why bother?

The weight includes an empty magazine, and I can just imagine the Glock engineers having wrestled with the G-26 problem, trying to figure out how to add enough weight to the magazine to bring the total up. Unfortunately, if they wanted to do it solely with the magazine, they were faced with the task of trying to add nine ounces at a minimum of extra weight to a magazine that in its original design weighed less than two! They probably spent a grand total of five minutes on it before giving up and moving on. The frame wouldn't be any help either, and trying to add that much weight to the slide would have been counterproductive. (There's no point in designing a pistol that makes the importation points but has a slide so heavy it won't cycle.)

Without the changes, all the subcompacts would have fallen short of importation

points. And that is why the G-25 and G-28, the .380 pistols, aren't imported for commercial sale. (Law enforcement officials can buy them, but you and I can't.) Because they are blowback, the G-25 and G-28 lose the five points awarded for a locked breech system. They also lose points from going down from 9mm to .380, another seven. The G-25 scores 66 points, even with a target sight and trigger. The new loaded chamber indicator extractor only adds five more, bringing it to a grand total of 71 points. "Missed it by *that* much!" as Secret Agent Maxwell Smart used to say.

Is there anything that Glock can do about all this? Not without making a big change in the design. A grip safety or magazine safety would do it, but how could Glock make them available on those two models and not the rest without arousing the interest of the civil liability lawyers out there? No, any change would have to be implemented across the board and therefore isn't possible.

Since it doesn't score enough points for import, the G-17T is a Law Enforcement Only item.

You may not like or notice the finger grooves, but they add import points.

Glock won't be bringing out any .22 rimfire models, either. A .22 long rifle Glock would score just the same as the .380s, not as big as a 9mm and with an unlocked breech. If you want a rimfire Glock you would have to get the upper from a source here in the USA. Or, once Glock has a US manufacturing facility up and running, you can clamor for the Glock G-25 and G-28 and perhaps a .22 handgun, too.

As for the competition Glocks, they already had plenty of points, and the third generation frame design just padded their totals.

Point totals for imports but not for domestic production. Restricted importation. Prohibited for commercial sale. Law Enforcement Only sales. You've got to wonder what the point of it all is.

But then again, it doesn't have to make sense. It's the law. ◆

Without the thumbrest and finger grooves (and maybe even an adjustable sight), this Glock subcompact might not score enough points to be importable.

The old extractor.

The new extractor, with its "loaded chamber indicator" that scores additional import points.

CHAPTER 7

Glock Numbers, Serial and Others

Your Glock is covered with tell-tale marks. The later ones don't have as many, but early Glocks can be quite interesting. Here in the USA, manufacturers are responsible for quality control and product tracking. In Europe, many countries have centuries of official Proof House regulations and law, not always with the intention of protecting the consumer. In the earliest years, Proof Houses protected the markets of the established gunsmiths by keeping lower-quality products (usually cheap imports) off the market. Firearms produced for sale would have to be sent to the Proof House, where they were inspected, measured, and test fired with a "proof load," which was a load with a higher powder charge than the gun was designed for.

Once a gun passed Proof Testing, it was stamped with the markings the current regulations or law required. Any firearm offered for sale lacking the proofs was suspect and perhaps even illegal.

To this day, those few firearms still for sale in England must have current proof marks or their sale will be disallowed. Ditto most of Europe. I've seen US-made firearms brought back by GIs from Germany sporting German proof marks. They weren't made there, but their sale there required the proof marks. The last one I saw was an S&W 586, unfired, offered for sale to a collector at a nice premium over suggested retail due to the Proof House markings.

Europeans – and the British, too – try to cover every firearm with proofmarks.

Glocks, being made in Austria, must have certain proofs. Early in production, all Glocks were manufactured and assembled in Austria

These numbers on the underside of the slide are a mystery. They're probably production marks or lot numbers, but Glock isn't saying.

A very early GH-17 with serial number, "NPv" proof mark and barrel production code date.

A .45 with caliber marking, serial number and Glock logo.

A later Glock with the NPv stamp replaced with the Glock logo.

before being brought to the USA. One proof mark seen on Glocks made before 1991 is the "NPv" or Nitro Proof after assembly. With proof regulations stretching back centuries, the proof houses have standards for both black powder and smokeless. The smokeless proof standards are known as nitro proofs. When pistols were assembled in Austria, they received both the barrel proof and the assembly proof. Once Glock began shipping parts to the USA and finishing assembly here, the assembled nitro proof wasn't required and was dropped. That's right,

the US "factory" is simply the assembly building, with all manufacturing done in Austria. The NPv proof mark location on the barrel was then replaced with the Glock logo. Once US manufacturing gets underway, we will probably see the panoply of proof marks vanish, and they will be marked simply "Made in USA."

The European custom of numbering everything has caused all kinds of confusion to the rest of us. In Michigan, for example, you have to submit your handgun for a "safety inspection," which is a registration system

so skimpily disguised that it wouldn't work in a "gentlemens' club" as a garment. The Michigan State Police are tasked with keeping track of the numbers appearing on a gun and finding the lost or stolen handguns that crop up in the system. The more numbers, the more confused the process.

And it can become quite confusing. The German Army, many firearms manufacturers and other armies used a "10,000" block serial number system. Each Luger (and every other pistol) received only a four-digit serial number along with a production block letter. The letter was a prefix or suffix that appeared somewhere near the serial number.

So, one day during the week the Michigan State Police might get a card in the mail, a new Luger registration: "Luger, 9mm, #0019" is on it. With much heavy sighing and muttered curses, a form letter and card go out to the new owner: "Please indicate all relevant features on said Luger pistol, such as manufacturing plant, year, language of markings and

This G-19 has the serial number, dual proof marks, barrel date and slide NPv mark.

other unique features." You see, the Luger in question could have been made at any time between 1908 and 1945, in any of a dozen plants. There can be as many as a hundred 9mm Luger pistols with the "serial number" 0019. The manufacturing code letter may only cut that number down to a couple of dozen. (Each year, the letter starts over at "a".) And what are the chances that at least one of those hundred "0019" pistols has been reported stolen in the last century? Almost certain. So the MSP wants to know if you have a0019, b0019, c0019, etc. And also the year in which it was made.

The first Glock off the line came into the world as number AA000. A thousand pistols later, it rolled from AA999 to AB000. One advantage to this procedure is tracking components. Each batch of 1000 can be strictly controlled as to which components go into it. A problem with front sight rivets? When did we start? If you don't intermix parts lots, you can accurately track production and component lots.

But what to do after the first 676,000 pistols, when you've run through the alphabet? I'm sure it was not a pressing thought on the mind of Gaston Glock when the first G-17 came off the line. After all, the Austrian Army wanted 25,000. The other Armies of Europe might want some. And the police departments of Europe might buy some. It wasn't until the Glock came to

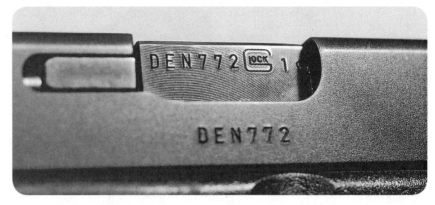

Another Glock mystery. Most modern Glocks have the serial number, Glock logo and the pentagon. The number 1? Glock won't say. Maybe it indicates a replacement barrel.

the US that the serial number ceiling became apparent. The State of Texas alone probably has more police officers than all the countries of Europe had in 1986 – probably more police officers than the armies of Europe had on active duty.

The obvious solution was the three-letter prefix. Once ZZ999 had been utilized, Glock rolled it over to three letters and three digits. Starting at AAA000, Glock has 17,576,000 serial numbers available to them, not even counting the 676,000 they've already used up. I think even at the rate they're making pistols, they've got some time to figure out a new system.

Part of serial number tracking concerns the parts upgrade for the trigger mechanism. The parts were upgraded to a better design, and the new parts designated by plating them with nickel. Also, the serial number plate was changed. The old pistols had serial number plates that were blackened, while the new ones were nickel plated. You can tell at a glance if a

pistol is old or new, provided the plate of an old one hasn't been polished bright. The parts upgrade may now be quite a few years in the past, but there are still plenty of old Glocks (now there's a phrase I never thought I'd be saying) that still have old parts in them.

The serial number prefixes that are the cutoff, that is, the last prefix made with the old parts, are:

G-17 XG
G-19 XK
G-20 WX
G-21 XM
G-22 YB
G-23 SL

I guess since all the G-18's are strictly controlled, Glock hunted them down and made sure the new parts got installed. Then again, maybe the parts in a G-18 are different enough that they needn't be changed. Since Glock isn't talking and I haven't had a chance to disassemble a G-18, we'll all just have to guess on this one.

Another G-19 with early barrel and its serial number, dual proofs and barrel date, but no NPv on its much-later slide.

Pistols produced after the cutoff prefix, and models that came out after the parts change was implemented, do not need an upgrade.

Another change concerns the angle of the ejection port and the extractors to fit them. The original ejection port is what is known as the "90 degree breech face." The rear face of the opening in the slide (and not the breechface itself) is cut at a right angle to the direction of the bore. Later production guns use an angled surface, tipped back (away from the muzzle) by fifteen degrees. The "15 degree" guns require a different extractor, also tipped back on its front face by 15 degrees. All the models were changed starting in May of 1995, and the serial number prefix cutoffs are:

G-17	BKK
G-17L	BMD
G-19	BKP
G-20	BKU
G-21	ALD
G-22	BKD
G-23	BKH
G-24/24C	BMD
G-26	BMX
G-27	BMY

Pistols with these prefixes and later have the new breech face and extractor design. Obviously, all models introduced after the change will have the 15 degree breech face and extractor.

Another change that came about later in production was the addition of the "US" suffix to serial numbers. The earliest guns, guns made for the Austrian Army and others,

did not have them. But all Glocks brought into the USA have them. I have inspected a G-17 made in May of 1986, and it has the "US" suffix. Why? Probably to satisfy an importation requirement, or perhaps to preclude "gray market" importation of Glocks to the US.

The suffix now means that your Glock serial number now looks something like this: XXX123US – unless your Glock comes to you courtesy the agency you work for, an agency that has custom-ordered a serial number block, in which case it will have a four digit block in the serial number. One such agency is the Miami PD, who ordered their pistols with the serial number block "MIA." With their order of .40 Glocks, the Chief of the Miami PD received "MIA0001US" and Armando Valdes got "MIA0002US." The Georgia Department of Transportation got theirs in the "GADOT" block. If you are offered a Glock with the serial number "GADOT0000US" you'd better be careful. It

Early Glocks had blackened serial number frames. They got nickeled when the trigger parts were upgraded.

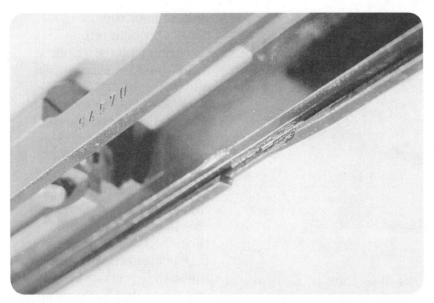

This .40 shows peening and has had the slide replaced. The "S4570" is the factory part number for a replacement G-23C slide.

belongs to the State of Georgia and may be stolen.

The Detroit Police Department went one better. They changed the direction the serial number runs. On all other Glocks you read the serial number with the muzzle pointed to the left. To read the Detroit guns, you hold it muzzle to the right. From a couple of different sources, the reason I've heard for the change is that the standard pistol racks in the precinct houses are designed to hold the guns so that the serial numbers can be read with the muzzle to the right. I guess if you order enough Glocks, you can have your serial number customized, too.

One aspect of the serial number you may not have known concerns the box and not the pistol. If you look at the box you'll see the serial number printed on a white label. Law Enforcement production guns are printed with blue labels. Glock gives wholesalers a discount on the law enforcement guns, which they are supposed to pass on to the agency buying them. Wholesalers who buy LE guns and then sell them as regular production will find themselves in hot water with Glock. No laws have been broken, but Glock feels the discount should be passed on and not pocketed by the wholesaler or dealer.

There are also yellow-label guns. Those are loaner guns, guns sent out to writers for test and evaluation, that Glock insists on getting back. Glock even has a full-page loan agreement that writers have to fill out, explaining that this is a loan, not a gift, and if you want to buy it you'll have to do more than just hang on to it.

You might encounter the occasional Glock with what appears to be a serial-numbered but not prefixed or suffixed slide or barrel, or the very rare mis-matched Glock. Replacement parts factory-fitted come with the factory part number on them. One I've seen is a slide that cracked on a range rental gun. The replacement slide is marked with the factory part number and not the serial number of

A rare gun. "J" indicates prototypes and factory cutaways, pistols not made in regular production.

the pistol is it fitted to. The slide prefix is "S," the frame "G" and the barrel "L". Very early G-17 and G-19 pistols have been reported with the model number cast into the polymer of the trigger guard. However, the G-17 that I inspected with a build date of May 1986 did not have the model cast in it, so I have to assume that marking was dropped before May of 1986, perhaps only for US importation.

I have had occasion to inspect a G-20 that had been violently taken apart by factory ammo. It had been shipped back to Glock, who had words with the ammo maker. In the end, the owner got a repaired Glock. What he got was his old slide and barrel on a new frame. A new frame with a new serial number. (Since this was in Michigan, the owner had to re-register his "new" handgun, an interesting story in itself.) As long as he retains the paperwork, he has a documented and rare factory mis-matched Glock that some collector might offer him a lot of money for in the future. The new frame did not have a "G" suffix, just a standard serial number of the time period.

A note to future collectors of Glocks: If you expect your mis-matched Glock to have any value beyond that of a shooter, get a letter from Glock documenting the mis-match. (Oh, the headaches this sentence is going to cause the factory.) Their repair and warranty records should cover the facts of

and the date of repair. If they don't, then you simply have a gunsmith-ed or recovered pistols parts gun.

A serial number prefix that is a rare duck indeed is the J prefix. J guns are pre-production samples, sales samples and prototypes. The prototypes are not supposed to exist outside of the Glock plant. How they might get out is a mystery (but we can speculate) and if you encounter one for sale you should buy it. One J series pistol I've seen is an early (1st generation) G-17 cutaway in the JQ series.

One set of marks rarely seen are the barrel production dates. The barrels used to be marked with the month of production. Strange, since the barrels were made at the same time as, and serial numbered to, the pistols they were fitted to. The code is simple: a set of letters assigned to each

month and to the numbers "0" through "9" to designate the year:

Month Code		Year Code	
E	January	O	0
L	February	W	1
N	March	K	2
B	April	R	3
S	May	F	4
Z	June	M	5
G	July	H	6
P	August	Y	7
I	September	T	8
C	October	D	9
V	November		
A	December		

So, if we were to use the Glock barrel code to designate the month I was elected to be the President of my gun club, January 1983, we would have a code of "ETR." Should you encounter a Glock barrel with a mysterious three-letter code in addition to the proof marks and serial number, try the

Own an E-series Glock? Call them and ask if they have a replacement frame for you. If this one were replaced, the gun's serial number would then be "1EUN114US." Would be barrel be marked that way? Probably not.

code and see what you come up with. The G-17 traced with a letter to Glock on the serial number, built in May of 1986? It has a barrel code of STH, May 1986.

The E Series Recall

Well, not really a recall. We now have more information on the recall and the reason for the replacements.

There are three machines that stamp out the rails for the frames of Glock pistols. One of the three was apparently re-built, cleaned, adjusted, (who knows) and when it was up and running again it was not making rails to spec. The rails are supposed to have a small radius on the underside of where they are bent so the steel is not stressed. This machine was making rails with a right angle at the bend, not a small radius. The right angle would stress the rails, and breakages might occur. With the rails all being mixed in the E series pistols before the problem was caught, Glock didn't know which were which.

The upshot of this is that some lots in the E prefix series might be prone to having the rails break from the frame. The Bernalillo County Sheriff Department (California) had four of their pistols do this. One Glock test pistol undergoing durability testing had it happen. (But it continued to fire 4,000 rounds after breaking.)

Glock will replace all frames in the affected production lots. Not all E-series pistols are likely to have this problem. (And apparently not much of a problem at that, based on 4,000 rounds after breakage.) The solution is to phone the special number that Glock has for the program. If your Glock is in a covered block, Glock will replace it. They will tell you when to send your pistol in. You will get your pistol back with a new frame, and the serial number will be slightly altered to reflect the change. As an example, if you find your Glock EXS123US is covered, you'll get it back with the serial number 1EXS123US.

Any problems you might have with the local authorities concerning the change in your serial number are strictly between you and the local authorities. Glock is making sure there isn't a black market in duplicate serial numbers and preventing future phone calls on the same pistols. Those of us in Michigan will have to re-register, no doubt. Or, perhaps in future decades, the Michigan State Police will have a card for Glocks just as they do for Lugers: "Please contact the Glock Corporation concerning the recall on your E-series pistol. Once obtained, re-register with this office via your wireless T-1 line."

Other Numbers

Each part in your Glock has a number. The part number is there for the armorers to know which are old and need replacing, and which caliber yours is. It would not do to have (for example) a .40 ejector in a 9mm Glock, if it would even fit. Those working in gunshops or as armorers for departments keep extensive lists of parts numbers on hand. They can then use the lists to determine if a sample Glock in front of them has all the current parts it should or if any are out-of-date or have been replaced.

Had I the permission of Glock to reprint their intellectual property, I could add the many lists to the book. But despite my asking, they have not yet given their permission. So, get yourself off to a GSSF match and let the armorer there look them up for you. You'll have a fun time shooting, you'll meet all kinds of other Glock owners, and the Glock armorer there won't charge you for the small parts. If you have something major, like a busted barrel (unlikely) he'll have to charge you.

Slide Markings

The next time you have your Glock's slide off, turn it over. On the underside you'll find a line of very small numbers. I managed to find out that they are production code numbers. They indicate the steel lot number, heat-treat and Tenifer lot numbers, which CNC machine the slide was milled on, and more. Those numbers are probably written down or printed out in a looseleaf binder in Austria that resides in a safe in the plant. From what I know of Glock, there

A .40 with factory replacement slide.

are probably a dozen people who are authorized to see that book. So don't expect any explanation of what each entry means. Just know that Glock is tracking all those variables.

And Yet More...

Apparently Glock has been busy since the first edition of this book. In working with the newest models I came across yet more markings. If you have a new G-21SF, or a G-37, G-38 or G-39, you can take a look for yourselves. (They might and probably have marked the others as well. It would make sense, as they all come out of the same moulds in Austria.)

Remove the slide and look at the top of the frame, next to where the locking block fits. You'll see a string of numerals. Why? You've got me. I can imagine they represent some sort of process control on the mould. The newest fashions in manufacturing have the production line tracking all sorts of variables. So there they are, that string of numerals, hidden from sight.

But wait, there's another place. If you remove the ejector block and look at the rear curved surface, you'll see a set of punched marks. Those are a two-dimensional equivalent of a bar code. What do they mean? Heck if I know! Unless it's an assigned pattern of the recognized code, and you have a scanner/dot reader wth the full inventory log in it, you could spend the rest of your life trying to decode it. It is entirely likely that it is a NATO code for inventory purposes (but why on the inside?) and is there because it is required to be for military acceptance in Europe. ♦

CHAPTER 8

Buying a Used Glock

Not everyone buys new guns. A used firearm can have a great deal of useful life left in it, provided it had a decent amount of care from previous owners. Glocks are not different in that regard. A horribly abused Glock may not be worth much even as a parts gun. (Unless, of course, that horribly abused Glock is the only firearm you can lay hands on in the city of Dirt, Carjackistan, when the terrorists are trying to kick down your hotel room door. Then it may be literally worth its weight in gold or more.) A like-new-in-the-box used Glock may not cost much less than a brand-new Glock.

However, the durability of Glocks, and the lower percentage of their owners who experiment with them, tends to mean more Glocks survive in good shape than other firearms. Should you be offered a used Glock for sale, the main dance is settling on a price. There is hardly anything on a Glock that can't be repaired, replaced or factory upgraded, and many of the factory upgrades are free. As a result, advice on buying used Glocks tends to be a lot less involved than that of buying other firearms.

What you are looking for are bargaining points. The small ones are things that are wrong or need upgrading, things that the factory will take care of free or at little cost. A G-17 with the old trigger parts can be fixed for free by Glock, but the same repair with new parts that have been experimented on will cost you should you send them back to Smyrna.

First, give the used Glock a good visual external inspection. Look to see if there are any signs of abuse, neglect and/or experimentation. External abuse would be things like the corners of the slide being chewed up and or dented from being dropped. Dropping the slide when it is off the frame can bend the

Glocks are less likely to have been victims of home gun-wrenching than a 1911.

If you drop your Glock slide, it can bend if it lands on the muzzle end extension for the recoil spring. Check this area before buying a used Glock.

recoil spring retaining tab or the relatively fragile (for a Glock) back ends of the rails in the slide. Neglect would be indicated by rust (rare) or a cracked slide from too many hot reloads (even rarer). Experimentation would be something like the slide being machined to take some other sight system than the factory one or milled for ports other than factory.

The good news is that the cracked slide might well be replaced by the factory for free or at little cost. The others? You're on your own. Glock isn't going to help you with a dropped slide, and the one that was machined will have a voided warranty. Don't worry about the factory sights; Glock sights are cheap and easily replaced. At the current pricing, an armorer's

cost for a new set of sights is only $3!

A scarred and chewed-up frame can be cleaned up but Glock won't replace it just because it got scraped along a curb during a fight. It will replace it, regardless of condition, if it is one of the E-series Glocks that were made from September 2001 through May 2002.

With the permission of the owner, cycle the slide and dry fire it. Try firing it without depressing the trigger safety. It should not fire. Try pulling the trigger normally and then hold it back and cycle the slide. Does the trigger return when you subsequently release it? If not, it may be due to a broken/bent trigger spring or a "trigger job" gone awry. The parts don't cost much, so bargain the price

down as much as you can but don't expect the owner to budge much.

Disassemble and inspect the slide and barrel. Is the barrel clean? Unmarred? Look down the bore. Do you see dark rings? Those are bulges in the barrel from lodged bullets being shot free. A new barrel costs money. At the armorer's cost, a Glock barrel runs $95 to $125, with compensated barrels running up to $140. Aftermarket Match barrels can run up to $200. If the barrel is bulged, bargain hard, for a replacement won't be cheap.

Look at the slide, in the breech face area. Inspect the area around the firing pin slot. In a very high-mileage 9mm, fed many rounds of +P or +P+ ammo (as some police departments use), you may find the area around the firing pin slot eroded or even peened back. The erosion comes from pierced or blown primers jetting hot gases back at and through the firing pin slot. If you find those signs you should remove and check the firing pin to make sure it is in good shape. The peening comes from the high pressure setback of the primer. The wall

Checking the Glock action. The safety plunger is blocking the firing pin.

The firing pin being cocked.

The firing pin fully forward.

Too bad you can't look inside a Glock this easily. Check inside by going through the safety check drill.

Check for a bulged barrel. Your Glock will probably still work (unlike this unfortunate SIG) but a replacement can be expensive, so check and bargain down if you find one.

The design of the Glock barrel (*bottom*) eliminates the need for a barrel link as found on the 1911 barrel (*top*). It's also simpler to machine than the S&W barrel (*middle*).

between the breechface and the firing pin tunnel isn't thick (it can't be) and the repeated hammering from a steady diet of P or +P+ loads can peen it back. Yes, the Tenifer makes the slide hard, but the substrate isn't hard or thick. If the area is made too hard by Glock, it may break. If it is too soft, it may peen. It must

keep Glock engineers awake at night, worrying about it.

If a Glock with a peened or eroded breechface still works fine (you won't know until you test-fire it) then you can use it. But the drag on the empty case from the primer expanding into the bulge or erosion can create malfunctions. Glock may or may not replace the slide. If they do, and they charge you, it can get expensive. The old armorer's manual listed slides and frames as parts that could be ordered. The new manual does not. Aftermarket slides can cost as much as the barrels do, up to $200.

Check the underside of the slide for peening from impacts with the locking block. A small amount is OK, but very heavy peening indicates something is wrong. Perhaps the previous owner fired a great many hot loads through it or experimented with recoil springs, using lighter-than-normal

springs for some perceived advantage. As a result of those changes, other parts of the Glock may have been stressed. Look at the front of the slide. The excessive recoil may have stressed the front of the slide where the recoil spring assembly bears on it. A crack there is very bad and cannot be repaired. The slide must be replaced. Bargain the price down. Also, the slide is thin on the ejection port side, and a steady diet of +P or +P+ loads may have cracked it there.

If you have a cracked-slide Glock, I'd suggest a letter and some photos first. If Glock is willing to replace the slide for free, ship it. If they want to charge you for it, find out how much. A replacement Caspian slide can be had for $140 for a G-17, and you may want to go that route if Glock will charge you more. But if they already have your pistol and won't ship it back without repairing

Look at the breechface for erosion or damage.

it, you won't be able to exercise the Caspian option.

Check the firing pin safety for function with the slide off the frame. Press the striker back, then try to push it forward. If it goes forward

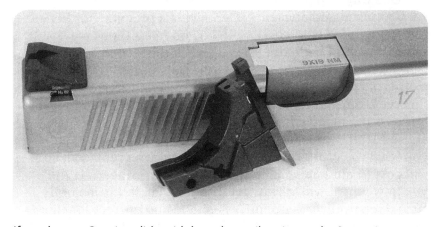

If you have a Caspian slide with barrel, recoil spring and a 9mm ejector, you can turn your .40 into a 9mm. This one, with the Heinie Straight Eight sights, is marvelous.

past the firing pin safety the firing pin and its safety need inspection and replacement.

The extractor merits a look. A chipped extractor may not function 100 percent, but a replacement isn't very much, $10 at armorer's cost. What you may need is the armorer to replace it, as Glock needs to know serial number and caliber to use the correct one. Extractors have changed a bit through the years, and one size does not fit all.

Look at the trigger parts. Black? Silver? Black means old, and a black trigger must be replaced, but Glock will do it for free. Check the trigger safety engagement. Press the trigger bar forward and listen for the safety clicking in place. While still pressing forward, pull the trigger and ease the bar back. If there is a problem, it may be very dirty. Then again, it may have been polished, ground, filed or otherwise experimented on.

Inspect the frame forward of the locking block. Gently flex the recoil spring housing

Older Glocks may need the trigger upgrade or other upgrades. Check for them and bargain down if you find one in need.

right and left, up and down. Some guns, especially the major-caliber compacts and subcompacts, have been known to crack near where the serial number plate is inserted. A cracked frame will be replaced by Glock, but this gives you an opportunity to bargain the price down. It also gives you an opportunity to create a collector's piece. If Glock returns the gun with a new serial number on the frame, but uses your old slide, barrel and other parts, keep the paperwork. You have a factory mis-match, and it may bring a bit of a premium at some future time – but only if you have the paperwork to prove it. Without the

Flex the frame to check for cracks.

Magazines can get dinged up. If it still works, Glock won't replace it. (This one did.)

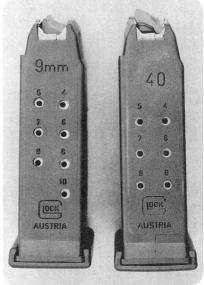

Make sure you get the correct magazines for the Glock you buy. Sometimes they get mixed up, and your .40 won't work with 9mm mags.

paperwork, what you have is a "parts gun" that no one will pay a premium for.

Recoil springs on Glocks don't give up the ghost very

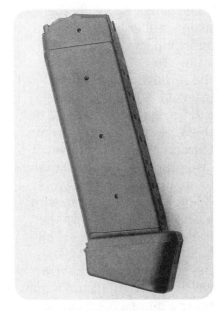

Check the magazine for abuse. This one has the aftermarket mag extension assembled incorrectly.

easily, so looking at the spring won't tell you much unless you have a Glock so old that it pre-dates the switch to the captured recoil spring assembly. (It probably has the old trigger parts, too.) A new recoil spring assembly is inexpensive, so don't worry about it. Keep bargaining.

One way to have fun and get your used and abused Glock upgraded is to go to a GSSF match. There, the factory armorer will as a matter of routine upgrade all the free stuff, and repair at low cost the mangled and abused stuff. He can also tell you what the other repairs will cost (if any) and can tell you how long it will take to get such a repair turned around. And you can shoot the match, have fun, and maybe even win another Glock.

Magazines are almost always part of a handgun purchase. Pistols don't work very well without magazines. Inspect the magazines to make sure they are as stated. Old style or drop-free? If they are drop-free, do they drop? Insert them in the Glock in question and see. Make sure they are Glock, especially if you are paying a premium for honest to goodness Glock mags. Check the feed lips to see if the polymer is still attached. (Glock won't replace them if they're ugly but still work.)

The magazine's internals and baseplates can easily be replaced, so your main concern is the tube itself. If it is in good shape and correct for the pistol you're buying, then shake over a price and have fun with your new toy. ◆

CHAPTER 9

The Glock G-17 and G-17L

he first, and for many shooters, the only Glock is the Model 17. Well, for a lot of you any Glock in 9mm is the only Glock, but the G-17 is first and foremost. As I've already mentioned, the G-17 was developed for the Austrian Army trials as a replacement pistol for their aging P-38s.

The first pistols, quite naturally, went to the Austrian Army. However, you can't have a hot new product like a service pistol without thinking of selling it in other markets besides your own army. After all, if you were the head of a corporation with a hot new product coming off the line, it would be the height of irresponsibility to neglect looking around for more outlets. The first lesson anyone learns either in business school, or in running a business, is that the pupose of the business is to create a return on the stockholders investment. Eveything else is secondary. If you have a hot new pistol that can make the

stockholders a lot of money, you would be negligent if you didn't at the very least explore your options.

And Glock was anything but negligent. Even before the first contract for 25,000 pistols was finished, other organizations had expressed an interest in the Glock. (You don't beat out the established manufacturers in any field without raising a lot of interest.) Not all of the organizations expressing interest were end-users such as the Norwegian army, which adopted the Glock

in 1984 and was one of the first non-Austrian services to adopt the Glock. Between late 1982, when Glock had enough excess capacity to start offering the G-17 on the European market, and 1985, no fewer than 36 different importers had expressed interest in becoming agents to bring the G-17 to the American market.

After looking around, the Glock company decided to form their own subsidiary in the United States to handle importation. (Exporting the product is always a problem

One of the first. This G-17 came in within the first few months of US importation.

for any manufacturer: do you let someone else handle importation and sales of your product, and the headaches that go with it, or do you shoulder the cost and headaches and do it yourself? It is not always an easy answer, as there are advantages and disadvantages to both.)

The Glock line, when the company's US offices were set up in January of 1986, was simple: the G-17, magazines for it and spare parts to keep them running. And there was an Armorers Kit, which consisted of one tool. (For a while, one of the Glock ads that ran in firearms magazines was simply a photograph of that tool, a 3/32" punch with a moulded-on polymer handle.)

G-17 vs. 1911

Let's get this out of the way right now: in the first edition of this book I got some flak from some quarters about spending "so much time" comparing the Glock to other pistols. If you thought that was bad, it is worse now, for Glock has a lot more competition. The dedicated Glockophiles may want to simply read a gushing list of why the Glock is so good, but I can't oblige them. The rest of you who may have a Glock but also other firearms, or are simply looking to see which works best for you, can read on.

The three main competitors the G-17 faced in its early years were the 1911 in its various sizes, the Beretta M-92 and the S&W M-59 series. The 1911 comes in three main sizes: the Government, Commander and the Officers. The G-17 is not quite on par in size and proportion to the 1911, the pistol so many older shooters were familiar with in the mid 1980s. At 140mm, the barrel is just under (.01" under) four and a half inches. This puts it on par with the Colt Commander in barrel size. In size and bulk, the best comparison for the 1911 shooter would be a Lightweight Commander. The weights are comparable (but in the favor of the Glock) while the height, length, width and overall bulk are quite similar. The grip of the G-17 is a little more raked than that of the 1911 pistols, but not enough that switching from one to another is difficult.

Some like to complain about the difference in grip angle. They point out that the Glock "points low" and isn't as natural as the 1911 (or some other pistol). They should get over it. The Glock points where the Glock points. Anyone who depends solely on pointing as a means of getting hits in a match or gunfight is setting himself up to lose. And yes, I say that knowing that all the "point-shooting" and "instinctive" shooting advocates will gear up to prove me wrong.

The overall slide length of the Glock is greater than that of the Light Weight Commander, allowing for a longer sight radius. The extra length of the G-17's slide overhangs the hand, going out into the space that the hammer on a 1911 would occupy; thus the longer slide doesn't mean a longer overall length. Indeed, stood on their muzzles, the LWC will be longer, the extra amount depending on what kind of grip

The Glock (*top*) is shorter than the 1911 it's resting on and holds more rounds. But is it better? That can start quite an argument.

safety is installed.

Compared to a full-size Government model, the Glock is king. Lighter by 10 to 12 ounces, the G-17 is also shorter by an inch. The added length of the Government model doesn't help the sight radius as much as you'd expect, since the sight on the 1911 doesn't reach to the back of the slide on the 1911. A fixed-sight Government 1911 will have almost the same sight radius as a G-17.

The Officers Model is a compact 1911, and is best used as a comparison to the G-19 and G-26.

And as for capacity, well, we all know that answer. A

If your police department issues 9mm subguns, then a 9mm handgun makes ammunition procurement and issue a lot easier.

Comparable in size, the Glock is lighter and holds more rounds than the P-35.

THE WONDER NINE

Again, the matter of the caliber. For many of the decades of the twentieth century, many European police and military organizations had been content with smaller calibers. Indeed, when the German Army had rolled into neighboring (and not so neighboring) countries during WWII, they simply continued making the local sidearm – be it .32, .380 or even odder – and issued them to soldiers and policemen. Many a soldier or policeman felt well-armed packing what we Americans would consider today to be a pocket pistol. Even after the war things didn't change much. The German police establishment wanted to upgrade their pistols in the 1970s and 1980s, to simplify the profusion of sidearms and make ammunition purchase and distribution easier. What they ended up doing was drawing up the specifications for the most advanced pocket pistol ever made and, in the process, creating a new caliber, the 9x18 Ultra. Within a few years the 9mm Ultra and its pistol were being sold as surplus on the American market.

What with the increase in crime, and the threat of terrorism, the German police (and many others) were abandoning their .32s and .380s and getting (or planning to get) 9mms from their military. Seventy years after it had been invented, and after decades of dissing from Americans who felt the 9mm was some kind of wimpy caliber, the 9mm was getting accepted as a sidearm cartridge. And in the midst of all this, even the Americans switched.

The makers of reloading dies have for years published the sales order of the various calibers. When I started reloading back in the 1970s, and for many years after, the 9x19 or 9mm Parabellum barely broke the top 25 or 20. For a bunch of years now, it has consistently been a top-10 caliber, and often makes the top five.

The 9mm Parabellum: a century old and a still a happening thing.

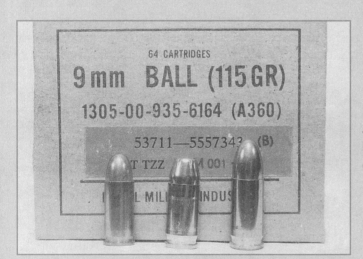

Left to right: The .32 ACP, .380 ACP and 9mm Parabellum. All three have been used as European military cartridges.

Commander or Government model will have the same capacity, nine rounds of 9mm in the magazine and one in the chamber. The G-17 holds 17 and one. With special magazines (Chip McCormick) and loading .38 Super instead of 9mm, (you also have the change the barrel on the 1911 to accomplish this feat) you can get 10 rounds in a magazine and one in the chamber. Still, for all your work you've got 11 rounds to the Glock's 18.

Not to beat a dead horse, but at this point I can't understand the complaints about comparing the two: right now the Glock has the advantage: more shots, lighter weight, longer sight radius and simpler manual of arms.

There are going to be those who will object to the comparison, complaining that the 1911 was designed for the .45ACP cartridge, and comparing it to a high-capacity 9mm isn't fair. Well, on the one hand they're correct. Comparing a 9mm to a .45 isn't fair. However, the comparison is one that many shooters make anyway. After all, while it is comforting to have the power or bullet weight of the .45 cartridge in your sidearm, the lure of the extra rounds is there. And, the 1911 system is available in 9mm/.38 Super, so the manufacturers themselves have left it open to comparison. Given the option, would I carry 18 9mm rounds or nine .45's? (Carrying 10 or 11 9mms in a 1911 would be a distinct third choice.) I have done both. The question of caliber is a different chapter. While I do feel that with all other things being equal, bigger is better, I have read enough good things of the high-pressure 9mm loadings that I wouldn't feel naked carrying one. Especially 18 of them, with another magazine on my belt.

Browning fans will object to comparing the 1911 and its nine rounds of 9mm and propose the Hi-Power with 13. Yes, a good choice. But for all intents and purposes, the P-35 is (and I'll get hate mail on this one) just a 1911 with a big magazine. While a very good choice, it didn't offer the huge leap in performance and operation that the G-17 did.

G-17 vs. M-92

The Beretta M-92 is the culmination of design efforts over more than 20 years. Starting with the Beretta Brigadier or Model 951 back in the late 1950s and early 1960s, Beretta gradually improved the design. Back at the beginning it had been a single action, single stack all-steel 9mm with a crossbolt safety and a magazine catch button in the heel of the grips. By the early 1980s, when it was entered in the US pistol trials being put on by the JSSAP (Joint Service Small Arms Program) it had become a double action high capacity 9mm with an alloy frame and American-style magazine catch position.

What didn't change was the locking system, derived from the P-38. The locking system featured a tilting wedge under the barrel. The wedge locked the barrel and slide together for a short distance during recoil. When the barrel-locking lug stops against the frame, it unlocks from the slide and allows the slide to continue. The system is quite reliable but suffers from two faults. One, it is tall. The locking lug has to ride under the barrel, and the frame has to accommodate the locking lug, the barrel rails, slide rails, etc. Two, the impact of the locking lug against the frame can be stressful. I've seen Berettas with the frame cracked at the locking lug stop recess, a permanent breakage. (M-92s or M-9s broken this way are useful only as a source of spare parts for the remaining M-9s in inventory, as the frame cannot be repaired.)

But the Beretta is quite popular, and there are a large number of them in use. How does it compare to the G-17?

First, it is longer. It has a barrel half an inch longer, but in overall length it is over an inch longer. The extra length is partly slide, but also the tang behind the grip, to protect the shooting hand from the hammer. For all of the extra length, the Beretta's sight radius is less than that of the G-17. The grip angle of the two is just about the same.

The Beretta trigger design comes one of two ways, traditional double action/ single action with a slide mounted decocker, or DAO.

Remember how we were talking about the height of the pistol and the need to accommodate the hammer and its pivot point into other designs? The Beretta M-92 is a perfect example of the situation. If you were to lay a Glock directly over an M-92 so that their barrels were parallel, you'd see a big difference in the curve of the frame where the web of your hand rests. (For those of you who do not have both a G-17 and an M-92 on hand, please look at the photo.) The Beretta, in order to provide room for the hammer pivot pin and the trigger parts needed for the double action mechanism, requires that the tang curve start lower than the Glock's curve and far tighter.

As a result, your hand rides lower under the bore, and you must reach a longer distance to the trigger. I'm 6'4" tall and wear a size 10 or 11 glove (depending on who the government contractor is) and for me the Beretta trigger reach is manageable. For someone smaller, or with smaller hands, it can be too much. Part of the reach problem is the grip/frame size. The trigger mechanism runs on the side of the frame, outside of the magazine. Those parts are covered by the grips. The bulk of the grips adds to the reach, and makes the Beretta larger still. Now, when the Beretta hammer is cocked the trigger rides farther back in the trigger guard, reducing the reach. When cocked the Beretta has a shorter reach than the Glock. But you've got to get it cocked somehow, and with the Beretta getting it cocked

means firing it that first time.

If you can reach the uncocked trigger, the cocked trigger is significantly shorter. If the cocked trigger position is comfortable, then reaching the trigger for the first shot is a long reach. Either way, it is a lot more work than with a Glock.

In magazine capacity, the Beretta falls a bit short. While the Beretta's magazine is the same height as the Glock's, it is slightly narrower and lacks two rounds. The narrowness is probably not a stacking design consideration of the 9mm cartridge as much as it is a need to keep the frame width down. If you were to make the Beretta magazine as wide as a Glock's (perhaps adding a round or two) you'd have to make the frame wider, and thus the grips wider, and you'd end up with an even wider pistol.

In weight the M-92 comes in right in the middle. It tips the scale at just under thirty one ounces, midway between the Glock/LW Commander and the steel Government model.

I've carried an M-92 for various classes and as a carry gun. As a somewhat bulky, high-capacity 9mm that can handle +P or +P+ ammo, it can get the job done. When on the road for classes, I select one or the other depending on what the PD I'm going to uses, so I can borrow magazines if need be. (And so I can teach using the same sidearm they carry, always important.) But were I in the position of

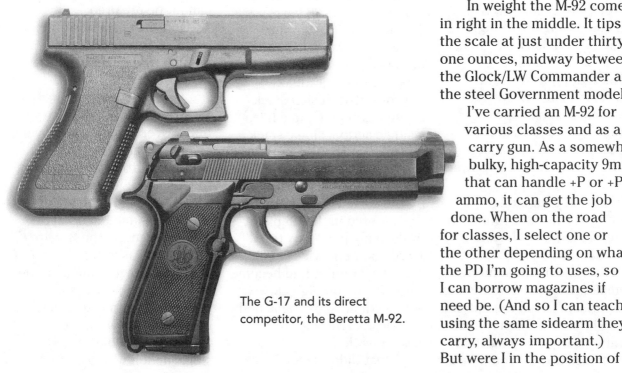

The G-17 and its direct competitor, the Beretta M-92.

being "stuck" with a 9mm, and had the option of feeding it a steady diet of +P or +P+ ammo, I'd definitely go with a G-17 instead. If my hands were a bit smaller, I wouldn't even consider the Beretta.

As a last strike against it, and in favor of the Glock, the height of the locking system puts the bore axis higher above your hand. As a result, the front of the pistol moves more in recoil. It has more leverage, and firing the same ammo in both, you'll notice the greater muzzle whip of the Beretta.

G-17 vs. M-59

Smith & Wesson has been developing and improving their double action pistols even longer than Beretta has been working on the M-92. The initial design started with the M-39, a single stack pistol in 9mm that they designed and developed at the request of the US Army. Forward thinkers right after WWII had expressed the idea of switching from the .45 caliber 1911 to a double action, alloy framed 9mm. (No, they were not summarily burned at the stake.) The idea was that 9mm was "good enough" and lighter to carry and easier to shoot. A lighter pistol would be easier to carry, and the double action mechanism would be "safer" in the context of the cramped confines of landing craft, armored vehicles, aircraft and bunkers. With the extremely tight quarters in many military situations, it isn't always possible to have

The G-17 has made great inroads into the M-59's territory.

a safe direction to point a weapon while you're handling it. A DA action prevents accidental discharges, or so it was asserted. (I've seen a few ADs, and they happen regardless of the mechanism involved.)

S&W got to work and made the pistol, and the powers that be decided that since they'd just finished a war, and had millions of 1911 pistols in warehouses, buying a new pistol just wasn't a prudent financial decision.

S&W continued improving the M-39 and convinced some police departments to adopt or allow its carry by their officers. In 1972, they came out with the M-59, a high-capacity 9mm development of the M-39. Developments since then have been cosmetics and variations.

The DA mechanism of the S&W series is a marvel. Someone decided back before most of the readers of this book were born that the new design should be adaptable to all needs. (Good choice, as it has worked out well.) By using different safety cams, or making slight alterations to the frame (easy to do now with CAD/CAM machining centers) the S&W mechanism can be a traditional DA/SA, DAO, DA-decocking, single action with slide safety or single action with frame safety.

Our concern is with the DA/SA and the DAO. In an alloy frame, they come in at just under 29 ounces (unless you get the adjustable sight variant, which adds a couple of ounces) and has a four-inch barrel. The S&W barrels tend to be short and shorter. The

Yes, 10-shot magazines are now curiosities, but they're rugged, durable, reliable and cheap. Stock up on them for practice.

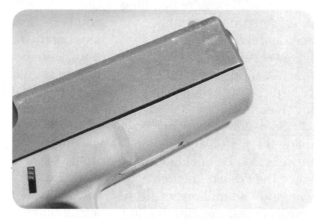

New model grip frames are still the same shape as the old, even with the finger grooves. A longer magazine still works in the shorter frames.

Old frame with the smooth snout, minus the new light rail.

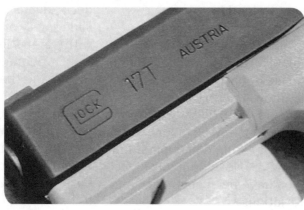

This G-17T has a light rail, perfect for law enforcement training applications.

standard 9mm and .40 caliber pistols have four-inch barrels, while the compact ones have barrels a half-inch shorter. If you want a longer barrel, you have to go to a bigger caliber, like the 4500 series in .45ACP.

The sight radius is shorter than that of a G-17; the grip is at a slightly less raked angle; and as with the Beretta, the grip area under the tang has a curve that starts sooner and arcs tighter than that of the Glock. As with the Beretta, you have a long first pull, then a shorter and lighter pull on the DA/SA models. On the DAO models, the trigger pull is always long.

The S&W bore axis is higher than that of the Glock, but not as high as that of the Beretta. So you'll see more muzzle rise with a 59 than a G-1, but not as much as with an M-92.

Why a G-17?

If there are more compact pistols, or bigger-caliber pistols, why the G-17? Why not one of the others? Until the G-17L and then the G-34 came along, the G-17 was the biggest Glock in the smallest caliber and therefore had the softest recoil with any given ammunition. The sight radius was the longest (again) until the G-17L and G-34 came out. For many shooters, the competition Glocks (17L and 24) are an attractive option. For target competition. For someone who wants a pistol that can be used for both competition and daily carry, trying to pack a G-17L or G-24 without getting a backache is impossible. (I carried full-size 1911s for years, and gladly switched to a Light Weight Commander when I had the chance. I'm tall, but I can't imagine trying to pack a G-17L or G-24 concealed.)

The G-17 is a nicely balanced package between capacity, size and ease of use. A smaller pistol can be harder to learn to shoot, especially for a new shooter. A larger caliber can be tougher to learn. Combine the two, and a new shooter can be scared off. The G-17 makes it quite easy. Yes, a G-17L or G-24 would be even easier, but then there is the pesky thing called expense. How many shooters are willing to buy another pistol just because it is a bit easier to learn with, then buy another, smaller one for carry? (Yes, yes, a bunch of you are more than willing, but you missed the point.) For someone looking for a do-all pistol, the G-17 can quite nicely fit the bill.

The G-17 frame has gone through all three generations of design, starting with the first, a pebble finish that seems secure but isn't. Get your hands wet, sweaty or bloody and the frame squirms around. But then again, so do a lot of other pistols. The second generation frames came out with textured frames, sort of a polymer checkering. The third generation frames have the finger grooves, the thumb rest and the checkering where it fits in with the rest. The third generation frames also have the accessory or light rail. A tactical light is quite the thing these days, and having the light attached directly to your handgun can be quite useful in some circumstances.

The G-17 can take longer barrels, but for the cost, a "poor man's G-17L" is not that much of an improvement. After all, you don't get the longer sight radius of the G-17L by simply plugging a longer barrel into your G-17. However, you can put a G-17L or G-34 upper assembly on

> ## For someone looking for a do-all pistol, the G-17 can quite nicely fit the bill.

a G-17 frame. The .40 caliber uppers would also fit, but unless you have a newer frame with the two-pin locking block design, putting a 40 caliber upper on your G-17 will break things with high volume shooting.

Oh, and the very earliest G-17s had what are now called "pencil" barrels. The barrel diameter was much smaller and the slide was bored accordingly. If you have one of those, and you need a new barrel, you're pretty much out of luck. Glock doesn't have any more, and everyone who makes new barrels makes them to the new dimension. You could find a gunsmith with a lathe who could turn down a new one to fit your old slide, but it would cost a bit of change.

The Glock G-17L

The first of the competition Glocks, the G-17L came out in April of 1988 as a worked-over G-17. The frame is a G-17 frame, and you could own one frame and two top ends and swap them back and forth without worry. The slide and barrel were lengthened for a longer sight radius and slightly higher velocity. The slide and barrel are each a fraction more than 1.5 inches longer than those of the G-17. (They are also longer than the slide of the G-18 by the same amount, and I once had the amusement of listening to a gun show "expert" talk of how Glock had made a whole bunch of slides for the G-18 on contract before the Sultan who asked for them had backed out. As a result, so he said, Glock re-worked the slides into the G-17L competition guns to sell to America. I had to leave before I started laughing out loud.)

The slide of the G-17L differed from those of the G-17 and G-19 in that it was machined open on the top, forward of the chamber but behind the front sight. The removed steel kept the weight down. The G-17L tips the scales at just under twenty four ounces. In weight it matches a LW Commander, but in size it is bigger than a 1911 Government model. For a short time, the G-17L was "the" Glock competition pistol. With its longer sight radius, and being shipped with 3.5-lb. connectors instead of the 5-lb. connectors the G-17 and G-19 had, shooting it was much easier. Indeed, Armando Valdes used his in the IPSC World Shoot IX in 1990 in Adelaide, Australia, to place 49th overall and come in as the First Place Stock competitor.

The arrival of the G-22 changed all that. One of the peculiarities of practical competition is the scoring, where a larger caliber is scored higher than a lesser one. Known as "Major" and "Minor," it is extremely difficult to compete and do well shooting a Minor caliber against someone shooting a Major caliber. 9mm is Minor. The new .40 caliber pistols could make Major. Glock took their time (four years) following the introduction of the G-22 and G-23 with a competition .40, the G-24. Shifting equipment developments and rules changes in practical shooting (the change to red dot optics, high capacity frames in .38 Super and high-capacity 1911 type frames) caused the L series to languish. No one wanted to shoot Minor, so the G-17L didn't sell well. Those who wanted to shoot Major usually went with a high-capacity 1911 frame and spent $1000 to $1500 more than they would have for a G-24, but that's what they wanted. For a short time, there was some intense experimentation going on with the G-17L for IPSC Open competition. By using a barrel half an inch longer and installing a compensator in it, velocities could be boosted to the Major level. (Back then, a 130-grain bullet would have to be going 1350 fps to make Major.) Reaming the chamber to 9x21 dimensions got around the pesky rule of 9mm Parabellum not being allowed to shoot major. The mechanical problems could be overcome, but the trigger and magazine ones couldn't. The G-17L with a 3.5-lb. connector is still not nearly as nice in feel and delicate in use as a 1911 trigger can be tuned to be. And the magazines held "only" 17 rounds. With other pistols going up to 25 (later 28) rounds, a Glock shooter could be at a disadvantage in a large field course. The makers of capacity-extending baseplates had all they could do to satisfy the desires of those shooting 1911s and it was a while before any were made for Glocks. Glocksters could have caught up, given enough time, but in 1994 the law was changed, and it was too late for Glocks in Open, and the use of Glock pistols in Open faded away for a while.

With the shift in the late 1990s to USPSA Limited 10 and Production, and IDPA shooting, the G-17L and G-24 could have made a comeback but for one pesky little rule: the IPSC box. In order to keep the equipment race under control, the International body uses a maximum dimension as an allowable pistol size. The G-17L wouldn't fit the box, nor would the G-24. To get in on

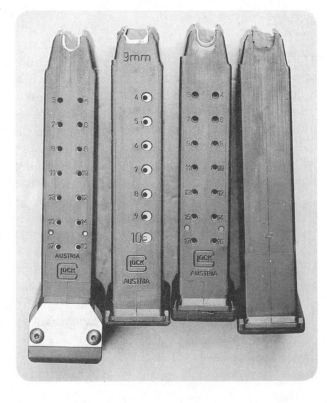

All Glock magazines work with Glocks if they fit the frame. *Left to right*: Old G-117 non-drop with Taylor Freelance extension, newer 10-shot Glock, non-drop Glock, no-name copy.

the new equipment Divisions, and garner competitors in the matches, Glock altered the size and came up with the G-34 and G-35. The new pistols were .70" shorter in slide and barrel than that of the G-17L and G-24, but still longer than the G-17 or G-22.

They were an instant hit, so much so that Glock dropped the G-17L and G-24, although you can special order upper assemblies. I suspect that "Special Order" means one of two things: either Glock has a parts bin full of slides and barrels they made up when the G-17L was the hot gun to have, or it simply takes some time to schedule a G-17L cutter order into the CNC mill and make sure a long enough chunk of bar stock is ready for the slide cutter and the barrel mandrel.

If you have a G-17L and want to use it in some other capacity, you are in luck. The frame is simply a G-17 frame, and can accept upper assemblies or barrels from other models. Well, upper assemblies, since the barrel length at 6.02" is the longest Glock offered, and all others will fall short. They'll fit on the back end but won't reach the end of the slide, and thus would be unsafe to use.

However, if you lucked onto a slide assembly from a G-17 or a G-34, they would fit right on and work just fine. You might be tempted to install a .40 upper assembly, but you shouldn't. First, you'd have to change the ejector to

Paint, non-skid tape, stickers – but it's still a box-stock Glock.

work with the .40 cartridge and clear the .40 slide. The G-17L frame is an old style G-17 and lacks the second locking block pin. If you shot such an assembly a lot, you could end up breaking the locking block pin your frame, which is the reason Glock added the second pin when they built the .40 Glocks.

The G-17L serial number cutoff for the six part trigger upgrade is the "XG" prefix, the same as the standard G-17.

Recently there has been interest in loading 9mm Parabellum ammunition to make major, called "9mm Major." The interest is due mostly to lower-cost brass. The 9mm Major fits a G-17 or G-17L magazine, and with the magazine extension makers now offering high-capacity extensions, you can get 26+ rounds in an Open Glock.

The Glock G-17S

This is the pistol Glock collectors and gunsmiths have been asking about, and trying to build: a Glock with an external safety. Why? After all, after his having designed a sidearm that didn't need one, you'd have to be pretty bold to ask Gaston Glock to then modify his pistol into one with a safety. But then, it is a 1911-centric world out there. Apparently the customer demand was enough for Glock to fill a contract with a police force in Tasmania (perhaps there is only one police force in Tasmania) for a Glock with an external safety, the G-17S. No details are known about serial numbers, nor could I track down a photo of one. I have heard of some gunsmiths experimenting with external safeties, but none have caught on yet. As you can imagine, such experimentation voids the factory warranty right away.

It does seem odd, but then if enough customers demand it, who knows?   ◆

CHAPTER 10

The Glock G-19 and G-26

The question could not have taken very long in coming up. As a matter of fact, it probably didn't take any longer than the first day the first Police Department was looking at the G-17, for someone to remark, "this would be really great if you made it smaller." (Meanwhile, someone at the other end of the table was no doubt remarking to the other Glock rep, "Hey, this is neat. When are you going to make it in .45?")

Introduced in March of 1988, the G-19 is just what it appears to be: a shorter G-17. The frame is made shorter simply by shortening the mould when machining it out of its steel block, the result

coming out 11mm shorter in the butt than the G-17. Up top, the barrel is shorter by 12mm (102mm vs. 114mm) and the slide is shortened a like amount. In shortening the slide, the sight radius gets cropped by (you guessed it) 12mm, since the sights are not just the same but located at the same positions relative to the front and rear ends of the slide as they are on the G-17.

In weight, the G-19 loses just one ounce from its big brother, as the hollow polymer frame cropped weighs next to nothing and the slide and barrel sections lost are simply hollow steel sections. The slide loses 12mm of "U" shaped length, and the barrel loses 12mm of tube, hardly large amounts of steel.

The slightly shorter G-19 frame requires a shorter magazine to match, and the G-19 specific magazine has a capacity of "only" 15 rounds of 9mm. The big concern some shooters had when they first heard of the G-19's introduction turned out not to be one at all, as the G-19 can use the same magazines as the G-17. (But not vice versa, as the baseplate of a G-19-only magazine won't fit past the

A G-19 with a Glock holster makes a pretty good carry outfit. And you've got 15 shots at hand.

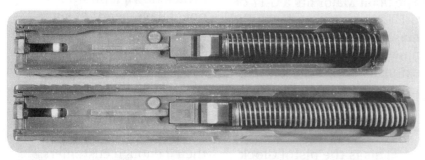

The difference between a G-17 and a G-19 slide is essentially one of length. The barrel and recoil springs are different, but not a whole lot else.

bottom of the frame of the G-17's magazine opening and cannot lock in place.) Thus for concealed carry, you (or a detective on a PD that has adopted Glocks) can carry a 15-shot magazine in the pistol, and have a 17-shot magazine or magazines on the belt as spares. Or even more rounds, if you used a G-17 magazine with an extended base pad on it.

In all other regards, the G-19 is just like the G-17 in takedown, parts replacement, operation and reliability. (The guy asking for a ".45 Glock" had to wait a few more years before he could lay hands on one.)

The feel of the G-19 is much the same as the G-17, except for those with larger than normal hands. A shooter with average hands might not notice the difference between frames, but the big-fisted shooter will. The shorter slide creates a slightly different feel in recoil, in that the G-19 feels a little bit "snappier" than the G-17. Of course this purely subjective impression can be altered by using different ammunition. And for a lot of shooters is completely unnoticed. Switch to a round that feels a little softer in recoil and your G-19 can feel as soft as the G-17.

The G-19 is a little smaller and lighter than a 1911 Lightweight Commander, coming in at 21 ounces compared to the LWC at between 22 and 24.

Why a slightly smaller pistol? Why not a greatly smaller one instead? (That

A G-19 with a factory mag and +2 extension. Eighteen shots (17+1) and still very compact.

The same G-19 (same hand, too) with a G-17 mag with a +2 extension. Twenty shots!

Okay, this is getting a bit much for carry, but a G-19 with a G-17 magazine and a Dawson extension gives you 24 shots carried (23+1) and 23 on the reload!

A G-19 in an in-the-pants holster makes a smaller package than a 1911 Light Weight Commander – and it gives you more shots, too.

The Streamlight light with a third generation Glock. Slide the light onto the rail.

came later.) The hardest part of a pistol to conceal is the butt. The hardest part to get comfortable with is the muzzle. A too-large butt (no wisecracks, please) makes clothing tent or bulge. The outline of a pistol's grip was the big giveaway when we were playing "spot the gun" on our customers at the gun shop. In addition to being a giveaway, the grip texture would over time wear and tear at clothing. Expensive suits can be ruined in short order by rubbing over checkered grip panels. The earliest Glocks had the "pebble" texture on the frame and would not wear cloth as quickly, but they too could eventually shred the lining of a suit jacket.

As for the muzzle, it jabs you. It doesn't matter if the holster is an outside or in-the-pants model, the muzzle end of things is going to ride against your body. On some people, the holster acts as a cantilever, where the rubbing muzzle pivots the grip around the belt and into your ribs,

Press to the rear until it locks. . .

. . .and keep moving your hand back until you have a firing grip.

and vice versa. The last one is a particular problem of mine. Years of martial arts training and weight lifting, but sensible eating, have left me with (how can I put this and be delicate?) a slightly larger ratio of "seat to belt" in my trousers. Many holster designs, coupled with long-barreled or slide pistols, pivot on me. I end up with the back end of the slide trying to gouge out my kidney.

By shortening both ends, Glock made the G-19 much easier to carry, so much so that the G-19 is in many cases allowed as an alternate duty weapon, even in uniform. And some departments use only the smaller Glock. (The same phenomenon can be seen in departments that went with .40 cal Glocks. If the G-23 is easier to carry, then why have the bigger one?) The usual pattern is for a department to authorize or issue the G-17 for uniform use, and the G-19 for detectives and off-duty carry. However, many officers argue that the G-19 is easier to fit on the belt and in a car. Since it uses the same magazines as the G-17, and since they can qualify with the G-19 (and most courses are easy enough there is no change in score) then why not use a G-19 for uniform carry?

Why not, indeed? The NYPD decided on the G-19-only route, authorizing it and not the G-17 for on- and off-duty carry. With 40,000 officers in the combined NYPD force, some 25,000 of them have decided to go with the Glock instead of one of

The G-19 can be used as a competition gun, but some competition changes alter its compact, easy-to-carry profile.

the two other choices available to them.

In the competition arena, the G-19 doesn't offer any of these advantages. While the smaller grip is a grasping problem only for shooters with very large hands, the shorter sight radius can be a problem for all. Remember, in a departmental qualification course, or a shootout, hits count. The idea is to post a "Q" score high enough to demonstrate proficiency. (And quite frankly, most police qualification courses are easy enough that an enterprising shooter using a pair of cowboy guns could shoot a passing score.)

On the street you need to win by hitting the bad guy sooner, more often, and with more certain results than he can manage on you. This shootout may never come. And in the 20 years or more that a police officer may be carrying his sidearm, comfort is an actual issue, while passing the Q course is an annual one and surviving a shootout is in the minds of many a theoretical one. Quite often, comfort wins. In a match, however, a few points here or there can make a big difference in the final outcome. Many competitors who opt for a Glock in 9mm, go with the G-17L or the G-34. The longer sight radius lets them score more points or shoot faster. The smaller size of the G-19 is not something

This G-19 has had an excellent low-mount job done to blend the Bo-Mar sight into the slide. It must have been hell on the cutting tools getting through the Tenifer.

tested in any meaningful way at a match, so it isn't often seen, except at GSSF matches, where the Glock-only focus allows for more specialization.

One development that came about shortly before the first edition of this book was the spate of Class 3 malfunctions that NYPD experienced. The result of the malfunction was that the extracted empty was impaled on the barrel hood as the slide attempted to close and chamber the next round. In its most severe manifestation, the pistol had to be pried apart with a screwdriver or knife, or whacked with a hammer. The malfunctions were not frequent (as mentioned, NYPD has 25,000 officers using G-19, and they all qualify annually) but the problem happened enough to gain attention, especially when a couple of instances happened during shootouts.

At first Glock (in the opinion of some) dragged their feet, and apparently it took NYPD asking another firearms manufacturer for a quote to replace all G-19s in service to get the full attention of Smyrna.

Glock ended up installing a dedicated machine shop at the NYPD range, and as officers came through for their annual qualification, malfunctioning pistols were modified. In the end, Glock modified 10,388 pistols. As an apparent modification, Glock changed the shape of the extractor and the rear of the barrel to match, which is how we came to get the "fifteen-degree" extractors.

If you have this problem, then yours is a rare Glock indeed. Sending it back to Glock for warranty repair (accompanied by photographs of the predicament) should get your problem handled in a timely manner.

The change from the G-17 required more than just a shortening of the barrel and slide. Since the front of a Glock slide does not have a long recoil spring tunnel

> ### As Glock makes the frames as "one size for all calibers" in each, you can swap uppers of the same size.

(as does the 1911) when the slide gets shortened the recoil spring abutment gets moved back also. The recess for the recoil spring must accommodate the spring, and the recoil spring has to handle the same amount of force, but in a smaller package. As a result, you can't swap a G-17 upper onto a G-19 lower.

Can you install a G-17 (or longer) barrel onto a G-19? Good question, and the answer is: maybe. Some say yes, some say no. Some say the cam angles on the barrel locking surface (and the locking block) are different and can't be changed. The locking block part numbers show some patterns, but not enough to tease out the truth. For instance, the locking block number for the G-22 and the G-31 (same size, .40 and .357) is the same, but that for the G-17 and G-22 are not. As Glock makes the frames as "one size for all calibers" in each, you can swap uppers of the same size. That is, you can take a G-22 and drop a G-17 upper assembly on it. (Don't forget to change the ejectors.) But larger and smaller frames and upper assemblies? They won't work. A G-17 barrel in a G-19 slide and gun? It probably will work fine, but I don't see the point.

Some even say the parts differ, but the difference between the G-17 and 19 is so small it doesn't matter. Me, I would be cautious. I wouldn't go swapping a longer barrel into a shorter gun unless the barrel maker made it to do so. That is, if you want a longer barrel on your G-19, go get one from Bar-sto (and tell them what you're doing) rather than fit a G-17 barrel to a G-19.

As for upping the caliber by building a G-19 into a G-23, you should be careful. Unless you have a new 9mm frame with the double locking pins on the locking block, the .40 caliber round will over-stress the 9mm frame and its single pin. You'll break things. Not a good idea.

Early G-19s can predate the trigger parts upgrade. To see if your G-19 needs the upgrade, look at the serial number. If your has a prefix under "XL" in sequence ("XK" is the cutoff) you should check your trigger parts. If the trigger bar is not dull or bright nickel in color, you need the six parts upgrade. You can either send it back to Glock or have the upgrade done at the next GSSF match. The G-19 change from the 90-degree breechface to the 15-degree breechface happened at the BKO prefix block. BKP and later G-19s have the 15-degree breechface and thus require a 15-degree extractor.

The Glock G-26

Introduced in July of 1995 along with the .40 caliber G-27, the G-26 was the first of the subcompact Glocks. The idea of an ultra-concealable sidearm for concealed carry has been one with a long life. Back before WWII, Colt and various gunsmiths were making "Fitz Specials," revolvers with the hammer spur and front of the trigger guard cut off, the barrel shortened and all sharp edges removed. With clothing styles heavier back than as compared to today, and those clothes being made of thicker and heavier cloth, carrying a sidearm in a pocket was a favored approach. A snubby revolver tucked in a pocket was comforting back then. (Still is; you just have to dress properly for it.)

The G-26 is short enough that those with large hands may find their pinky fingers floating in air.

But with a mag extension, the G-26 now has a place for your little finger.

Pocket carry has mostly gone by the wayside, both due to the lighter nature and fabric of clothing, and for safety. (Who wants their keys getting tangled up in the trigger guard of their pocketed handgun?) The G-26 offers 12 rounds of 9x19 in standard (for the frame size) magazines, and can use G-17 magazines holding 17 rounds, or extended magazines with more. As currently shipped, the G-26 comes with stubby 10-shot magazines as mandated by some few states that have their own version of the spectacularly pointless and nonsensical Assault Weapons Ban that expired at the federal level in 2004.

In overall length the G-26 is a full inch shorter than the G-17 and a half inch shorter than the already compact G-19. The height is an inch and a third less than that of the G-17, and three quarters of an inch shorter than the G-19.

In function is it just like every other Glock model extant, save for the G-18 and its selector switch. All internal parts except for the barrel and recoil spring are interchangeable with other Glocks of the same caliber. You can install all the standard and optional sights that fit other Glocks. If you find that the frame is just a bit too short, you can install magazine extensions (not

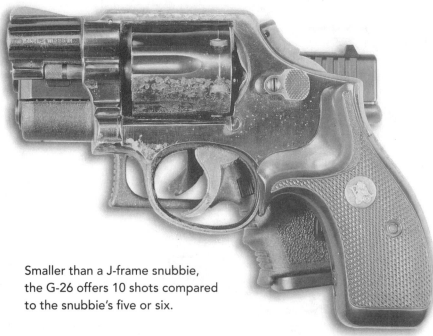

Smaller than a J-frame snubbie, the G-26 offers 10 shots compared to the snubbie's five or six.

there is no real difference between them. If there isn't (and Glock wouldn't tell me anything, let alone answer this) then a standard barrel that fits a G-17 or a G-19 could be installed and trimmed to whatever length you feel is needed.

If they are different, then what can you do? It seems to me the problem with the short guns is keeping them closed long enough to let them cycle properly and not get beaten up by functioning. The cam angle of the G-26 (operating strictly in a theoretical mode here) would keep the gun closed longer. Installing a G-17 or G-19 barrel would have the effect of opening the action sooner. Except for one thing. The extra mass of the longer barrel would act to slow down opening. (Oh, if only Glock returned my calls, to answer the burning question put to me by exactly three readers!) I guess if you wanted a longer barrel then you should have gotten a G-17 instead of a G-26.

any that increase capacity over ten shots, please, if you happen to live in Kaliforniastan or the People's Republik of New Jersey!) in order to get a better grip, like the Pearce or Scherer

baseplates. If you want a longer barrel, the matter gets a bit more complicated. One Glock rep told me that the cam angles were different. Other reps, gunsmiths and barrel makers have told me

One big difference between the G-26 and its Glock big brothers in 9mm is the recoil spring. On the bigger Glocks it is a single spring wound around a center pin, and on anything since the very early production, is a captured assembly. That is, the spring and its guide rod are fabricated so they do not come apart when out of the pistol. On the G-26 it is a spring within a spring assembly. The dual spring design keeps enough spring

For lots of extra rounds, the G-26 takes G-17 and G-19 magazines with extensions.

The front of the G-26 is beveled to make it easier to carry and to slide into the holster.

Ten shots of 9mm Parabellum+P+ all ready to go.

force to work the action within the space available. To try to use a single spring would create problems. With a single-piece spring made of steel thick and large enough to properly cycle the action, the fully-compressed spring might not fit within the confines available within the frame of the G-26.

What is the G-26's utility? For one thing, it can replace a snubnose .38 or .357 revolver. For the same size as the revolver and its six shots, you can have the G-26 and its 10 or 12. And on the reload, up to 17. As a primary concealed carry gun for someone who feels that a 9x19 is good enough, the G-26 shines. As a backup gun for someone who carries a bigger Glock, the G-26 can be perfect. All the controls are the same, and if your main gun is a 9mm, then the bigger magazines work in the littler gun.

The G-26 post-dates the trigger bar upgrade, so you should only have a nickeled bar in your Glock. If you have a G-26 with the old blackened bar, then you either have

a factory gun that slipped through or your gun had the old parts installed after it left the factory. In either case you should get them upgraded. G-26s should all have the

15-degree breechface cut and use the 15-degree extractor. The beginning of importation was July of 1995. The change to the 15-degree extractor was July, 1995. The beginning of

A G-26 easily beats a 1911 Commander for compactness.

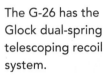

The G-26 has the Glock dual-spring telescoping recoil system.

the change was with the prefix "BMX," and any G-26 prefix before that will have the old 90-degree extractor. An old-style 90-degree extractor will not be appropriate for most of the G-26 pistols extant.

I have had several shooters and Glock reps tell me that the subcompacts can be more touchy in ammo selection. The Glock mechanism is an efficiently locking one, and working the mechanism

properly takes hot ammo. The double recoil spring makes the guns even more dependent on hot ammo. Use of wimpy reloads, or soft factory ammo, could cause a malfunction called "smokestack." In a smokestack jam, the empty brass can't quite get out in time and gets trapped by the closing slide. Commonly it sticks straight up, and has to be swiped out of the way. The mechanical cause is low slide velocity leading to slow or insufficient ejection speed. The slide goes back slowly, doesn't throw the empty out briskly enough, and then begins closing before the empty is clear.

Disassembly for the G-26 is the same as it is for other Glocks: simple.

G-26-specific magazines fit flush with the frame.

The black oxide finish may rub off, but the Tenifer is still there.

My shooting grip is quite rigid, and I rarely have any pistol smokestack on me, even many prone to it. So I cannot report from my own test firing that I encountered any instances of it. But it is something to be aware of, and if you encounter the problem, your first attempt to fix it should be to try some hotter ammo. If the problem then goes away, you have an easy fix.

If not, then you've got some 'splainin' to do, having caused a perfect Glock pistol to not work 100 percent. A bit of practice and training could also make the problem go away. If your grip is too limp, letting the pistol move too much under recoil, then a firmer grip can solve the problem. ♦

CHAPTER 11

The Glock G-34

The G-34 exists for one reason: The IPSC box. In International Practical Shooting Confederation competition, a pistol that is to be used in the Standard category has to fit within the "IPSC Box." (So does a pistol in Modified. However, those handguns used in Open, Production and Revolver don't.) Neither the G1-7L nor the G-24 fit the box, both being a bit too long. The G-17 does, but the shorter (than other brands of competitive pistols) sight radius made the G-17, if not a non-competitive choice, then a "less competitive choice than it could be."

To get the Glock name back into the forefront of competition, the G-34 came out of Austria in 1998, along with the .40 caliber competition version (the G-35) at the same time as the standard, compact and subcompacts in .357 SIG. (There is no competition model in .357. No need for it, as none of the competitions other than GSSF have a place for it.)

In length, the G-34 is as long as possible to fit the box. The slide is 8.15", the barrel 5.32" long. Yes, the barrel is longer than that of a government model 1911. The top of the slide is opened for lighter weight, to balance the action for use with 9mm ammo. The frame is a third generation G-17 frame, and what with the adoption of the two-pin locking block feature of the G-17, the G-34 will also have the newer locking block. (Collectors, take note: old guns-one pin, new guns-two pins. Start planning for the future now.)

The G-34 comes standard with the 3.5-lb. connector. While you could install heavier ones, or the New York trigger, why would you? As a competition gun, the G-34's lighter connecter is held to be better by many shooters. As a carry gun, the G-34 is a

A standard G-17 or G-22 rattles around inside the IPSC box, but a G-17L or G-24 wouldn't fit.

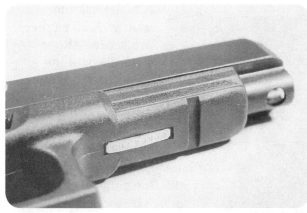
The G-34 sight rail. The G-34 is built on the standard G-17 frame.

bit large. Anyone who makes barrels for the Glock probably makes one for the G-34, although it is .830" longer than the G-17 barrel.

If you want to use the Glock in competition, then the G-34 is the ticket for IDPA SSP Division and USPSA/ IPSC Production Division. Using a G-34 or a G-35, Dave Sevigny has simply dominated practical shooting competition in the Production or production-like (as in IDPA SSP Division) since 2001. Basically coming out of nowhere, he has spent the better part of the first decade of the twenty-first century being untouchable. The margins may be getting smaller, but Dave keeps winning.

The G-34 post-dates all the modifications, the trigger part update, the change in extractor/breechface angles; the only one it might be affected by is the E-series recall. Phone Glock and find out if yours is one of those covered. However, the G-34 has to be carefully considered for use in international competition. First, IPSC competition in Standard Division is scored "Major" and "Minor." The smaller 9mm Parabellum cartridge is scored Minor, which means hits on target that are not in the center zone will earn you fewer points. (Slightly offset by your ability to shoot somewhat faster.)

The rules specifically prohibit your reloading the ammunition to greater power

Dave Sevigny won Production at World Shoot XIII with a box-stock G-34.

The G-34 is a regular G-17 frame with a longer slide and barrel.

the Major/Minor worry, as all calibers are scored Minor regardless of the power they generate. (Provided you meet or exceed the minimum threshold.) However, in Production you must use the Glock 5-lb. connector, as trigger pulls in Production cannot be lighter than five lbs.

The G-34 uses standard 9mm G-17 magazines, and will not take any from the compacts or subcompacts. It will also accept extended magazines. The capacity of a G-34 magazine is sometimes limited by the competition

to exceed the threshold to be scored Major. (You cannot load 9mm to major except in Open or Revolver.) However, if you go to use the G-34 in Production, you do not have

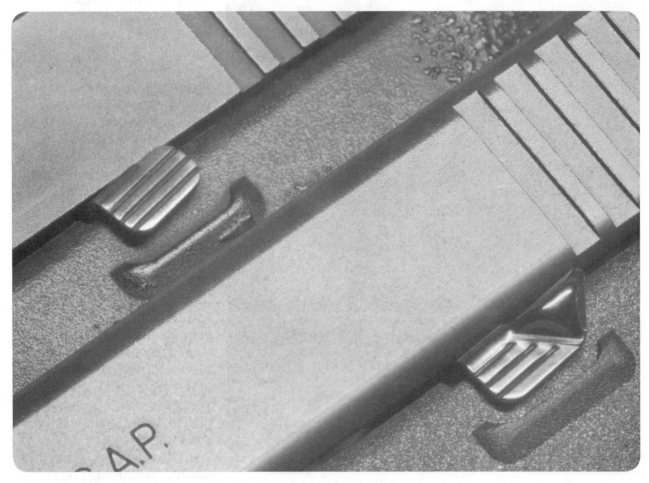

Glock makes a very slightly larger slide stop lever for competition use.

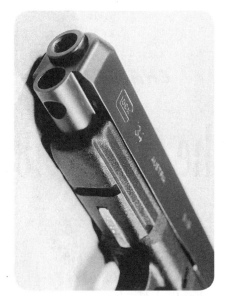

The longer barrel and slide of the G-34.

The G-34 comes equipped with a new and improved Glock adjustable rear sight.

Current G-34s can use 10-round or 17-round magazines.

you want to enter with it. If you're shooting in a GSSF match, it doesn't matter, as you won't be allowed to load more than 10 anyway. If you're shooting in international practical matches you'll have to stick with standard magazines of 17 rounds. Any longer and the pistol won't fit the box. If you shoot your G-34 in USPSA matches in Limited, you're limited to a 140mm overall length, which gives you 22 rounds or so. But you'll be scored Minor in Limited due to the 9mm cartridge. If you enter a USPSA match in Limited Ten or Production, you're back to the 10-shot capacity limitation.

However, in any of those arenas, the G-34 will serve you exceedingly well. When I went through the Glock armorer's course, I was given the option (as all graduates are) to purchase a pair of pistols at wholesale. One of the two I selected was the G-34. ♦

The G-34's slide is open on top to reduce its weight to that of a regular G-17 or G-22.

CHAPTER 12

The Glock G-18

f you think shooting is fun, then shooting a G-18 is the most fun you can have with your clothes, glasses and hearing protection on. Developed for the Austrian counter-terrorist Cobra Unit, it came about because they wanted a "concealable submachinegun." (Ignore for the moment that a suitable trenchcoat on a tall man can almost conceal a Browning Automatic Rifle and fully conceal a host of other choices.) The idea was that a handgun could be used in the role of a submachinegun if it had a selector switch. (The fact that the idea had

For compact, controllable firepower, something with a shoulder stock leads the list. This Beretta is fun and controllable.

been tried repeatedly since the introduction of the 1896 "Broomhandle" Mauser, and been found pretty much wanting, did not deter anyone involved in this latest episode.)

The G-18 is a select-fire 9mm handgun, with a very quick (even by machinegun standards) cyclic rate, and is somewhat hard to control. Oh, you will see photos of tight groups fired, even tight groups of full-magazine bursts, but don't be fooled. If you give me enough time to practice and shoot, I could fire a tight group full-auto offhand with that BAR mentioned earlier.

Smallest to largest, all 9mms, all select-fire (although the Beretta is three-shot-burst only). The largest is the easiest to shoot well.

Here's the Glock G-18 in three-burst mode (note the airborne empties). Not as controllable as a true subgun.

The Beretta with three shots off. A slide that close to your face can be disconcerting.

Practicing would be a real fun afternoon, too! That doesn't mean the BAR is of use as a target rifle, despite its known record of accuracy.

You can mount a stock to a G-18, but that defeats the purpose of its compactness.

I'm not one to classify firearms as either in the "useful" or "useless" category, but the G-18 comes awfully close to getting into the second column. I have managed to shoot three different G-18s through the years. The first was at the Second Chance bowling pin shoot, brought there by its owner for an afternoon of fun. (I look back and could slap myself for not having my camera gear along at the time.) The second was a privately-owned G-18 that I was privileged to shoot but not take apart and inspect. The third was a factory gun (a ported model, to boot) at a tactical officers association get-together.

In all three cases, even the ported one, I found much the same situation: With preparation, muscle and good technique I was able to hit what I was shooting at, often with the whole burst. But for all that effort I could have put nearly as many shots onto the target, nearly as quickly, with a regular Glock 9mm. Were I in the situation of having to hose an area with fire to deny it to the bad guys (we're talking strictly military applications here, as no police department in the USA could countenance such an exercise) I could do it with a G-18. Then again, I could do it with anything else in the military arsenal, too.

In that last episode, the assembled tactical officers had great fun (especially the "dunk the smoking-hot G-18 into a cooler full of water" part) but had much less success in shooting it. Despite being only about 10 yards from the target, they routinely shot through the target sticks holding the cardboard.

One end-user who has a lot of experience in the law enforcement end of things told me that it was adopted for airport security in Europe because it didn't look like a submachinegun. Those of you who haven't traveled overseas don't know what you're missing. Even before 9/11 it was common for police officers to be walking a beat, or ambling along the concourse of an airport, with slung MP-5 submachinegun. To say that such officers are obvious is an understatement. They're supposed to be obvious.

The idea of the G-18 was that if the bad guys burst on the scene, they'd deliberately target the officers with MP-5s first. (I can imagine that scene at morning roll call: "OK, who wants to be the designated first targets today?" Just how many volunteers can you get with such a job title?) With the G-18, full-auto firepower was available without advertising it. With all due respect to the experienced operator who told me this, as a handgun the G-18 offers false hopes of firepower. As a submachinegun it is not very controllable (not at all controllable to those who haven't put their time in with good technique, even tactical officers, and who then must practice regularly) and without a stock you can't get much else out of it.

But boy is it fun!

Any pistol is going to be smaller than any submachinegun. The laws of physics follow as a result: the full-auto pistol will generally have a higher cyclic rate and thus be less controllable. One approach to control is the Beretta machine pistol. With a quick-attaching stock and a three-shot burst setting, it can be controllable. But not all that much, and again, a properly trained shooter using a regular handgun can do just about as well and with less hassle, paperwork and ammunition expenditure.

In layout it is basically a G-17. The factory has made changes to the slide, barrel and frame so G-18 parts can't simply be dropped into G-17 frames. (The G-18 specific parts won't fit any other model Glock than another G-18.) On the left side of the slide is the selector. Up is Semi, down is Full. There is no burst control other than your finger. In firing, I have found that my grip is too

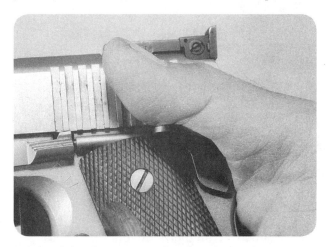

My usual thumb position when firing a handgun. . .

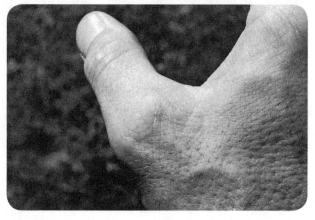

. . .makes my thumb take a beating when firing the G-18.

high for the G-18. The selector switch nips my thumb going back and forth, and after an afternoon of shooting I was just short of bleeding on the knuckle of my thumb where the selector switch on the gun "got" me. (When I mentioned this to another shooter he pointed out it was a "small price for full-auto fun." OK, he had a point.)

The frame exterior is just like any old Glock, with the oldest ones being first generation frames and the later ones being second and third generation frames. When I was trying out the latest one, the one at the tactical officers' get-together, I neglected to notice if it was built on a single pin or double locking block pin frame. (I'd

The first shot of a three-shot burst. Note that the muzzle is still on target.

bet double, as all frames were going that way at that time.) The only apparent difference is the selector switch, and on the back of the slide, the extra plunger for the detent for the selector switch.

On the ported one, I didn't notice that it helped all that much. Not that Glock is at fault, but porting a 9mm pistol just doesn't get you much for your efforts. First, there just isn't that much gas

Three more empties just forward and above. (I can shoot three-shot bursts with trigger control alone. It just took practice.)

to work with, and the leverage available isn't all that great.

The porting was out through the top of the barrel, where the slide had been cut away like the G-17L and later long models. The earliest G-18s had extended barrels with transverse slots as the ports, but operational problems led to those barrels being withdrawn from service. Now, if you really wanted a controllable G-18, you'd get Bart-sto to make an extended barrel, and then put a slide-shaped muzzle brake on the end of it. The actual work itself wouldn't be too difficult, and most any gunsmith who is conversant with USPSA/IPSC Open guns could manage the work. The real trick is having both a G-18 to have the work done to, as well as a gunsmith who is willing to do the work. Oh, and once you've locked your compensator in place, you are stuck with a comped G-18 until you "un-stick" the comp.

In operation, function and disassembly, the G-18 is much like the G-17. As for photos of the model-specific parts, you are out of luck. The owner of the privately-owned G-18 is understandably reluctant to allow clear photos of the internals. The Glock representative who had brought the factory G-18 to the tactical officers' association demo session would not even allow closeups of the outside. So, no crisp, clear photos, no detailed drawings with dimensions of the altered parts; just my

This MP-5 is lots more comfortable than the G-18, but at nearly 10 lbs. you'd expect it to be. A lot of fun – but light it ain't.

impression of the G-18: Not too hard to control, not worth the effort for the "firepower" you get, and probably worth the paperwork to own one, were Glock (and the Feds) inclined to allow it.

If you do entertain the idea that you'd like to own a G-18, you'd better start by winning the lottery. Glock has always been a stickler when it comes to the law. They are not the least bit worried about the shooting public grumbling over their "keep 10 miles away from the line" approach to observing the law.

G-18s were sold only to Class 3 dealers, and then only to be sold to police departments. Most were sold only to police departments directly from Glock. The entry of Glock to the US market was just beginning when the infamous (to gun owners, anyway) Hughes Amendment to the Firearm Owners Protection Act of 1986 was passed. The amendment prohibited the production of new machine guns for commercial sale. Law enforcement and the military could still buy

them, but not the rest of us. The price of "transferable" machine guns since then has skyrocketed, as anyone who didn't sleep through Econ 101 could tell you. Whereas an M-16 would sell for $600 in 1986 ($100 more than an AR-15) today the same would easily cost you $15,000. A G-18? As I have heard figures between five and 50 of the total number of transferable G-18s in the US, you can count on one of them costing you a lot more than $15K. Definitely in the realm of yachts: "If you have to ask, you can't afford it."

As an interesting aside, the Glock Armorers Manual makes no mention of the G-18. No cutoff prefixes for trigger parts, no parts listings in the back of the manual, no date of introduction or technical specifications. If you were to literally go "by the book," you'd have no idea it existed.

If you ever get the chance to shoot a G-18, don't walk away from it. Even if you have to buy new, factory ammo to feed it – as the owner will probably insist – the experience will be worth it. ♦

CHAPTER 13

The G-22 and G-24

The development of the .40 S&W cartridge (the heritage of which Glock does not acknowledge, simply calling their pistols ".40") took the firearms industry by surprise. As mentioned in the chapter dealing with calibers, the .40 came about from the FBI work on the 10mm cartridge. While Glock was in the middle of the development of the G-20 and G-21 (10mm and .45, respectively) the .40 came as a complete surprise to all at the 1990 SHOT Show. (No fault of Glock: the developers, Winchester and Smith & Wesson, wanted to spring it as a surprise and thus gain a market advantage.)

In the long run it didn't help, as Glock beat S&W to market with .40 caliber pistols and later ran away with the market in the police segment. In the scramble to get pistols out, Glock and all the other manufacturers dove into the problem of fitting the bigger cartridge into their standard 9mm platforms, and all were faced with the good news and the bad news. The good news

is that the .40 will fit magazine tubes and frames designed for the 9mm cartridge with only a little work on things like magazine feed lip spacing and breechface dimensions. The bad news? The same.

While all 9mm pistols had the benefit of decades of testing, development and refinement, the .40s in 1990 were a "gotta have it right now" proposition. As soon as anyone heard about it, everyone who carried a gun

for a living had to have one. And why not? Nearly the power of the .45, in a package sized for the 9mm? With almost the capacity of the 9mm? Who wouldn't want it? The G-22 and G-23 became available in May of 1990, ahead of the 10mm G-20 and .45 G-21, both of which had been in development for some time before that.

While the G-17 has been refined through the years to meet market expectations,

When the .40 came along, there was doubt whether it would unseat the 9mm or .45. Today, handgun makers probably make more .40s than the other two.

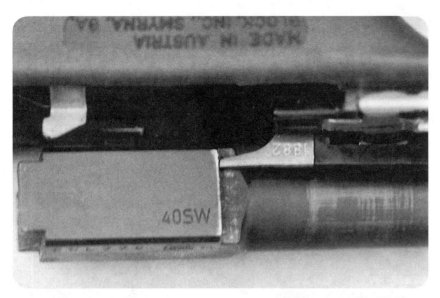

Some earlier guns are marked ".40SW." Currently, they're simply marked ".40."

the .40 has had improvements made to it due to the nature of the cartridge itself.

Before we go into the problems that had to be dealt with, let us look into the problems the cartridge poses to the firearms designer.

Power and Mass

"For every action there is an opposite and equal reaction," postulated Sir Isaac Newton. He was and is quite correct. The .40 in standard trim launches a bullet fully 45 percent heavier than the 9mm does (180 grains vs. 124 grains). It pushes said bullet more slowly, but not much (950 fps vs. 1150 fps). By any measure, that is a lot more work. And that work is done within the same distance, as the barrels are identical lengths. To get the bullet going that fast, the .40 works at the same pressures a 9mm does. Some shooters assume that because it is bigger than

the 9mm, the .40 operates at a lower pressure, as does the .45. Not true.

When you fire a round, the bullet leaves the muzzle and the barrel, slide and frame have to deal with the momentum created. If you use a 9mm barrel and slide for your .40, then the slide velocity will be much higher in the .40 than in the 9mm.

(You can't get something for nothing. More action out the muzzle means more reaction to deal with.) The .40 must therefore have either a heavier slide, a heavier recoil spring, a less-efficient locking cam angle, or some combination of the three.

What the G-22 has over the G-17 is a slide that weighs 1.1 ounces heavier, about eight percent. To make the situation tougher, the barrel of a G-22 actually weighs less than that of the G-17, eight percent of a smaller total. So the total unlocking mass of the G-22 versus the G-17 ends up at a bit more than four percent greater. That's why your G-22 has a different, and heavier, recoil spring than your G-17.

You, as the designer, also have the problem of shoving a fatter round up out of the magazine, across the feed ramp and into the chamber. Fatter, that is, than the 9mm cartridge the design was initially intended for.

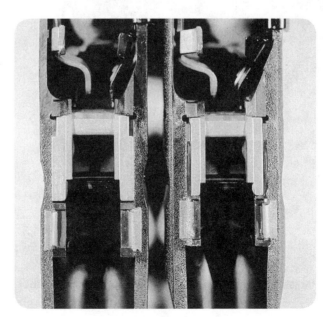

When you change calibers, you need different locking blocks.

G-22 Specs

In size, the G-22 is indistinguishable from the G-17 unless you look at the caliber designation. Indeed, if you swapped the ejectors you could change a G-17 to a G-22 and vice versa. Holsters, magazine holders, sights, internals that aren't caliber-specific, all interchange. The caliber-specific ones have to change in concert with the caliber you're using. One question, if you want to change, is can you use the existing locking block? The part numbers differ in the current Armorer's Manual, but the one I have pre-dates the adoption of the double pin frame for the G-17. The pattern of parts listings for locking blocks show that similar frame sizes usually (but not always) get the same block, regardless of caliber. Blocks are listed at 15 dollars,

Here's the kind of peening some .40 slides get. This is a high-mileage rental gun, and Glock will not replace the slide (again) because of peening. Only when it cracks or becomes otherwise damaged will Glock replace it.

so I'd say get the caliber-specific one for the caliber you want to swap to (unless the part number for both applications is the same, then you're home free).

As for trigger pull, the G-22 can be built to target specs, with a 3.5-lb. connector, or beefed up with the NYPD-2 spring for a long double action feeling trigger.

The G-22 Drama

The first big problem shooters noticed was the peening on the bottom of the slide. Under recoil, the frame flexes. The flex can (with some rounds more so than others) cause the locking block in the frame to bang against the bottom of the slide, causing the peening. The good news is that it reaches a certain point and stops. Apparently recent production G-22 pistols have that area of the slide bevelled slightly to reduce the peening.

In any group, there will be those who shoot a lot more than others. The high-

The G-22 is virtually indistinguishable from the G-17 except for the caliber designation.

Very early G-22s were made with single locking block pin frames. Once Glock determined that those guns broke pins, they went with the two-pin design. Recently, they have upgraded their 9mms to a two-pin design.

volume shooters began to find a problem with the .40s. The locking block banging against the slide caused breakage of the locking block retaining pin. To prevent the breakage, the G-22 and G-23 (and all subsequent models) were changed to have two locking block pins. Very early in the 21st century, the G-17 was changed to include the dual pin design. The move was not made for strength but for production ease. Why have two otherwise identical

frames (the G-17 and G-22), but have one with one pin and the other with two? And I'm not even sure that at the factory they even distinguish between 9mm and .40 frames until it comes time to marry-up the various parts.

The last problem has to do with the chamber. The chambers on G-22 barrels are larger than other .40 cal pistols. Is it a necessity for feeding? Or is there some other reason? I don't know, and Glock isn't saying. The

end result is that brass from a Glock .40 can be expanded too much to then chamber (even after resizing) in other .40 caliber pistols. If Glock has changed the chamber dimension over time, they have stayed mum on the subject.

Despite the reservations some had, the .40 S&W cartridge has gone on to be the de-facto law enforcement standard. Some departments stick with 9mm and some allow .45, but many if not most have gone to .40.

A Curious Problem

When I first heard of this problem, I stuck it in the "nice, but urban legend" category: G-22s with accessory light rails and a light installed had feeding problems. Then I taught a class where I had the problem confirmed by a DEA agent. It seems that some pistols, with some ammo, and some lights, in the hands of some shooters, will malfunction some of the time. He'd experienced it on occasion. What pistols? What ammo? Which lights? No one knows except on a department-by-department and shooter-by-shooter basis. The problem shows itself in a pistol when the shooter has it happen.

The solution is to replace the spring and follower with a stiffer spring from Glock and a new design follower. The spring and follower reduce magazine capacity by one round. The magazine with

Despite being bigger, .40 brass is not any stronger than 9mm brass and it runs at the same pressure. The .40 on the right has an interior that comes down closer to the extractor groove than the 9mm on the left.

the new spring and follower will work in other G-22s. If an unmodified magazine gets into the recalcitrant Glock, will it work or malfunction? Only experimentation will tell. You can tell the springs you have by counting coils. A standard G-22 magazine spring will have 10 coils, and the new spring will have 11.

G-22 Upgrades and Changes

The G-22 introduction predates that six-part trigger upgrade we mentioned earlier. A G-22 with prefixes prior to YC should be checked for the old parts. Again, if you see silver, you're safe. If you see black, send it back. The G-22 post-dates the change to the second generation grip design (1988), so you won't see any G-22s with the smooth pebble finish frame. They will all be either the second generation checkered, or the third generation checkered and finger grooved. The third generation guns came along in May of 1998, at serial number prefix CRT.

What you might see are rare second generation one-pin frames. The initial production G-22 (and G-23) was made with one locking block pin. After breakages occurred, the design was upgraded to include a second pin. The change happened relatively soon, so there aren't many one-pin guns out there. If someone offers you a rare Glock G-22 with one pin, check the serial numbers. If the slide

The G-22 leaves lots of room in the IPSC box but it can be a very competitive pistol.

and barrel don't match the frame, the odds are it's a 9mm frame with a .40 upper.

A change that Glock made concerns only armorers, or those who through the use of hot loads have chipped an extractor and must replace it. G-22s past the serial number prefix BKD have a 15-degree breechface and require a 15-degree extractor.

The G-22 is quite popular with USPSA/IPSC shooters who want to shoot either Production or Limited 10. In Production you can load it with soft reloads to diminish the difference between it and the 9mm pistols common there. For Limited 10, it can make Major and you won't have the scoring disparity that you'd have if you wanted to use a G-17 in Limited 10. It is not as popular as the bigger G-35, but for those who already have one, the G-22 will do quite nicely.

The Glock 24

When Glock rushed the .40 caliber pistols into the marketplace, they brought not just the service pistols, but a target pistol as well. The service pistols came first, but making a competition .40 was no big deal. In design, the G-24 was simply a G-17L in .40, with the reinforcing pin on the locking block, and the correct barrel and ejector. The problem was, there wasn't much of a competition need for it. The G-24 came out in January 1994 just one competition season after IPSC shooters were embarking on a six-year tear of experimenting with high capacity pistols in .38 Super with red dot sights and loud, obnoxious compensators on them. If you weren't shooting a pistol with a 25-round (later 28-round as the details got worked out) magazine with a dot and

Put a competition slide stop on a G-22 and you're ready to shoot in matches.

a comp that blasted paint off of props, you were not competitive. Who wanted a .40 caliber iron-sighted pistol that held 15 shots? Even when the Limited class was introduced, competitors simply took worn-out Supers and built them into .40 caliber pistols using new slides and barrels, with iron sights and no comp.

Had the G-24 come out a year sooner, it might well have carved a place for itself in competition shooting.

It wasn't until the introduction of Production and Limited 10 Divisions late in the 1990s (brought about by IDPA success in garnering shooters) that the G-24 had a chance. However, as mentioned in the G-17L

chapter, the G-24 wouldn't fit the IPSC box. So Glock shortened the barrel and slide by .70" to get it to fit, and the G-35 was a roaring success.

With the introduction of the G-35, the G-24 was soon dropped from the line, but you can still special order an upper assembly. As with the G-17L, the G-24 is simply a G-22 with a longer slide and barrel. Thus, you can re-fit your G-24 with the upper assembly from a G-22 or a G-35. And, if you wanted to, you could install the upper assembly from a .357 SIG G-31. If you're willing to change the ejector, you can also install a 9mm upper on your G-24 frame, selecting from the following: G-17, G-17L, or G-34.

With a bit of luck in finding suitable uppers, you could have a three-caliber Glock: 9mm, .357 SIG and .40 S&W.

The G-24 post-dates the trigger part change, and the transition to the second generation frame, so you won't see any G-24s with pebble finishes. They came out before the breechface change, so you'll have G-24s both with 90-degree breechfaces and 15-degree breechfaces. It's a problem only if you need to replace the extractor.

They'll take all the trigger parts, so you can if you want you can swap out your light match trigger for a NY trigger to use your G-24 as a carry gun. If you aren't going to be shooting in international matches, then the G-24 is actually a better choice for practical competition here in the States than the G-35. The longer barrel (G-24: 6.02", G-35: 5.32") gives you the same velocity with less powder (slightly less recoil) and the longer sight radius (G-24: 8.07", G-35: 7.56") allows for more accurate shooting.

As a Limited gun, with extended magazines, or a Limited Ten gun with the low-cap at-one-time-federally-mandated magazines, the G-24 could be a match-winning machine, provided you're up to the task.   ♦

CHAPTER 14

The G-23 and G-27

When the G-23 was rushed to market, the Glock lineup already included a compact model in 9mm, the G-19. To complement it, the G-23 came out as an identically sized pistol, save for the caliber. As with the G-17/G-22, the G-19/G-23 are identical in every dimension except for the chamber and the hole through the barrel. As a result, any holster, magazine pouch or accessory that fits the G-19 fits the G-23. As with the G-19, the G-23 can use the longer magazines standard for the G-22, so your carry gun could have 14 rounds in it (13+1) and your spare magazines could have 15 rounds – more, if you used a sufficiently durable magazine extension on a legal hi-cap magazine.

As you'd expect with a compact pistol and a powerful round, the G-23 can be a handful to shoot. But with practice it is certainly manageable.

The G-23, since it came out in 1990, predates in some pistols the trigger upgrade. For the G-23, the cutoff prefix is SL. SM and later are fine. Before that, look at the trigger bar. If it is black it should be upgraded to the nickeled bar, and associated parts. G-23s made after prefix BKH have the 15-degree breechface, something only the armorer who may need to replace your extractor needs to know.

The G-27

Q: *What fits in your pocket, holds 10 rounds of .40 ammo, and weighs less than your first cell phone?*

A: The Glock 27. At just under 20 ounces empty, the Glock is lightweight but comforting to have when you just might need a firearm. The G-27 offers the extremes in a concealable carry gun. It is the smallest gun in a big caliber, offering the most ammo in the shortest grip. And since it uses magazines with the same upper dimensions and

The G-23 is a shortened G-22, just as the G-19 is a shortened G-17. This G-23C is ported for competition shooting.

A G-27 with a G-22 magazine with a Grams extension: 21 rounds of .40 at your command. If you can hide it, great; otherwise, this is your reloading magazine.

This is a curious G-23, with a four-numeral serial number. Collectors are going to have a field day in the future.

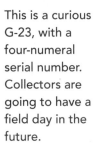

locking slot location as its bigger .40 brothers, you can carry a 10-shot pistol that you can reload with 15-shot (or larger) magazines from your belt at a moment's notice.

This compactness and handiness for carry comes at a price, however. The small frame offers a small place to hang onto when shooting. Shooters with large

hands might find it a bit disconcerting to grab a pistol and find that their pinkie finger has no place to hold onto. For those shooters, a Pearce or Scherer mag extension that offers a finger rest but not more than one extra round of capacity will make the G-27 more comfy.

During the AWB-94 period the magazines were made to hold nine rounds, but the Law Enforcement Only magazines held 11. Why not a factory 10? I can only surmise (since Glock has declined to answer any questions) that there is something about the geometry of 10 that makes it too easy to hold an eleventh round. The manufacturers were extremely reluctant to even give the impression that they weren't complying with that now-expired law. (Why do you think it was so hard to get that tenth round into so many beauracratically-mandated 10-shot magazines? So there will be no change of George Strongthumb getting an eleventh round in.)

The subcompact G-27 lacks the light rail found on larger third generation Glocks.

At right, a custom G-23 barrel and night sights; at left, those of a box-stock Glock.

The G-27 is so short, it's all I can do to get my middle finger on the frame.

A Pearce mag extension aids in giving my fingers a place to rest.

On the happy day when the law sunseted, we all went out and bought bigger magazines for our G-27s. The Glock spec book now lists a standard magazine as holding only nine rounds, but what with the "law enforcement only" restriction having been lifted, we can buy all the 11-shot magazines we want. Certain jurisdictions excluded, of course.

The slide is a full inch shorter than that of the G-17/G-22 (7.32" vs. 6.29", and the barrel is likewise an inch shorter (4.49" vs. 3.46"). In the back, the height of the G-27 from the top of the slide to the bottom of the frame is an inch and a quarter less than the original Glocks. (5.43" vs. 4.17") Those differences have a big effect in the concealability and comfort when carrying.

With the hottest .40 loads, the G-27 can be a handful, but no more than you can learn to deal with given a bit of practice.

The recoil spring of the G-27 is the double spring telescoping system that allows Glock to fit a full-power recoil spring in the short space available. It can be a bit touchy, and give some feeding problems with light-loaded ammo. But even then a firm grip and stiff wrist will keep it running. Fed full-power defensive ammo you'll have a hard time keeping a G-27 from running.

As an extremely cut-down G-22, the G-27 makes it perfect as a backup gun for

A real snubbie – small, but offering nine shots of .40.

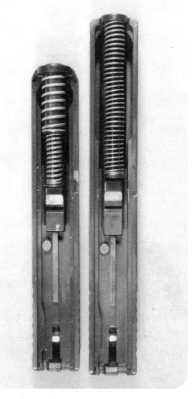

The G-22 slide at left, with a G-22 slide showing different length and recoil spring design.

many police officers. If the department issues or allows a full-sized .40 Glock, then the G-27 in reserve operates the same way, with the same controls, and in a pinch uses the same magazines as the main gun. And for the law abiding citizen with a CCW, the G-27 as the main gun can be perfect.

Introduced in July of 1995, the G-27 post-dates the trigger part upgrade, so your trigger bar should be the bright nickel part. If it isn't, someone has changed it and you should have it re-upgraded. July of 1995 was the cusp of the change from the 90-degree breech to the 15-degree breech, and the

G-27 cutoff for the change in extractors to match is prefix BMY. Remember: before, 90 degrees, after, 15 degrees. ◆

The Scherer mag extension adds size, so you must choose between compactness and capacity.

A Scherer extension, one that gives you a place to grip while boosting capacity from nine to 10.

CHAPTER 15

The G-35

ntroduced in January of 1998, the G-35 found the home that had been denied the G-24 four years before in January of 1994 and the G-17L back in April of 1988.

In 1988 the state-of-the-art competition handgun for the practical minded shooters was one of two calibers, one of two types, in one model. The choices were a 1911 in .45 for Stock competition, or a .45 or .38 Super with a compensator for Open competition. (There were no optical sights in use in 1988, except for the author, who shot the Masters Long Range Event with a scope-sighted 1911A1. I did not start

Easy to use and soft in recoil, the G-35 can win if you can.

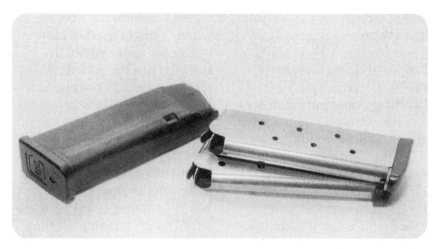

You can have one magazine or two. Total capacity is close to the same in 9mm, .40 or .45.

a trend.) And not all IPSC clubs in 1988 had Stock as a possible entry. Ours did, because we were a maniacal bowling-pin and IPSC shooting club and when shooting pins at Second Chance you needed a Stock gun as well as a Pin gun. Your Pin gun could double as an IPSC Open gun if it was in .45. (At least for a few more years. By 1990 even the stoutest .45 diehard had to

admit that the .38 Super was the way to go in Open Division competition, and .45 was only useful as a Stock gun.)

But everyone would still have been shooting 1911s in 1988. The DA/SA guns were out of the picture, and even the Browning Hi-Power had fallen by the wayside. The hurdles in 1988 for the G-17L were great: you had to shoot Minor, thus you were taking

a scoring handicap. Many clubs were still smarting from a recent acrimonious dust-up over eight-shot magazines for .45 and the brand new 10-shot magazines for .38 Super, so few were willing to set up a match where a 17-shot pistol would have an advantage – especially not the polymer wonder. And you couldn't put a comp on it easily. In 1988 the .40 didn't exist, just the 10mm, and the sheer size of the G-20 (not available in 1988) kept it out of the hands of many competitors.

In January of 1994, when the G-24 came out, the competition world was in the middle of a sea change, with hi-cap guns in .38 Super sporting comps and dots winning everything in sight. The world was shifting, as the Springfield P9 (a CZ-75 clone) was all over the place, and people were loading and shooting 9x21 ammunition at a brisk pace. Despite all that, a hi-cap stock gun like the long-barreled G-24 had no place to shoot and wouldn't for a couple of years. You could shoot it in Stock, but against the highly-tuned 1911 and hi-cap 1911 clones, it wouldn't stand a chance, would it? (This was before Dave Sevigny took up shooting.)

Unfortunately, the G-24 would not (like its smaller-caliber brother, the G-17L) fit within the IPSC box. You could not use it in International competition, except in Open, a losing proposition. By 1998 Production Division and Limited Ten in the USPSA

Even in the fast-shooting sport of IPSC, Glocks can win – and the G-35 should be your first choice for some categories.

The G-35 is identical to the 9mm except for the breechface, bore and chamber.

and Standard Service Pistol in IDPA provided a ready home for the G-35. In USPSA-Production and IDPA-SSP, the 9mm cartridge is not a handicap, but some shooters download the .40 in order to shoot with their .40 Glocks.

The 10-round magazine restriction kept everyone on an even playing field in Production and SSP, and for those who wanted to invest in them, the hi-cap mags could still be used as carry magazines or to shoot in Limited at Minor. To shoot Limited or Limited Ten in Major, the .40 in factory trim or reloaded to make Major meant a G-35. Why the G-35 and not the G-24? The IPSC box. The longer G-24 couldn't fit the box. The IPSC box

doesn't exist in the USA, where a pistol used in Limited Division thus need not fit the box. But the relative low numbers of G-24 pistols, and the interest in the G-35, meant that what you'd mostly see on the range were the latter.

The G-35, or "Practical Tactical" as Glock likes to call it, was made to fit the IPSC box. The barrel is longer than a G-17/G-22, but shorter than a G-17L/G-24. At 5.32" it is the Momma bear compared to the G-17L/G-24 and G-17/G-22 (6.02" and 4.49" respectively)

As far as the frame goes, the G-35 came across the Atlantic in January of 1998, so it is a third generation frame, with all the frames made with the double locking pin. (It is a .40, after all.) It post-dates the

Dave Sevigny, using a stock G-35 in Limited Division, shooting his way to another nationals championship at the 2006 USPSA Nationals.

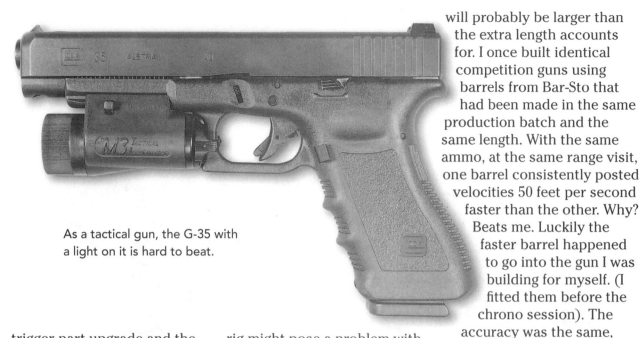

As a tactical gun, the G-35 with a light on it is hard to beat.

will probably be larger than the extra length accounts for. I once built identical competition guns using barrels from Bar-Sto that had been made in the same production batch and the same length. With the same ammo, at the same range visit, one barrel consistently posted velocities 50 feet per second faster than the other. Why? Beats me. Luckily the faster barrel happened to go into the gun I was building for myself. (I fitted them before the chrono session). The accuracy was the same, tackdriving, with one inch groups at 25 yards. After that experience I don't worry about the velocity boost a longer barrel is supposed to provide.

trigger part upgrade and the extractor/breechface change, so all G-35s will have the 15-degree extractor.

As a carry gun the G-35 is a bit large. After all, you can have the same 15 rounds in a G-22 or G-23, without the extra slide length to poke you when you sit down. At least as a concealed carry gun. If you're in the position of carrying openly, your duty

rig might pose a problem with the slide length and car seats. As far as a tactical thigh rig is concerned, the extra length doesn't matter.

Theoretically, the longer barrel of the G-35 over that of a G-22 should mean more velocity. However, the extra length is just over three quarters of an inch, and the velocity variances between barrels and individual rounds

The extra sight radius of the G-35 over the G-22 is a gain, although not as much as that of the G-24.

The G-35 slide is milled open on the top, to make it the same weight as the G-22 slide. The competition Glock also uses the same recoil spring assembly as the G-22, and as an added bit of interest, the G-35 barrel will fit and work in a G-22. It would be too short to fit in a G-24.

How well has the duo of G-34 and G-35 done? Well enough that for a few years many felt that USPSA Production Division should have been named the "Glock Division." You saw mostly Glocks there, and those you saw were mostly G-34 and G-35s. Dave Sevigny used a

The G-35 is full-size and not the easiest handgun to conceal.

As a competition gun (here with a Seattle Slug), the G-35 is a crowd-pleaser and a game-beater.

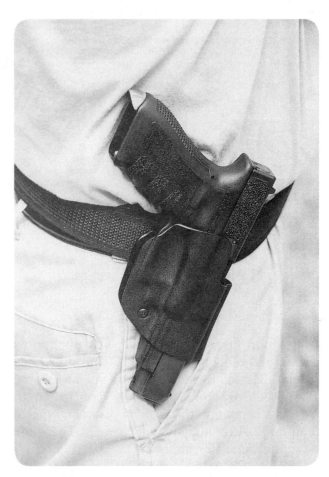

For some competitions, a selection of 10-shot magazines is all you need or are allowed. So get them cheap, abuse them during practice and don't worry about them. They're Glock. They can take it.

G-34 to win 14 USPSA and IDPA National titles between 2001 and 2007. Also, he took on the hegemony of the hi-cap 1911 in Limited Ten Division in 2005 and won the USPSA Limited Ten Nationals. That's right, using a $600 G-35, a 3.5-lb. connector and standard factory .40 S&W ammo, he beat the other assembled Grandmasters, with their $2,000+ hi-cap 1911s and custom-loaded ammunition.

Then, in 2006, he took them all on again in Limited Division, and won again – this while still kicking butt in Production coast-to-coast.

You've got to love a performance like that. ♦

CHAPTER 16

The .357 Glocks

he .357 SIG (to give it its correct name, something Glock neglects to do on their pistols) didn't exactly burst on the scene. The .357 exists because of a mechanical peculiarity: no one makes an autoloading pistol in .357 Magnum, or hasn't since the Coonan company stopped making a 1911 clone in .357 Magnum. In the esoteric world of stopping power study, the .357 Magnum loaded with a 125-grain jacketed hollowpoint bullet is the hallmark. The goal to aspire to. Depending on the person doing the studying, that load has up to a 95 percent stopping power rating. But you can't fit the .357 Magnum, a revolver cartridge, into a standard pistol. The squeeze to fit it into the Coonan was not easy, and the 1911 grip isn't for everyone.

Achieving the .357 performance in the 9mm Parabellum wasn't possible. The "Mag" scooted its 125-grain bullet at 1450 fps out of a 6" revolver. The best a 9mm could do with standard ammo was a 125-grainer at 1100. To go to a +P or +P+ load might boost that same 125-grainer (most went with 115 grains) up to 1300 fps. Close, but not close enough. More case capacity was needed, but the .38 Super wasn't a prospect. The Super gets closer, but its overall length precludes its use in a 9mm-size magazine.

The introduction of the .40 S&W in 1990 changed all that. If someone wanted to neck down the .40 case (and SIGARMS apparently did), the resulting case has enough volume to boost velocities

The .357 SIG had the capacity and velocity of the .357 Magnum. However, the SIG fits in a pistol mag designed for a 9mm. The Magnum? Not a chance.

Left to right: The .357 SIG, the .40 S&W and the .45 ACP.

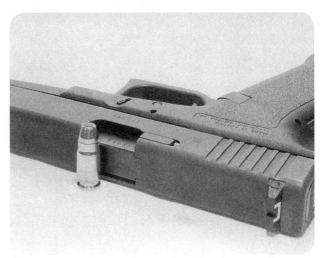

The .357 SIG fits in any .40-caliber Glock, just by changing barrels. It's the easiest caliber change of all.

right up to the .357 Magnum level. And the necked-down case fits in a 9mm double stack magazine tube. Barely. Any bullet loaded into a .357 SIG case must stay within the overall length of the 9mm, which means the longer 9mm hollowpoints won't work. The short neck and short maximum overall length don't allow short-seating longer or heavier bullets. The .357 is a 115- and 124-grain bullet cartridge.

G-31

The full-sized .357 was introduced in August of 1996, and is for all purposes a G-22 with a smaller hole in the barrel. Same size, same weight, all the standard interchangeable parts, and in addition, the G-22 and G-31 also use the same locking block, ejector, recoil spring and extractor. Swapping a .40 to a .357 couldn't be simpler, as all you need to change is the barrel. (It goes without

saying that they take the same magazines.)

What do you get with the .357? The recoil is a bit different. Even if you're accustomed to shooting 135-grain rockets in your .40, going to the .357 is a change. The shot will be noisier, with a higher pitch to the sound, and the recoil will be a bit softer but snappier.

Recoil will be greatly lesser in the Glock than in a

.357 Magnum revolver. First, the frame is better shaped to deal with recoil and spread the impact into your hand evenly. Second, the slide cycling spreads the time of the impact over a greater period than the revolver would. Third, with the bore closer to your hand than on any revolver, the Glock has less leverage to pivot the muzzle up, a visible and psychological aspect of recoil. You'll get a

The Glock .357s all use double-pin frames.

A single-pin frame would quit in short order on a .357.

flatter trajectory than with any other cartridge, although the difference might not be immediately noticeable. With a 100-yard zero, your point of impact at 50 yards will be around three inches high. Zero at 50 yards, and at one hundred you'll be three inches low. If your club has a long range match, the .357 can win you loot and glory.

You'll get lots of stopping power in a specific performance envelope. When the scholars of stopping power consider performance, they are almost always concerned with its ability to stop the aggression of two-legged predators. If you are going to be out in the great wild, and depending on a handgun for some level of protection against wild critters, the .357 will not be a wise choice. The stopping power generated comes from the violent expansion of the 125-grain bullet. Expansion

The .357s feel like hot-loaded 9mms in a Glock.

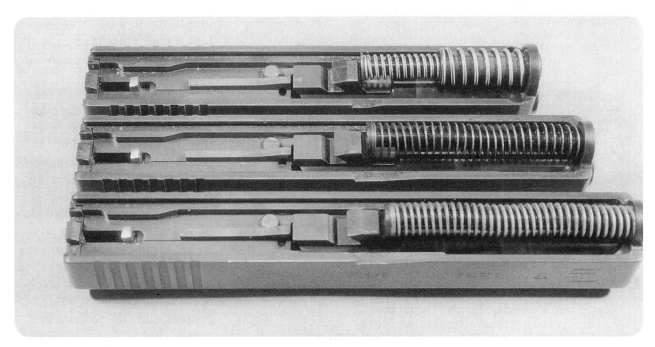

The slides of the .357s are just like those of the .40s and could be interchanged without a problem.

limits penetration. If you need to scrape an angry bear off your leg, you want penetration, not expansion. (In which case you should be using a G-20, with your 10mm ammo loaded with 200-grain truncated cone solids.)

Velocity does gain you penetration of chance obstacles. When the Chicago Transit Police went with the .357 SIG cartridge, they reportedly did so because it, and it alone could penetrate the seats and windows in the trains. .40 couldn't, nor could .45, but the speed of the .357 could.

The G-31 and all other .357 Glocks post-date the trigger parts upgrade and the change to the 15-degree extractor. They also are all built on two-pin locking block frames. And all frames are third generation frames with the finger grooves. First

arriving as they did after the Assault Weapon Ban, all Glock .357 marked magazines made before 2004 will be 10-shot only. Since then, they'll be full-capacity magazines, 15 rounds each. Any hi-caps marked .357 you come across that were made in that time period will be marked LE-Only. Regardless of the timeframe and source, .40 cal mags work just fine in the .357 pistols.

G-32

This .357 Glock fits the G-19 mould (literally) as it is simply a shortened G-31. While the recoil and noise in the .357 is tolerable in the G-31, in the G-32 it is starting to become objectionable. It takes all the parts and accessories that the G-31 does and can use the larger magazines. Since it uses .40 mags, you could even use a 29-round Scherer magazine loaded with .357

ammo. A magazine bigger than the gun, but you would not lack for ammo.

In barrel length the G-32 is giving up a bit of velocity, but not much. The half-inch shorter barrel still keeps the velocity well above that which a 9mm +P+ load can generate, and certainly more than the 9mm+P+ would give you in a G-19. The G-32 uses the same parts as its .40 caliber cousin,

The same magazines that work in your .40 will work in your .357, complete with the magazine extensions.

and the same magazines as the larger .40s and .357s.

G-33

The pocket rocket of Glocks. An ultra-compact pistol in .357 is not fun to shoot. Yes, you can hang on, and even do good work with one, but it won't be fun. The magazine capacity in the subcompacts is nine rounds, with a tenth in the chamber. The same size handgun in .357 Magnum would hold only six rounds, and your reloading to get six more would take twice as long as reloading the Glock for nine more. Or 15 more if you reload with a full-size G-22 or G-31 magazine.

The greatly reduced barrel cuts down on velocity. The G-31's at 4.49" is just a bit more than an inch longer than that of the G-33 (3.46"). While an inch generally doesn't make much of a difference, the already short G-31 barrel is just barely long enough. Compared to a 1911 in .357 SIG, the half inch shorter G-31 gives up 50 feet per second. The extra inch of the G-33 gives up almost another hundred. For all the noise and recoil, the G-33 with factory .357 ammo is not much ahead of a 9mm G-26 loaded with +P+ ammo. And both are objectionable to shoot. (You can't get extreme performance out of a subcompact pistol without taking your lumps. Noise and recoil are the payments you make for velocity in a subcompact.)

Some might argue that the noise is an added psychological benefit in a gunfight, but I doubt it.

For someone who will carry a lot, shoot a little, and wants the power even at the price of recoil and muzzle blast, the G-33 is impressive. ♦

CHAPTER 17

The 10mm Glocks: the G-20 and G-29

The experiments of the crew at *Guns & Ammo* with a mid-sized pistol cartridge in the mid 1970s finally bore fruit in the early 1980s. The idea was to make an updated 45 ACP, one that boosted the older cartridge's performance without having to go to an entirely new mechanism.

The earlier Automag pistol had done so, but it was a Ferrari that needed a lot of maintenance for its performance, and Jeff Cooper and others wanted a Chevy. Or a Mercedes. The Bren Ten didn't have a long life, but the Colt Delta kept the 10mm from fading out of sight. Once the FBI decided to go with 10mm, the race was on. Who

could build a gun to satisfy the sometimes conflicting requirements of the most prestigious law enforcement agency in the U.S.?

The G-17, as versatile as it was, couldn't do the job. There just wasn't room "under the hood." But a scaled up G-17, now there was something else.

The Glock 10mm was almost ready to be introduced when the .40 S&W cartridge pulled the rug out from under everyone.

The big bruiser Glock, the 10mm.

The 10mm, center, flanked by the 9mm (*left*) and the .45 ACP.

If you're going out in the timber and need a handgun, then your first Glock choice should be the 10mm in the form of the G-20.

Introduced at the 1990 SHOT Show, the .40 S&W immediately and completely changed the face of defensive shooting, pistol design and police acceptance. Everyone had to have one or be left in the dust, whether manufacturer or end user. In the scramble to get a .40 out, the 10mm ended up getting to the USA later than planned. Not much, but coming in after the .40 didn't do anything good for the 10mm's sales prospects.

The G-20 is a scaled-up G-17, sized to fit the 10mm cartridge and handle the power.

G-20

You want power? You want lots of it? Great. Only one question: Do you have a big hand? The frame of the G-20 was scaled up from the G-17 proportionate to the cartridge it had to hold. Too bad, as it ended up too large for many shooters. The G-20 is comfortable to shoot, even though it is lighter than other 10mms. At 30 ounces empty it weighs six ounces less than my Colt Delta Elite, but

A successful whitetail bagging machine: a G-20 with a Tasco Propoint.

the recoil of the Glock 10mm is much lighter. It has more surface area bearing against your hand, the polymer frame flexes and takes up recoil, and the heavier slide also dampens felt recoil.

But that grip. I wear gloves in Large, and the G-20 is a bit of a reach for me. If you have average or smaller hands this Glock may be too big for you.

The only reason for the G-20 is power. If all you're going to do is shoot 180-grain bullets in the 10mm reduced load, at roughly 1000 fps, why not just go with a .40? Or a 1911 in .45? In power, you want 180-grain bullets at 1200 fps, or the original Norma specifications of a 200-grain bullet at 1200 fps. If your plan is to go hunting in the thick timber and you want a backup gun, then the G-20 is the tool for you. If any handgun can be considered good enough for bear, a hard cast or full metal jacket 200-grain truncated cone 10mm at 1200 fps will do. And if you have the original full-capacity magazines to use, then you've got 15 rounds of power at your disposal.

Coming out in July of 1990, the early G-20s are subject to the trigger parts upgrade. The prefix cutoff comes after "WX." The extractor/breechface change happens after prefix "BKU." They also pre-date the Assault Weapons Ban and magazine change, so there were hi-capacity magazines available during the ban. Now

On the G-29, the magazine floorplate comes flush to the frame.

The Major Subcompact, the G-29, lacks the sight rail of other third generation frames but doesn't lack power.

that the ban is done and gone, the full-capacity magazines are back. The early G-20s are the second generation frame.

The G-20 is large enough that several companies do custom work to reduce the grip size. In general terms, the process is simple: fill the hollow backstrap with an epoxy resin formula that adheres to the polymer of

The G-29: 10 rounds of 10mm in the smallest possible package.

For a magazine with one more round (for a total of 10), you can go with an oversized baseplate.

the frame. Once it is cured, then cut and grind the frame to a smaller size. The main company doing it is Robar, in Phoenix, Arizona. They can make the frame enough smaller that even those with average size hands can handle the G-20. However, having this process done to your G-20 voids the warranty (except for the "E" series recall). It also precludes using the gun in a GSSF match.

The G-29

And for those who simply must have the loudest of anything, we have the G-29. The G-29 is a compact 10mm with a barrel nearly an inch shorter. The G-29 was not an immediate outgrowth of the G-20, coming out in October of 1996. It came out after the AW Ban had been passed, so at first only 10-shot magazines were available

The G-29 oversized baseplate isn't marked with a part number. An oversight? Who knows?

for it. Since then, we've discovered a curious thing: apparently only 10 rounds fit in the magazine anyway. Either that, or the sales of the G-29 have been so slow that the factory has seen no need to re-engineer the magazines to add one more round. In between the full-sized 10mm and the compact 10mm, we had the G-24, G-26 and G-G-27, and the G-31. Once the FBI had shifted from the 10mm, there wasn't the red-hot interest in a compact 10mm as there had no doubt been in December of 1989 before anyone knew about the .40.

If the G-33 in .357 is a pocket rocket, then the G-29 is a pocket Saturn V rocket. In size and weight it is just about the same as a Colt Light Weight Commander, but holds 10 rounds of full-power 10mm ammo. You can't get the LWC in 10mm, and even if you could, or used .45 ACP+P+ ammo in a .45 LWC, neither you nor the pistol would like shooting for very long. As a concealed carry pistol it is great, until you have to shoot it. With the noise and recoil, you need regular practice to be able to handle it well. If you aren't going to practice enough to stay on top of it, do yourself a favor and go with something easier in recoil.

Due to its introduction date, the G-29 post-dates all the upgrades and changes.

G-20 SF?

With the introduction of the Short Frame in .45 ACP, one of the first questions that

Without the oversized baseplate, there is barely enough room for your little finger to get on board.

occurred to me was "Will there be a G-20SF?" I have yet to receive an answer from Glock. The 10mm slide, barrel and other parts will certainly fit on the SF frame. You could even modify a 10mm ejector block to fit the frame well opening, and thus have a G-20SF of your very own. There would, however, be one catch: magazines. You see, the new SF frame cannot use old-style magazines. The new SF magazines will work in older guns, but the older mags in new guns? No-go.

So unless you figured a way to modify your old 10mm magazine to lock into place in the new SF frame, your 10mm SF project would come screeching to a halt.

You still can, however, send a G-20 off to Robbie Barrkman and have him do his grip reduction package on it. ◆

CHAPTER 18

The Glocks in .45 ACP and .45 GAP

Americans are in love with the .45. Since the introduction of the Colt Single Action army in 1873, a .45 caliber handgun has been considered by many to be the ultimate in defensive handgun equipment. There have always been contenders. When Colt was selling revolvers like pancakes at a charity breakfast, the .45 Colt chambering was the biggest seller. The second and third places went to the .44-40 and .38-40 cartridges, and those two together did not sell as many revolvers as the .45 Colt did.

When the US Army was looking in the early

twentieth century to replace its revolvers with pistols, the then-recent brief experiment with the .38 Colt cartridge convinced them that they wanted to stick with a .45 caliber cartridge. That insistence caused all kinds of headaches for Georg Luger, who found he just couldn't make his design work in .45. The testing board even went so far as to let him use his own ammunition, rather than the test ammo loaded at the Frankfort Arsenal that all the other contestants had to use. He still couldn't make it work and gave up. The other would-be service pistol designs also could not be made to work, and so it fell to

Colt to provide the Army with a new service sidearm.

The resulting 1911 and subsequent 1911A1 pistols were the mainstays of the US Armed Forces until 1986, when they were replaced with the Beretta M-92, called the M9. There are still units in the services who refuse to give up the 1911 and have them rebuilt again and again, to provide the performance they desire. Good for them. When the ongoing fracas in Iraq was relatively new, we found we needed a lot more handguns than the TO&E (Table of Organization and Equipment) called for, and the services scoured the various depots and warehouses, and lo and behold, there were still 1911s in storage, some new and unissued.

For shooting competition, the 1911 was king. It had to be used in the Service Matches, and Bullseye shooters slaved over and swore at and by theirs in centerfire matches. When the new sports of combat shooting (later to be called practical shooting) and

Since the .45 isn't a proprietary round from one of Glock's competitors, Glock marks its guns with More than a simple ".45."

Many competition shooters go with a pistol like this STI Edge. It holds as many rounds as a Glock but costs three times as much. For many shooters, the cost/benefit advantage goes to the Glock.

pin shooting came about, the early proponents used 1911s in various trim, chambered in .45.

So, why did it take so long for a .45 Glock to reach our shores? It didn't, really. The original Glock came out in 1982. The G-17 wasn't imported to the United States until 1986. Four years after that, there was a .45 Glock. Introduced in December of 1990, the G-21 came out later than expected not because the .45 wasn't wanted, but because the .40 S&W had been sprung as a surprise. And for those who love little tidbits of information, the G-21 is actually a 10mm turned into a .45.

All other 10mm pistols started life as .45 pistols. The Colt Delta came from the 1911A1 and its variants, with a different breechface and barrel, and heavier recoil springs. The S&W line of 10mm pistols came from their 45 series, the 4506 and its progeny. The first Glock .45 was designed originally as a 10mm, and then modified to be a .45.

If your G-30 can't put lots of ammo downrange without malfunctioning, you should try different ammunition.

The G-21

The big Glock, it shares external dimensions with the G-20 10mm. The size is required to deal with the power of the 10mm cartridge. A 10mm in full-power factory ammo starts a 200-grain bullet at 1200 fps.

A .45 ACP factory load with a 200-grain bullet will be at or just under 900 fps, while a .45 ACP+P load with a 200-grain bullet will max out right around 1000 fps. While an adventurous reloader could probably exceed the 10mm's performance in a .45 ACP by a

The G-21's slide is machined on the inside to reduce weight. You can clearly see the step down, forward of the locking lever.

Ten-round magazines are cheap and plentiful. Get some for range use, to save wear and tear on your hi-caps.

judicious selection of powders and bullets, the .45 maximum is just that: maximum. If you as a firearms designer build a pistol sufficient to deal with the power of the 10mm, it probably won't work very well with standard .45 power ammo. To make it work properly, you have to change things. One way would be to change the cam angles of the locking block and the recoil spring so the .45 unlocked sooner. However, the G-20 and G-21 use the same locking block and recoil spring. (Probably a manufacturing decision: fewer parts to keep in inventory and keep track of.)

So, you're shooting a lighter load (.45) in a pistol with a recoil spring and locking block designed to deal with the power of the 10mm. What to do? Lighten the slide. Unlike the long slide models of the Glock family, the .45 isn't lightened by cutting a big hole in the top of the slide. It is lightened by thinning the sides of the slide forward of the ejection port. The net result is 1.4 ounces less of steel. The G-21 cycles well with full-power .45 ammo, but if you start loading your own and going down the power scale you may have problems. With a stiff grip

you can keep it cycling, but if you limp wrist the big Glock you can cause a smokestack malfunction. It isn't the pistol's fault; after all it was designed for full-power ammo.

And it is big. As with its big 10mm brother, the G-21 grip is large, and if you do not have large hands the reach may be more than your hand can manage. The large frame does distribute recoil well, so you can use the hottest .45 ACP ammo you can get off the shelves and not worry about either its ability to handle it, or your comfort in hanging on.

The G-21, coming out well before theassault weapons ban of 1994, originally came with magazines that held 13 shots. You can easily use magazine extensions on those tubes to provide several more. After the ban, Glock provided 10-shot single stack configuration magazines which you should not try to extend for increased capacity. Yes, the ban is dead, but the magazines really were designed to be difficult to expand. If you want more than 10 shots, get the normal-capacity magazines, and expand from there. After all, it isn't like Glock magazines are all that expensive.

The Glock G-21 10-round magazines have to be the most durable magazines ever made. To restrict capacity the internal metal liner is kinked in, and as a result the polymer exterior walls are even thicker than on the original magazines. I'm not sure you could hurt these with a ball

G-21 third generation guns have the light rail.

Showing its 10mm origins, the .45 barrel has a cam surface to ensure easier unlocking. The .45 is a lot less powerful than the 10mm.

peen hammer. For practice, and when used in GSSF matches or the like, use the 10-shot magazines, Put your practice wear-and-tear on those, the most durable ones.

The G-21 cutoff prefix for the trigger parts upgrade is XM. Before and including that, you should check for the old trigger bar. Glock will gladly upgrade them for you should your G-21 need it. On the extractor, Glock went a step further in the change from the 90-degree to the 15-degree breechface/extractor. Not only did they change at prefix ALD, they also decided to upgrade

The Robar grip reduction makes the big G-21 and G-20 smaller in the grip, but there is only so much even Robbie can do.

The new G-21 is plenty accurate enough, although it won't be winning any events at Camp Perry. But Bullseye-level accuracy is not the be-all and end-all of a defensive pistol.

any older G-21s to the new standard. So, a Glock armorer will replace a chipped, worn or broken extractor, but if given the opportunity he will ship it back to Glock (as you can) to have the slide machined to the new 15-degree configuration.

They will also reduce the pickup rail. The pickup rail is the small ridge running along the bottom of the slide, right behind the breechface. It captures the top round in the magazine on feeding, and strips it forward towards the chamber. The new configuration is better because, well, Glock is still getting back to me on that.

One small note on the G-21 upgrade. The prefix dates for the upgrade for all the other models range from May through July 1995, from BKD through BMX. The G-21 cutoff date is May of 1993, the ALD series. Two years earlier? I can only glean from that that Glock had not made any G-21s from May 1993 to May 1995. The .45 Glock is, after all, a US-only pistol. Who else wants it and insists they need it?

For all of its low cost, reliability and accuracy, why hasn't the G-21 made more inroads in practical shooting competition? First, the matter is size. For the girth, the Glock only holds 13 rounds. In a slightly more svelte STI, the .45 holds an identical 13. Yes, an STI Edge easily costs two to three times what a Glock G-21

does, but the STI's accuracy is greater (not much, but true competition shooters want it all, not just a cost-effective portion) and it's got a lighter trigger, adjustable sights, and more gunsmith-able options and parts. And a need for that gunsmith. For less than half the cost, no need of gunsmithing, and plenty of accuracy, I can't see why more wouldn't shoot a Glock. Except that it isn't a 1911.

One approach to the overly-large G-21 grip frame is the grip reduction by Robar. Robbie Barkkman (or his crew of skilled gunsmiths) fills the hollow rear of the G-21 frame, then carves it back and textures it as well. The result is a noticeably smaller grip, but unfortunately one that can still be too large for the small-handed shooter.

The problem Robbie runs into is that the ejector housing on the inside of the G-21 frame projects into the space Robbie needs to really carve on in order to make your frame smaller where it really counts: the top. As a result, the grip is smaller, but only those of us with average or larger hands can take advantage of it. Still,

for many years Robbie did lots and lots of those grip reductions.

I remember being at the SHOT show one year, standing at the Robar booth with Robbie, while he was talking over gunsmithing options with a couple of Special Forces E-7s. Gaston Glock walked by with his entourage, and on seeing Robbie, veered over and lit into him. "Why do you modify my perfect pistols?" he asked. "Why do you change the receivers?" Not receiving an answer, Herr Glock walked off. At that point Robbie turned to us and said "Because people pay me perfectly good money, that's why." And so it was for 15 years after the G-21 was unveiled, and for nearly 10 years after I witnessed that meeting. It took a while, but Glock finally changed the G-21, and made the G-21SF: Short Frame, not Special Forces.

21SF

As organizations go, the US government is pretty indecisive, which is probably a good thing. In the first few years of the twenty-first century there have been several proposals to drop the 9mm (and thus the M9/Beretta 92) and get back to something bigger. Something the caliber designation of which starts with ".4." In fact, something in .45. Despite the many advantages, those in the military who want a

> The pickup rail is the small ridge running along the bottom of the slide, right behind the breechface.

.45 are not interested in the .45 GAP. Gnash your teeth, argue all you want, they aren't interested. Why? Well, for one, the established base of knowledge. The .45 ACP cartridge is a known quantity, with almost a century of manufacturing, use, storage and interoperability behind it. Call it prejudice, but they know what they want.

So, given that the .45 ACP might be the next choice (and the .45 GAP would certainly not be) what was Glock to do? The G-21 is a durable, reliable piece of machinery that would do pretty much all the military wants, except for a few little details: since the G-21 was unveiled, the military has insisted on additional capabilities.

For one, it has to fit average and even smaller-than-average hands. Big problem there (no pun intended) as the G-21 and G-20 are a handful even for those of us with large hands. Second, the military is very big on ambidextrous everything. They want controls to be useable for either hand without the need to rebuild the gun. Again, argue all you want, but their minds are made up. Last, and easiest, they want light rails. Lights, laser, and who knows what in the future, are all going to fit on pistols in the future. So have a rail on your gun. And not a proprietary one, but a mil-spec picatinny rail.

To stay ahead of the curve, and in anticipation of the military someday getting off its bureaucratic butt and deciding on something, Glock came out with the 21SF, or "Short Frame." For those who have a cursory idea of what goes into firearms design, the 21SF was a "no-brainer." Or, as we gunsmiths like to chuckle morosely at each other: "All you've got to do is...."

The idea is simple: make the curvature of the backstrap shorter, that is, pull that surface towards the frontstrap. After all, "all you have to do is... ."

Well, not quite.

The external indication of the new gun is the marking on the frame, "SF" for short frame.

One of the problems gunsmiths like Robbie Barkkman had with the grip reductions on Glock frames was that you can only move the web-area of the frame forward so much before you start cutting into the space taken up by the ejector block. But Glock found a way around that: they changed the shape of the tail of the ejector block. The bottom, instead of being squared-off, is tapered. That gives them more space in the back to move the web area of the backstrap forward. Me, I would have done a much more radical trimming of the ejector block, but I'm not the one who has to go out and sell a truckload of them to justify the new mould costs.

The new 21SF mags will work in older guns, but older mags won't work in the new guns.

Weight Comparisons Between Glock Models and Some Other Handguns

(All weights in ounces, to the nearest tenth)

Model	Total Weight (Empty, w/o Magazine)	Barrel Weight	Slide Weight	Upper Assembly Weight
G-17	22	4.1	12.5	17
G-22	22.9	3.8	13.6	17.7
G-21SF	26.4	4.1	16.6	21
G-37	26.1	3.9	16.7	20.9
G-38	24.2	3.6	15.6	19.5
G-39	22.3	3.2	14.4	18.1
1911 #1	38.3*	3.3	13.4	18.6
1911 #2	36.5*	3.4	14.4	18.5
P-35/9mm	29.4	3.3	11.2	14.9
P-35/40	31.4	3.2	13.2	16.8
HK P7	27.6	n/a	10.2	n/a

* The steel frame of the 1911s is the cause of the large disparity in gross weights.

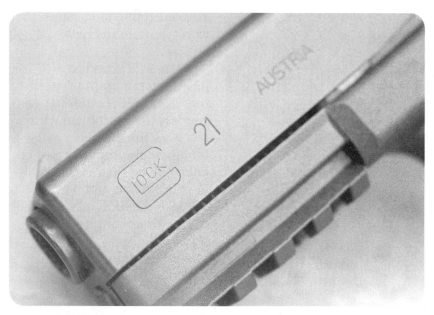

The slide is marked as all G-21s are, but the light rail is a picatinny rail.

Glock sent me.

So there might be a G-20SF in the offing, except for the magazines, but more on that in a bit.

The need (desire/wish/ fantasy) for an ambidextrous magazine release on the part of the military services makes a magazine catch design a tough one. It is easy to make them swappable, but not so easy to make them work from both sides. Glock has done it by making the catch shoulder on the magazine tube be out front. The new magazines still retain the old catch, so a new magazine will work in both the old and new guns. But old magazines will only work on old guns. And that's the problem with building your own G-20SF: no magazines.

Here's where it gets interesting: the new ejector block has a new number, and it also has a newly-shaped ejector. Despite the new ejector shape, an old G-21 assembly will slide right on to a new G-21SF, and work just fine. I did just that with my G-21 and the loaner G-21SF

The 21SF uses a different-number (and shaped) ejector block, but old upper assemblies will fit right onto the new 21SF frames.

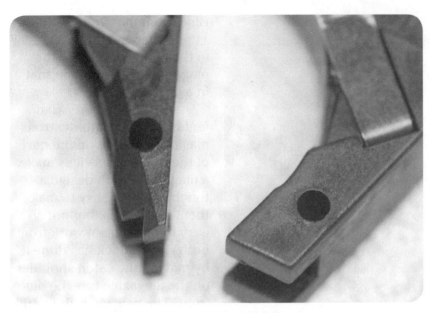

On the left you can see the new, slimmed-down lower tip of the 21SF ejector block. That is what allows Glock to make the frame smaller even than a grip-reduced old 21.

The old 10mm magazines won't work in the new SF frame.

The 21SF also has a picatinny rail up front, not the Glock rail of old. That can cause a slight problem with some, as the picatinny rail is a bit larger. But the only way to know for sure is to try a 21SF in your holster and see.

Will the 21SF take off? Will the government buy it? Only time will tell.

The G-30

The "30" is a chopped G-21. It comes in surprisingly small, with a slide a fraction shorter than a G-19, and

The 21SF will be a lot easier for some to shoot than the parent 21, but not as easy for a lot of others as anything in .45 GAP.

The G-30 is a lot smaller than a Government-size 1911 yet holds more rounds.

effectiveness comes with the last hundred feet per second of added velocity with the bigger (bigger than .38 Special, that is) case. In the .45, with a 230-grain bullet at a nominal 825 fps, losing some velocity and dropping to 775 fps hardly matters. Although it may not seem like you're losing velocity when you experience the recoil. Compact, lightweight handguns chambered in powerful cartridges can be work to shoot.

The G-30 came out in October of 1996, postdating all the upgrades and changes. You should call Glock if you have an "E" series G-30, but you needn't worry about older trigger parts or 90- or 15-degree extractors. The magazines all came after the Assault Weapon Ban of 1994, but the size of the G-30 made that now-defunct law a moot point. Even without the magazine capacity restriction you couldn't get more than 10 rounds in a G-30 without an extended-length magazine.

height shorter than the G-19 by almost a quarter of an inch. In it you get 10 shots of .45 power. As a carry gun for someone who isn't keen on the 9mm or .40, but wants a small gun, it really rocks. And, it uses the same magazines as the G-21, so your 10 shots can be quickly replaced with 13 or more.

The G-30 and its magazines will fit the same holsters and magazine pouches as the G-21, so if your department allows the big .45 as a duty gun, then the G-30 would make a great backup or off-duty gun.

The velocity loss with the shorter barrel is small, not because the almost seven-eighths of an inch doesn't matter but because the .45 works its stopping-power magic from bullet weight more than velocity. Cutting back a .357 hurts, because the real

The G-30 frame is so short that your little finger needs the magazine for support.

The standard magazine baseplate barely gives your little finger a place to rest.

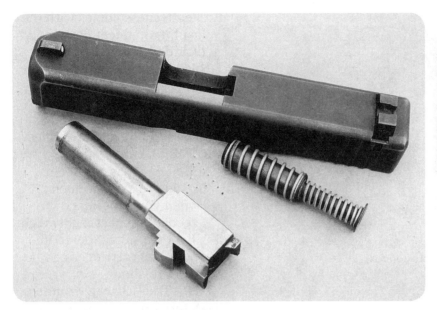

The G-36 uses a dual-spring recoil system. It may be touchy with soft target ammo.

Here is the bottom of the Pearce extension. Put this only on nine-shot magazines.

The G-36

Almost the first moment someone in the USA got their hands on a G-21 (or perhaps a G-20) the cry went up that the frame was too big. And they were right. The combat shooter's gold standard would be a Glock that was the same size as a 1911 pistol, with a slim frame, single stack magazine and chambered in .45. When the first news of the G-36 was being whispered about, the excitement was high, for it looked as if the real 1911-slaying Glock was to appear. It wasn't. The G-36 turned out not to be a 1911 in Glock guise, but an even more compact G-30. In their disappointment, many shooters overlooked what the G-36 really was: a slimline Glock. It may not seem like much on paper, but the difference in width matters in the hand. The G-30 (and G-21, G-20 and G-29) is 1.27" wide. The G-36 is 1.13" wide. The first two 1911s I measured for width came in at 1.25" and 1.30". Glock has made their latest pistol one slimmer even than a 1911 with slimline grips on it.

The bad news is capacity. The standard magazine only holds six rounds. And the G-36 does not use G-21/G-30 magazines. It can't. However, Pearce makes an extension that adds a round, bringing the magazine to seven rounds, for eight total in the gun. Still compact, and holding as many rounds as a 1911. Not bad.

The Pearce Plus One baseplate is much more comfortable to shoot on the G-30.

A compact big-bullet launcher, the G-36 is slimmer than any other Glock. It's as thin as a 1911.

The G-36 with a Pearce extension on the magazine. The whole package is the size of a 1911 Officer's Model.

The G-36 came out in January of 1999, and post-dates all modifications.

Call Glock for the "E" series change.

The G-36 could be the perfect big-bore carry pistol if the barrel and slide were extended just a bit and

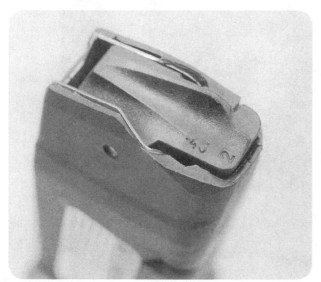

There have been several generations of followers. The armorer at a GSSF match can tell you if yours are up-to-date.

The price of the G-36's svelte lines: six shots maximum unless you install an extension like this Pearce.

the frame and magazines lengthened. Making the G-36 about the size of a 1911 commander size would produce a slim, compact, big-bore pistol that would be easy to carry and have the Glock standard of toughness and reliability. We can hope, but that's about all.

.45 GAP Pistols

A few years back, Glock had a small problem: they didn't have a .45 that people wanted. Oh, the G-21 was a fine gun, and the compacts were certainly great, but they were all big. The compact .45s sold well, but they didn't sell like the .40s did and the 9mms had. In fact, all .45 pistols combined sold at about a

Box-stock, ready to go, and a lot less expensive than a Colt 1911 .45 ACP.

third of the rate that the .40 pistols sold.

So to solve the problem, Glock took a different approach: Instead of trying to shrink the gun to fit the cartridge in use, they shrank

Initially, the .45 GAP was available only with 185- and 200-grain bullets. But it didn't take long for the ammo makers to figure out how to make a 230-grain bullet fit and work.

Glock unveiled the .45 GAP in all three frame sizes.

the cartridge to fit in the guns in use. The approach is not without precedent. The first is over a half-century old; the .308 is essentially the .30-06, but shorter. The idea was to do two things: the US Army would shorten the case, and using the (then) new ball powders, be able to fit enough powder into the shorter case to replicate the velocities of the .30-06. A shorter overall length would mean they could make (or have made for them) a weapon with a shorter receiver, shorter bolt travel, shorter operating rod travel; a more compact rifle. And since they were making a new case, make the rim of the new case thicker and thus stronger, so it would be more useful in future automatic weapons.

A similar thing happened with the 10mm and 40. By the time the original 10mm had been throttled back to the ballistics we now know as typical of the .40 S&W, there was so much dead air space in the case that the whole thing could be significantly shortened.

In a similar fashion, Glock shortened the .45 ACP to fit it into a G-17/G-22 platform. Not that it was as easy as "opening the breechface and make new mags," which is how one so-called expert described it. No, the new .45 Glock Automatic Pistol cartridge had to have a heavier slide, new extractor, new magazines, recoil spring and ejector. There was also the little matter of getting a brand-new cartridge type-approved by SAAMI,

the Sporting Arms and Ammunition Manufacturers Institute. Not that you have to have their approval to make a cartridge, but if you expect any police departments or the military to buy any you surely need their seal of approval. Also, by having a cartridge SAAMI-spec'ed you can then have ammunition makers make ammunition for your new guns, all knowing they are making it to the specs laid down.

The initial loadings were not quite up to .45 ACP. The velocities were, in the bullet weights available, but the first-blush .45 GAP only had bullets up to 200 grains in weight. If you're going to make a new .45 to replace the old .45, then you have to have the bullet weight that "made the bones" of the first one: 230 grains. The ammunition engineers here in the USA are a clever lot, and it didn't take them long to figure out what it took to get the 230 up to velocity within the pressure limits of the .45 GAP.

The pressure is another difference. The initial pressure of the .45 ACP was quite low, in keeping with the thoughts of the time: heavy bullets, moderate velocity, low pressure so you could use it anywhere and not have a climatic problem. So the pressure of the .45 ACP was limited to 17,000 CUP, which under the new system is measured in punds per square inch (psi); specifically, 21,000 of them. Only relatively recently was the .45 ACP

bumped up with the "+P" loading to 23,000 psi. (Recent as in the 1980s, when it had been lower for most of the twentieth century.)

Considering that the standard 9mm runs with a "redline" of 34,000 psi in the USA and over 40,000 psi in some NATO loadings, when other handgun cartridges are commonly run even higher, 17,000 is quite modest. To match the velocity figures of the .45 ACP in a smaller case, the .45 GAP had to be run at a higher pressure. The marvel isn't that they are running the pistol at a mere 23,000, but that they can match the standard .45 ACP ballistics while *only* running at 23,000 psi.

The .45 GAP case is shorter, pretty much 9mm Parabellum in length: a nominal .775" compared to the .45 ACP at .898" in length. (Both, and all cases made for both, will actually be shorter. It's simply an unavoidable result of manufacturing tolerances and the result of cases being fired and resized.) The maximum overall length of the .45 GAP loaded is 1.070", shorter than the 9mm, a result of the blunt .45 bullets in use (hollowpoints) and the need to feed the stubby little rounds through an envelope originally designed for a 9mm.

Published ballistics may be a bit misleading. The industry-standard test barrel for a .45 ACP is five inches, while the standard for the .45 GAP is four. So if you're looking over printed data, and find the .45 GAP just a bit behind, that is why.

There is some talk of the "rebated" rim of the .45 GAP. A short primer on rim diameters: a cartridge has to have a rim so it can be extracted. On a revolver cartridge the rim is larger than the case diameter (the so-called rimmed cartridge) so the extractor star can lift the case when you want to remove it.

The .38 Super is a rimmed pistol cartridge; it has a vestigial rim that projects a few thousandths outside the case diameter. A case that has the rim the same diameter as the case body is called "rimless" and you find most pistol cartridges here; the 9mm and the .45 being two examples. Except they aren't. The 9mm is usually a true rimless, with the case the same diameter. However, the .45 ACP often has a rim a few thousandths larger than the case body.

A rebated rim, on the other hand, is a case where the rim the extractor grabs on to is significantly smaller in diameter than that of the case body. This is usually done by the designers so they can fit a large case into a chamber, but not have to greatly increase the side of the bolt and breechblock. It almost invariably brings feeding problems unless the designers are very careful in adjusting the feeding system to accommodate the rebated rim. You see, the bolt/breechblock rides on the case body as it cycles. If the rim is too small, the cartridge may not have time to pop up into the pickup rails path as the slide or breech goes forward.

I have a cartridge on my desk as I type this, grabbed at random. It's a loaded factory

Left to right, we have the 9mm, .40, .45 GAP and the .45 ACP. You can see the GAP is the length of the other, smaller-bore cartridges. Now if Glock had only done this back in the late 1980s, the world would be so different....

round and the case body just above the extractor groove is .468" in diameter. The rim? .470" on average. So the .45 ACP is "sort-of rimless." A loaded .45 GAP right next to it measures .470" just above the extractor groove, and has a rim of .466" in diameter. That means if you were to stuff the cases (the loaded round wouldn't fit) into a .45 GAP magazine, the rim of the .45 GAP would be a mere .002" lower than that of the .45 ACP case. I really doubt that the pickup rail of the Glock slide is even going to notice a .002" difference in rim location. If it is, then Glock has made an incredibly fussy pistol, which

has not been their habit over the last 25 years.

So don't worry about the "rebated" rim.

The .45 GAP is viewed by some as a ".45 ACP Short." Close but no cigar. Just like the .40/10mm matchup, if you were to chamber the shorter .45 GAP in a barrel made for the .45 ACP, you'd have excessive headspace. Possibly, the extractor would hold the case in place firmly enough to fire the round. More often, however, it would both ignite the cartridge and push it off the extractor, into the chamber. When the pressure built up and launched the bullet, the case would get

slammed back against the breechface. In other pistols, the result would usually be a pierced primer. As the Glock primer can't protrude enough to pierce the primer as the 1911 does, you wouldn't see that. But it would still be bad for the pistol.

However, in revolvers the effect is exactly the same as the .38 Special/.357 Magnum. In the S&W revolvers that use the .45 ACP, with moon clips to hold the rounds in place, you can swap .45 GAP for .45 ACP with no problem. The moon clips snap onto the cases around the extractor groove and hold the rounds in place. I just shot the USPSA

Here I am, shooting with .45 GAP ammo in the USPSA Nationals, in the mud of Tulsa. Thank you, Herr Glock, for this interesting cartridge.

Nationals in Revolver, using Cor-Bon .45 GAP ammunition. This is getting a bit esoteric for a bunch of Glock shooters, but why would someone do it? Simple: the shorter cases have a shorter distance to fall into the chambers, and a shorter distance to be extracted on reloads. As revolver shooters are constantly reloading in practical shooting matches, reloads mater. Anything that can shave even a small amount off the time, adds up.

What does this mean for Glock shooters? After all, "it's a G-22 with a new barrel," right? No, the G-37 is most definitely not just a G-22 with a new barrel. No, the "rebated rim" isn't so the .45 GAP fits on a G-22 breechface. The .45 GAP rim is (see above) .465" while the G-22 in .40 S&W is set up for a rim diameter of .425" – not even close. I took the liberty of taking apart some of the Glocks sent to me

(don't worry, I'm a factory-trained Glock armorer) and weighing the various parts. I used a rugged old Pitney-Bowes postal meter, good to a tenth of an ounce, to weigh the parts in question. As you can see, they are not simply modified "whatever" parts.

While the G-37's barrel is almost the same weight as the G-22's barrel, and they are both lighter than the G-17 barrel, the slides are quite different. The slide of the G-37 is a quarter again as heavy as that of the G-22, and a third again as heavy as that of the G-17. In fact, the G-37 slide is heavier than that of two other 1911 slides I had along to weigh. The unlocking mass (combined weight of barrel and slide) for the G-38 is 12 percent higher than that of the 1911, an impressive difference when you consider the fact that the barrel of the G-37 is half an inch shorter

than that of the government model 1911.

One item that I found quite interesting was the relative weights of the G-17 and the Browning Hi-Power slides and barrels. While the G-17 slide is only 11 percent heavier than the Hi-Power, the barrel of the G-17 is fully one-quarter heavier. That would make unlocking slower and less violent. While they are not radically different, they are different.

Also, experience has shown us that older (forged, not cast-frame) Hi Powers are relatively fragile and considered by many to be short-service-life pistols while the G-17 has an enviable record for longevity. It's a striking demonstration of what the differences in materials technology and manufacturing have brought us. ♦

CHAPTER *19*

Compensated Glocks

The idea of jetting gases from somewhere near the muzzle to dampen felt recoil and muzzle rise isn't a new one. I recall reading the old Herter's catalogs, where they had their muzzle brake for the M1 Garand that made it possible for a nine-year-old boy to shoot a .30-06 without being knocked to the ground. (To which I say harumph! It doesn't kick that much.)

But compensators never really caught on that much. Two things changed that, both a result of Larry Kelly. Larry Kelly liked handgun hunting, but even a .44 Magnum was underpowered for the kind of game he had in mind. Yes, a .44 Magnum was plenty for whitetail deer, but he was thinking of moose, elk, dangerous game and even bigger critters. The problem with more power wasn't the cartridge or guns, it was the recoil. Larry was an aerospace machinist, and he came up with a neat idea about how to "machine" firearm barrels without marring them.

He used a process known as electrical discharge machining (EDM) Simply described, it involves using a carbon electrode and a huge electrical charge. Once the charged electrode is brought close enough to the surface of a conductive material, an arc leaps the gap. The arc erodes the material. Properly applied, you can burn a hole through a barrel without kicking up burrs, disturbing heat-treating or even marring the finish.

With recoil dampened via EDM barrel porting, handgun hunting could really take off. It even had an effect on the then new sport of metallic silhouette competition.

With the path now clearly open, other experimenters tried different approaches. One other one was to affix a ported cage on the muzzle to capture and redirect the muzzle gases. Called a muzzle brake in the old days (think artillery muzzle), it now goes by the name of "compensator" or "comp." For competitive shooting, a comp or porting offers such an advantage in recoil reduction that those matches that allow it keep ported and unported guns in separate categories.

Larry Kelly and his company Mag-na-Port soon had revolvers pouring in and out of their door. But how to port a pistol? The ports go directly through the barrel, but the enclosing slide complicates things. Through

Compensated Glocks are clearly marked.

Comping a 1911 takes a lot more work, like this one from Nick Sevastian of Canada. A very efficient comp.

residue onto the top of the barrel, where the slide had to ride over the deposits in cycling. Given enough blast-deposited powder residue, even a Glock gets cranky. The first G-18s had barrels that extended beyond the slide, with the ports cut as slots across the top. (Early experimenters on the 1911 and Browning Hi-Power had tried this and dropped it as less effective than other methods.) Apparently the slots on the G-18 blackened and even blew off front sights. So, the first ported Glocks were not successful and were quickly withdrawn.

Then in February of 1987, the G-17C was introduced. It was followed in quick order by the G-19C, G-20C, G-21C, G-22C, G-23C, and the G-31C and G-32C.

The new Glock ported models differ from the older designs in one important regard: the orientation of the ports. The old transverse ports created mechanical and operational problems. (which the early 1911 experimenters quickly discovered). The slots rub across whatever bearing surface the barrel rides on. In the 1911, that is the bushing. On the Glock, it is the upper surface of the clearance hole in the front of the slide. Each gap presents its edge to the bearing surface, adding friction and rubbing the muzzle residues on the surface. The friction and wear create service life problems for the pistol, and as an added insult, the slots aren't that effective.

experimentation (and persistent customer requests) Larry found that by making the barrels ports one size for efficient porting, and making the slide ports larger for gas clearance and powder residue blast, he could port pistols and not gum them up.

Mag-na-Porting was particularly sought after by Pin shooters, as you could port a pistol and still use it in the Stock category provided you didn't change its basic external dimensions. However, a ported pistol was not stock for USPSA, Steel or other competitions, so many shooters had a specialized pin gun, stock gun, and then extra pistols for the other matches. (The clever ones simply fitted a spare barrel or barrel/slide combo for pin shooting.)

The first ported Glocks were the G-17L and the G-18, back before 1990. The G-17L ported barrels were dropped with rumor having it that they were cracking. Glock says no but won't say why. I figure they had problems with the slots blasting powder

Even compact Glocks get comped.

Here you see the dual barrel slots and slide clearance slots.

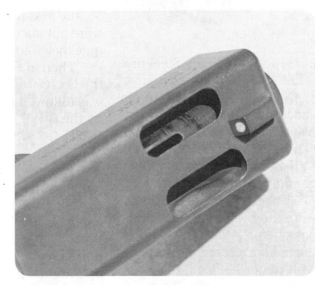

The slide slots provide lots of room for the powder gases and debris to get clear.

Here a shooter at World Shoot XIII is hosing the targets with his comped and scoped Glock.

The use of longitudinal slots solves many problems. The slots do not present multiple ridges to the bearing surface. Since the 12 o'clock part of the barrel is not pierced, the bearing surface is not even rubbing on the slots unless it is a very tightly-fitted bushing. With the slots on the upper sides, the muzzle residues are not blasted directly onto, and wearing against, the bearing surfaces. The large openings allow much of the residue to simply blast off of the gun into the air. The bearing surface on the slide acts as a plow, scrubbing a path through any powder residue that might be on the barrel.

How well do they work? Well enough, as mentioned that competitions have separate categories for ported guns. But what about loss of velocity? Or accuracy? From extensive experimentation with Mag-na-Port and pin shooting in the past, I can state that there is no loss of either. The amount of gases lost to porting is small enough that it does not affect velocity. There is no loss of accuracy. That said, the amount of gas diverted for recoil control is too small to change velocity, and as a result it is not the most effective recoil reducing method available. If you want true reduction, you have to divert more gas. And that can either affect velocity, cost more money, or both.

The first method is the compensator. A comp is a cage on the muzzle that scavenges

This racegun Glock, set up for Open, has an extended barrel and a comp on the muzzle. With those threads, not legal in California!

The Hybrid spine, to give the rocket nozzle ports thrust surfaces.

The comp ports (and blast shield) on a gun built for International Modified class.

A Ned Christiansen Hybrid and compensator system. This setup is so efficient that with some loads it recoils down, not up.

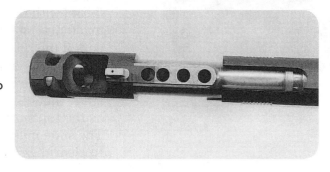

gas from the muzzle blast and re-directs it. On the Glock, you have two problems: One, to thread a barrel for a comp you need a longer than normal barrel. At least half an inch, and you can't use a Glock barrel because no one can cut the Tenifer finish to thread it. (At least not without a severe wear problem on their cutting tools, which you, the customer, will end up paying for.)

Second, as the Glock barrel is removed through the rear for disassembly, a locked-in-place comp makes disassembly of the slide and barrel impossible. You have to clean them while juggling

Unlike the old cross slots, the new dual slots don't smoke up the white dot front sight.

A red dot sight and ports – and it still fits the International IPSC box.

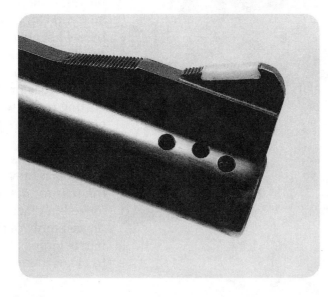

Don't drill your own ports. Even if you can get a drill bit through the Tenifer treatment (don't bet on it), you'll make a mess of things.

the slide and barrel back and forth. Until recently I would have thought those were the only problems, but the state of California has thrown us a curve. In their apparently never-ending attempt at making the world "safe" from anything and everything firearms-related, California has banned barrels that are threaded. The legislators, in a futile, uninformed and bizarre twist, seem to feel that threads alone are indicative of an intent to install a silencer.

Stop laughing. I'm not kidding. They banned barrels threaded at the muzzle. Since they seem to lack a grasp of grammar as well as mechanics, the law is worded so that even if you have a compensator soldered to your threaded barrel, the threads underneath are sufficient to be a banned object. Attempts to convince the committee members to allow an exemption for competition handguns were met with no success. As a result, you can't have a Glock with a threaded-on compensator in California. (Without threads, you can't assemble it to get it in the slide.) One manufacturer who makes 1911s (which disassembles out the front of the slide) is STI, who makes a barrel with the compensator machined integrally on the end of the rifled portion.

Another approach is to fabricate the barrel with a spine that extends as far up as the top surface of the slide. The slide must be machined to clear the spine. The extra depth of the barrel along the spine allows ports to be cut that are shaped like rocket nozzles, to redirect the gases upwards efficiently. Called a "hybrid barrel," it can be very effective but requires major surgery to the slide. As with many things, some people make compromises. To get the hybrid effect without machining the slide to accommodate the spine might work. But it take very delicate machining, and in the end you might find that you would have been as well served by simply buying a new slide and hybrid barrel to match, rather than cutting your Glock slide and voiding its warranty.

Both comps and the hybrid barrel require a different ammunition approach to be most effective. The comp works by scavenging gas at the muzzle. So to make a comp work, you have to load in your ammunition a slower-burning powder than you might otherwise select for that caliber. The slower powder extends the burning curve (and thus the peak pressure curve) towards the muzzle, and the extra gases at higher pressure (than they would otherwise have been) work better in the comp. The hybrid drains gas off sooner, so again you have to load a slower powder in order to keep the gases pushing the bullet through the barrel. Otherwise your barrel pressure drops off too quickly, and you lose velocity.

The most effective method is to combine the

If you want to shoot this G-21C as a stock gun, just drop in an unported barrel and you're ready to go.

two into a "hybriport" gun. The problems here are that you must now shovel large amounts of powder into the case to feed both the hybrid and comp, and the resulting pistol is loud, objectionably loud to some shooters' ears. But if you want a fast-cycling gun where the red dot doesn't lift much then the hybricomp approach can be for you. (All comped guns fall into the Open category, and if you don't have a red dot sight you're out of the game.)

If porting is so good, why should you pay so much money to have it done or buy another Glock to get it? Because home porting comes under the heading of surgery at home: Messy, expensive, painful and prone to error. Do not simply retire to your workshop with a carbide drill in your drill press, expecting to drill your own ports. Tenifer is too hard to allow it, and even were it not you

would ruin a good barrel. I've seen it, and it isn't pretty.

If porting is so good, why doesn't everyone do it? Because not everyone wants it, and some competitions don't allow it. All ported guns have one problem: they're ported. In a defensive situation, the ports aren't going to cause a problem for most shooting, but there is one case where it can be a big problem: shooting with retention. All defensive shooting instructors will tell you that there are times when you may have to shoot while holding the handgun right next to you. Such as when someone is trying to take it away from you. Holding the handgun right next to your belt keeps it away from them, but puts the ports right on you. For that reason, some defensive shooting instructors suggest you not use a ported gun as a carry

The bearing surface of the slide is between the slots, not riding over them.

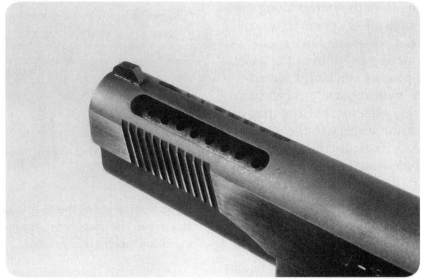

Other pistols also come ported from the factory, like this Springfield Armory .45 Super.

gun. Some simply flatly refuse to allow their students to use ported guns in a defensive shooting-oriented class.

The standard Glock ports don't require a slower power, nor do the Mag-na-Port ports, but they do gain greater effectiveness from using a slower-than-usual powder for the each particular caliber. Just don't expect as much recoil reduction from a "C" model as the comps or hybrids provide.

Glock "C" models all post-date the changes in trigger parts, and the breechface 15-degree modification. They all use all the standard parts and accessories and magazines of their unported brothers.

And, if you wanted to shoot a "C" Glock for fun, while still having the option of shooting Stock in a competition, you have an easy route: install an unported barrel. All the competitions I've consulted feel that simply dropping a stock unported barrel into a C model Glock is good enough to bring it to stock configuration. You aren't gaining any advantage with a slightly lighter slide (due to the debris-clearance ports in the slide) and so long as you install a Glock barrel and not a match tube from say, Bar-Sto or KKM, you haven't violated the spirit of the GSSF rules.

Other competitions might not even object to your using a non-Glock barrel. Be sure and check the rules of the particular competition before investing in a new barrel. ◆

CHAPTER 20

The Training Glocks

n the course of teaching defensive tactics, or instructing on an Armorer's course, it may come to pass that muzzles get pointed at people. We work really hard to make keeping the muzzle pointed in a safe direction a constant habit, ingrained at the genetic level. But sometimes it can't be done, and sometimes you simply must. For instance, when you're teaching police officers on weapon disarming or retention techniques, muzzles will get waved all over the place.

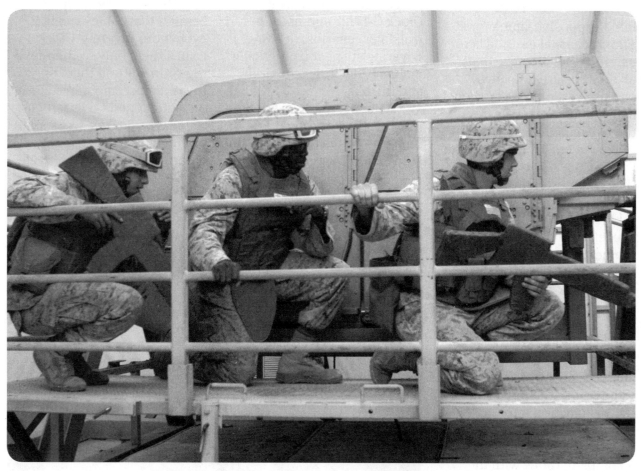

The Marine Corps has lots better things to do than bust up perfectly-good Marines and rifles, hence the need for training dummies. Police departments feel the same way, and thus we have training Glocks. (Courtesy U.S.M.C.)

There is also the problem of wear-and-tear on live, expensive weapons. As a result of the ongoing Global War on Terror, we find our service man and women have to deal with tipped and rolled-over Humvees. The Marine Corps built a special training simulator to allow marines to train in this particular emergency skill, without having to tip over real vehicles. They also use foam-rubber M-16 training dummies, partly to save wear-and-tear on the Marines themselves, but also to save busting up expensive new rifles.

What to do besides build expensive simulators? The traditional method is to carefully check to see that all firearms are unloaded, and use cattle prods to keep live ammunition away from the training area. (A bit tongue-in-cheek, but a method I've considered using from time to time.)

The typical plastic replacement training tool is useful, but not always the best. How to train in malfunction drills with a solid rubber gun?

Enter the red Glock. Red has been the customary color for inoperative or fake firearms, so the red Glock is simple to make by introducing red dye into the polymer before injection into the mould.

The Glock G-17T-Red is a complete Glock with the exception of a few critical parts. The barrel bore is not drilled out to act as a barrel. Indeed, the sides of the exposed barrel when you open the action are drilled crossways, to amply demonstrate that the barrel is a dummy. There is even a huge hole in the top of where the chamber would be were there one, as additional assurance that what you're looking at is a dummy gun. The slide is not drilled through for the firing pin to protrude, and the 17T-Red firing pin lacks a tip. In all other regards it handles just like a "real" Glock. (It is, after all, a real Glock.) With it, an Officer can handle a sidearm that has the same weight and balance as his Glock G-17/22 and use it in training scenarios, drawing, covering suspects, practicing malfunction clearance drills and the like.

An instructor can handle it, or face it, knowing it is inoperative, and the class can study shooting positions and retention techniques without worrying about being on the wrong end of the muzzle. He/she can stand in any location watching a students draw and dry fire practice, to see the process from every angle in safety.

The barrel is serial numbered (again, it is a real Glock, so it has a serial number) to match the frame, so a quick look verifies that it doesn't have a live barrel in it. The question comes up, could you re-activate a red Glock as a live firearm? Yes. It is in all paperwork matters and mechanical function (except for firing) a real firearm, and Glock treats it as such. No, scratch that: Glock treats it even more severely. Glock issues them only to their field reps and will sell them only to law enforcement agencies on a direct and on letterhead-request basis. Yes, I as a state-certified law enforcement firearms instructor can't get

A G-17T, perhaps the rarest of all the Glocks.

one from Glock. The agency I'm teaching at could, but I can't personally.

Obviously, accuracy testing, chronograph work and reliability testing are all functions that have no meaning for the G-17T-Red. Dream all you want, this one is a Law Enforcement Only model, and the distribution is strictly controlled. Introduced in December of 1996, it would be superfluous to consider whether a particular G-17T is in need of the trigger parts upgrade or what extractor angle it takes. No, the only considerations are, does it have the original barrel? Has it been dropped too many times and not work? Can we send it back to Glock if we break it?

So, what to do if you have need of a training Glock and are not a police department? Call up Dave Manson at Loon Lake Precision (aka Manson Reamers) and ask

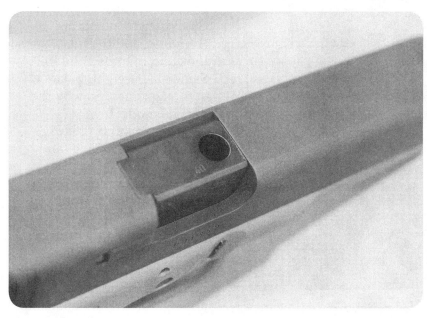

This G-22 Red Glock is a training dummy for non-firing training. Those aren't compensating ports on the sides of the barrel.

for his training barrel. Dave makes aluminum Glock barrels that fit in your G-17 or G-22. They're anodized red. They have no chamber; they protrude past the slide enough to identify the gun as a dummy; and were you to drill one out (a lunatic proposition, I might add) it would not survive firing. With the red stub of the barrel sticking out of your Glock, you can do everything the G-17T can do, without the onerous restrictions Glock insists on.

You wouldn't have the cool red frame, but you can't have everything. And the Manson barrel is a lot cheaper than a Glock G-17T.

Blue Glocks

Sometimes you simply have to have a projectile. Draw and dry-fire practice will only do so much. You need the verification of a projectile and its relationship to its intended target. The problem is, live ammo isn't always the solution.

Getting students to agree to force-on-force training with live ammo is impossible. (It is what many in the military call "on the job training" and the idea is to train your side to win and the other side to lose – not to train your people at the expense of greatly reduced recruitment and ever-increasing D&D benefits.

The non-firing training Glocks have a huge hole in the chamber to indicate that they aren't live guns.

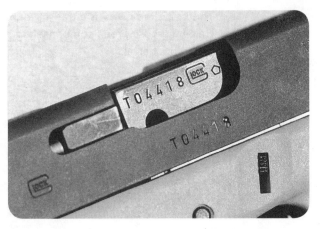

Serial numbered, proofed and marked just like real guns – because Blue Glocks are.

The bore of the Blue training Glock is angled upward to compensate for the nonexistent recoil.

For that, marking bullets are the solution. However, despite all the safeguards, using live firearms for non-live ammunition presents a problem. You can take a group of students and shake them by their heels until everything falls out of their pockets, and sooner or later a live round will slip by. It would be better if the firearms involved couldn't use live ammo at all.

Thus the blue Glocks. The G-17T-Blues are chambered for two different training cartridges, the 9FX and the 7.8x21AC. Both are blowback pistols, since the cartridges don't generate nearly enough force to cycle a locked-breech action. The frames are standard-size G-17 frames that have had blue dye introduced into the polymer before moulding.

Other than the odd calibers and blowback operation, the Blue Glocks operate just like any other Glock. The controls are all the same, and the magazines look and operate the same. Same size, weight, balance and magazines. So why the special model?

In the course of law enforcement training (and other areas of defensive firearm use), training occurs in three methods: static, dynamic and interactive. At the bottom is static training. Static as in standing in one place and repeating the same motion or motions until they are ingrained. Marskmanship drills fall into static training, as do malfunction drills.

Training Glocks come with training magazines, with color-coded baseplates to match. This Blue Glock has a blue baseplate and an LEO-marked magazine.

In dynamic training, the shooter, or the targets, or both, may be moving. Or they may not be moving, but the targets react to being hit. One example of targets that don't move except when hit would be falling plates or pepper poppers. In dynamic training, shooters must analyze the results of their actions and adjust their plan accordingly.

The polymer in the frame of training Glocks has blue or red dye mixed in before it is moulded.

Interactive training is done with other people who can adjust their behavior as a reaction to yours. No steel plate can realize it is going to be flanked and retreat to a better position, but another person can. A form of interactive training that many competitors would be familiar with is paintball. In paintball, no one stands still and lets the other side shoot at them. Competitors are constantly evaluating, adjusting and taking advantage of their opponent's mistakes.

Police do the same thing. At least, those lucky enough to have something like the Blue Glocks. In the really old days, force-on-force training was done with revolvers, where the rounds were loaded with primers only, and cotton balls stuffed into the otherwise empty cases. In order for it to be done safely, everyone had to wear hearing protection and glasses (still a good idea) and all participants would have to funnel through a single doorway, to be relieved of their duty weapon, backup gun, knives, brass knuckles, blackjacks, mace, etc, etc.

There could be no possibility of live ammo getting into the training area. (Not even the Chief, the Mayor or his bodyguards could get in with live ammo.)

Even with the Blue Glocks, such precautions are a good idea. Why did the idea fall out of favor? One, police departments stopped using revolvers. Two, cotton balls are good, but they don't offer enough incentive. Paintball pellets sting when you get hit by them, and the sore spot acts as a reminder.

Both of the Blue Glock calibers come in two varieties: paint and rubber. Paint is meant for animate targets, and rubber for inanimate. The paint rounds fire a small, frangible pellet of paint-filled plastic that breaks when it hits and marks the struck object. No more arguing about who got in the first shot or asking the referee who was on-target. The paint tells all. (Instead, the referee decides who shot too late from being struck, and

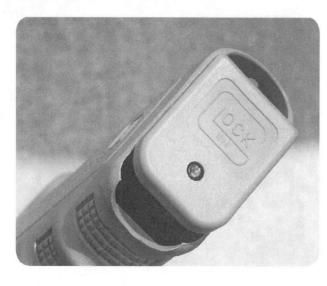

The baseplate may be blue, but the inside retainer plate is still basic black. Training Glocks are as interchangeable with "real" Glocks as they can possibly be.

thus was "dead" before pulling the trigger.)

Police can construct scenarios with trainers where an officer or SWAT team has to deal with a role-playing opponent or opponents. Unlike paper, cardboard or steel, which simply wait to be struck, the role-player can argue, threaten, move and hide. If the officers involved make a mistake, the role-player will take advantage of it.

The paint pellets are not completely innocuous. You can get hurt by them. They will sting and raise a welt, and you could suffer eye injury if you aren't protected, so eye protection is mandatory and protection for the other delicate parts of your body are highly recommended. But other than the face mask and perhaps gloves and a trouser insert, a police officer can wear his (or her) normal gear, and use a handgun that feels just like the standard duty sidearm. (The paint is water-soluble and washes out. One hopes the lessons learned last longer than the paint marks do.)

In the course of force-on-force training, the idea isn't to send the SWAT team in after some Rambo-like player who deals death and destruction at every opportunity. To do so is to teach the team the wrong lesson, or really, really depress them if the "bad guy" is a top-notch IPSC shooter. No, the bad guy has a basic script, and as long as the SWAT team does everything

by the book he goes along with them. However, if they make a mistake, it is his (or her) job to take advantage of the opportunity. Once done, the team and bad guy get debriefed and summarize the lesson learned. Properly done, it isn't just an afternoon playing paintball.

What of the rubber bullets? They are not meant for force-on-force training but for dynamic training on paper or cardboard targets. The rubber bullets, since they don't break on impact, hit harder than the paint pellets do and hurt a lot more. They also present a possibility of greater bruising than the paint rounds would. What they do allow is training to occur in locations that

It may be Blue or paint- or rubber-firing, but it's still a Glock all the way.

Even the magazine of this cutaway Glock used for armorer's training is sectioned to show the metal liner. (This one is a very early Glock witha non-drop magazine.)

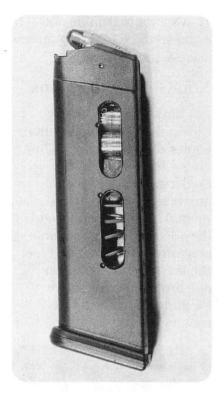

Cutaway but still functional, this Factory Cutaway is one of the rarest Glock magazines.

otherwise might not allow it. For a SWAT team practicing a bus, plane or boat rescue, using real ammo is not an option. It's not just that no one will allow such valuable equipment to get shot up, but who could haul them to a location where there is an impact berm in all directions?

With the rubber bullets, a SWAT team could practice in an office building that has been built but is not yet open for business or closed until it has a new tenant. They could practice in an abandonded house ready to be torn down without worrying about endangering the neighborhood with live ammo. They could practice in the station house, using a set of offices set aside that day

or weekend for the specific purpose of training.

One option that I think holds real possibilities for departments is the use of the rubber bullets for remedial marksmanship training. When someone needs a basic grounding in marksmanship, an eight-hour day spent out on the sweltering range is not always the best way to do it. Long, grueling training sessions do not always impart knowledge. (Well, they do, but often the "lessons" learned are that shooting is no fun, the instructor is an ogre, and qualification is something to dread.) However, the same amount of training, broken up into shorter (15 minutes to one-hour blocks) and spread over consecutive days, can be much better. But how to get to the range? Not every department has a firing range right out back of the precinct house. (As a matter of fact, most don't have anything like it.) However, a suitable cardboard backstop (even tucked into a closet) can serve as a stop for the rubber bullets.

A daily sesson, under the watchful eye of the firearms instructor, right there in the station, can bring someone along very quickly. And rubber-firing before going out on shift can keep skills fresh even when the department only has annual qualifications.

All of this is fun, but I know there are those burning to ask, "Why two different calibers to do the same thing?" Why 9FX and

7.8x21AC rounds? Those Austrians are crafty, that's why. The 7.8x21AC uses compressed air cartridges to propel the bullet rather than primer and propellent. Each round is a pressurized container with air and a bullet. There are locations where the minute amounts of Lead or Barium that the primer or powder might contain could be a cleanup problem. Compressed air has no such problem.

As you would expect, the air-propelled pistols are quite rare, as the idea that lead is as dangerous as plutonium has not quite proved to be true. (Except in California, where it apparently has extra-lethal qualities that are not apparent in other locales.) Yes, airborne lead can represent a health hazard, but not so great that it must be expunged from the shooting world.

A few curious things about the rubber and paint pellet-firing training Glocks: one, the barrel bore is drilled off-axis and points up. In all pistols, the line of the bore is actually pointed under the intended point of impact. As soon as the bullet begins moving, the pistol reacts to the recoil in a simple demonstration of Newton's Second Law in action. The pistol whips upwards in your hand, and the bullet is released from the muzzle exactly at the point where it can hit what you aimed at. The recoil of the training pistols is miniscule or non-existent, and thus there is no whipping. They have to start out pointed at the target and not under it.

Second, Glock also treats these Blue trainers as actual handguns. They have serial numbers and their distribution is as closely controlled as the Red Glock. If you are ever offered the opportunity to handle and shoot one, do not turn it down. You may never get the chance again.

It occurs to me that I may be a bit too hard on Glock here. After all, as blowback guns they fall short of the importation point requirements, and as such can only be sold to law enforcement agencies. And it wouldn't do any good to provide conversion uppers to those who might desire them, as the uppers could be used to assemble cartridge-firing uppers on regular Glock frames. The only way training uppers would work would be if Glock were to re-engineer the uppers, make the slides out of aluminum, and make them only in a proprietary cartridge that wouldn't accept regular ammunition.

That's a lot of trouble and expense to go to for not much sales activity.

Non-Glock Blue Guns

Ring's makes training Glocks that are simply rubber copies of Glock pistols. They are so accurate that the markings, including serial numbers, can be read on them. They don't cycle, and they do not have removable magazines, but you don't feel the least bit put out when one drops onto the parking lot during a force-on-force training session. ♦

Here, Henk Iverson of Strike Tactical shows how to disarm an opponent. Do you want him doing this with your Glock? I don't!

CHAPTER **21**

The .380 and 9x21 Glocks

There isn't a lot known here in the United States about the .380 Glocks, the G-25 and G-28. They were originally made for sale to various markets/countries that do not allow their citizens to own military caliber pistols. In order to get the pistols to work with the low-power .380, the basic Glock design had to be re-done as a blowback pistol. As an unlocked mechanism, they fall below the importation point requirements for the United States.

Despite being the same size as the G-19 (as the G-25) and the G-26 (as the G-28) the loss of points of the not-locking blowback mechanism puts them out of civilian reach, and makes them law enforcement-only guns, except for a batch that somehow slipped through and into the hands of some members of some Glock collectors associations. The Glock rep whom I was interrogating almost lapsed into profanity at the mention of the episode. It seems some people in the organization in question had done some questionable things

(not illegal, but contrary to Glock family custom) in order to be able to lay hands on the G-25s, and a number of noses were put out of joint. Needless to say, the process they used is now closely scrutinized, and the people involved are *persona non grata* with Glock. (Or so I've heard. As with so many things Glock, you can hear at least three sides to any event, episode or technical change in the products.)

In size, weight, and function, the two .380s are identical to their larger cousins. While their specifications are in the Glock Armorer's Manual, their parts are not. If you have a G-25 and need a part for it, you'd better hope a G-19 part works, for Glock isn't acknowledging that parts even exist for the .380s. And may I say: you lucky devil, you. You have perhaps the rarest of the rare. It was my understanding from the Glock rep that there are fewer G-25s in the country than there are G-18's.

I have heard rumors that when the long-awaited US production facilities get up and running, we may actually see the G-25 and G-28. Not

because they will be hot sellers (but they probably will be) but even if they don't sell any better than the lesser lights of the Glock lineup, they'll be offered certainly because Glock doesn't want to give up any market share they can acquire. Making the G-25 and G-28 would be quite simple, and without the import point restrictions to throw a wrench into things, why not?

9x21

The rarest Glocks outside the factory are three special G-19s made for investigators in the US Naval Investigative Service who had been stationed in Italy. Italy is one of those countries where civilian possession of military calibers is prohibited. Working undercover, they did not want to have 9x19 pistols, so they requested the 9x21 chambering instead. They own the three only known factory-marked 9x21 pistols. I wonder if the Navy will let the investigators keep them when they retire.

And will they be able to hide them from the Glock collectors? ◆

CHAPTER 22

Magazines and Magazine Accessories

Like the Glock when it first came out, magazines for the Glock are unique. The magazines for the first model G-17s were very odd affairs to the American shooters who encountered them. Not only were they "plastic" but they were squishy, too.

The first Glock magazines were constructed by pressing a sheet metal shell into shape on three sides for the magazine tube. (Front and sides, no steel in the back.) The sheet metal channel was then held in place in the mould when the polymer was injected. The sheet metal acted as the inner walls of the magazine tube and provided shape and durability to the polymer tube.

The design had many advantages. First, it was highly corrosion resistant. The only part that had any chance of rusting was the liner, and it wouldn't rust easily. (The liners are nickeled spring steel and are meant to last a long time.) For its size, the Glock magazine had greater capacity than other magazines. The additional capacity was partly due to the Glock magazine being a fraction longer than other magazines of high-capacity 9mm pistols. Also, the shoulders where the double stack was funneled down to a single feed position are higher on the Glock tube. The third aspect that gave the Glock a few more rounds was that the tubes were a little larger in diameter. This was possible due to the polymer frame. (Some magazine pouches for 9mm high-capacity magazines won't take Glock mags, due to the slightly larger diameter.)

Most pistols have a frame that encloses the magazine, which then has grips attached to it. The drawback to the frame-and-grips design is that everything you do constricts the design envelope left over for the magazine tube. For all of its wonderful feel and shape, and for being a huge advance at the time, the Browning Hi-Power only holds 13 rounds. (Interestingly, John Browning's original design appears to be large enough to hold 17 rounds of 9mm ammunition. Wouldn't that have turned heads in the late 1920's?)

The polymer Glock magazine is metal-lined.

For an equally comfortable grip, the Glock G-17 holds 17 rounds. There is and was one drawback to the original design. The magazine would swell when stuffed full of 9mm ammo, and not fall out of the frame even when the magazine button was pressed. It was also a snug fit inserting it in the grip of the pistol when fully-loaded.

You see, in Europe, where the Glock was designed and intended as a military and police pistol, letting magazines fall to the ground is considered very bad form. In some circles it is even considered an abuse of issued equipment, and letting a partially-loaded magazine fall to the ground will get you a stern talking to. So, the first design of magazine would not fall out of the pistol. Well, sometimes it would, and sometimes it wouldn't. Consider the "falling" status of your magazine as a contest between the magazine spring trying to push the magazine out, and the magazine tube swelling when loaded. When full, it wouldn't fall out, too swollen. When empty, it wouldn't fall out – the spring couldn't push the lightweight empty tube hard enough to overcome the friction.

With just enough rounds to add weight, but not so many as to swell the tube, your old-style magazine will drop out when you press the magazine button. How many rounds? It's a question you'll have to answer for yourself. Some magazines drop with three or

Practical competition shooters drop the magazines in the dirt, mud, sand, etc. We expect them to take it, and Glock magazines do.

DROP IT!

"Drop free? We don't make drop free."

If you talk to a sufficiently indoctrinated Glock employee or rep, you will cause him just a bit of concern when using the term "drop free." The factory designations are "Non Fully Metal Lined" and "Fully Metal Lined." And there is only a passing thought paid to the various generations of designs, but there's great concern that you might be installing a magazine baseplate to add capacity in places where it isn't legal. The original intent was to keep the magazines in the gun, and the need to alter the design to accommodate the peculiar concerns of the American shooters came later. All other designs were made to improve the magazines for good, engineering reasons. That's us: as good Americans we're always causing trouble.

You'll find Glock magazines of all vintages, but as far as the factory people are concerned, there are two: the originals, and those "American magazines."

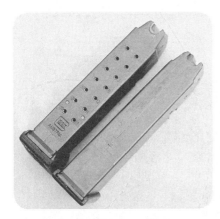

Yes, the hi-cap on the right is a no-name knockoff of the Glock, but the owner has tested it thoroughly and found that it works.

four rounds, others as many as six, some as few as two. And some will never drop.

If you needed to reload while using one of those first magazines, you had to use your fingertips to pry it out of the gun. Remember, we're talking of a design offered for the Austrian military trials, where the potential buyers are considering its issue to soldiers. A machinegun crewman is not going to be trained in speed reloads, and if after using his pistol for a few shots in an emergency he has to pry the magazine out to top it off, so what?

In the USA, that attitude didn't go over very well. American shooters considered the magazine as almost a disposable part. When it was empty, especially for practical shooting competitors and law enforcement trainers, getting it out of the gun as fast as possible was the highest priority. Indeed, they were used to magazines that launched themselves out of the pistol when empty.

Where an Austrian soldier is issued one spare magazine and one in the gun for the pistol he is handed, and some European police departments issue only one magazine with a pistol, American shooters, competitors, and law enforcement officers viewed owning three or four magazines as an absolute minimum.

As an aside, when I first went through the Glock Armorer's course, we were offered guns and magazines at very good prices. Hold onto your chair, because back in those days, we were offered the opportunity to buy high-capacity magazines for $10.50 each. That's right, 10 dollars and 50 cents. The storage box for the original Glocks is a dead giveaway of the European attitude. One pistol, two magazines: one in the pistol and one beside the pistol.

The solution to the peculiar American insistence

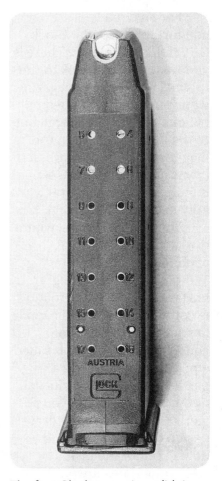

The first Glock magazines didn't even have the caliber markings – just cartridge holes and the Glock logo.

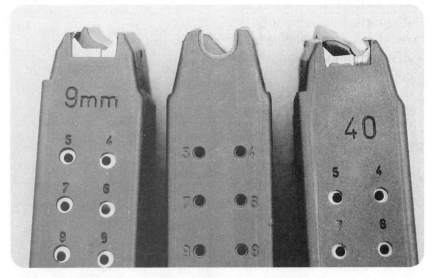

Two drop-free mags flank a very early 9mm mag – so early it isn't even marked "9mm" because that was all Glock made at the time.

MAGAZINE DISTINCTIONS

So which Glock magazine do you have (in case it isn't marked) and how can you tell if the feed lips are within specs? Measure the feed lip gap with a pair of dial calipers. If your magazines lips have spread (or been dented, bent or altered) you can tell quickly. Measure the width of the lips with a dial caliper.

The allowable dimensions are:

9mm: .325" to .335"	.40: .360" to .370"	10mm: .360" to .370"
.357: .360" to .370"	.45: .425" to .435"	

If you have other magazines on hand, you'll quickly find that Glock magazines hold their rounds tighter and in some cases the feed lips extend forward farther than other designs do. Nothing good or bad either way, just the way it has to be for a particular mechanism.

One peculiarity: A .40 magazine can hold 9mm ammo, and feed it into the pistol. As a stopgap measure to keep a 9mm running, I would put it up there with running your car with the tires flat. What it does mean is that if you get some 9mm ammo mixed in with your .40 ammo, it will feed and chamber. It may even fire. It won't cycle the .40, and it won't damage the pistol – just your reputation as the "high-speed, low-drag" shooter at your club. More than once I've watched a Glock-shooting competition shooter have the dreaded "Nines in a Forty" malfunction. The pistol is immediately reduced to a hand-operated single-shot pistol. And if the range officer or safety officer figures out what is going on quickly enough (as in before the shooter finishes the stage), the shooter's score could suffer as well as his reputation.

One small detail long-time Glock owners have noticed, on their pistols and magazines, is the reluctance of Glock to give their competition any space. The pistols are not marked ".40 SW" but are only marked ".40." Ditto the .357 SIG, which is simply marked ".357" for caliber. Publications under the control of Glock make no mention of other manufacturers, even obliquely in the caliber designation. I don't blame them. I just find it curious. Is S&W going to die of envy because Glock won't mark their pistols with "S&W" or "SW" even in the caliber designation?

As with the other parts, there are upgrades to followers. The armorer at a GSSF match can upgrade your mags for you.

Nothing new in it, though. Colt for a long time marked their revolvers ".38 Special" instead of ".38 S&W Special." And even earlier than the .38 Special cartridge, they offered revolvers in ".38 Colt" and ".38 New Police" to avoid using the dread phrase "S&W" in the caliber marking or cartridge designation. Even today, the curious custom continues. Ruger refers to its .40 pistols as "40 Auto," and so marks them on the chamber of each.

on drop-free magazines was simple: make the sheet metal pressing a four-sided, solid internal affair, and insert the new tube into the mould before encasing it in plastic. The exterior of the magazine was changed slightly so as to make it possible to determine which type a magazine was without having to insert it into a pistol. The giveaway is the notch in the upper rear where the slide passes through to feed a new round, right above the caliber designation. (Some very old magazines won't be marked with the caliber at all, since when Glock only made 9mms they didn't bother to so-mark the magazines.)

The old magazines that wouldn't drop free have a rounded U-shaped notch. The drop-free magazines have a square U-shaped notch. Later iterations of the drop-free design have the sidewalls of the notch tipped outwards,

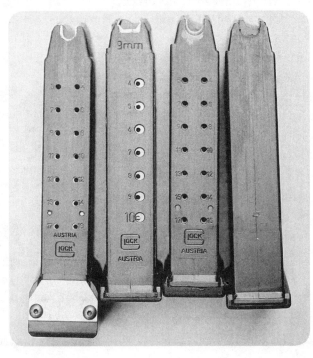

Two non-drops, a 10-shot, and a no-name copy of the Glock magazine.

so it is an angular slot. One other change made to the tube when going to the drop-free magazine was another American shooter-induced requirement. The top edge of the magazine shoulder was altered so it acted as a positive stop to magazine insertion.

Again, it is common in Europe to insert magazines with the slide forward. Or, if the slide is locked back, to carefully press the magazine in place. In the USA, we shoot until the slide locks back, drop the old and "slap" in a new one. (And sometimes slap it hard.) The old magazines could travel farther up into the frame than intended. The new shoulder prevented that problem. (If the magazine goes too high it wedges in place, sticks up too high, and the slide then can't go forward.) The stop ledge also solved a minor problem again caused by the American insistence on

slamming the magazines into place. The magazine riding too high could cause wear and damage to the retaining notch of the magazine tube, and the ejector and magazine feed lips. With enough wear the magazine might bind when inserted, or fail to stay locked in place when fired.

One other change was to make the composition of the polymer of the magazine tube stiffer. The old magazines had a lot more flex to them, actually bulging when stuffed full of ammo. And in hot weather, partially-loaded old magazines could disassemble themselves when they were dropped. The stiffer polymer led to other problems, but we'll get to that in a bit.

When the new magazines hit the market, everyone who could do it ditched their old magazines in favor of the new. When the Assault Weapons Ban law was enacted in 1994, a whole lot of non-drop free magazines came back onto the market, and you are as likely to find the magazine you are looking at to purchase is an old non-drop as a new drop-free mag. After the ban sunset, we saw a flood of new, non-drop magazines, such that the older ones are probably going to become curiosities. They still work just fine and can be had cheap in many instances. If you come across some in good shape don't pass them up just because they don't drop free. As practice magazines they work just fine.

In competition, having a mixture of the old and new

can be a problem. If you don't pay attention to the sequence in which you use your magazines, you may find yourself halfway between shooting boxes, trying to rip a non-drop magazine out of the gun against the clock. Also, since the old ones swell when loaded, you have to press them the entire length into the frame in order to seat them. A new-style Glock magazine is like any other pistol's magazine in that once you give it a running start it will whack in place and lock up without you having to press it the whole distance. In daily carry, a non-drop magazine can spare you the embarrassment of having your magazine drop out at inopportune times. I've never had the exquisite embarrassment of having a loaded magazine clatter to the floor in a public place, but I've talked to those who have. It is something you should avoid, if at all possible. An original non-drop magazine isn't going to fall out even if you remove your magazine catch entirely and do cartwheels down the hall. If you use a non-drop magazine as your carry magazine, just don't be needing a speed reload when the shooting starts.

As good as they are, Glock magazines still need TLC.

Why All the Fuss?

There has to be at least one reader out there who is scratching his (or her) head. Why all the fuss and exhortation over magazines?

Well, without trying to start an "old shooter vs. new shooter" schism, unless you were shooting actively in the early 1980s (or earlier) you just can't realize what magazines used to be like. Early magazines were so bad they were considered almost disposable. Well, not all, but many.

For example, if you chose to shoot IPSC with a Browning Hi Power (the P-35) back in the "good old days," you could count on good magazines. They were expensive, but good. Since the good ones came from Browning, you could count on them. Wartime surplus P-35 magazines were often quite good. Other pistols were not so lucky.

Ever wonder why the Luger, for all of its good feel and great looks, never caught on in practical pistol competition? The magazines. (Okay, so the wrong-way safety, pitiful sights and creepy trigger were problems too.) If you had a Luger with a magazine with matching numbers, you never let that magazine get away from that pistol. Other magazines, even those made before wartime production was hurried, couldn't be counted on to work reliably.

Many other pistols had the same fault. Indeed, the entire reputation of pistols as being less reliable than revolvers is based on crappy magazines.

What of the legendary 1911? You could always tell a new practical shooter back in the early 1980's; he was the one throwing his "gun show bargain" magazines into the weeds. The first article I was ever supposed to be paid for concerned itself with the detailed and continuing struggle of finding and keeping good magazines running properly. And one of the first bits of advice I offered was to not be cheap with magazines – go ahead and pay the $12 it took to get good ones. (What can I say, they were 1979 dollars.)

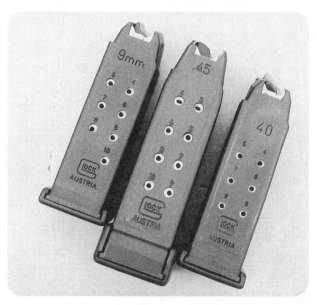

Increasing the capacity of compact models makes the magazines a lot longer.

THE FIVE TYPES OF GLOCK MAGAZINES (AND TWO VARIANTS)

The ages of Glocks mags so far are five. The first ones were 9mm only, didn't drop free, and weren't even marked as to their caliber. They also had a baseplate without an internal retaining plate. The baseplate was held on by the sidelugs only. The first magazines are 9mm only.

The second magazine was the transitional non-drop. It came into being with the introduction of the G-22. Transitional mags have the caliber marked and a retaining plate inside. The baseplate has a hole through it so you can poke the retaining plate out of the way on disassembly. The transitional magazines have three sides of metal on the interior and do not drop. The rarest of these are the .40 caliber ones.

The third age of magazines are the drop-free. They have square slots on the top rear. The baseplate and retainer look the same as the transitional ones do, but the part numbers are different. Don't put Type 2 retainers and baseplates on a Type 3 magazine. The tolerance differences can lead to self disassembly.

The fourth magazine is the 10-shot. Ten-shot magazines are all drop-free. They use a different follower and magazine spring than their hi-cap brothers and sisters, but the retaining plate and baseplates are the same. The 10-shots were made during the Assault Weapons Ban and for a while were common as dirt. What with the expiration of that odious law everyone with any spare cash has gone out and bought hi-cap magazines.

The fifth magazine is a curiosity. It is a hi-cap made during the time of 1994 to 2004, marked "For Law Enforcement and Military Use Only." It simply is a drop-free magazine with the warning machined into the mould. If you weren't an LEO or military person, it was a crime to own one of these back then. It still is, in some jurisdictions.

The latest Glock magazines; the .45 GAP, are only of one kind: they are drop-free, tipped-out stripper slot, not marked LEO Only.

The two variants come in the drop-free and the 10-shot magazines. Some drop free mags have a square slot on the back. There are also drop-frees with what cowboys would call a "Lazy U" slot, where the sides are angled outwards. Why the change? No word from Glock, but one Glock representative I talked to said the change was made to indicate that the magazine incorporated a new design in the inner tube assembly.

Another change first appeared on the 10-shot mags and involves the side of the taper. To make fast reloading easier, part of the taper was cut away to a sharper angle.

Yes, you can obsess over magazines. You could even spend time collecting nothing but magazines. Keeping them running is pretty easy: strip ands scrub them now and then, don't drop them too much, and don't loan them out.

The only things most owners worry about are 1) will they work, and 2) did I get them all back when I'm done shooting?

On the right is an early 10-shot 9mm magazine. On the left is the upgraded tube shoulder design.

Some magazines could always be counted on. S&W magazines were always dependable, but the DA/SA trigger of the S&W line was viewed back then as a hindrance to "good shooting." The trick was finding good magazines for a pistol that was suitable for competition or carry. The problem would quickly go away with the changes market forces brought about. Just as Glock was entering the market, the 1911 world was changed with the introduction of the Wilson-Rogers magazines. (Now sold in an improved version by Wilson as the 47D, and now replaced by the #500.)

Ruger entered the centerfire pistol field with their durable and reliable P-85 soon after the Glock appeared. In a few years the whole idea of cheap, crappy and unreliable magazines being the norm for pistols was overturned. The lousy ones still exist, but they aren't what shooters expect to be their usual gun purchase fate. Lousy magazines are to be strenuously avoided, because good ones exist. Such an attitude and situation was not the case before the early 1980s.

Today, you can buy ultra reliable and durable magazines for less than what they cost back then. But in the early 1980s, the idea that a high capacity 9mm pistol could be had with magazines as tough as rocks was almost as radical as the idea of a pistol with a plastic frame.

Disassembly

I know of more than one Glock owner who has never has his magazines apart. Partly because they never fail (at least in 9mm) but also partly due to the sometimes difficult disassembly procedure. While stripping the pistol is a piece of cake, getting the magazines apart can sometimes be a real hassle. The nature of the polymer is the problem. Since it is a slightly flexible material, the interlocking parts of the magazine have to be relatively large and strong to take the load. The magazine is composed of five parts; the tube, follower, spring, retainer and baseplate. (Some very old magazines were made without the internal retaining plate.)

The arrangement is the same as any other pistol magazine, the follower rests on top of the spring, the retainer on the bottom. The baseplate slides on the lips on the bottom of the tube, and the retainer locks the baseplate. On the Glock there is an additional retaining design. The lips on the bottom of the tube have square shoulders, that catch in the baseplate. The retainer, inside the tube at the bottom, prevents the tube from squeezing inwards and releasing those shoulders from their notches. That's your mission, should you choose to accept it, to get those shoulders out of the way.

The start is simple. Look at the bottom of the baseplate. Is there a hole? If

You want to make sure you have the correct baseplates on your magazines for proper function.

so, you have a later magazine. If there is no hole, you have an early magazine. (Or, curse your luck, an early baseplate on a later magazine. Get ready for some struggling.) On the later magazines, take the unloaded magazine and insert your handy-dandy Glock disassembly tool into the hole in the bottom of the baseplate. Push upwards on the retainer until you have pushed it up and out of the way, and it has

After you've pressed the internal plate out of the way (if it has one), squeeze the tube and slide the baseplate off.

Once you get it past the slide tabs, the baseplate moves easily.

snapped to the side or front of the tube.

Now squeeze the sides of the tube bottom while sliding the baseplate forward off the tube. The older, non-drop-free magazines were sometimes a struggle. The new ones, with their stiffer composition, can be even worse: a three-handed job. You have to squeeze strongly and flex the tube enough to clear the notches. I have seen some shooters who didn't have enough hand strength to accomplish this resort to using pliers or even a vise. Careful! You can crush the tube (not easily, but you can) and then you'll be in the position of explaining to the Glock warranty department just how it was you came to mangle a magazine. They

might replace it. They might not. They aren't in the business of replacing perfectly good magazines just because you got a little heavy-handed in disassembly.

The early magazines lacking the internal plate are simple: Squeeze the sides to release the tabs from the notches in the baseplate, and slide the baseplate off. The softer composition of the early magazines does make the task easier, but it is not always easy.

With the baseplate off, remove the spring and follower. Wipe the dust, crud, grit and powder residue off everything. Refrain from lubricating it. Oil will simply attract dirt and grit, and you'll have to clean it sooner. If you

want to use something to keep your magazine running smoothly, Mag Slick from Krunch Products is one option. As a synthetic and non-tacky lubricant it will smooth the internal parts function without attracting grit.

Reassembly is the infamous reverse order. Install the follower and spring, making sure you get them pointed in the right direction. Press the spring down, put the retainer in place (correct side: the little bump towards the baseplate) and start sliding the baseplate on. You'll need both hands and some dexterity. The trick is sliding the baseplate on, and keeping the retainer pressed out of the way, while you squeeze the rails to clear the little shoulders on the rails for the baseplate to slide fully into place.

After a few times, you'll either get the hang of it or you'll wait until your magazine malfunctions to go through it all over again. It will be a long wait in 9mm. In the G-22 you may have a shorter wait, as I have heard their springs don't last as long as they do in the 9mm magazines. My G-22 magazines and springs are 15 years old at this point, with a few tens of thousands of rounds through them, and are still working fine. But your mileage may vary.

Oh, and if you want to strip and clean your magazines, do them one by one. Don't be in the position of having a jumble of tubes, springs, followers

The Pearce extension does not increase the capacity of this G-26 past the former legal limit. It does make it easier to shoot.

and baseplates on the table, and not remember which ones went together. It may not really matter, but it is asking for trouble to mix parts in magazines that were working before you started. As a friend of mine has been known to comment: It's Murphy's Law, not Murphy's Suggestion.

Other Magazines

In the world of firearms accessories, it isn't unusual to find a bunch of manufacturers making parts, and parts only, for firearms they themselves don't make. The biggest example is the 1911 pistol. There are a dozen people who make magazines for it, and most every manufacturer (three dozen or more) of the pistol offers its own magazine as well. (The pistol manufacturers' magazines almost certainly comes from one of those dozen magazine makers, but since they buy hundreds at a time they can have their name put on them.)

You could buy a 1911, and then buy a lifetime supply of magazines for it, and not have two of any maker's magazines.

Not so the Glock. The reason? Polymer. The other magazine makers are all set up to make magazines out of steel. Whether they fold and weld or extrude the tube, they all make them out of steel. If you're set up to process sheet steel into magazines, making a new model for a different pistol is a matter of buying or making new pressing forms. If you want to make polymer

magazines, you have to invest in a plastic injection moulding or casting machine (no small or cheap thing, by the way) and buy or make moulds for each magazine you plan to offer.

Why not make steel mags for Glocks? A steel magazine tube and the polymer magazine catch on a Glock don't go together well. The weight of a loaded magazine, the spring pressure pushing down on it, and the recoil of shooting all act to tear up the polymer magazine catch in short order when using a steel magazine in a Glock. There are metal and metalized polymer magazine catches, but why install a different mag catch just to use a non-Glock magazine? Also, the steel magazines need a bit more care.

Serious shooters who use steel-tubed magazines, especially the high-capacity ones, fuss over their magazines. You see, steel bends. Bend it far enough, and it takes a set, and it does not spring back from the bend. A serious competitor will measure the width of the feed lips of his or her magazines and note the distance in their log book. Once a month, or just before a big match, they'll measure the width again to make sure the lips haven't been dented or spread from use. If need be, they'll carefully adjust the feed lips.

All of that worry and fussing is wasted on Glock magazines. The lips don't bend, as the polymer coating

offers enough protection to keep them from getting whacked hard enough to bend them. The polymer also acts to support the steel liner against fatigue from constant use. The polymer may peel away from the steel, crack, break off, flake or otherwise become very ugly looking. As far as Glock is concerned, as long as it still feeds reliably (defined by Glock as 100 percent) and locks the slide back when empty, it is not in need of replacement.

The best magazines for your Glock are factory originals. I have never had much luck with the steel aftermarket mags, but I have had good luck with one brand of aftermarket polymer, called Scherer. They made good polymer mags for the Glock, and the ones I have work flawlessly.

Capacity

You'll run into a lot of magazines that will only hold 10 rounds, despite the tube and frame size potentially allowing more. For those of you who have already forgotten, there was a law passed back in 1994 that mandated ten round capacity. Called "the Crime Bill" or "Assault Weapon Ban" or simply "the Mag Ban," the 1994 bill made the new manufacture of "high-capacity feeding devices" (government speak for magazine) against the law. New magazines up to 10 rounds could be made, and the old high-capacity mags could still be owned, bought sold and traded. But no new ones could be made except for law enforcement agencies and the military. And the magazines produced for them had to be specially-marked so there was no doubt as to what they were.

Passage of the law simply caused prices to skyrocket. For a while, original-capacity Glock magazines were being sold for over $150 each. Then a few things happened. One, common sense crept in. A hundred and fifty dollars is a lot of ten-shot mags and

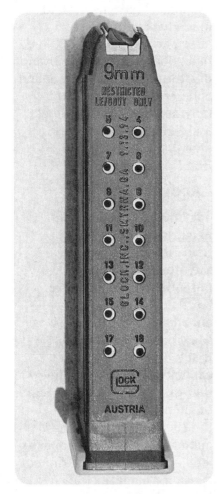

Do you really need high-cap magazines? Perhaps not, but since you can have them, why not?

ammo for practice, and shooters stopped being so eager for hi-caps. Second, the firearms wholesalers started working with police departments to trade up. A wholesaler could offer to trade a bunch of .40 caliber Glocks to a police department in exchange for their 9mm ones and all their magazines. To sweeten the deal, the wholesaler might even throw in night sights or compact versions for full-size guns. Having traded gun for gun, the wholesaler would then sell the guns to retailers with one high-cap magazine each, and offer the extra magazines at a fair but profitable price. After all, his cost in the traded-to-the-police new magazines is less than $15 each, so he can afford to be generous and sell the old ones he gets for a mere $40 wholesale.

So, for those looking for magazines on the used market, that explains why most of the hi-caps you saw from 1994 to 2004 were 9mm. For a while, there was a huge screaming match going on about pre-ban magazines. You see, the law merely stated that magazines produced before September 13, 1994, were legal, and those made after were not but it made no mention of made where. That's right, the argument concerned overseas magazines.

By a strict reading of the law, every magazine on the planet manufactured before September of 1994 was a legal hi-cap magazine. Under the law, Glock could have traded

those magazines from their current owners (with new, hi-cap ones for countries where there wasn't a capacity ban) and then imported those magazines here, and thus had an immense stockpile of legal hi-caps. They could have owned the pistol market in those 10 years.

When those in the government who hadn't previously figured it out found out, they kicked up a fuss and you'd have thought Glock and all the other importers were trying to import nuclear weapons or something. The end result was that the import paperwork never left the desk of whoever was supposed to

With luck, we won't have any more hi-cap bans and "LEO" markings such as this will simply be collectors' curiosities.

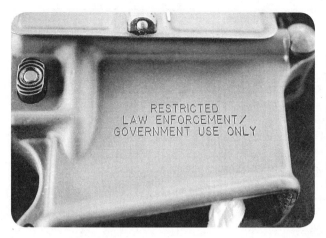

Magazines weren't the only article restricted by the Assault Weapons Ban of 1994. This isn't even a select-fire rifle!

approve the transfer. Well, it was a good try. Now it is all moot, as the law has expired.

One wag has suggested that we not adopt the terminology of the enemy, and thus we shouldn't be calling the 17-round G-17 magazines "high-capacity" magazines. They should be called "standard-capacity" magazines or "normal capacity and the 10-round ones should be "under-capacity" magazines. While I appreciate a good tongue-in-cheek joke, the government back then had defined them as "high-capacity" and any attempt at changing the terminology will probably get you branded as some sort of loony curmudgeon.

Some states still have a hi-cap bans on their books. The poor unfortunate souls who happen to reside in these places cannot get new hi-caps and cannot even buy old ones unless they had bought them before the state law was passed.

What to do now? Buy lots of hi-cap magazines, and get involved in politics to keep future bans from happening.

Join groups, donate money, and send an occasional letter to your representative.

New Tubes for Old

In the old days, you saw tubes offered in magazines and parts catalogs offered as replacement magazines. Somehow, a tiny spark of rational thought had crept into the bill that became the Assault Weapons Ban of 1994. While new magazines were banned, old ones were still legal to buy, sell and trade. And existing ones could be repaired or replaced. Those tubes you saw for sale were to repair or replace existing magazines. It was against the law to use them to build a new magazine. The supply of replacement tubes for Glock pistols had not been as great as that for other pistols due to design. If you make magazines for, say, a 1911, you make them by bending sheet metal. To make some other design you modify the tooling that bends the sheet steel and make the new design.

To make Glock magazines, you need the sheet metal

bending equipment to make the liners, but you also need the injection moulding equipment to finish the job. A much bigger investment.

The current maker of replacement tubes is Scherer. I have had good luck with their magazines. They are lined polymer and they work. You can also buy complete magazines now that the hi-cap law has sunset. You probably should lay in a supply of spare parts, if for no other reason than that you might lose or break some while cleaning. And you never know, if some sort of law ever passes again, you may find those spare parts very useful.

If your magazines break or fail to work, you can send them back to Glock. However, be aware that they will not replace magazines that are out-of-spec due to normal wear-and-tear or that have obviously been abused. What you're likely to get is one of three answers: 1) your magazines are used-up, it isn't Glock's fault, and you need to buy new ones; 2) your magazines work, and despite their shabby appearance they meet the Glock performance specs so you'll have to pay for shipping them back; or 3) they are worn-out and cannot be repaired, and how many new ones do you wish to buy?

Do you need hi-caps?

Ah, that's the question, isn't it? Yes, for some applications you sure do. For self-defense, law enforcement, and military applications, having a hi-cap mag is very

A QUESTION OF EXTENSION

The question always comes up, "How much does an extension increase capacity?" In order to answer that question at least partly, I used two of my own magazines as test subjects. One is a 9mm for a G-17, the other a .40 for a G-22. The test was simple: load them to maximum capacity with each of the extensions installed, and see if I could seat the magazine.

Since each round decreases the available space in a magazine by a constant value, why would seating be a problem? It is possible, if the variables stack up just right, to get the last round into a magazine without any extra space to compress the stack under the slide. You see, the rounds have to rise up into the slide's path. That means when the slide is fully forward it rests on top of and presses down the stack of rounds and magazine spring. If the stack doesn't have any extra travel left, you can load the magazine with X number of rounds but can't get it seated no matter how hard you try. In such a case, that particular magazine has a capacity of "X minus one" and you must take care when loading it. Otherwise you could load it up, forget about stripping off the top round, and find in the middle of a match that you can't get that magazine seated no matter how hard you hit it.

The situation is one that many AR-15 shooters are familiar with. It is possible to stuff magazines with one too many rounds. Some 20-round magazines will "hold" 21 rounds, and 30s will "hold" 31. I use quotation marks because while you can get 31 rounds in (as an example) and even get the magazine to seat (only with the bolt locked open), firing the first round will create a malfunction as the friction is too great for the bolt to overcome.

So I loaded the two magazines with each extension to as many as it would hold, then seated and fired the first round. I then pulled out the magazine and stuffed it full again. And then fired one round, repeating until I had fired each magazine 10 times fully-loaded. Why do all this to just one magazine of each? Magazines can vary in their capacity. I know, I know, they are industrial products created to be as identical to each other as possible. In the single-stack world, it isn't a problem. If you buy a truckload of Chip McCormick eight-round 1911 magazines (just as an example) you will die of boredom loading each to check capacity. They will all hold eight. No more, no less.

However, in hi-cap magazines, things are different. Otherwise identical tubes can hold a round more or less than other tubes. (Smaller rounds, especially the nines, and the rounds are double-stacked) If I used one extension on one tube and another extension on a different tube and came up with different capacities, I'd have to swap and try again. Better to simply do the check to one particular magazine in each capacity and see what happens. The resulting capacities are as follows:

9mm
Taylor Freelance +4: 23
Arredondo: 23
Grams: 23
Dawson: 22

.40
Taylor Freelance +4: 20
Arredondo: 20
Grams: 19
Dawson: 20

comforting. Were I to be in the position of going through doorways on a SWAT team for a living, or riding a helicopter on the payroll of the Army or Marine Corps, I'd sure feel a lot happier with more than 10 shots per in my magazines. (I'd also be comforted by the presence of lots of other firepower carried by those riding along with me.)

However, there has been a counter-current in regard to demand. In the 1990s, a large number of states changed their CCW laws to Shall-Issue from May (or Never) Issue. Carrying a full-sized gun concealed isn't easy. It is harder still if you are average or smaller in size. I'm 6'4" and 205 pounds, and I used to carry a full-sized 1911 all day. At the first opportunity I switched to a Light Weight Commander. When I got my hands on my first compact Glock, it was smaller and lighter still. Many other shooters who have CCWs have figured the same thing

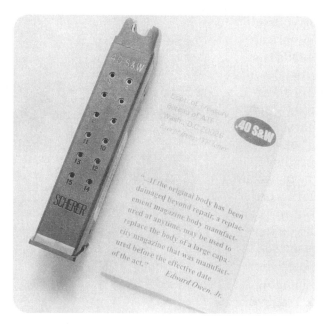

Scherer makes replacement tubes and assembled magazines. They're good, although snobs might prefer Glock-made mags.

out. If you're going to carry a compact pistol, you aren't going to get 17 shots anyway. Since you can reload quickly, 10 is probably enough.

As an unintended consequence of the switch from 1994 to 2004 to 10-shot mags and compact carry guns, interest in the big calibers is greater than ever. After all, if you're going to be carrying only 10 shots, they might as well be the biggest 10 you

can wrestle into the gun. Ten shots of .40 or .45 are a lot more comforting than 10 shots of 9mm. With the new magazines, the calculation gets a lot more interesting. Eight or 10 .45 bullets, vs. 15 9mm? And if those 9mms are +P or +P+?

In many competitions, you don't need more than 10, then or now. In GSSF competition and in USPSA Limited-10 or Production Division, or IDPA matches you can't have more than 10 rounds in a magazine. In The Steel Challenge, if you need more than 10 you're losing in your class. (Some might argue if you need more than five you're losing, but we won't go there.)

But in some competitions, more than 10 is not just nice but a must. If you're shooting bowling pins and are in the 9-pin category, 10-shot mags are a definite handicap. Shooting Open or Limited in a USPSA match with 10-shot magazines is a sure way to end up

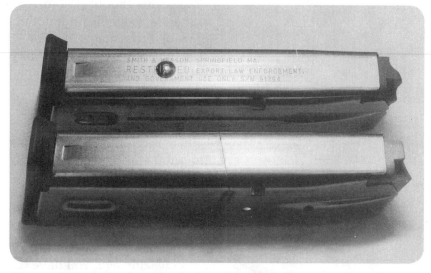

All manufacturers had to comply with the 1994 AWB, not just Glock.

losing. And limiting yourself to 10 shots at the American Handgunner Shoot-Offs is s sure way to lose crucial bouts in Open or Stock Auto. We now have the option, which we didn't for 10 years.

As I mentioned before, using a non-drop original magazine as a carry magazine makes sense if you're worried about dropping your magazine inadvertently. If all you have are drop-free magazines, a bit of paper tape can keep the magazine in and still allow you to do a reload. Yes, I've heard people argue that 17 is enough, and expecting to still be in the fight and reloading after emptying one magazine is beyond optimistic.

My view on reloads is that I'm not as worried about running out as I am about other problems. If you have only one magazine, and anything, anything at all happens to that mag, you're done for. Falling, having

The Pearce extension on a G-36 bumps capacity from six to seven shots of .45 ACP and gives your (or at least my) little finger a place to rest.

the gun or holster struck, whacking the baseplate on a door frame during the start of your fracas – oh, many things can render the magazine in your pistol inoperative. A spare magazine makes sense. If anything, the spare should be bigger than the one in the gun, not the same size or

smaller. Packing and keeping concealed a magazine is a lot easier than concealing a pistol.

Non-Hi-Cap Baseplates

Even in the polymer world of Glocks, there is a perceived need for metal. One way to get empty or partially-empty magazines to eject cleanly is to increase their weight. Brass magazine pads do that quite nicely. The CPMi Glock brass baseplate for a G-20/21 weighs 1220 grains (about .174 lb.) and adds a significant amount of weight to a magazine. For someone who wants durability without too much extra weight, CPMi's aluminum baseplates will keep your magazine togethe, and add only a fraction of an ounce to the total empty weight of 2.75 ounces for a G-17 magazine.

The only drawback to getting aftermarket baseplates, whether they increase capacity or not, is magazine age. You have to know what version magazine

You can use hi-caps in smaller guns. This G-27 with a G-22 mag and Grams extension holds 20 rounds of .40 ammo.

This G-30 .45 magazine already holds 10 rounds.

For USPSA/IPSC Production Division competition, this G-19 and its 10-shot magazines are very competitive. And they make a great carry package, too.

you have in order for the maker to get you just the right baseplate. (It goes without saying you're going to tell him model and caliber.)

On the other hand, if you want a larger pad for more-certain insertion but don't want to increase capacity and aren't too keen on adding metal to your polymer pistol, then Arredondo has the answer for you. (They have the answer even if you don't have an aversion to using metal accessories.) The Arredondo standard basepad fits both 10-shot and high cap magazines and doesn't add any capacity while doing so. The basepad is in two parts and uses the standard spring and follower. Disassemble your Glock magazine and set aside the factory baseplate and locking plate. Slide the upper half of the Arredondo

pad over the top of the mag and press it down to the bottom. Press the bottom half over the magazine spring and hook the fronts of the two halves together. Now compress the rear ends toward each other. You may find using the included disassembly tool is an aid to getting the tab on the assembly compressed so the two halves can click together.

Once clicked, they will stay together until you use the disassembly tool. To take them apart, use the tool to compress the rear tab and unlock the halves. Pivot the halves apart, and slide the upper off the tube.

Increasing Capacity

There are a few ways to increase capacity. One is to go

The CPMI extensions can add a round or two, or not, depending on which one you get. They are frame-specific, so get the ones that will fit your Glock.

out and buy higher-capacity magazines. The other is to increase the capacity of the magazine you have.

Before we go any further, I would be remiss if I didn't tell you the following: DO NOT put any of the capacity-increasing gizmos we will be discussing onto a post-ban 10-shot magazine if you live in some place like California or New Jersey. Even if it works, it is a violation of state law, a felony, and subject to stiff fines and severe prison sentences. Back during the federal ban I almost bolted for the door the first time someone showed me how they had wrestled a +2 basepad onto a 10-shot magazine. Doing so in some states now is the same thing, differing only in the uniforms of the guys busting down your door.

The first of the capacity-increasing accessories were the Glock +2 baseplates. A pyramid-shaped hollow baseplate, the +2s simply replaced the existing flat baseplate and added two more shots to a magazine's capacity. (That is, two more 9mms and one more .40. They were

Clockwise from upper left: a Dawson; an Arredondo; an Arredondo 10-shot-only; a Grams; and a Taylor Freelance.

never made for 10mm or .45.) They fell out of favor for a few reasons. One, they only added two shots. Two, they came off. If shooters were going to fuss over a new baseplate and add more shots, they wanted more than just one or two; they wanted as many more as possible. Now, if what you want is only an extra round or two, with minimum extra bulk, then the CPMi hollow Glock pads work for you. They add a round or two while adding less than half an inch to the overall length of your magazine. And they won't come off accidentally.

Manufacturers of competition replacement baseplates made them as long as the rules (if any) for those competitions allowed. Thus, capacity jumped up to +4, +6 and +8. Also, as I mentioned, the original +2 baseplates suffered an embarrassing problem: they came off. With the weight of the ammo, and the tension of the spring, the baseplate was under a lot of stress. The pyramid shape allowed for more leverage if something whacked the Glock +2. It isn't at all uncommon

for police officers to whack their holstered gun against door frames, car doors and frames, vending machines and the like. The +2's had a tendency to pop off and spew the spring, follower and ammunition all over the floor or ground.

I'm not picking on police officers when I bring things like this up. They were the first ones to go into Glocks big, and you learn a whole lot of interesting things when you issue a thousand of anything to people who wear them all day and keep records.

If you have a +2 extension that has never come off of one of your magazines, great. Don't swap it to another tube. I've seen competitors at matches with duct tape applied to keep their +2s on. (Yes, it is an ugly sight. No, I don't know why they insist on using gray duct tape instead of using something more suitable like black.)

The higher-capacity baseplates like the Taylor Freelance, Arredondo, Grams and Dawson use a more secure method of attachment than the factory +2 arrangement and are not prone to sudden disassembly. The first three feature plastic machinings or castings, while the Dawson is machined out of aluminum and anodized in an array of colors.

The Taylor +4 and +8 extensions (actually +5 and +9 9mm rounds) use an aluminum plate they call the Fort Knox retainer, one that is bolted onto the back of the extension with a pair of cap screws. You couldn't knock it off with a ball peen hammer. Machined from blocks of delrin, they add very little to a mag's weight.

The Taylor Freelance isn't caliber-specific, as it uses the factory follower. But you will have to specify if you are using a 9mm/.40 tube or a 10mm/.45 tube. Also, tell them if it is an original or drop-free tube.

To install a Taylor Freelance, disassemble your magazine and set aside the baseplate, inner place and spring. Place the follower on the new spring, and insert into the magazine tube. Unscrew the locking screws from the Freelance extension and set the screws and retainer aside for the moment. Slide the bottom of the spring into the Freelance extension. Line the spring up so one of the forward coils is at the front of the tube, and wriggle the extension onto the mag tube rails. Once it is in place, screw the Fort Knox locking plate down. Disassembly is the traditional "reverse order."

The Arredondo extension uses an upper moulded collar and a clip-on bottom and comes with a new spring and a disassembly tool. As it does not replace the follower, you need only specify if it is a 9mm/.40 tube or a 10mm/.45, and whether or not it is a drop-free.

To install, disassemble your magazine and set aside the baseplate, inner place

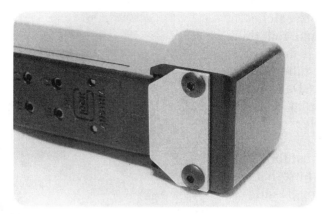

The Taylor Freelance Fort Knox retainer. This puppy isn't coming off accidentally.

and spring. Place the Glock follower onto the Arredondo spring provided in the kit. Slide the upper collar over the magazine. It will stop on the bottom lip of the magazine tube. Insert the follower and spring. Then press the Arredondo baseplate onto the extension, compressing the spring between them. Once both sideclips have locked into place, you're done.

To disassemble, use the provided tool to simultaneously press and unlock the sideclips. (Unload the magazine first, and keep your hand over the baseplate, as the spring will try to shoot it off the end of the tube.)

The Grams uses a pair of interlocking delrin parts that are held together by a steel "U" clip that passes through them. Disassemble your magazine. Replace the old spring with the new, longer spring and Grams follower. The Grams magazine extensions are caliber-specific, so you'll have to order the ones you need. You won't be able to swap them back and forth between 9mm and .40 unless you're willing to use the factory follower.

Slide the upper assembly down over the mag tube until it rests against the bottom lips. Use the Grams baseplate to compress the spring, and once nestled together, press the stainless U clip through to secure the assembly. Again, it's a bank-vault solid assembly that won't come apart when you drop it. To disassemble, pry the U clip out of the closed position, and pull it free of the assembly. Once free, the baseplate will try to shoot off, so restrain it.

The Dawson lives up to its nickname, "Team Awesome." It is a beautifully machined piece of aluminum with a sliding door as the retaining latch. Dawson machines a dovetail on the side of the baseplate and then machines and fits a door/latch that rides on the dovetail. The best part (besides the anodized colors)? The door has a retaining pin so it doesn't come off the baseplate.

To install, strip your magazine and place the factory follower on the Dawson replacement spring. Insert follower and spring into the magazine and compress it with the Dawson baseplate.

Tilt the baseplate to catch it on the rightside tube rail, then tilt it back until it is flush with the bottom of the tube. Slide the door shut. The Dawson is so trick and cool that I know competitive shooters who switched all their magazines over to Dawsons just for the look. It didn't hurt that they are hell for tough and guaranteed.

For competition, any of these is a hot ticket. The +4 is still short enough to stay under the Limited equipment rules of USPSA, and the +8 stays within the Open length restrictions. A G-17 with scope and compensator, fed a magazines with a +8 on it, can be stoked with 27 rounds of 9x21 ammo, keeping up with the 1911 hi-cap frames (17, plus nine, plus the one chambered.)

Beven Grams in particular extolls his extension as being "impact resistant." Thinking about it, I recall that every range I've been to West of the Rockies (Beven Grams is based in California) has range bays composed of river rock and parking lot gravel. (Here in Michigan we have sand. Sand, sand, and clay. In the rain they turn to mud.) I'm assured by the shooters in the Pacific Northwest that they have lots of slick mud. (In the rain, they use straw to cover the paths, leading their ranges to end up being composed of paths of stucco until the straw wears out or sinks out of sight. "Paths of Stucco." Sounds like the title of a romance novel.)

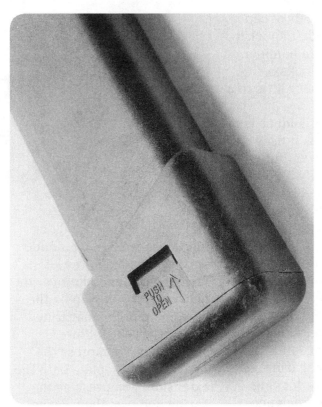

The Arredondo extension is easy to assemble, requires their tool to disassemble, and works like a champ. Tough, too.

While thinking this over, I could feel a test protocol forming in the back of my mind. Back when I was getting my degree, we used to play a game between classes called "Stopper Hockey." Back then, chemistry students had to form their own glass for reactant vessels, and many vessel designs required rubber stoppers. The bigger ones were the size of a hockey puck, so we'd kick them down the aisles between the chem benches. I decided to play a little "magazine hockey" as well as some other cruel abuses of fine pistol magazines.

I first borrowed seven magazines from a local law enforcement officer (he too wanted to know The Truth) and we met at the range. I borrowed from him four

9mm and three .40s, all full-size, hi-cap, LEO-Restricted magazines. (The test was first done during the Assault Weapons Ban.) We figured if we trashed the magazines he could always turn them back in to the departmental armorer for new ones. And the knowledge would be worth it. I also installed the Arredondo no-cap extension on one of my 10-shot Glock magazines.

What I didn't do was conduct the tests with a +2 baseplate. I already knew what the outcome would be and didn't feel like chasing magazine components around the range.

I installed one of each of the three (Taylor Freelance, Arredondo and Grams) hi-cap extensions on the 9mms and one each on the .40s. The Dawson I installed on a 9mm

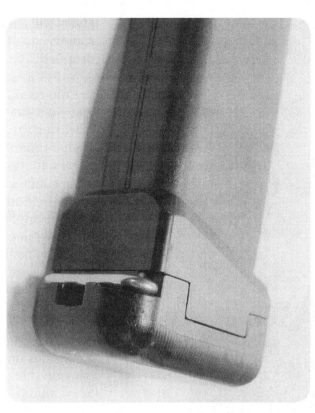

The Grams extension is machined delrin, tougher than a two-dollar steak, and easy to take apart and clean (if you ever need to).

tube. The installation went smoothly, and there were no problems in the few minutes it took to rebuild the eight magazines.

Before I describe the tests, let me tell you that I almost chickened out when it came to the Dawson extension. After all, it was aluminum. It wasn't going to break under anything I could come up with that would be a reasonable magazine test. But it was going to get gouged and scarred. It would look ugly when I was done. Did I want to do that to such an attractive manufactured object? Adding to my angst was the Dawson Guarantee. I was assured by Tom Hall at Dawson that they would replace any extension that I or anyone else was unsatisfied with. (I must admit that a little voice in the back of my head suggested abusing the extension and then sending it in for a pretty replacement. I slapped it down.) In the end, I figured that ugly was worth the knowledge.

Let the abuse begin!

The Tests

The Sweeney "I can't believe he's doing that!" test regime started out with some dropping. Our latest club range improvement uncovered some large rocks that we've hauled to the side. (There's one we dug up that's the size of a Yugo. It has about the same performance as a Yugo, without the smoke.)

I dragged a chair over and sat there, dropping the magazines, baseplate hitting the rock, for a few minutes. Nothing broke or fell off. Then I spent a few minutes standing over the rock, dropping magazines, picking them up, and dropping them again. Still no problem.

Time to up the ante. I loaded the magazines and started over. No breakage. What surprised me was how rarely rounds launched themselves from the magazines when dropped. Some magazine

This scarred old Dawson still works like a champ.

Sand and gravel didn't cause any of the extensions to falter.

The poor, abused magazines, hiding in their nest, hoping the author has run out of ideas.

Dropping magazines on rocks is bound to attract attention. But if you've got to know, you've got to know.

styles will launch one or many rounds each time they are dropped. I've seen dropped hi-cap 1911 mags that would snap the top round 180 degrees, leaving it rim forward. (Clearing the malfunction such a round creates can take a few minutes.) I've seen Colt 9mm submachine gun mags spew their entire contents when dropped. The Glock mags did fine.

Obviously, the rock problem wasn't much of one for the extensions and I was getting nowhere fast. I then went to the nearby range and proceeded to drop the magazines onto a steel plate lying on the ground. After a few minutes, I came to the realization that I simply wasn't going to uncover any problems. To soothe my disappointment I fired the rounds that were in the magazines, and was not at all disappointed. They all worked.

I set up a pair of steel drums adjacent to the lumber retaining wall of the enclosed range and proceeded to drop each empty magazine into the sand and kick it through the "goalpost." After a few attempts with each magazine I started over, "dribbling" each round with a series of kicks, then driving each through the "goal", impacting the lumber wall with a sharp smack.

On inspection, the magazines appeared fine. The extensions were intact and securely attached, and the feed lips of the magazines were unharmed. I wiped the exterior sand off with my hands, loaded them and fired the rounds, again without failure.

Time to get serious. I loaded the magazines to start over. On the first kick, I left the magazines where they were and went back to the truck. Deliberately kicking a loaded magazine with running shoes on is not a good idea. As a matter of fact, it hurts. I put on a pair of boots and went back to kicking. After a good aerobic exercise session, I wiped as much of the sand off on my trousers that I could and got to shooting. Does anyone care to guess how many failures I had? All of you who bet against "none" owe your shooting buddies a soft drink. That's right, none. At this point, having fired enough practice ammo and photographs for the day, I packed up and went home.

Once I'd done this, Robin Taylor, the editor of *Front Sight* magazine, asked me a sneaky question: "Got any aerosol gun cleaners?" Sigh. And just what does a degreasing/ gun scrubbing aerosol do to the plastic composition of the various extensions? Unfortunately, I had a bunch of cleaners on hand and a limited supply of extensions. I could not test all extensions with all chemicals. On the good side, I was positive that the makers of the extensions went to some trouble to find polymers that would shrug off common firearms cleaning chemicals. (After all, they are going to be gun parts, right?) And, we all know what

to expect from the Dawson extension, right? Any chemical cleaner that will attack the aluminum of his extension is something that will probably dissolve both the Glock magazine tube and you in the same few seconds. What you can buy over the counter won't have any effect.

So I dragged out the cleaners and installed the slightly scuffed extensions on my own magazines. Rather than kick the magazines I simply hosed the extensions and let them sit wet with the cleaner to dry in the warm air of the springtime breeze at the range. Once they'd been through the bath three times I proceeded to repeat the drop test. And to no great surprise, none of them failed. The pattern of what appears discoloration is simply the pattern of the cleaners as they evaporated off the plastic. The various extensions were not actually

discolored, as wiping them with a clean cloth brought them back to their original (now scarred) appearance.

So I now have a bunch of really high-capacity Glock magazines for use in competition. I'm particularly fond of the Dawson extension, both in its design and this one's current scarred condition. Anyone who looks at the scuffs and gouges on it has to figure that I'm some sort of lunatic who will do anything in practice or at a match in order to gain a few extra points or a second off my time. Looking at the Dawson they have to wonder if winning would be worth the effort of beating me. Let them wonder.

Mag Catch Notch

Under hard use, the bottom of the notch on the magazine tube will get peened. The usual cause is slamming

While the magazines may last forever, the mag catch doesn't, if you take it out all the time. This is the mag catch from the training gun I used in the Glock armorer's course. Looks like a squirrel's been at it.

the magazine into the frame when the slide is locked back. The magazine rides up past the catch, and the bottom of the notch bangs against the bottom of the catch. If the peened area causes a problem fitting it into the gun, you can use an exacto knife to cut away the excess. If the magazine otherwise locks in place and functions as designed, Glock will not replace it just from peening.

Magazine Springs and Followers

Springs will always be with us. If you are going to go and do some really high-volume practice or competition, you should invest in spare magazine springs.

The problem isn't leaving them loaded but in using them. The repeated cycling is what wears out a magazine, not leaving it stressed. (At least not good ones.) I've had good luck for a long time with Wolff springs and recently with ISMI springs. I've been putting tens of thousands of rounds through an ISMI recoil spring for a 1911 that has not showed significant compression set yet.

Swapping magazine springs is simplicity itself. Disassemble the magazine, pry the old spring off the follower, insert the new spring in the same orientation, then reassemble. The trick lies in knowing when to replace your spring. You could just do it every few years. After all,

at less than $10 per spring, if you replace them once every couple of years, you're still spending less on springs than you are on primers for reloading the ammo you shot in those same magazines. And springs don't cost anywhere near $10 each. The current Glock armorers catalog lists them at $3 each, with the usual shipping and handling charges.

At three bucks each, you should simply buy two spares for every magazine you own, and a couple of followers per caliber to round out the order. If you have magazine extensions on your tubes for competition use, you can get replacement springs from the makers of the extensions, or oversized springs from ISMI or Wolff and cut them to proper length. When cutting, don't go by overall length (the old ones may be shortened from use); rather, count the coils. The Dawson spring (which simply happens to be the one at hand as I type this) has 11 coils. So, when trimming a new, over-sized spring, cut it with sidecutters to 11 coils and bend the bottom coil to match the original.

The classic symptom of weak springs in 1911 pistols is when the otherwise reliable pistol stops locking open when the magazine is empty. That is also what Glock tells us in the armorer's course: if it locks back, it is bad. If it doesn't, it is fine. The dynamics of the Glock are slightly different, and what you'll likely see are feeding problems.

If you start getting rounds trapped under the slide and against the feed ramp, your spring is getting tired. The magazine extension baseplates come with their own, longer, springs. These springs have to lift an even heavier stack of rounds when you shoot. If you are going to use extended magazines in competition, invest in a set of spare springs and keep them with you.

As for the followers, you will be hard-pressed to wear them out. It is common for other pistols to have aftermarket followers that offer higher capacity. On some designs, changing the follower gets you one more round. No so the Glock. Can you wear out a follower? Theoretically, yes. I haven't seen one yet, but there has to be at least one high-mileage follower out there in constant use in a police training range that is ready to quit. They last so long that no one has been able to create a market for replacement followers, as there is in the 1911 world.

Abuse, however, is a different case. Sergeant Armando Valdes of the Miami PD described to me a failure he saw with their Glocks. It seems that some officers were not content to merely let their magazines fall to the ground during qualification or training. They would actually hurl the magazine down. "I saw them throw them down. Ripped out and thrown." He shook his head. "Gravity works. Why not just let go and let them drop?" The magazines would eventually break the tab on the follower that locked the slide back when empty. A new follower solved the problem. I don't know what he did about the magazine tossing.

Really Hi-Cap

For a while, you could buy Glock magazines up to 33 rounds in capacity. Made by Scherer and Glock (and probably others, but I haven't seen them) the ones I tried all worked fine. While the Sherer magazines were offered on the open market, the Glock 33-round mags were strictly law-enforcement only. Not that there was a law against them (at least not until 1994-2004); Glock just felt they were only suitable for LEO use and sold them only to departments. We can now buy them with wild abandon, at least the Scherer magazines. Glocks are still

controlled by Glock. Do you need them? As much as I hate to say it, probably not. They are quite large, bulky, and too long to pass muster for USPSA competition. But they are fun.

Magazine Reliability

All the old tricks for getting magazines to feed reliably went out the window when Glock mags hit the scene. In the old days (and even today for some magazines) we'd polish the inside, measure and bend or adjust the feed lips, deburr the inside of the tube and the follower, lube or coat the inside with some sort of non-sticky lubricant, and install extra-power magazine springs. Some magazines even came in for bending, sanding and polishing the exterior as well. I still remember the maker of my Caspian hi-caps squeezing the tube in a vise and then whacking it with a rawhide mallet to get the tube straight

enough to drop free. Definitely something the faint at heart should not watch being done.

The only one of those that applies to Glock magazines is installing an extra power or new spring. That and keeping your magazine clean is about all you can or need do to keep your magazine working 100 percent of the time.

If you shoot at a range composed mostly of sand, your magazines will get gritty after being dropped a few times. At matches, you'll see competitors pumping brushes in and out of their magazines to keep them reasonably clean during the match. When they get home they'll strip and clean their magazines. You should, too.

Inspect the follower for ground-up bits of polymer that might bind it. Instead of a file, use a sharp knife to trim the bits off, like clipping stray threads from your clothes.

Sometimes when installing the capacity

The Glock LEO 33-shot hi-cap built for the G-18.

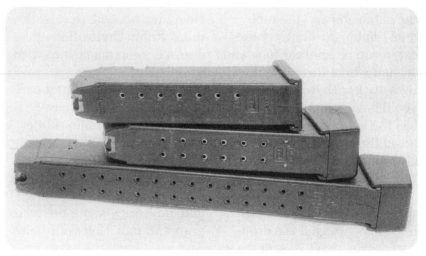

If you want the biggest, the 2- and 33-round magazines, the only way is to get them from Scherer. Glock sells their "big stick" mags only to police departments.

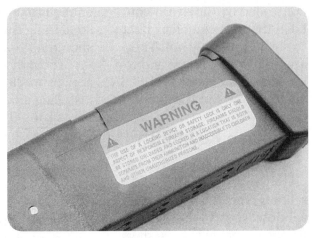

Just when you thought the warning labels were maxed out, here's another one.

Marking Your Magazines

At many matches, you'll go dashing through each stage, leaving a trail of dust, empty brass and expended magazines behind you. Especially if you're shooting with 10-shot magazines in Production Division and going through a large field course in a USPSA match.

Forty or 50 rounds later (I've heard of stages as big as 130 rounds!) you'll have your half-dozen magazines scattered behind you. You want to be sure and get all yours back.

So mark your mags. The easy way is to disassemble them and then degrease the baseplates. Once clean and dry, give them a coat of spray paint. No, it won't stick very well, nothing will, at least not to Glock parts. But enough will stick that you can tell which ones are yours.

The paint job can be renewed as needed and changed if too many others start using that color. You should also number your magazines. If you get into the habit of numbering them and then using them in numerical order (#1 to start, reload to #2, reload to #3, etc.) you can track down malfunctions. If you have an intermittent problem, but it always happens to #3, you can then test your adjustments on #3. By narrowing the problem to a single magazine you make your problem much less of one. If, on the other hand, you

extension, you'll run into a small problem: you don't get any increased capacity. When Glock designed their magazines, they weren't concerned with aftermarket capacity-increasing baseplates. (They probably view them as yet another point that proves just how strange the American shooters can be.) The dimensions of the bottom interior of the Glock magazine tubes are kept within tolerances that allow all Glock parts to fit and work. If your magazine doesn't allow the full increase, the insides of the extension and the tube aren't lining up. First, try the extension on another tube and see if it works there. If it does, then stick with it. If not, then you'll have to find the side that has the ledge and carefully bevel the corner there so the follower can ride down into the extension for full capacity.

If you have a magazine that sticks and doesn't drop free even though it is a drop-free design, don't go sanding it. While sanding is an accepted method of getting a steel magazine to gain clearance, the polymer of the Glock magazine won't sand. You simply kick up a fuzzy surface of fiber edges (sort of like velcro in appearance) and end up making your magazine even bigger and more of a problem.

What to do if a drop-free sticks? One solution I've heard of but never tried (I haven't had a drop-free stick on me) is to insert the offending magazine backwards into the gun overnight. By stuffing it partway (it won't fit far) front-to-back you're either squishing the magazine or stretching the frame and creating the clearance needed. (If it works, thank Robin Taylor. If it doesn't, swap magazines with someone else.)

One solution offered early in the Glock existence was to use an automobile rubber shine product to slick up your magazines. That one I never understood. First, if it is slick enough to go easily into the gun, how are you supposed to grab it to pull it off your belt? And what happens when your gooped-up magazine hits the dirt, sand, mud or gravel of the range floor?

A Glock LEO orange training baseplate.

One advantage to the orange baseplates is the ease with which you can mark them with a felt-tip pen. Too bad they're Law Enforcement Only.

have an intermittent problem but it never seems to happen to the same magazine twice in a row, then you still have a useful bit of information: the source is probably not your magazines.

Number your magazines with press-on numerals. Again, they won't stick for very long, but you aren't looking for a forever solution. You just want something that will stay on well enough to let you know which ones are which and that can be easily renewed when it falls off.

One trick I use on other magazines that doesn't last nearly as long on Glock magazines is to degrease the mag, stick the number on, then give a light overspray of clear polyurethane. The degreased surface lets the numeral stick. The polyurethane seals the edges of the adhesive on the numeral. Unfortunately, while the method works for months of use on steel magazines, the

Glock tubes flex enough that the numerals come off in a few range sessions. The lack of adhesion to plastic/polymer is one reason some shooters use aluminum basepads for their magazines. Aluminum holds paint, and the stick-on lettering adheres well enough (especially with the poly overspray) that you can get months of use out of them before having to scrub and reapply.

One of the shooters at our club uses a label making machine, the kind that spits out a strip of adhesive-backed plastic label material. He prints up his name and the magazine number and applies it to the side of his magazines. When they get too tired or scarred he scrapes them off and applies new ones.

Or you can use a paint pencil, a metal tube that works like a felt-tip pen, but dispensing paint. The paint pen lets you write on surfaces and thus number them.

Glock makes bright

orange baseplates for use in law enforcement training. By marking training-use only magazines with orange baseplates, a department can ensure that the heavy use and occasional abuse those magazine receive won't be cause problems on the street. The training mags get the dropping and kicking, and the heavy exposure to dust, mud and rain. Meanwhile the duty mags are tested, then left loaded in their pouches, protected. The bad news? The orange baseplates are LEO-only, and not for sale to the general public.

Could you paint your baseplates? (The Glock orange ones are colored by the use of dyes in the mixed polymer.) Yes. If you find a paint that sticks and stands up to range use, let me know, will you?

Magazine Funnels

Having reliable magazines is just part of the equation. Getting them into the gun as quickly as possible is the other part. While the basic design of any hi-cap magazine/pistol makes reloading easier than single stacks, funnels help. The tapered shape of the top of the magazine, and the larger than that top entrance in the frame, makes getting Glock magazines (and other hi-caps) into the frame a pretty smooth operation. But you can always make things better. If the magazine opening is larger, or larger and tapered, then getting the magazine in is even faster. And in some matches, faster is better.

The smallest "funnel" I have on hand is from Scherer. A simple plastic wedge that fits into the hollow rear of the frame, it helps guide magazines into place. Another simple method that also adds weight is the Seattle Slug from Taylor Freelance.

The Seattle Slug comes in two styles, brass and aluminum. The aluminum is light, and doesn't add much weight, but the brass adds a significant amount of weight to the Glock. Yes, light weight is one of the virtues of the Glock, but what is a virtue when you're carrying all day can be a liability when you're shooting in competition. The extra weight of the Seattle Slug helps dampen recoil, and the wedge lower portion guides your magazine on reloads.

The small Scherer mag funnel, inserted in the hollow of the frame.

In talking with Robin Taylor I found another use for the Seattle Slug. It seems police officers in his area have started using it, not to hit suspects with (very bad idea, by the way) and not just as an aid to speed-reloading. They plan to have it on their pistol as a tool to break car side windows. An officer in their area bought one right after he had to break a car window, and in the process of using his Glock sans Seattle Slug his magazine came out. The hard point of the Slug breaks windows and leaves the magazine intact.

For some competitions, bigger is better. (And for some competitions, no changes are allowed.) For the bigger ones, you need to go to something like the Grams or Arredondo magazine funnel. They circle the mag well, offering a funnel on the complete circumference of the frame.

The Grams comes in tungsten for a real addition

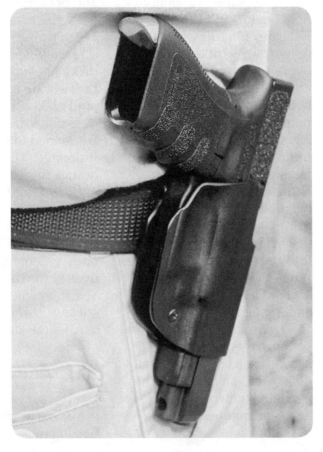

The Seattle Slug in a G-34 for competition.

The Seattle Slug locked into the frame. The shipped polish is so good you can see my hands reflected when I took the photo.

of weight. For real speed, Dawson offers their Ice funnel. The body of the Ice funnel is aluminum but the inner face, where your magazine impacts it when guiding, is a slick polymer. It's a big hole you can't miss, and a slick surface that your magazine can slide over as you do your high-speed reload? How can life get better?

Reloading Methods

Not all ways of getting more ammo into your Glock are the same. And some will be required skills in some competitions.

Reloads fall into two categories with two approaches in each. The two methods are Competition/ Speed reload, and Tactical/ Retention reload. In all methods, you keep the gun high enough that you can watch what you're doing and still keep an eye out for

trouble. You don't want to be reloading down at belt level, with your eyes off the world around you.

The speed load is the one we've all seen and marveled at. Properly done, you hardly have time to realize that the

shooter has reloaded. Properly done, the down time between shots can be as small as a second flat. The competition load goes like this:

When the competitor decides he (or she) needs more ammo, he lets go with the off hand and begins reaching for the next magazine. As he reaches, and if his hand is small enough to require it, he shifts the gun slightly and pushes the magazine release button. As the first magazine falls free, he is already grasping the next one. Before the magazine hits the ground, the new magazine is off the belt, inserted and slammed home.

The variant of the speed load used in law enforcement has one difference: Here, the magazine button isn't pushed until the shooter has ALREADY grabbed the

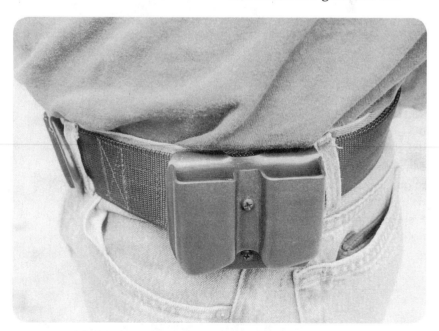

If you're going to carry or compete with a Glock, you have to carry spare magazines somehow. A belt holder is so much more convenient than your pockets.

next magazine. A small detail but an important one. In the rough-and-tumble of an actual fight (as opposed to a competition) you can lose magazines. It would be a real shame to dump your only magazine, to then find out your spares have fallen and can't be found.

The important detail in the speed load is to be fast-slow-fast-slow-fast. That is, get your hand to the next magazine fast. Slow down enough to be sure you have a good grip on the magazine. (I've seen more than one shooter throw a magazine across the range, from being fast but not having a good grip.) Get the magazine from your belt to the gun fast, then slow down to make sure it is lined up properly. (And I've seen shooters throw a loaded magazine past the gun, trying to insert it at warp speed.) And finish by inserting it fast and in one motion. (Don't insert it, then take your hand off it, and then slam the magazine home. Don't take two or three motions to do what one can do.) Done at top speed, it doesn't look like a good shooter is slowing down, but they are.

In the old days, we used to try and get photographs of ourselves with the classic speed-load elements: Two fired empties in the air, old mag in mid-air and new mag in the left hand on the way to the gun. And no cheating by shooting one-handed already holding the spare mag!

Tactical/Retention is different. Here, you aren't getting reloaded as fast as possible. You're reloading during a lull, or you're reloading on the line between firing strings. Or you're in an IDPA match and you aren't allowed a speed load. Why not? Simple: at the range you can pick up magazines and use them again. In a gun fight or in combat you may not be able to get back to where you dropped that magazine.

Infantrymen in combat units often have "dump bags," a bag where they can drop off their magazines once they've emptied them. Reliable magazines are not always easy to find. And you can never carry enough spare ammo, so ditching the few rounds left in a magazine (swapping mags before you run dry) is a bad thing. And dropping magazines onto the ground subjects them to dirt, dust, mud and potential damage. The less you abuse them, the longer they'll last.

So the tactical reload keeps your magazines on your person and saves every single round of ammo for future use.

There are two ways of doing a tac-load. The first, the old way, is often done by the old-timers who learned their reloading back when

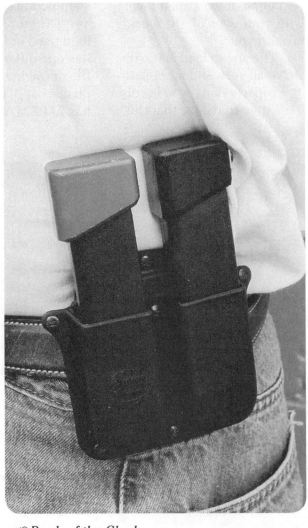

A hi-cap carry setup for competition or concealed carry. With a G-17 on the other side, this shooter has 64 rounds ready to go. (Dawson on the left; Taylor Freelance on the right).

Gunsite was still new. Here, you let go with your off hand, reach down and get your spare magazine, and then bring it up to the gun. Holding the new magazine between thumb and forefinger, you pop the old magazine out so it goes between your other fingers. Once you have a good grasp of it, you swap to the new one and insert it. The old magazine goes back into a pocket, *not* on your belt. Your mantra and standard procedure should be: belt magazines are fully-loaded, pocket magazines are partials. That way you don't go and reload a magazine into your Glock thinking it is full, only to find out is is only partially loaded.

The second method is to remove the old magazine,

pocket it, then get the new one and insert it.

Why the difference? Some feel the older method is too dependent on fine-motor control and prone to breaking down under stress. The simpler method doesn't require that you balance two magazines in one hand.

Where does the old magazine go? Again, a pocket, or down your shirt, or in a dump bag, but not back on your belt or in a magazine carrier. Not until you can top it off. My friend Mas Ayoob found this out the hard way back in the 1980s at the IPSC World Shoot held at Bisley, England. (Yes, there was a time when a Subject of the Crown was trusted with a handgun.) He was both in the match as a competitor and as

a range officer. He finished a stage, and then ran another stage. When it came time to shoot again, he checked that he had magazines in all of his mag pouches, and nodded that he was ready. Partway through the stage, he found out that some of the magazines were only partially loaded, and he set a record for number of speed loads per stage.

Is it a magazine you've shot some rounds from? Then it goes into the dump bag, or a pocket. Learn from the mistakes of others.

Glock Collectors

The field for collectors will be rich someday, assuming we can all own guns that far into the future.

Quick, wash the mud off that mag and find out if it is a collector's item. Oh wait, it's a Glock. You needn't wash the mud off, it will still work – and collectors haven't noticed magazines. Yet.

For instance, right now you can collect five different magazines for the G-17 alone. Now that the Assault Weapon Ban has been allowed to sunset, the LEO-marked magazines have added a sixth and seventh variant.

The five collectables right now are: Original Non-Drop Free, 1st Variant Drop Free, 2nd Variant Drop Free, 1st Variant Ten Shot, and 2nd Variant Ten Shot. The LEO-only magazines are those specially marked 1st and 2nd variant drop-free.

And each model adds three to five more to the total. The G-19, while it can use magazines designed for the G-17, has its own, including the 10 shot magazines. And the G-19 LEO marked magazines.

Some models will not have all the variants. Those models introduced after the changeover to drop free magazines (basically any model number 24 or higher) won't have the original design. And those whose size precludes capacity higher than 10 rounds won't have LEO marked or high capacity magazines. While the law was in effect, high capacity magazines introduced after September of 1994 were all marked "LEO Only," so as an example you couldn't find any .357 high capacity magazines not marked LEO until after 2004. When the law changed you could.

As you can see from the chart, during the time the AWB was in effect you could form a collection of Glock mags totaling 42 magazines. When the law sunset, the 12 LEO magazines immediately bumped the total to 59. (The real prizes would be the G-25 and G-28 .380 marked magazines) When the law changed and the high capacity magazines were once again available and manufactured without LEO markings in models where they haven't before been available, the total was 66. But wait, now the .45 GAP adds three more magazines to that – but no LEO, no 10-shot AWB/ 94-compliant magazines.

The real collectors, though, would set their goal on a higher prize: the transitional LEO magazines. The 1st and 2nd variant drop-free mags could potentially add another dozen to the total. On the matter of the 1st and 2nd variant LEO magazines, I had been assured by a Glock representative that the change to the 2nd variant had occurred after the Crime Bill went into effect in 1994. As a result, there were no pre-ban 2nd variant magazines extant, and no 1st variant LEO-only magazines. And yet the very next day one of my club members showed me his pre-ban 2nd variant drop-free magazine! Glock marked, with no funny business about LEO markings or somebody else's magazine tube.

So, for the purposes of collecting Glock magazines, all the variants are in the mix. The possibilities can make one dizzy, coming to a potential of 91 magazine variations! (And we haven't even considered the variations of the 33-round G-18 magazines that might exist.) And all this from one factory, starting with one design, just over 20 years ago. And who knows what's to come?

For the really serious collector, the future is brighter than ever. Many police departments have their magazines (and pistols) marked as to who owns them. As current officers retire, the supply of departmental-marked magazines trickles away. With 7,500 agencies using Glocks right now, if only one percent of them have Glock mark their magazines with the PD's acronym or logo, the collecting field opens even larger. ◆

CHAPTER 23

Holsters

The field of holsters for your Glock covers five areas: Concealed, Open/Field, Competition, Duty, and Military/SpecOps. It wasn't that long ago that the selection of holsters for a handgun fell into two categories: Concealed and Everything else.

Up until even the 1950s men (and women) wore clothes made of heavier cloth than today. And before then, several layers' worth. When my grandfather was going to work, every man who wasn't a field hand wore a suit or jacket to work. Even if work meant taking it off, he wore the coat to the plant. Concealment back then meant making sure your coat was long enough to cover your holster.

For law enforcement duty, for hunting, and even many military applications, a specialized holster wasn't so different from all the others. Even when my Father got the government's Grand Tour of Northern France and Germany, "concealment" meant something in a pocket, and duty meant a flap holster on the web belt. The only competitions that required a holster were the police courses, PPC and whatever (if any) qualification course the department mandated, and fast draw. You could do it all with one holster, and that holster was leather. You've heard the phrase "accept no substitutes"; well, back then there weren't any to accept.

Today? Anyone who wears a suitcoat to work or out in public is either a banker or an off-duty police officer. And what do women wear? The trend for modern clothing is definitely towards selections from the shrink-wrap collection. Hide a gun? Get real. I live in a university town, and the parade of brand-new fashions is something to see. And the

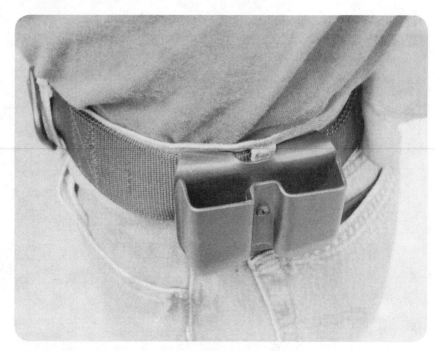

To keep your holster and mag pouches under control, use the belt loops on your trousers.

The injection-moulded Blade-Tech. Less expensive than the kydex versions, and nearly as indestructible.

trend has been to lighter cloth and tighter fitting, to the point where many women here couldn't hide a wallet or even a credit card.

Today some competitions require expensive and complex holsters, and the law enforcement community has gone almost entirely to "security" holsters. That is, holsters that require a particular draw stroke to release the two or three safety catches and are less likely to let an assailant simply snatch the gun away. The military has long since given up on belt holsters. Even a soldier who is overweight doesn't have enough running belt space to hold everything that could be latched onto a belt. Military holsters, and those used by SWAT teams (they have many of the same equipment transport problems) have moved to the thigh.

And they have all come to be offered in synthetics. Oh, the leather mavens will tell you that dead cow wrapper (except for the horsehide aficionados) is the only thing at a real man uses, but the legion of plastic, nylon, synthetic and other petroleum-derived holsters continues to grow. And what would be more appropriate than a polymer holster for your Glock? As the owner of more leather holsters than synthetics, I guess I'll just have to referee that particular argument.

Glock makes holsters for their pistols, but there are only two designs. Most

A skinny belt is not at all useful, regardless of the holster.

MAGAZINE POUCHES

Why a spare magazine?

You'd think, what with your Glock holding 15 or 17 rounds, you wouldn't need a spare magazine. In an ideal world, you'd be right. But then, in an ideal world you wouldn't need to pack your Glock all day, now would you?

In the North Hollywood shootout, where the bad guys were all duded up in multiple layers of body armor and had illegally-modified automatic weapons, the responding officers needed extra magazines. I know what you're thinking: "What are the chances I'll need to reload, finding myself in a raging firefight against guys with machineguns?" One responding officer didn't need a spare magazine for extra ammo; he needed it because the one he was using was damaged. The magazine that went into his AR-15 had one if its feed lips severely bent, and it fed in slow motion as a result. (The rest of his magazines? Left in his car, or strewn across the street, proving once again Sweeney's Third Axiom: "If it isn't in your hands or on your person when the balloon goes up, it might as well be on the moon.")

Violent encounters are not like range sessions. Your signal to "start the stage" in real life may be getting tackled into a wall, or knocked to the floor. And if your one-and-only magazine gets damaged in that moment, then what?

You carry spare magazines as much for the need to replace a damaged one as for the need to replace an exhausted one. Luckily, carrying a spare magazine is not nearly as much of a hassle as carrying the pistol itself is. Especially Glock magazines, which (at least outside of the big cities like Detroit) if seen when your coat flies open in the wind, might very well be mistaken for a pager or cell phone. I've found myself in situations where I've taken my pistol off for whatever reason, only to discover later that I'm still packing the magazine.

A magazine pouch can be quite comfortable. When you find one that works, stick with it.

A concealing jacket would keep the mags and light from getting taught on the chair.

of the real action is from the independent holster makers. After all, with millions of Glocks out there, a holster maker would be engaging in suicidal marketing if he didn't offer at least some styles to fit Glock pistols.

As long as you don't just carry your Glock around in a paper bag, I'm not sure you can go wrong buying a holster. A good one, that is. Don't be tempted by prices that seem too good. They usually are.

The Carry Ensemble

Whether you are carrying concealed, on duty, competition or in a combat zone, you need more than just a Glock and a pocket. You need the pistol, spare ammunition, a holster, a way of carrying the ammunition, and something to attach it all to your body. (And in combat you need maintenance gear in your rucksack.) Some systems are entirely self-contained, like a double shoulder rig. But with that exception or a gym bag, anything you use to carry a pistol requires more gear. Those who love gear rejoice. Those who don't, dread the shopping.

Belts

While a belt is optional for a shoulder holster, for all the others you need a belt. And not just any belt. A thin, skinny, flimsy dress belt is worse than no belt at all. A skinny belt can't anchor a holster in place. If you're trying to carry a handgun

and not use a holster (called "Mexican carry") you're acutely aware of the potential of dropping your gun. You check it, you pay attention to it, and you readjust it if need be. Holster or not, you need a belt. A skinny belt doesn't secure the holster but gives the illusion of security. Also, the flapping of the gun in its holster against your side as you walk and move (with a flimsy belt) can quickly prove tiring. And it shows the gun through your jacket.

A flimsy belt also make the draw more difficult. A flimsy belt doesn't keep your Glock in the same place, or at the same angle. It really slows down your draw to have to frisk your waist playing "find the Glock" after the buzzer has gone off in a match, or you've suddenly realized that the fellow at the local party store is not asking for donations to the local homeless shelter.

For the longest time, "belt" meant leather. I wore a leather gun belt as a trouser belt (and gun belt, too) for nearly 20 years. The same belt. When it finally gave up, I looked around and found that the synthetics revolution had gotten to belts, too. One I have tried lately and found quite useful is a design usually called an "instructor's" belt or a "rigger's" belt. The one I'm testing and wearing now (and probably won't send back because it is just too comfortable, convenient and well-made) is a Galco. It is a heavy nylon weave belt, usually with a stiffener in it. (I got the stiff one.) The buckle is a slip-lock affair, and there is velcro on the tongue as an additional locking space.

The heavy mesh is strong enough to keep a holster in the proper orientation, and you can adjust it for the perfect combination of comfort and security. With

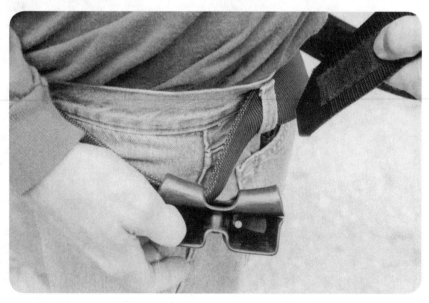

Getting dressed when you carry can take some time. But getting the gear "just right" makes the day so much more comfortable.

Glock makes their own holsters. They are spartan but serviceable.

the belt pulled tightly enough to lock the holster in place, it won't slide around your belt. And you don't have to exhale and go to the next notch as you would on a standard belt, if you needed a setting just a bit tighter than the previous notch.

While an instructor's belt like the one from Galco I have is very useful, and will pass muster if you wear jeans as standard work clothes, it won't go with a suit. For suit wear, you'll have to go with a leather belt and settle for a slightly Western look

Two double mag pouches, and you have plenty of magazines to get through a course of fire. Change to one double, and hi-caps, and you're set for life in the big city.

to your apparel. While you can get belts that are wide and thick around your waist, but narrow as a dress belt in front, I haven't found them comfortable. However, many shooters who carry do find such belts comfortable.

For competition, a holster and belt is something else entirely. The current state of the art in competition rigs calls for two belts. The underbelt is an all-velcro affair, and you slide it through your belt loops and pull it tight. Very tight. The underbelt locks to itself by velcro, and its entire exterior surface is a velcro attaching surface. The competition belt, with the holster and magazine

pouches already attached, then attaches to the underbelt with another swatch of velcro. But then for many competitions you don't have to worry about concealment at all. Only speed and security during movement. And for those competitions that require concealment, you just use your daily concealed carry equipment.

Concealed Carry

A very large subject, as the requirements for concealed carry are not only as many as those who carry, but can vary over time and place. When I was working at the gun shop, concealed

carry for me meant getting from the truck to the shop in the morning and back out at closing. I didn't carry concealed in the shop for a set of very good reasons: primary among them was that I didn't have to. But also I was in the back room most of the time fixing guns and had as many as five people at the front counter as my personal first line of defense.

Carry for me was simple and consisted of tucking my Light Weight Commander into my belt (in its Summer Special holster) and heading out. (I started packing before the Glock ever made it to the USA, even before Gaston Glock designed it. I stuck with

BE PREPARED

Carrying concealed is an awesome responsibility. And it can be a crushing legal burden. Many jurisdictions require a certain amount of class work, either range time for shooting competency, or classroom work for the law, before issuing a permit. While the legal minimum is not that hard to meet, it would be a good idea to learn more. For competency you can practice, you can take classes specifically to improve your shooting skills, and you can compete. Good competitions would be matches held under the auspices of the IDPA and USPSA.

Firearms classes can deal mostly with skills and tactics, such as at Gunsite, or heavily weighted towards legal responsibility and tactics, at Mas Ayoob's Lethal Force Institute. It would be a very good idea to invest the modest amount of money in getting a copy of Mas' "In the Gravest Extreme" (you can obtain a copy directly from Mas) which will give you a good grounding in the legal implications of concealed carry and lethal force.

And above all you should have an attorney. Find one, talk with him, make sure he understands what you do, why you carry and when you'll call him. The aftermath of a shooting incident is stressful enough without having to worry about how you're going to find an attorney at 2:00 AM to help you deal with the questions the nice detective has for you..

Glock mag holders can certainly get the job done.

my LW Commander for a long time after.) But selecting a holster isn't so easy for many people. Those with back problems may not be able to wear an in-the-pants holster. A crossdraw or shoulder holster may be comfortable, but for barrel-chested men and buxom women it may not be an easy draw.

The small-of-the-back is quite concealed, but don't plan on driving farther than across the parking lot while wearing one. A small-of-the-back holster is for those who stand and work. You also have to worry about falling while wearing one. The gun rides right over your spine, and a fall onto your back can be painful, debilitating and even end up with you losing the fight before it starts.

Ankle rigs? Fine, if you can get down and draw, and wear trousers baggy enough to cover the Glock and let you clear leather.

However you carry your pistol, it must remain concealed. Inadvertently letting your handgun show (let alone deliberately and incorrectly) is in most jurisdictions an offense called "brandishing." While it may only be a misdemeanor in many places, it is an offence great enough to quite often call for your CCW to be voided,

and even have the handgun confiscated. Yeah, the arresting Officer has heard "the wind blew my coat open" or "it must have ridden up when I picked up the box" and all the rest of the excuses. Forget them. They won't help you much, if at all, when someone takes offense and complains.

So if you're going to carry concealed, it had better be Concealed.

Fobus

Fobus holsters and Glock holsters are both entirely synthetic, made from polymer, and retain their shape from having been cast or moulded that way. The Glock holsters are moulded in one piece, while the Fobus holsters are assembled from moulded sections.

Made in Israel, Fobus holsters are exclaimed to be "Combat Proven." You've got to take seriously something used by people whose idea of being properly dressed is to

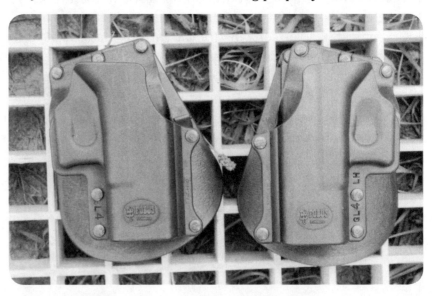

Fobus makes very good holsters at a very attractive price.

walk out of the house carrying an M-16.

The Fobus holsters are made by moulding sections as flat pieces, then using rivets to hold them together. While it sounds like a pretty cheap way to make a holster, don't be deceived. In the interests of scientific inquiry, and the readers need to know, I tried to tear one apart with my bare hands. Ten minutes later I wasn't very far along, and I had some ideas about making an aerobic exercise video.

On the paddle holsters, you've got enough leverage to bend the paddle pretty seriously, and if you were to work at it I'm sure you could eventually rip it apart. But you'd have to have hand strength a lot greater than mine (and I'm no slouch) to rip the holster body into its two pieces. The Fobus is plenty tough enough to wear every day for a long time. And if it does go to pieces on you, the Fobus line is so inexpensive that buying another one is cheaper than the ammo for your next practice session.

In attending classes given by those who have had a lot more experience than I, I've discovered some interesting things: first, I was going about "Fobus destruction" all wrong. They can be torn off of you, and torn apart, with a lot less work than the way I was going about it. So I have to consider Fobus holsters as inexpensive carry holsters in a controlled environment. Carry in your store, where you have a counter between you and the bad guys? No problem. Out on the street, where attacks will not have a counter in the way? Not the place for Fobus.

A paddle holster is designed to be an easy-on and easy-off holster. You don't have to undo your trouser belt to take the holster off – it slides between your belt

HOLSTER TESTING

In order to see what a holster can do, you have to go to the range and try it out. Draw and dry-fire practice only tell you so much, and actual range time is needed to get a full picture of a holster's performance. But you're only at the range for a few hours, and the range isn't a normal environment.

In order to see if a holster is comfortable for daily wear, I have to wear it for longer periods than just at the range. So, as I sit here and write, I'm wearing a holster. You'd be surprised how many chairs aren't comfortable while "packing" and how many normal daily activities are precluded or made very clumsy by wearing a holster. Each day when I sit down to write, I'll have something different on, with a Glock in it. Which leads to other problems. What to do when the doorbell rings? It may be the postman, with something I have to sign for. It may be the UPS or FedEx driver. (Both of my regular drivers are knowledgeable about guns and would be more interested in what holster or gun I have on than alarmed that I'm wearing it.) Or someone with a petition. As a result, I keep a bathrobe by the front door, and put it on before answering. I'm sure the postman thinks I'm some kind of a slug, answering the door at three in the afternoon wearing a bathrobe.

At least with the concealment holsters, I can put on a sportscoat, so the postman will think I get out of the house now and then..

and trousers. The standard Fobus paddle holds the Glock in a slightly muzzle to the rear angle, with the trigger just above belt level. Friction retention in the holster is created by the moulded recess for the front of the trigger guard. Retention on your belt comes from two tabs in the paddle that hook on the back of your belt. Once the guard snaps into place, you have a good level of retention. It isn't going to resist snatching, but you're carrying concealed, right?

If you need more or less angle, then the Roto Paddle is what you need. On the Roto, the standard paddle back and holster body have two additional parts between them. The two parts can be rotated to change the angle the holster sits at. You access the locking screw from the back. Loosen, adjust, tighten, try. Repeat until you've got it just where you want it.

The Fobus mag pouches are constructed the same way, with the pouches riveted to the backer. You can have a single or double mag pouch, and you can also have a light holder for the Streamlight M3 or M6 light. The Streamlight attaches to the light rail on the front of the frame of 3rd generation Glock pistols. You may not need light very often, but when you do you need it very much.

Galco

Some companies still stick with leather. Galco makes synthetics but believes that there is still a place for leather. The holster I have is the COP three-slot. It is a thumbbreak holster with a friction adjustment retention system. The adjustment screw is next to the triggerguard, and has enough adjustment that with it you can tighten the holster to the point where you couldn't get the Glock out. The point of friction and thumbbreak is to keep the

Fobus mag holders are as low-bulk and low-weight as they come.

A G-22 in a Fobus holster.

On the draw, the covered guard keeps your finger off the trigger.

The Galco COP holster, with two front slots for straight-up or canted positioning and the rear slot to keep the gun tight to your body.

Glock with you even during the rough and tumble of an altercation.

The three slots let you change the angle at which the holster sits on your belt. Some like a pistol straight up and down, while others like the "FBI cant" where the muzzle is pointed behind you. It all comes down to comfort and speed of draw. I'm tall, with a high waist and long arms. A straight-up holster for me can require contortions to execute the draw. Quite often I find that I need the FBI cant just to keep from having to dislocate my shoulder in order to get the Glock out.

For a magazine carrier, the COP mag pouch compliments the COP three-slot, and since Glocks have such high capacity I don't feel the need for two spare magazines. Instead, a combination magazine and

The Galco COP holder for magazine and SureFire light.

flashlight carrier lets me pack my SureFire Nitrolon 6P along with a spare magazine. The flashlight rests behind the magazine, a minor point of contention among concealed carry circles and CCW mavens. Yes you'll probably need the flashlight more often than the spare magazine and it would be nice if you could get the light out without revealing the spare magazine. But under stress your hand will grab the first thing it encounters during a speed reload, and you don't want to be trying to reload your empty Glock with a compact flashlight.

On the other hand, every time you produce the flashlight, you're risking flashing the butt of a magazine to anyone who happens to glance down as you grab for some light. As I've mentioned, brandishing is taken seriously in some areas. And many who have no love for gun owners will complain at even inadvertent viewing of hardware.

One way to avoid the problem of brandishing is to reach for your flashlight only with your strong hand. That is, with your right if you are right-handed, and the light (and spare mag) are on your left side. Reaching with the right you needn't brush your jacket back to grab the light. Or, if you use your left, practice reaching straight up under the edge of the coat, rather than sweeping the front of it back to the mag and light pouch. But we're getting dangerously close to training matters, and away from gear specific to Glocks.

The Galco COP mag holder has two tension adjustment screws, again to keep the gear on you. If you set them tight enough to retain them when you're running, you can still easily produce either the magazine or light when you need them. The light pouch has a nice feature: a hole in the bottom to clear the flashlight button. Surefire lights work from a push button on the end cap. The clearance hole ensures that you don't turn on your light simply by pressing it into the pouch.

Blade-Tech

The hottest thing (which was just on the horizon in the first edition of this book) is Kydex. A synthetic produced in sheets, Kydex is so tough that you would have a tough time piercing it with a heavy-

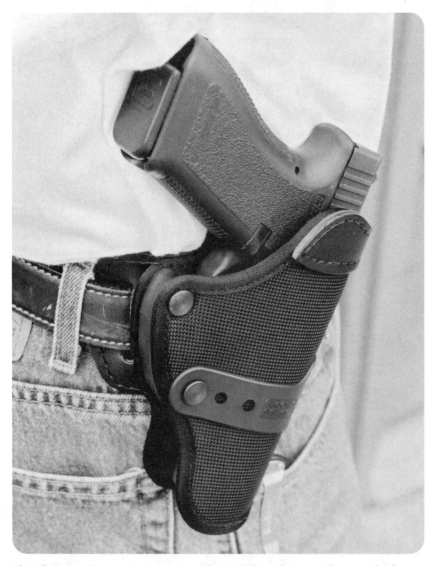

The Shooting Systems Avenger, with its trailing slot to pull your Glock close for concealment.

duty knife, or even driving a nail through it. Kydex fabricators like Blade-Tech fold the sheets and mold them to a dummy or real gun. They then use industrial cutting tools to create belt loops, relieve the trigger guard area, etc. The result is a holster with friction retention (you can get thumb breaks on some models) that is impervious to solvents, wear, impact, and can even be painted. (Ugly, but painted.)

For those who don't need a custom-molded holster, Blade-Tech offers injection-molded holsters as well. If the standard leather holster is a 3-4 on a toughness scale, the injection-molded ones come in at about 9, and the Kydex at 11.

Shooting Systems

The Shooting Systems Advanced Super Avenger is a dual-purpose holster. It can be a concealed carry holster, and it can be an open carry holster if you don't have to worry about attempted gun grabs. (A detective carrying openly might not find it secure enough, but someone packing in a less travelled but still dangerous area might.)

The Super Avenger is a holster in the style known as the Askins Avenger, with friction retention and a slight FBI cant. The back of the holster is wide and has a trailing slot that pulls the holster into you when you pull your belt tight. You won't find it wobbling back and forth as you walk or run. The open top ensures fast and clear access, and the adjustable retention keeps it secure.

The synthetic materials of the construction keep it rigid, yet washable. If you take a dunk, or sweat through your holster, you can scrub it clean. I don't know if it is "dishwasher safe" (the most common joke about Glocks) but washing it would be easily enough accomplished by dunking it in soapy water, dunking it in clear, toweling it dry and letting it air dry for a day.

Advantages and Disadvantages

The big advantage for most rigs is comfort, closely followed by concealability. A properly fit holster on your belt is going to be almost as

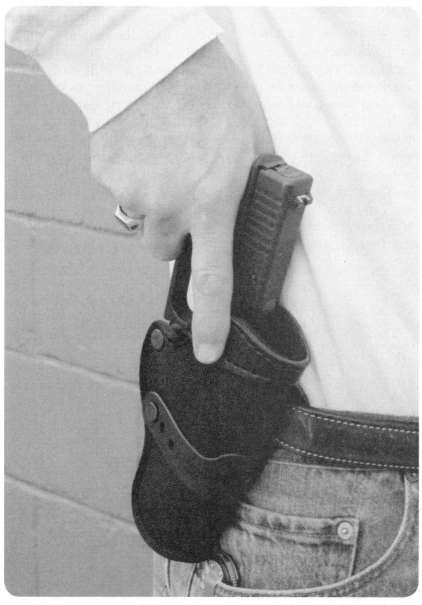

The stiff open top of the Shooting Systems makes it a snap to re-holster one-handed.

comfortable as you can get, although not as comfortable as the best open carry holsters. Except for women. The ladies will be hard-pressed to find a comfortable holster. The curve of their hips cants the gun in and presses the rear of the slide into the body. (Except for runway models, of course, who have no hips.)

For the ladies who have to carry, the way to get a good holster is to find a gun shop that is understanding, and try on all kinds of holsters. Also, ask around at your CCW class and at the gun club and see what the experiences of other women has been.

One example not to follow for the ladies is the television show which is now in syndication (and on cable somewhere) called "Silk Stalkings." The female lead, Mitzi Capture, always wears very tightly-tailored suits. In Miami (where the show was set) the heat and humidity would have been oppressive with any but the lightest fabric. The show expected us to believe she could carry concealed a full-size pistol like a 1911, Beretta 9mm or a Glock. I don't want to pick on the show too much, as every television cop show is guilty of it at one time or another. Just don't use television as your guide to what will cover your carry gun.

The draw can be be quick, and unless you are anorexic there is room to carry what you need. The disadvantage to concealed carry is the need for a jacket for concealment, even in the summer. (Q: How do you spot police officers off duty in the summertime? A: They're the ones wearing windbreakers, hawaiian shirts or an untucked tee shirt over another tee shirt.) Women will find clothing styles particularly unsuited for concealment of a firearm.

Fanny Packs

Yes, yes, we all know that fanny packs are merely "concealed" carry waist bags. Except not everyone knows that. And even those who do don't always think every bag they see is a gun bag. And even if they do, it is after all concealed.

The trick to using a fanny pack (and why do we call them "fanny packs" when we wear them in front?) is finding one both comfortable and quick while still being secure.

The London Bridge Trading Company #1528A on my desk is all that. Made of heavy-duty Cordura nylon, it promises to deliver years of use. The layout is the standard fanny pack/holster, with a circumferential two-tab zipper that acts as the breakaway for the outside. Once you position the zippers at the corner you need (upper right for right-hand use, upper left for lefties) you need only pull the strap with your off hand to open the pack.

One design feature I like on this one is the holster. Rather than stitch the holster to the backing, the backer is one piece of velcro and the holster is wrapped in the other half. You can remove the holster and position it where you want, at the angle

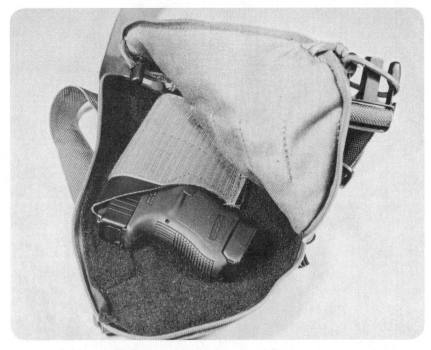

The London Bridge fanny pack. The velcro makes it possible to position the gun anywhere you want in the pack.

Just another fanny pack.

Pull the corner cord. . .

. . .and the cover peels away.

Hey! There's a Glock in there!

And now it's out.

you want, for best comfort and security. The front flap has several zippered compartments, with room for spare magazines, a flashlight, and whatever else you might want to keep in your fanny pack.

The waist belt is large enough to go around most users, with 56 inches of reach at full extension. (Nothing personal, but if you need the whole strap, you've got more pressing medical problems than where to hide a carry gun.)

One trick to wearing a fanny pack as a method of concealed carry is to keep the waist belt snug. If you let the strap out a bit, you'll find that when you go to break it open the bag will lift off your body and you'll have to really pull to get the leverage to open it. And a snug pack is less likely to bounce around while walking. A bouncing pack can beat you up in short order.

Another trick I learned while using fanny packs as a means of carrying camera gear is to add a carabiner to your waist. Carabiners are the spring-catch aluminum loops that rock climbers use. The spring-loaded clip lets you snap them onto many things. I snap one through a loop on the waist belt and then over my trouser belt. Since the buckle on the waist belt is behind us while we're wearing it, someone can quickly unsnap the waistbelt and make off with your fanny pack. The carabiner keeps it attached to you. The only

drawback is that if someone does try to snatch your gun-bearing (or camera-laden) fanny pack, they'll be trying to snatch it while it is still attached to you. It may be startling, but more so for him than you.

I wore the LBTC fanny pack on my trip to South Africa for the IPSC World Shoot in 2002. In South Africa, your firearms must either be locked in a safe or in your possession. Your import permit is your carry permit. I tucked a 10mm into the fanny pack for my trips outside of the match. If anyone spotted it for what it was, they didn't let on with any inadvertant facial expressions. As far as I could tell, I was just another tourist with a camera and fanny pack.

Advantages and Disadvantages

The fanny pack is a self-contained unit. The gun, spare ammo, the flashlight and anything else you carry in it are all there. And it all comes off and goes back in in a flash. But it is obvious. And it is also, like a purse, an object of attention even if it isn't recognized as a gun bag. Properly adjusted (snug to the body), a fanny pack is quite comfortable.

A couple of disadvantages with many styles is the model-specific holster that's built in, and many are built to be "handed," that is, right- or left-hand only. The London Bridge Trading Company model I tested can switch right or left, and if the holster

doesn't fit well enough you can inexpensively swap it with another replaceable holster to velcro to the fanny pack interior back.

Open/Field

The Open and Field category is something of a jumble. On one end we have places like Arizona with Open carry, and on the other hand we have once a year hunters who want a backup gun but want it protected from the weather and brush. As a resident of Arizona, or a working cowboy, you would want something comfortable, reasonably secure (but not necessarily snatch-proof), reasonably quick, and good looking. And did I mention comfortable? As an Open carry holster, where you'll be wearing it all day, comfort is just as important as it is for concealed carry. But you don't have to worry about it being bulky as long as it isn't so large as to get in the way. A good Open Carry/Field holster is also one that you can conceal if you need to.

There is one drawback to a very comfortable holster: you forget it's there. How can this be a problem, you ask? When I went through the handgun class at Gunsite lo, these many years ago, one of our club members who was in the class had turned his trip into an expedition. After the Gunsite class he was going to go to the West Coast and do some scuba diving. (Glenn was ambitious, and we were all younger then.)

After the week's class was over he piled into the car with the rest of his group and headed out. Glenn fell asleep, and when they stopped for gas, he volunteered to go get coffee. Walking across the parking lot, he entered the local fast food place and started barking out the coffee order. (Glenn can be an overwhelming experience to the first-timer.) When the kid behind the counter didn't move, he asked "What's the problem?" The teenager pointed at his belt and said "This is California." Glenn was still wearing his .45! After a quick trip back to the gas station to stuff his gun, holster and spare magazines into the trunk of the car, he collected the coffee, and they zoomed out of there before anyone else could ask questions.

I've had to leave my gun in the car on several occasions when I forgot I had it and found I needed to enter a place where its possession was forbidden. And more than once I remembered just as I was reaching for the handle to the entrance, with its no-guns reminder sign.

A working cowboy also has to worry about the handgun (a Glock in our example, in case anyone has forgotten what the title of the book is) staying in place while riding, walking, working and occasionally falling. One other type of open carry would be a high-risk occupation where the idea is to make it clear you are armed, and not hide the gun. A gun shop, pawn shop or jeweler in a rough neighborhood would carry openly. (If the law allowed it.) I've seen owners in party stores (the corner snack, liquor and lotto store) who carried openly. Maybe it's just a Detroit thing, but it doesn't bother me. However, in many places it isn't allowed even in your own store. Check your local laws before deciding to work while armed. (and consult your attorney.)

Many holsters in the Open/Field category, like concealed carry, depend on friction as the retaining method. Since many shooters don't trust friction, you'll have quite a selection of holsters with thumbstraps. Hunters want a reasonable amount of comfort but are almost always looking for more protection.

Protection comes at a price, as the only thing that really protects a handgun

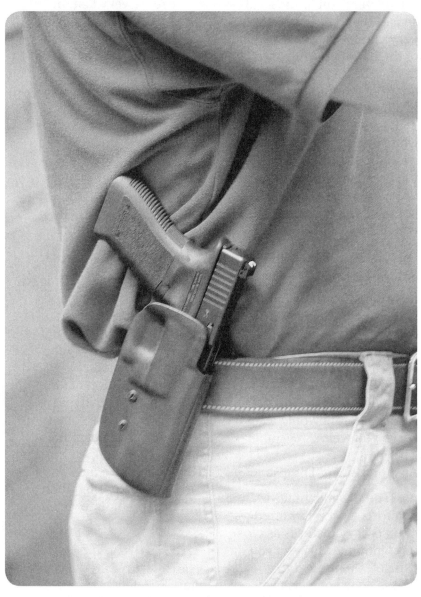

An open carry holster can be so comfortable that you forget you have it on.

is a flap. A flap holster is going to be slower than any other holster. In many jurisdictions, you can't get protection by carrying your handgun under your coat while hunting, as it is then concealed. In many places carrying concealed is tacitly approved while hunting, but in others it is forbidden. And if you're counting on your hunting activity protecting you while carrying concealed (protecting you in the legal sense) then you'd better be very careful to divest yourself of the handgun as the first act to end the days hunting. I have heard of more than one case of a hunter carrying concealed (legally so, while hunting) who was "too tired" to take the handgun off for the drive home, and found themselves in hot water when they stopped for a cup of coffee.

The Shooting Systems Super Avenger mentioned earlier would make an excellent open carry holster. It's secure from accidental loss, fast on the draw, comfortable and durable. You would get many years of use out of it. The Fobus holsters would also serve you well.

Advantages and Disadvantages

The big advantage is comfort. A properly fitted open carry holster is as close to un-noticed carry as you can get. Un-noticed to you, that is. Everyone else will see it. Arizona is an Open-carry

State, and I remember one instance where I was filling my truck up with gas on the Interstate. I was inside the store stocking up on road snacks when the fellow who had been hanging around and chatting up the counter help leaned over the counter and whispered to her, "He's got a gun!" She replied in a normal voice, "Looks like a .45. This is Arizona."

A good open carry rig can also be very fast, but at the expense of security. An open-topped holster doesn't present any barrier to someone attempting to snatch it, so you must always keep an

> **Security holsters are more than pouches to hold a pistol.**

eye out for people getting too close. An open carry holster with a flap for protection, such as a hunting rig, would offer more security, but at the expense of speed.

Your situation dictates the style holster you invest in. If you're living in Arizona (you lucky dog) and carry daily, then an open-topped holster will do. If you're only going to carry when hunting, then a more secure holster is for you.

Duty

The Duty category is simple to define: police officers in uniform. The

proliferation of gear has added much weight to the belt of police officers, to the point that there are now suspenders to hold up the belt. One weighty addition is the security holster. Security holsters are more than pouches to hold a pistol. They depend on multiple security straps, or a rocking motion to unlock the pistol. The idea is to make it difficult for an unauthorized user (read: bad guy) from snatching the pistol from its holster.

The extra security adds weight. How secure can they be? Properly locked in, you can suspend your weight from the Glock locked in its holster. You can let someone yank away to their hearts content, and your Glock won't leave the holster. But they do weigh some.

And if you are going to use a security holster you must practice with it. If you are accustomed to a straight-up draw, then the rocking motion or the extra straps you'll have to defeat will be new. You must practice a couple of hundred times (thousands would be much better), spread over a couple of weeks, to accustom yourself to the new holster. If you do not, the security rig will be secure from you, too, and not just the bad guy.

Competition

For the most part, competition means speed. When the results of a match hinge on a few tenths of a second difference in shooting times, speed of draw matters. However, dropping your pistol in the dirt is not just a bad show but a match disqualification. So even while fast, a competition holster has to be reasonably secure or there isn't much point in using it.

In the early days of competition, friction was king. Holsters kept their pistols and revolvers (this was pre-Glock) by friction, usually an adjustable tension screw that drew the leather tighter around the muzzle or trigger guard area. Competitions that call for real-world holsters still depend on friction. An IDPA-approved holster (you can only use a holster on the approved list in an IDPA match) will depend on friction.

As mentioned before, the holster and its magazine pouches are attached (in some cases clamped and screwed right to) an outer belt that then velcros to the underbelt.

The holster and magazine pouch are not positioned for comfort. They are positioned either for maximum speed and accessability, or in some rare instances positioned to meet the location requirements of the match. A full-house competition rig will have a shooter bristling with gun and magazines. They may not even be able to sit down comfortably. And the only way to carry such a rig concealed would be to use a poncho or tarp.

A competition holster is so minimal it might not even be recognized as a holster.

A thumbstrap will keep your Glock in, but it's secure only against gravity. In a struggle, your gun will come out as easily for the bad guy as it will be for you.

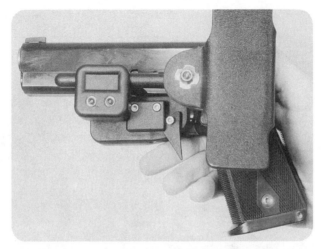

The Garcia Universal latched.

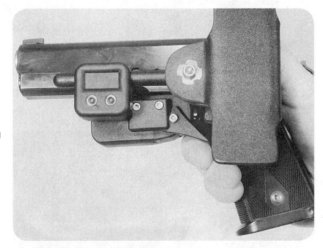

The Universal has a rear latch that your finger unlatches and you grasp the pistol and swipe it.

At a three-gun match, your holster had better be secure or you'll be DQ'd. This shooter (Mike Voigt) has a secure holster.

Modern competition holsters use a different approach than friction to keep you and your Glock together. The current speed approach is to use cammed locking latches that hook onto the trigger guard. Think of the latch on the door to your house. The cam on its front lets it swing shut and latch. The lack of a cam on its rear surface keeps it latched. The trigger guard latch uses a cam with the two surfaces at right angles to each other, rather than opposite each other. Your Glock can go down into the holster and come up out of it but can't tip forward and fall out. (At least not when properly adjusted.) At the muzzle, a rubber muzzle plug keeps your Glock stable and positioned for the draw.

Many competition holsters are referred to as "skeleton" holsters. Since they don't depend on anything except the trigger lock and muzzle plug, there is no cover or wrapper. You have the belt plate, the trigger lock and cover, the muzzle plug and whatever bars are needed to bolt them together. From a distance your Glock appears to simply float next to your belt.

One essential feature of a skeleton holster is the lock. While the draw is fast on a skeleton, security is not always so good. So, there is a setting (lever, knob, button) that locks the Glock in place regardless of what you're doing. Well, almost regardless. If you're in a 3-Gun match (rifle, pistol, shotgun) and have to carry your handgun while using a rifle or shotgun, be careful. Even locked in, if you strike the Glock with enough force (swinging rifle, butt whacks pistol, pistol goes flying) you can drop the pistol. In every instance, you will be disqualified and your shooting for that match is over.

The skeleton holster I use is a Universal, with all aluminum construction except for the muzzle plug. The locking is done by a "press-turn" setting on the side knob. Once locked, the Glock won't come out without a serious impact. Unlocked, it is secure enough for walking around and helping on the stage with your squad.

Some holsters even dispense with the rubber muzzle plug. instead they use a pin in the base of the locking block, and you must drill a small hole in the front of your trigger guard. The pin rides in the hole, and keeps the Glock from rotating out of the holster. A short lift and the Glock is free, but until you lift it won't fall out.

A non-plug holster that doesn't require drilling your trigger guard is the Arredondo. The locking hook is not just spring loaded, but cammed into place by the front of the trigger guard. On the front top of the housing, Arredondo has installed a tension adjustment screw. The nylon screw bears up against the dustcover of your pistol, and keeps it from pivoting out from under the hook. While

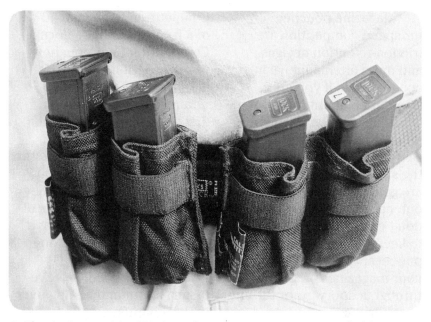

California Competition Works makes a very secure magazine holder.

plenty secure, it still gives a speedy draw.

Another holster of this type, which I must confess I'm growing fond of, is the Universal Shooting Academy "Xtreme" holster. The Arredondo and Xtreme holsters both can give a new shooter quite a scare. From a short distance there doesn't appear to be a holster at all: the gun is somehow attached, but not enclosed. The cammed hook and the locating screws keep the gun in place. The Xtreme also features a locking lever on the rear of it.

If you want to have extra security at the small risk of not being able to draw from the still locked holster, leave the lever down. When you go to draw, your fingers grasping the frame should push the lever out of the way. When it works, it is 'way fast. When it doesn't, you'll give yourself a wedgie. Most shooters lock the holster between stages and leave it

unlocked after loading and before the start buzzer.

For a lot of shooters accustomed to a holster actually enclosing a handgun, a competition holster can be a scary thing. Properly adjusted, it is as secure as any other holster. But it's fast, really fast.

For the competitions that require speed, like the Steel Challenge, IPSC and the American Handgunner Shoot-Off, a skeleton holster is almost a requirement. As one example, in the Steel Challenge your holster selection can make or break your match standings. The match requires up to 25 draws against the clock. If your holster slows each of your draws "only" by two tenths of a second, your total match time is already inflated by five full seconds. In a match where a few tenths can mean the difference between winning and not winning, five seconds is an eternity.

Magazine pouches for speed competition are friction-retention designs, and quite often minimal in construction. If you are a prudent competition shooter, crank the tension knob until it takes a healthy yank to get each magazine clear. Under the stress of competition you are going to get that magazine out, no problem. But if you don't crank the tension knob to keep the magazines in their pouches, you might swipe your magazines off going through a doorway, or turning a corner.

One design of magazine pouch comes from California Competition Gear. Instead of a friction knob, California Competition Gear pouches use the friction of a tight fit of their nylon straps to retain your magazines. At first, you distinctly feel as if you are going to need help getting the magazines into the pouches, and how will you get them out? But while they feel tight, under the stress of competition you won't have any problem snatching one out.

Of all the goodies we're talking about and lusting over in this chapter, competition gear is by far the most expensive. An underbelt and

When USPSA/IPSC decided to get "practical" they disallowed holsters that used tie-downs. Then police and military decided they needed to put pistols there, so what to do?

top belt can easily run $50-$75. You'll need at least three mag pouches (four or five if you shoot a 10-shot gun in Production Division) and they run close to $20 each. The holster itself can easily run $150, and some are closer to $200. Before you've even pulled your Glock out to start shooting, you've dressed yourself in over $350 worth of leather or plastic. Add the cost of a Glock, three hi-caps or five 10-shot magazines and the ammo to fill them, and you've gotten pretty quickly to the $1000 level.

Some feel the cost of shooting is high enough to scare off new competitors. All I can do to offer a comparison is ask if anyone has priced the cost of rebuilding or replacing a blown engine on a dirt bike lately? Or looked at the cost of anything with an internal combustion engine on it? (My next door neighbor goes through $6000 worth of tires for his little race cars each season. Expensive to shoot? Compared to what?)

Fun costs money, at least in our capitalist system. For the cost to fun ratio it provides, shooting is a very inexpensive sport.

Military/SpecOps

One recent article I read on military equipment likened the modern infantryman to a pack mule. The amount of gear each soldier or Marine has to carry is impressive. Rucksack aside, the weight and volume of the personal gear of rifle, rifle ammunition and magazines, grenades, canteen or canteens, personal medical pouch, bayonet, entrenching tool, an extra knife or two, a flashlight or weapon-mounted light, and all the pouches and web gear to carry – it is all quite impressive. (Let's not forget the body armor, which is getting lighter with every generation of progress, but still weighs a few pounds.)

And he also has to carry his share of the team equipment. That gear can be machinegun ammo, an extra barrel for the machinegun, map, GPS unit, radio, mortar rounds or other mortar parts, pop flares and smoke grenades, and such mundane gear as spare batteries for anything electronic. (The modern military uses so much gear that requires power that

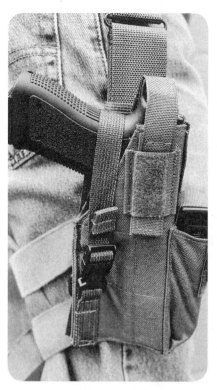

A London Bridge tactical with the airborne strap. note the mag holder on the front of the holster and the quick-secure velcro second strap.

With the quick-secure strap out of the way an the airborne strap unlocked, the draw is quick with the thumb break strap.

London Bridge leg straps are elastic, and you can attach extra gear to them with the velcro strips.

The Naval Special Warfare model, with full flap.

Velcro holds the flap up once you've unlocked it.

A flap keeps the gun protected so you won't grind it up on pavement or walls.

a rifle platoon carries the equivalent of a shelf-full of batteries down at the local big-box store.) Add to that load any of a vast panoply of military gear for special occasions, like night vision equipment and specialized grenades or explosives, handcuffs or plastic zip-strips, a gas mask or supressor for his main or backup weapon, and you can see why some joke that at least one meal a day should be oats and hay.

The SWAT officer doesn't have to carry stuff like belted ammo or spare barrels for the machinegun (can you imagine living in that city, or working in a department that needs belt-fed machineguns, let alone one that needs spare barrels for same on a call-out?)

The London Bridge elastic airborne strap.

Once you're on the ground (or off the boat, etc.) pull the tab or the strap and get it off the gun.

Again, the final security is the thumb break strap.

mortars and other military gear. But every officer does need to carry a mace canister, handcuffs, a radio, gas mask and the team equipment.

With all this gear, where to put the handgun? In military units it isn't a universal problem, as not everyone who is in the armed forces is authorized to carry a sidearm. However, a lot more carry sidearms now than when the first edition of this book went to press. The requirements of the war in Iraq and Afghanistan find our soldiers, airmen and Marines in close quarters quite often. Also, they spend a lot of time riding in vehicles.

There are a lot more pistols in use now than just a few years ago. Every SWAT officer carries a sidearm. (And a radio, another piece of gear to lash on somewhere.) And there isn't any room on the belt.

One possibility is to build a holster into the equipment carrying vest. We have been seeing a lot more vest-mounted holsters in Iraq. The main reason: vehicles. As with WWII GIs, and every war since, American servicemen and women do not walk. In an up-armored Humvee, trying to get a rifle out of the "ready" rack and onto the bad guys can be impossible. But a holstered handgun, in a holster on the vest, can be drawn and fired out the window. I've even seen some handguns simply tucked into the mag pouch of the vest. The obvious utility there is that it can be turned to be right or left-handed without re-rigging a holster. Still, with a holster somewhere besides the vest, taking the vest off still leaves you with a handgun, a comforting detail in many locations and situations. The obvious solution is to pack two handguns. However, that is a solution that is subject to departmental regulation, availability of said second pistol, and a willingness to pack the extra weight.

The London Bridge NSW mag pouch has a full flap for more protection.

The NSW pouch closed, using velcro and a snap.

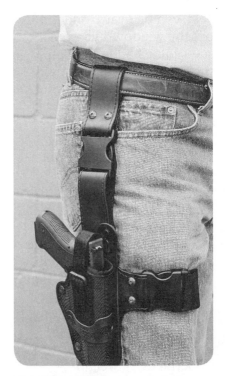

The Shooting Systems tactical holster. Fastex buckles and elastic keep it secure. A thumb break snap keeps the Glock in.

Also, in military use the gear attached to the trouser belt is generally considered to be personal or "bug-out" gear, Level One gear. That is, if you have your trousers on you have enough stuff to give you a chance at getting to more equipment in an emergency, or escaping and getting to another unit.

But the waist is a location packed full of gear, and a waist belt or trouser belt-mounted handgun holster can interfere with web gear or an equipment vest. (And for those of us with a trim waistline, the available space is limited indeed.)

So, the thigh holster came into being. And a curious thing it is. You see, when Westerns ruled the movie screens, holsters went down the leg. For a fast draw with a hanging arm, low is good. And since the climactic shootout was a staple of the Western script, a holster had to be fast or the wearer couldn't prevail in the shootout. Low, however, can be clunky for everyday use. When IPSC was organized, one type of holster specifically disallowed was the low-mounted holster that wasn't attached directly to the belt, and required a leg strap. The idea was to get rid of the irrelevant western fast-draw rig.

Enter a couple decades later the military/police tactical thigh holster. Yes, it can be a bit clumsy, but compared to mounting it in a trouser belt or waist belt, it is a suitable solution. Slower than a belt holster, it is still fast enough.

The best units have an adjustable drop. Not everyone has the same length leg, and to get the holster in the right spot requires adjustment. The leg strap should be wide, at least an inch and a half wide, so it doesn't roll up or bind. And you should have a solid thumb break strap to secure your Glock.

One addition that is vital if you need it, and a curiosity if you don't, is the airborne strap. Jumping out of perfectly good aircraft isn't easy on equipment. What with the banging of stuff on the aircraft while getting in and getting out, and hitting the ground upon arrival, things can get lost. The airborne strap offers an additional level of security while jumping. Once down, you unsnap the strap and fold it out of the way. On the ground, you depend on the thumb break strap for security. (The airborne strap is also insurance while rappelling.)

All tactical thigh rigs have a spare magazine pouch. Reaching around to get the spare magazine isn't fast, or sometimes even elegant, but the desire is practicality. If you have the holster, you have the handgun and spare ammunition for it. Mounting the spare magazine pouch someplace else can make the reload faster, but at the risk of separating the pistol and its spare ammo. (Some might argue that a speed reload in such a situation is a highly optimistic attitude, but I feel you can never get more ammo into a defensive weapon too quickly.)

Do you need a tactical thigh holster? Unless your job requires it, probably not. Can you use it for competition? Some of them, but not all. Do they look cool? That depends, and you should never discount the "cool guy gear" factor when it comes to selling equipment. Do the holster makers sell lots of them? You bet. Are they comfortable in use? If you don't have any room on your belt, nothing beats them. The tactical thigh holster is a demonstration of the convergence of military and police operations and equipment needs. Both are adopting all kinds of gear (radios, night vision gear, etc.) and both face the problem of where to wear it.

Two models from London Bridge Trading Company exemplify the tactical thigh rig. Both are made of Cordura nylon with heavy-duty webbing as the backbone. The first of them is the #372A. It has a drop strap with plenty of adjustment. Both the belt loop and the hanger attachment have plenty of velcro and overlap for adjustment. As sent, the holster is set up with seven and a half inches of drop, enough drop to get the holster down on my leg instead of riding up. (I'm tall, and many tactical rigs lack enough adjustment to get the holster down my leg far enough to prevent binding in delicate personal locations.)

The leg straps are one and a half inches wide, and have an elastic construction for a tight fit and comfort. The straps also have retainers to keep the loose ends from flapping around, a nice touch. Many tactical holsters use straps that are sewn to the holster, and you're stuck with the buckles wherever they may fall. This LBT holster has straps that slide through the holster, so you can adjust the buckle position. Also, the backs of the straps have sewn-on rubberized fabric panels, to keep them where you place them. No sliding around, no riding up.

The body of the holster is stiff, so it doesn't collapse when the Glock is out. The shape-retention makes reholstering a breeze. The retention strap is a velcro-adjustable thumb break, with a metal reinforcement on the strap to make sure it stays stiff. The thumb break strap has an additional security strap that can be folded over it. My only complaint about the one I have is that the velcro to secure it out of the way is too short (*vis a vis* the strap length for storage) and the stored strap thus has a

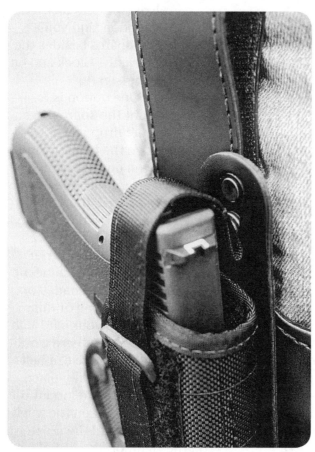

The Shooting Systems' thumb break is adjustable and secure.

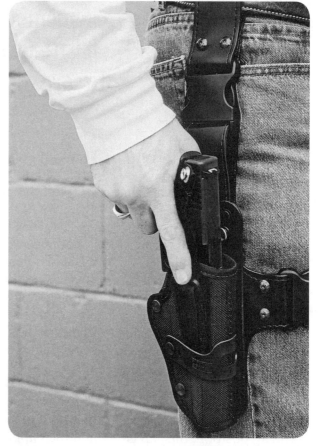

On the draw your thumb opens the strap, and the holster keeps your trigger finger straight.

loop to it, a loop that might catch on stuff.

The 372A has an airborne strap, a buckled strap that loops over the frame and keep the pistol (one of our test Glocks) in place even when jumping out of a perfectly good aircraft. It would also serve as a security strap for any other highly active transport, such as small boat or helicopter. The only thing to keep in mind with an airborne strap is that you must drill into yourself the habit of undoing the airborne strap as soon as you reach solid ground. (For you airborne types: land, secure the 'chute, check to see that all your limbs work, unstrap the pistol. Then proceed with the rest of your duties.) If you don't, you will not be able to draw your Glock, no matter how strong you are.

The spare magazine pouch on the front of the holster is velcro-closed, and large enough to hold either a single Glock magazine or two single-stack magazines.

The 372E Naval Special Warfare Model has the same basic construction and dimensions. It differs in having a flap, modified leg straps and a different airborne strap. A flap holster? Yes, for the same reason you have an airborne strap: for extra security and protection. The flap buckles down, so it obviously isn't meant as full-time protection. In the up position, the flap is held up by a velcro strip on the belt loop. When you need

the protection, pull the flap down off of its velcro security position and buckle it in place or pull it completely off (it is secured to the holster with a pair of snaps) and stash it in a pocket.

I found the flap quite useful in a recent Law Enforcement AR-15/M-16 class. I went to sitting to deal with the targets on a particular course, and without the flap the grip of my Glock would have been ground up and marred by the concrete slab I happened to be sitting on. The airborne strap on this model is an elastic strap that loops over the butt of the Glock and

> **Remember, in combat it isn't always possible to save your magazines.**

keeps it in place. (Once you land, fold up the flap, pull the strap off the butt and let it swing free.)

The magazine pouch is both velcro-secured and has a two-position snap. The cover is not just a strap, but a pouched cover that offers additional protection. And the leg straps have velcro-secured cargo straps that let you attach extra gear or a clipboard to the leg straps. The extra gear pouch would be useful to an infantryman, and the clipboard to a chopper pilot. In all, both are versatile and useful pieces

of gear that will give you many years of service. Both also offer you the option of removing the drop strap, pulling the leg straps out and using the holsters as regular belt holsters. The 372E in particular would make a very useful hunting holster, with its full flap offering plenty of protection for your Glock.

Spare magazine pouches become a real issue: how many do you need, and is that number greater than the holster itself can provide? Remember, in combat it isn't always possible to save your magazines. Getting extra ammo doesn't help much if your magazines are scattered all over the Area of Operation, and you'll need spares besides the ones in the Glock and on the holster.

One option is to mount the spare mags on the drop strap, above the holster. I'm not too keen on that, as it could interfere with the draw. Another option is the other thigh. While convenient, that location is often taken over by a spare magazine carrier for the rifle or submachinegun or flashbangs or grenades or by the gas mask bag or dump bag. If you have your left thigh free, then a pouch there would work great. Otherwise, a belt mount will be the only place. One possibility is to mount the spare pistol mags on the thigh straps, forward of the holster on the right, or forward of the other spare main weapon mag pouch or gas mask bag, on the left. While the mag pouch might slide around, and isn't much of an option for pilots, the thigh top can be a convenient location.

Shooting Systems offers their Advanced Tactical Holster, a thigh rig with some differences. The drop strap uses a fastex buckle to attach. If you want to take the holster off you don't have to go ripping apart your carefully-adjusted velcro straps, you just unbuckle it. The leg strap is a single, wide strap that has a single elastic thigh strap. But it is wide enough, and the drop strap is stiff enough, to keep the holster from moving around.

The holster itself is a standard Shooting Systems holster secured to the tactical webbing. Instead of a unitized and organic structure, the Shooting Systems approach uses their regular holster and the extra webbing. As a manufacturing approach, it has benefits.

The cost is that for some shooters, the holster doesn't quite fit. I had no problems, but some of my testers found they couldn't get the holster just where they wanted it and make it stay. By the time they got it secured it was tight enough to chafe. The Shooting Systems holster isn't quite as "sexy" as the others, but it is a durable and useful holster – and good enough that one of my testers insisted on taking it home.

Advantages and Disadvantages

The big advantage of the tactical rig is that it gets your Glock off your belt and out of the way of other gear, which is also its disadvantage. Especially in a vehicle, a thigh rig can be a real hassle to draw from. Your arm doesn't have much room, with the seatback in the way.

When I'm geared up, with a tactical thigh holster on, spare magazines or other pouches on the other thigh, I can't fit into the seat of many automobiles or trucks. You wonder why your local PD uses honkin' big SUVs to get around in? Because they can't fit into anything smaller with their gear on. Once you've crammed two officers fully geared up into the front seat of a Chevy S-10 or a Ford Ranger, you can't get the doors closed. Also, with a tactical thigh rig if you go prone and your holster isn't adjusted tightly enough (or lacks the rubberized non-slip strap backs), it will roll around your leg until it is lying on the ground.

But the thigh rig is here to stay, and if you want to look cool, you simply have to have one.

Lanyards

A lanyard used to be something we saw in our grandfathers photos of the Great War. A lanyard is simple: it keeps the gear attached to the owner. For a mounted soldier, it made a great deal of sense. It's a long way down to the ground, and the horse may not be all that enthusiastic about going back to get dropped gear. But after cavalry turned in their horses for internal combustion engines, the lanyard fell out of use. Oh, some units still had them, but for the most part they were old hat.

Not any more. What with all the gear, the high tempo of operations, and the exhaustion of soldiers, a lanyard can be a smart thing to have. When I first noticed that suddenly everyone had one, I asked some friends in the know what the deal was. It turns out that not only had lanyards made a comeback, but in one fashion or another they had never left. One friend remarked to me, "Pat, I've been so exhausted on a

The Wilderness Safepacker looks like a map case.

The Blackhawk Industries lanyard tied to the Glock frame with 550 cord. The next step is sealing the ends with a match or lighter.

Ranger Op that I would have forgotten anything not tied to me." Not only had this soldier gone out on patrol with a lanyard on his sidearm, he had the belt-fed machinegun attached to his web gear with 550 cord. Called, unflatteringly, a "dummy cord" it kept him from having to explain the loss of, and reimburse the government the cost, of, that M-60.

The Glock pistols have a lanyard hole. The earliest G-17s didn't, or so I've been told. And the compacts and subcompacts don't, either. (A portable drill can take care of that, should you greatly desire a lanyard hole on your compact Glock.)

The Blackhawk lanyard I have on my desk is pretty simple: a webbing loop with velcro attachments goes around your belt right behind your holster. The coiled cord ends in a nylon cord loop. At

first I couldn't figure out how this was supposed to work, so I asked the folks at Blackhawk. "Tie it together with gutted 550 cord." was the reply.

Ah. You see, in military units (and a lot of police and Sheriffs departments) 550 cord is common. More common than duct tape. Originally parachute cord, it has the multiple virues of being easy to cut, soft on the hands and gear, and quite strong. Yes, the name gives it away, it has a breaking strength of 550 pounds. To attach the lanyard, take a six-inch section of cord and pull the white core out of it. The outside you're left with won't be as strong as the full 550 pounds, but it will be strong enough. Loop the 550 skin around the nylon lanyard and through the Glock frame hole. Loop twice if you can fit it through the hole. Then tie a square knot. Trim the ends, and use a match or lighter to

melt and seal it. The melted ends won't unravel, and the square knot, done right, won't loosen.

Now so long as your belt is on your Glock is with you. If you have to remove the pistol from the lanyard, just cut the 550 part of it (not the lanyard itself) and it's free. You can always reattach with a new section of 550. One small detail on lanyards: if you use an airborne strap, you must use the buckle style with a lanyard, not the rubber loop slip-over type.

The Joker in the Deck

It doesn't matter how carefully you describe your categories, someone will come up with something that defies description, or covers more than one. The Wilderness, out of Phoenix, makes the Safepacker holster. It is not just a holster, it is a pistol case and a packing case. Used as a holster, it looks like a map case or oddly-shaped fanny pack. Rectangular and flat, the large flap is big enough to hold a wallet, map, or other goodies. And that compartment can be accessed without exposing the pistol. Unbuckle the flap, and the Glock and spare ammo are right there.

If you don't want to wear it on your belt, you can clip a shoulder strap onto it and use it a a shoulder bag or purse-like carrier. It has a built-in hand strap for when your shoulder gets tired, or you want a different carry. The hand-carry is sort of like a clutch purse with a retention strap and takes a little getting used to.

And it is also a gun case, capable of protecting your Glock while it rides in the trunk of your car to the range.

The really trick option is to strap it to a rucksack or backpack. On the outside of a ruck, the larger ones look like a map case and the smaller ones look like a cell phone or first aid kit pouch. As long as someone doesn't make it for a gun case, your handgun is secure but available. If you think it might be "made" then you can tuck it into an outside pocket of the backpack. Yes, it would take an extra step to get your sidearm, but it would be secure and safe from impact as well as ready to go. You can't just dump your Glock (or any other handgun for that matter) into a pouch or pocket on a rucksack, as you can't then control the direction of the muzzle nor access to the trigger. In the Safepacker, you can control both.

Just to prove that I can't think of everything, the first wheelchair-bound shooter I showed it to immediately started wondering about locations on his chair where he could strap it. Chair, car, boat, truck, let your imagination run wild. (Limited, of course by local law, or regulations the chief, sheriff or commanding officer might insist on.)

Spare Gear

In most applications, you needn't further burden yourself with extra stuff. For daily concealed carry, you can leave the cleaning tools and repair parts at home. At a match, they reside in your gear bag. For a police officer on duty, or in a SWAT callout, cleaning equipment and spare parts can stay in the car. In the event your handgun goes

Unsnap.

Hand in.

Glock up.

Support hand under.

down on duty, you transition to your backup, go to cover, depend on your partner, or all three. Especially in a SWAT response, your Glock is your backup to your rifle, smg or shotgun, and if you are in the position of having to transition to your Glock and find it also fails you, I'd say you were having a really bad day.

But three situations would call for extra gear: camping/hiking, working outdoors in the wilderness, and military. For a hiker depending in his or her handgun, going back to the cabin or truck isn't an option. Ditto for a working cowboy riding the fence, several miles from the bunkhouse. And a soldier or Marine on the perimeter or out on patrol isn't going anywhere except where he's needed, regardless of what happens to his Glock.

What could happen? Something as simple as having to ford a silty river, or taking a tumble into a mudhole. Or even more miserable, out in the rain for days on end. Or riding in the back of a truck for a day, getting covered in dust. Yes, a good holster will help, but there is only so much you can expect even from properly-

designed and made tactical nylon. Thus, the cleaning kit and spare parts roll.

You'll need a cleaning rod or cable, patches, oil (even though Glock says "no oil" you'll need some) patches in a sealed plastic bag, and a few spare parts. The rod that comes with your Glock will serve nicely. Get a bronze bristle brush and keep it in a plastic tube to keep it from getting crushed. And seal your spare parts in a plastic bag, to keep dust off them and to keep them all in one spot.

What parts? Since nothing is likely to break, carrying spares to replace broken parts is not smart. The only spare I'd carry against breakage would be an extractor. The rest of the parts in my kit are there against loss in cleaning, and to clean. In addition to the cleaning equipment I carry a disassembly punch, a spare set of striker cups, disassembly pins, firing pin spring and a firing pin sleeve. In all, not a lot of stuff, and a compact enough package that I can simply lash it to the holster and have it handy when I need it. The pouch can be switched from the holster for military classes, to a rucksack for backpacking.

One of these days I'm going to assemble another package and simply leave one with the rucksack and one with the holster, and not have to switch.

As for the need, I was reminded at the last World Shoot just how bad things can get. The range was 50 or 60 acres (ranges alone, then there was the rest of the range property) of freshly bulldozed earth. In that part of South Africa the dust was so fine as to make talcum powder look like beach sand. Everyone who intended to keep their pistols going cleaned them every night. And some cleaned them at lunch, too. Those who neglected cleaning found themselves subject to the random and puzzling malfunction, even when using a Glock.

My cleaning gear went into the rucksack I was packing, rather than on my belt or holster. At a match I can always count on being able to walk the few feet to my "ruck" and get what I need.

In a military setting, however, the rucksack may be the next hole over or a couple of miles off. If you need stuff cleaned, you need it done now, and you can't wait.   ♦

CHAPTER 24

Sights for Glocks

ights are this radical new innovation. Well, you'd think so, when you see some people shoot. As my wife once remarked when watching shooter after shooter working over a plate rack to no avail "What do they think aim is? A four-letter word?"

Glock sights are radical, in that they are composed mostly of polymer. The front sight is a parallel-sided pyramid, while the rear is a flattened pyramid. The front is entirely plastic and is held on in a manner that first-timers view as inadequate. The front sight has a split post underneath, and the post goes through the hole in the slide provided for it. Once through, the sight is held in place by a tiny polymer wedge that gets pressed into the split in the sight post. Trust me, it will stay if you press the wedge in properly.

The sights are a reflection of the era in which they were designed. In the late 1970s and early 1980s, white outline sights and dot front sights were all the rage. Compared

to the traditional European military sights (small, rounded, negligible bumps of steel on the top of the slide) the Glock sights were a marvel of design. And if you don't like the dots or bar, it is easy enough to make them go away with the judicious application of a felt-tip pen. Me, while I love a McGivern gold bead and white outline rear on a revolver, on a pistol I want black on black. Silly, but I shoot better with plain sights.

Neat, simple and easy to make and replace, Glock sights are plenty durable enough for their intended users: police and military. The low weight and tough composition of the polymer allows the sights to shrug off many of the impacts that sights get in use. In the Glock system, all sight changes are made by working on the rear sight. Windage adjustments are made by moving the rear sight from side to side. To adjust bullet

Despite the advances in optical sights, here is why you want iron (or polymer) sights on your defensive handgun. I'm not blaming the maker of this sight (a very good one, by the way) but if you drop a pistol out of your holster, you've got to expect this kind of thing to happen.

White dot and rear outline: its's soooo '80s! But unlike the music back then, these sights still work.

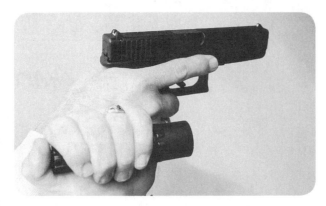

impact up or down, Glock makes rear sights in different heights, noted by markings on the side of the pyramid.

But still plastic. OK, polymer. They'll stand up to police or military use, but the kind of wear that American competition shooters subject them to is something else again. (I can imagine Gaston Glock sitting in his office, mulling over the problem of the American competition shooter. No matter how carefully he designs things, they want something different. No matter how durable he makes it, they insist on greatly exceeding the design parameters or expected service life. But then, they do buy a lot of Glocks.) Chuck Taylor, in his long-term testing

of a Glock G-17, did thousands and thousands of draw and dry-fire repetitions, and gradually wore his front sight down due to friction with the holster. If that is a problem for you as it was for him, go with a replacement front sight made of steel.

Armando Valdes, who must do as many presentations as Chuck Taylor does, has not worn his sight down. He prefers the factory sights. He likes the dot front sight. "My draw is so grooved that the sights come up aligned and I just use the dot

on the front sight as if it were a red dot sight." (A grooved draw is one of the big secrets of the Grand Master shooters, by the way.) "If I need a finer sight alignment, for a far shot or a tight one between no-shoots, then I go with a classic sight picture. Otherwise I go with the front sight dot."

The rear sight is polymer, with a steel plate cast into it to grab the dovetail on the rear of the slide. The sight is moveable by pressing it back and forth in its slot. You cannot move it by traditional methods, however. Usually, if you need to move a rear sight (or a new front sight dovetail design) you use a brass or plastic drift and a hammer. Tap the drift against the sight and thus move it. Won't work on a Glock sight. Whack it, and it spreads under the impact, wedging tighter in the slot. If you want to move a Glock sight, you must use

The Glock front sight, with the split post and wedge.

The Glock front sight installed.

either a Glock sight pusher or the MGW sight pusher. Both use a large screw press to move the sight.

If you need a higher or lower rear sight (to change the bullet impact vertically) you need to swap your current Glock rear for a different Glock rear.

Look on the side of the sight. You'll see a bar or set of bars. The standard 9mm and .40 sight will have a single bar on it: "—" is what it looks like. The standard 10mm and .45 sight will have that bar with a shorter one above it. A still taller one will have the regular bar and two shorter ones above it. If you want to raise bullet impact, go with a sight that has more bars (provided they are shorter bars above the long bar).

For a G-17, each change in sight creates a 2" difference in the point of impact at 25 yards. If you find your bullets are hitting too high, then the sight with a short bar under the long bar lowers point of impact by two inches. The click adjustable sight spans the gap from the shortest to the tallest of the fixed sights. The new click adjustable sight from Glock is far superior to the old adjustable sight that was made solely to comply with the silly US importation regulations. It actually works as a sight, and it isn't so fragile you can break it just getting the Glock out of your gun bag and into your holster. (I've seen the old ones get snapped off, just getting hooked on a belt.)

The trend in 1911s is to use a dovetail front sight for ease of changing and durability.

A longer pistol, such as the G-34 or G-35, will have less change in the point of impact with each change of sight, due to the longer distance between the front and rear sights.

Some people don't favor a plastic sight, and I can't say that I blame them. Not just the wear of plastic but also the banging around a handgun gets in service use. For taking a beating, nothing works like steel. And if you're going to go to steel, you might as well get some night-capable sights too. The Heinie Straight Eight is one example.

The problem with standard three-dot sights in the dark is that when you're faced with three dots, how do you know that what you're seeing isn't the front sight outside of the rear sight, instead of nestled between the rear dots? You don't. The Straight Eight is simple. There is a tritium capsule inside the front sight blade and another one underneath the rear sight slot. To aim, you place one dot on top of the other. If you dip the front sight too much, you lose the dot and see only one. Ditto if you point to one side enough for the rear blade to hide the front sight. If you raise the muzzle too much, you can see the gap between the dots.

The rear sight in its dovetail.

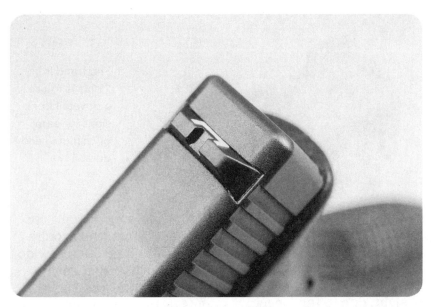

The rear sight in its dovetail.

The rear sight markings. A short bar over the long bar means one step taller.

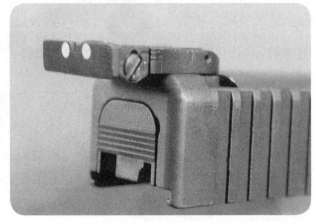

Some adjustable sights offer adjustments at a risk. In a match, this sight risks getting snagged on the draw.

Scott Warren also offers steel sights, and Dave Sevigny uses them to great effect. While we can't lay all of Dave's competition success to the sights he uses, he would not select them over others if he did not feel they offered him an advantage. That's the secret to all success: you select the gear that gives you the greatest advantage, and the practice, practice, practice.

Installation is easy. To take the Glock front out, use a dental pick or sharp and narrow awl to pry the wedge out of the sight post. Glock says to toss and use a new one, but I've had 100 percent success re-using the old ones. What can I say? I'm cheap. Press the Glock sight out.

A steel front sight blade for a Glock is unlike any other sight out there. Obviously, what with the mass of a steel front sight, we can't go with the wedge-and-slot method used on the polymer sights. We can't machine a Glock slide, so the cross dovetail method is out, too. Press the Heinie or other steel sight through the slide.

You'll notice the post is drilled and the hole threaded. The bottom of all steel sights for the Glock are machined to be a tight fit in the oval milled through the slide. The sight is secured in place by means of a hex-headed bolt. To attach the sight properly you need the correct thin-sided wrench to tighten the bolt, or a delicate touch and narrow needlenose pliers.

The Heinie Straight Eight sights.

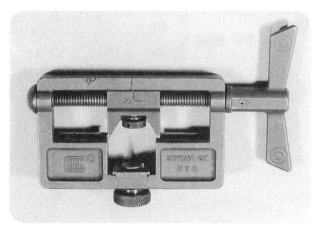

The Glock sight adjustment tool.

Once you have the Glock sight out, check the fit of the steel sight. If it binds in the oval, use a small safe-edge (no teeth on the side) file to clean up the oval boss of the sight until it fits snugly. Don't remove too much or your sight will be loose.

Once the sight fits correctly, try the fit of the hex bolt. When you screw the bolt in (don't tighten it yet) does the sight fit tightly in the slide? In the rare event that it is loose, you'll have to shorten the bolt a small amount, enough to let the bolt pull the sight tight to the slide.

For the rear, you must use the Glock or MGW sight pusher or destroy the old sight removing it. Check the fit of the Heinie or Warren rear sight pyramid to the Glock dovetail, and if needed file with a safe edged three sided file to adjust. (You aren't going to get the file to bite on the Glock slide, so you have to file the sight.) Once the sight starts, use the sight pusher to move the sight to the center of the slide. Range test to see if you need to make any minor corrections.

Now, all you have to do is pay attention to the sights when you shoot, and you won't miss. ◆

The Heinie rear sight fits right into the dovetail with a little judicious filing.

The MGW sight tool.

CHAPTER 25

Barrels

So, why would you want to take a perfectly good Glock barrel and replace it with something else? Good question. The curmudgeonly answer would be that American shooters are a cranky and unsatisfied lot and are always looking for ways to make what they own "better." Which is true. But it is also true that the search for things "better" has resulted in many improvements in firearms, ammunition and gear through the decades.

What is wrong with Glock barrels? From the point of view of many shooters, and Glock themselves, nothing at all. For a police department or military organization, Glock barrels are more accurate than the unwashed mob of personnel they have to supervise, and expending more of a limited budget getting "better" barrels is a waste of time, effort, paperwork and money.

Considering the generous scoring rings on most law enforcement targets, any Glock made can place every shot fired in the center zone at any reasonable (and some

unreasonable) handgun distance. Since the limiting factor for police use is the operator, and not the barrel or ammunition, the budget is better spent on ammunition and training. And since each pistol comes complete with a barrel, why add more to the inventory? And if someone breaks a barrel it is easy enough to replace it, so what's the big deal?

On reading this again, I wonder if I haven't been a bit too harsh. "Unwashed mob?" "Generous scoring rings?" Some of you must think I'm a hopeless cynic and condescending snob. Not at all. While I might have spent too much time around really good shooters, that does not negate the reality that most police departments strain to meet the minimum standard allowed by law or custom. Any more is money that could be spent elsewhere, to "better effect" in the opinions of those in charge. Qualification course? As long as everyone passes, it's no big deal.

For many shooters, the deal is big indeed. And the matter of replacement barrels

for Glocks always ends up coming down to three areas of inquiry: accuracy, ability to use lead bullets, and chamber size. In the search to solve these problems, some shooters will be willing to spend a quarter to a half of the cost of the purchase price of their Glock in order to have a better barrel.

Before we go looking at replacements, let's take a tour of Glock barrels.

The Glock Barrel

Glock barrels are formed by the cold hammer forging method. The method is simple. A bar of steel is drilled through, and the hole precision-reamed and polished. The exterior is also turned to a precise dimension and finish turned to a specified level of surface smoothness. The barrel section (a thick walled pipe at this point) goes into the barrel forge. The forge machine (all automated) inserts a "mandrel" into the hole. The mandrel is the exact shape and dimension of the

Each barrel is marked with the serial number of the Glock it goes into, before it ever sees the slide and frame.

bore-to-be, right down to the rifling and chamber.

The forge then hammers the blank down to shape over the mandrel, forming the barrel interior, complete with chamber. The simultaneous forming of the chamber is to ensure precise alignment, at least as precise as the lathe grinder that fabricated the mandrel. (In today's manufacturing world, that's pretty precise.) The barrel then is slid off the mandrel, and automatic lathes and mills finish machine the exterior to final dimension.

Once shaped, the barrel is then gauged and proofed, marked with the test-fire proof mark, caliber and serial number, and then Tenifer treated and sent on to assembly where it is mated with a slide, frame and the rest of the parts to create a Glock pistol. Serial numbered, then Tenifer treated, then mated to its pistol? Yes. The design and the manufacturing standards of Glock ensure that any barrel will fit any Glock (of that caliber and size) regardless of when it was made. As a result, the barrels can be serial numbered before they are assembled.

If barrels are utterly interchangeable, why put a serial number on them? European custom and tradition? The military

The Glock barrel is hammer-forged and then machined to shape.

While many Glock parts are interchangeable, barrels usually are not.

requirement to keep barrel inventory tracked? Busywork to keep jobs at the plant? I don't know, but I suspect the reasons are most likely in the order I've listed. In the early days, barrels were also marked with the date of manufacturing, using a three-letter code. Now, they're simply marked with the Glock logo.

Starting at the rear, you see the block of the chamber and locking lug section. On the very rear, top and bottom, you have the barrel hood and integral ramp. The hood acts to keep the tip of the bullet under control when it snaps upwards in feeding, and guide the slide onto the barrel at the end of the forward slide cycle. Could Glock have made it wider, as in full width? Probably, but there would not have been any advantage. And it would make the machining process slightly more complex. The ramp is the complete section needed to guide the cartridge up out of

the magazine. Unlike the 1911 pistol, with the ramp divided between frame and barrel, the Glock ramp is all on the barrel.

On the chamber section is the pistol's serial number, proof mark and caliber. Depending in when it was made, the caliber may be on the right or the top. The chamber itself is a bit larger than many competition shooters would like, betraying its military origin. A service

pistol has to keep working regardless of the conditions it is in. So, to accommodate a certain amount of dust, dirt, mud, rust and other debris, the chamber is a little bit large. The somewhat oversized chamber can be a problem with the .40 and .45 caliber pistols, but in 9mm it is no big deal.

The leade (the tapered portion of the rifling and bore just in front of the chamber

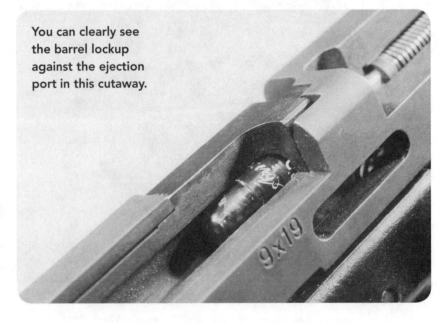

You can clearly see the barrel lockup against the ejection port in this cutaway.

9x19

The bottom lug, showing the cam and the assembly and recoil spring recesses.

The G-17T training pistol, with its off-center bore to compensate for the lack of recoil when firing paint or rubber bullets.

proper) at the front of the chamber is, again, different from what competition shooters would like. The leade is steeper than on other pistols, and the leade and early part of the bore can attract a buildup of lead from cast bullets. Military ammunition is always jacketed, and a steep leade is of no consequence.

Underneath and forward of the ramp section is the cam of the locking lug, with the assembly notch and recoil spring notch at its front. The cam runs the barrel up or down the locking block when the slide cycles. The recesses on the front are not interchangeable. The recoil spring assembly must be inserted in its semicircular notch. If the recoil spring is inserted too high or too low, assembly will be difficult or impossible.

Forward of the chamber, the barrel exterior is cylindrical to the muzzle. The muzzle is crowned with a flat face, and the rifling is recessed by means of a short tapered section. The rifling is polygonal. Instead of the gear-like segments of typical rifling, the Glock rifling is composed of curves as seen in cross-section. The polygonal rifling gives a better seal, which is the main advantage proclaimed. My suspicion is that polygonal rifling is easier to fabricate on hammer-forging machines, and so Glock makes a virtue of necessity. The rifling works, so who cares, right?

Left: a Glock barrel with polygonal rifling. *Right*: a cut-rifled barrel suitable for use with lead bullets.

On all calibers but the .45, the polygonal rifling is hexagonal, that is, six lands and grooves. (If you can call a series of curves "lands" and "grooves") The .45 rifling is octagonal, or eight-segmented. The smaller flats of the octagon give a better seal for the .45 bullet. I suspect that what Glock found was that the six-segment barrel dimensions allowed too large a gap at the "corners" and that they were finding .45 bullets that wouldn't bump up to fill the gaps. One solution would be to make the whole bore tighter, so the bullet would be swaged down, or squeezed to fit. (The chamber pressure of the .45 ACP is not large enough to do much bumping up of the bullet to fit larger bores, as some calibers can be counting on doing.)

But the combination of a tight bore and hard bullets (some jacketed .45 bullets can be quite hard) would greatly increase chamber pressure. Not that the pressure would be a problem for the Glock (after all, the G-21 is basically a 10mm with a bigger hole through the barrel) but it could be very hard on the brass. More segments means a tighter fit without squeezing the bullet and producing higher pressures.

With a few notable exceptions, the rifling twist for Glock pistols is the same: 9.84", or 250 mm. That is, the bullet makes one complete rotation every 250 millimeters of travel down the bore. A twist slightly faster than 10 inches for a 9mm, 40 or 10mm is faster than optimal, as the calculated standard (one that many other barrelmakers use) is one turn in 16 inches. A 10-inch twist instead of a 16-inch twist isn't a big deal, as many pistols will shoot quite accurately with a fast twist. However, six models use a different twist: the G-21, G-30, G-31, G-32, G-33 and G-36. The G-31/G-32/G-33 are all chambered in .357 SIG. The G-21, G-30 and G-36 are made in .45 ACP.

The twist rate for the .357 SIG pistols is 406mm, or 15.98". The .45 ACP model has a twist rate of 400mm,

You can't thread a Glock barrel (the Tenifer is too tough), so if you want an Open gun like this one, you have to use a custom barrel.

OVER A BARREL

Can you change barrels? Should you?

In some competitions, changing barrels is not allowed. And even within some competitions, the different equipment Divisions can have different rules. For instance, if you are shooting in a GSSF match, using a non-Glock barrel moves you out of the Stock category into the Open category regardless of any other equipment you might have on the gun. In USPSA competition, using a replacement barrel is allowed in all Divisions: Open, Limited, Limited Ten and Production. So, you can improve accuracy or use lead bullets with impunity in those categories (good luck using lead in Open, as lead and comps can be an unhappy marriage). The idea for Production is to be the category of choice for those who don't want to be beholden to a gunsmith in order to compete. However, even Production shooters want accuracy and can wear out barrels, so replacement barrels in Production are allowed.

In IDPA, internal modifications for reliability or accuracy are allowed, but barrels that are heavier than factory, or use a cone shape instead of a bushing, are not allowed. Since the only barrel that will work in a Glock is one with near-identical external dimensions (perhaps slightly larger for a tighter fit) then any barrel would work, provided you don't have a muzzle brake on the muzzle or ports out the top.

In still other competitions, no one cares what barrel is in your Glock. Go to the American Handgunner Shootoffs and tell the match officials that you have a replacement barrel, and the reply is likely to be something like this: "What's that? A Bar-Sto barrel in your Stock Auto category Glock? Is is ported or comped? No? Then good for you."

If you were to shoot Bullseye with Glocks, you could shoot the .45 in Any Centerfire portions, but the Service Pistol (1911's in .45 Only, or Beretta 9mms, no others need apply) would be closed to you.

Changing barrels in some competitions tosses you out of Stock.

Still, if you are going to compete with a Glock then it would be a good idea to get a copy of the rules for the match and read them. Then, if you have any questions you can ask the match officials before you show up. Doing so can save you some embarrassment. If you show up with improper gear, the match officials at a club match will usually let you shoot, but your score won't count, and you may be in for some gentle ribbing by your fellow competitors. At a larger match, you may find yourself entered in Open, or not being allowed to shoot at all.

or 15.75". I can understand changing the .357 SIG twist, as the too-fast twist of the old rate, combined with the additional velocity that the .357 SIG imparts to its 9mm bullets (up to 350 fps more steam) could have been too much for lightly-constructed hollowpoint bullets. After all, there is no point in getting more velocity from a bullet if you're going to watch it break apart on the way to the target due to a too-fast twist, or fragment on impact. So, the slower twist for the .357 SIG was a wise choice.

Why use the same twist for all the others (.380 Auto included)? Manufacturing uniformity. Remember, the barrel blanks are produced on a cold hammer forge machine. With a different program selected, the bin full of barrel blanks that have been hammered can be turned into barrels to fit any model. A barrel blank could theoretically made into a barrel to fit a G-17, G-17L, G-19, G-26 or G-34.

Since the chamber is hammer-forged along with the bore, the .380s have to be done separately, unless all chambers are forged to .380, and the 9mms reamed to size, a wasteful and unsatisfying manufacturing decision that I can't imagine Glock making. Ditto blanks in .40 and the G-22 and its derivatives, and the other calibers. As for the "wastage" – the extra barrel cut off – so what? In holding the barrel blank for turning and machining, some portion

forward of the muzzle has to be retained as a clamping surface. If that surface is only an inch long, then in cutting from a G-17 barrel to a G-19, an extra .47" of steel tube is cut off. Compared to the steel cut away to create the barrel, the extra .47" isn't much at all.

In the .45, I'm puzzled. The fast twist may have been too fast for the wide range of .45 ACP bullets: 185 to 230 grains. The faster twist may have been too much for the high-speed (relatively speaking) 185-grain .45 loads. At 1150 fps (a velocity the Cor-bon reaches easily in a full-size gun) the 185-grain jacketed hollowpoints may have been over-rotated and fragmented upon impact in tests or field study. Glock may have simply gone with the twist rate of so many American barrel makers. As with so many things, Glock remains mum on the subject.

Now let's look over other barrels and the considerations that compel other shooters to spend good money upgrading their Glocks.

Glock Accuracy

Ask the Glock masses, and they'll extol the virtues of the "match grade" Glock barrels. You'll be told of spectacular groups and wondrously accurate pistols. I have to remain a skeptic, as I haven't seen any of those pistols. Don't get me wrong, I find them quite accurate, just not the tack-drivers that enthusiastic owners claim.

I recently bought a used G-17 because I wanted to. I was at Double Action Indoor Range, in Madison Heights, Michigan, and had just found out about a promotion. So I splurged and bought a gun. Al Allen had a very clean G-17 at an attractive price, so I gave in. I took that pistol to a law enforcement class, and had no problems hitting steel plates out to 75 yards with it.

In testing the new .45 GAP models I shot them over sandbags at 25 yards. They produced nice groups, but nothing spectacular. However, you must keep thing in context. To me, a "spectacular" group is five shots into one ragged hole at 25 yards. Not many pistols will do that, and most of those I've seen that would, had a custom, match barrel artfully installed by a top-ranked gunsmith. My G-17, and those .45 GAP Glocks would, however, produce groups at 25 yards that subtended less of an arc than the apparent width of the front sight.

And as accuracy goes, groups less-wide than the width of your front sight blade are very good indeed. They just aren't the best that money can buy.

What Is Accuracy, Anyway?

For a lot of competitors, there is no such thing as "too much accuracy" provided it doesn't come at the cost of reliability. Just what constitutes sufficient accuracy is a matter of debate, but many shooters

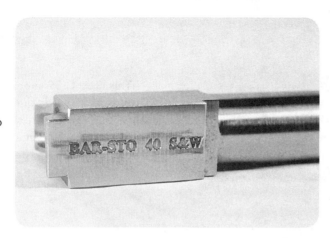

You want accuracy? Bar-Sto can deliver.

Properly nestled in the Ransom's grip adapters, your Glock will shoot to the best of its ability.

You can learn a lot with careful bench shooting, but the real test of accuracy is the Ransom rest.

simply want more. Can a new barrel get you more accuracy? It sure can.

A small subset of the shooters looking for accuracy also want some sort of recoil control as well. For them, an extended barrel with a threaded-on compensator offers both more accuracy and recoil control. The only drawback is that securing the comp to the barrel makes cleaning your Glock a bit of a hassle.

A replacement barrel manufactured in smaller batches than Glock barrels (hundreds of barrels vs. hundreds of thousands) can be machined to tighter tolerances. Combined with a slower twist to aid accuracy, and tightly fitted to the slide, a replacement barrel can improve accuracy from a small amount to a lot.

In the interests of discovering just what accuracy improvements can be gained by installing a match barrel, I enlisted the aid of Irv Stone at Bar-Sto. He sent me a barrel for my G-22, and I tested it with the factory barrel and the Bar-Sto barrel. Rather than prejudice the test with my poor attempts at shooting like a machine rest, I used my Ransom rest. The flex of the Glock polymer frame makes getting the Ransom rest set up and settled in a bit more work than with a metal-framed handgun, but not a lot.

When I did the accuracy testing for *The Gun Digest Book of the 1911*, it took as few as two or three groups to

This little G-39 shoots groups at 25 yards that are smaller than the apparent width of the front sight. How much more accuracy do you expect?

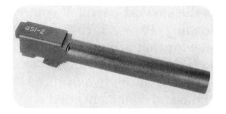

The Dave Manson/Loon Lake red aluminum training barrel. No chamber or bore, and bright red for no confusion.

get a pistol settled into the grip inserts. With the Glock, the initial settling in took five or six groups, depending on which range trip it was (some five, some six, one seven) but once settled in, I only had to fire the usual two groups when switching ammo to re-condition the bore.

I first tried the G-22 for groups with factory ammo with the Glock barrel, then took off the upper, swapped to the Bar-Sto barrel, re-fired the settling groups and then proceeded to try again with the factory ammo. The experiment was quite gratifying, as the Bar-Sto barrel markedly improved some ammo performance and slightly improved others, but was always better.

Lead Bullets

Then there is the matter of lead bullets. As I mentioned before, only American shooters are in the position of using lead bullets. Only we reload in volume enough to consider the economy of lead bullets. In many countries, reloading is prohibited. In others, the amount of reloading components allowed on hand is so small that reloading is more a matter of crafting perfect little jewels than loading buckets of practice ammo.

Glock didn't consider lead bullets as a viable choice, as they were building guns to satisfy NATO specifications and to serve the European market.

So the matter of lead doesn't come up elsewhere in the world. Here in the USA, not only does it come up, but there is a simple solution. Swap barrels. The barrel makers who provide Match barrels and aftermarket barrels are quite familiar with the use of lead bullets. As a result, they can provide a barrel that can

While many pistols get along fine with both, Glocks are much happier with jacketed bullets rather than lead.

easily handle your lead bullet reloads, assuming you load dimensionally-correct ammo. How economical is the option of swapping barrels? First, you have to be a reloader, and thus compare lead-bullet reloads to jacketed or plated bullet reloads, and not to factory ammo. If you are going to compare reloads to factory ammo you should add the investment of a reloading setup to the cost.

When reloading lead vs. jacketed, the only real cost difference is the bullet itself. The brass life is the same, the primer is the same, and the amount of powder used is so close to being the same that the cost difference hardly matters. (In 9mm, I find I have to increase a powder charge by .2 grains [from 4.2 to 4.4] to get identical velocities going from lead to jacketed. At $15 per pound of powder, that adds 43 cents to the cost of loading 1,000 rounds. Not enough to break the bank.)

The recent increase in critical metals on the world market has made ammunition a much touchier subject than it has been.

Before the War, the rise in Chinese and Indian production, and the first edition of this book, a savvy buyer could find 9mm ammunition for $120 per thousand rounds. Now, you are hard-pressed to find any at all for less than twice that. Lead bullets can still be less-expensive than jacketed, but the numbers are always shifting. That they are going up simply makes reloading more and more attractive.

The cost in bullets can be significant. At the extremes of bullet cost, I can buy lead 125-grain 9mm bullets for $60 per thousand. (All comparisons of reloading will be done with 9mm, as it is the least advantageous to reload for. All other calibers recoup your investment sooner. Some calibers a lot sooner.) The expensive jacketed hollowpoint match bullets are $150/K.

A better example (since you probably won't have an in with a volume bullet caster and won't be shooting Hornady XTPs in practice) is lead at $75/K and jacketed at $120/K. The $40-45/K difference pays for a lead-specific aftermarket barrel in the expenditure of 3,000 rounds of ammo. That may seem like a lot of shooting, but it isn't. An annual consumption of 3,000 rounds only means 250 rounds a month, and one range trip can use up that much ammo. Many serious competitors go through 3,000 in a month of dedicated practice.

Once the barrel has been paid off through lower ammo costs, the savings either stay in your pocket or can be plowed back into more practice. After all, if you were used to paying $125/K for your components for reloading jacketed (bullets, powder, primers) then the same $125 gets you 1,600 rounds of lead-bullet reloading components.

If you want to go from factory ammo to reloading, then the investment of a reloading press should be added in. The best (and most common for high-volume loaders) is a Dillon. If you go economy but still keep volume production, then a Dillon Square deal B and all the needed extras runs $450 or so. The Dillon 550B would run you $550 with the extras needed. (The big advantage of the 550B is the ability to easily change calibers. If you're sticking with one caliber, the SDB might be all you need.) Factory ammo can run as much as $200 per thousand rounds.

At reloaded lead ammunition for the total cost of $90/K (bullet, powder, primer) and factory jacketed at $125, you'll need to shoot 7,500 rounds to pay for your SDB reloading press. The 550B requires just over 9,000 rounds. Using jacketed bullets in your reloading delays the break even point. As I mentioned earlier, 9mm is the slowest payoff. If you're loading .40 or .45, you can pay for that SDB or 550B in less than 5,000 rounds. Add to that the two or three thousand rounds needed to pay off the new barrel, and you can see why some shooters don't switch. And others don't reload.

Chamber Size

The Glock chamber on the G-17 was designed to NATO specs. The idea of any military firearm is that it will be used in a stressful environment. Not just the stress of combat, with other people trying to mess with your carefully-laid plans of staying safe, but the environmental stress of dust, dirt, mud, rain, rust, blood and sweat, snow and ice. If a firearm won't work when it gets a bit dirty, it isn't much use. And in the field (let alone combat) a firearm can't always be pampered as so many

Brownells carries a full line of gunsmithing tools and accessories and has shelves of Glock barrels on hand. This is one corner of just one building.

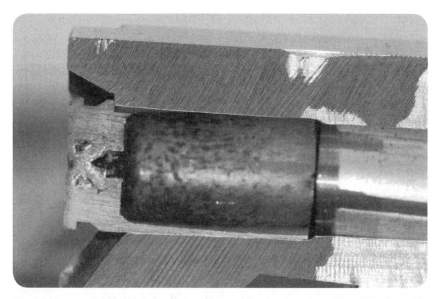

The closeup of this sectioned chamber and case (*courtesy Bar-Sto Barrels*) shows how close to the edge you're running even with a full-supported case. Toss tired brass and a large chamber in the mix and it could lead to trouble.

competition firearms are. A chamber has to be loose enough that a modest amount of grunge doesn't keep it from firing. But a too-large chamber is bad for accuracy and can be unsafe. The G-17's chamber is designed to gobble up any ammo fed it, under any climatic circumstances the soldier it is issued to can survive.

The large chamber can pose a problem to reloaders. A case is not fully supported all the way down to the extractor groove. It can't be and still provide a compact feeding mechanism. The base of the case is relatively unsupported (some designs and calibers provide more support, others less) – and therein lies the rub. A hot load, or a relatively soft

case, can expand or even bulge at the base. The expanded base isn't enough to keep it from working in the Glock it was fired in but may be too large to fit in a tighter chamber in another pistol or one that offers a bit more support.

No problem since the case is re-sized when you process it for reloading right? Actually, it can be a problem. You see, just as the chamber can't support the case right down to the extractor groove, most sizing dies don't reach that far, either. The die has to have some taper at the mouth to funnel each case in. The case has to be held by a plate called a shellholder. One sizer does go all the way, the EGW base sizer. But the rest don't.

What happens when a base-expanded case gets into a pistol with a tighter chamber? It doesn't close, and the impact of trying to chamber the round usually wedges it in tight. Shooters who reload and feed more than one pistol in a caliber, find that changing a stock Glock barrel with its generous chamber to an aftermarket barrel with a tighter chamber can prevent many problems with their reloaded ammo. By using the tighter-chamber barrel in place of the looser-chamber Glock barrel, they can avoid having to sort ammo or brass for particular pistols.

The problem is particularly evident to other shooters at your range in .40S&W, and to the original owner in .45. The Glock chamber is overly generous to ensure reliable feeding. The

The EGW die has a shorter taper, so it sizes down the case farther.

.40 cartridge is just as high a pressure round as the 9mm, but with a larger surface for the case to deal with. Many competition shooters who shoot .40 pistols that aren't Glocks have match barrels with tight chambers. Typically, .40 brass that has been fired in a Glock is useless to them unless it has been sized down all the way to the extractor groove. And if they overlook a round, it will stop their pistol cold, and usually right in the middle of a match.

Competition shooters with non-Glock pistols will sort their brass and discard any that show signs of having been fired in a Glock. The .45 has such a large chamber that even though the cartridge operates at a very low pressure (for a firearm), the brass is overly expanded on each firing. Sized down it works fine, but working the brass so much each time it is reloaded shortens its useful life.

Barrel Fit

Many drop-in barrels will improve accuracy enough, in conjunction with the improved brass life, to make them a worthwhile investment.

For the greatest increase in accuracy, a barrel should be fitted to the particular pistol it is to be used in. Barrel fitting is an advanced gunsmithing/armorer's process, and you shouldn't be working over your $200+ match barrel with stones and files in order to fit it yourself. Yes, a gunsmith will charge you to fit it, but that is the admission price to

greater accuracy. How much accuracy? Groups an inch smaller at 50 yards, maybe. (Three inches instead of four, according to a recent test session.)

If you think you need that much accuracy, consider the cost. Then consider how much actual need you've had for that level of accuracy at recent matches. Do you really want to be spending $300+ for a couple of extra points at a club-level match or two a year? If you do, congratulations, you are a hard-core competition shooter.

Glock considers barrel fit to be something the factory has already taken care of. The factory barrel will already fit the factory slide, so no fitting is needed. Indeed, in the Glock Armorer's Course, barrel fitting is simply barrel reassembly. "No fitting required" is the mantra. You will only have to worry about barrel fit on a replacement

barrel not of Glock origins, like a Bar-Sto from Irv Stone III. While Irv (and other barrel makers) make drop-in barrels, they also make over sized barrels that require precise fitting to your particular Glock. (Even some drop-in barrels might require fine-tuning.)

For those who want to give it a go, or those curious about how it is done, here is how your barrel is fitted by the gunsmith. In its details the process is much simpler than fitting a barrel to a 1911, the standard many would compare it to. Simple because of the Glock design, and simple because Gaston Glock had all the previous models of the twentieth century to use as a guide.

First, the gunsmith attempts to assemble the barrel as if nothing was too large. (If it goes into the slide without binding, "fitting" is finished. Many drop right in.)

You can see the barrel cams in this cutaway. The front cam will unlock as the action cycles, and the rear cam rides up, locking the barrel into the ejection port.

Closeup of the barrel locked into the ejection port.

In the rare case of the barrel being too large to fit into the hole in the front of the slide, he'll have to polish it down. Depending on how much he has to take off, he may simply polish the barrel on its cylindrical section, or he may lathe-turn it.

Barrel fit at the muzzle for a Glock is a much simpler matter than the 1911 due to all the delicate machining that's already been done to the slide. The slide is machined at the front barrel hole for the barrel's pivot when it unlocks, and for its lockup when it closes. Unlike the 1911's barrel, the Glock's barrel itself must only be a cylinder. Turning or polishing a clearance section behind the muzzle on a Glock is not very useful and can be counter-productive. (It is common to polish the 1911 barrel down in diameter behind the barrel bushing seat section, to prevent binding on cycling.)

If the barrel slides into the slide but won't close and lock into the ejection port, the fitting begins. A visual inspection will tell him where the barrel is binding. It will be one or both of the hood width and chamber box length. He'll measure the distance from the front shoulder of the chamber section to the rear of the hood and also measure the width of the hood. He will then compare these measurements with the size of the openings in the slide, the hood width and the front to back gap in the slide. The comparison is made to the slide and not the existing factory barrel! After all, you want the new barrel to fit better than, not merely as well as, the factory barrel that is in it.

The common method of correcting a too-long hood is with a file, but a gunsmith with an end mill or lathe could dress the hood back the required length in about two or three minutes. The usual method is to file the hood back (and narrower, if needed) to the measured dimension or a thousandth longer, then start pressing it to fit. By smoking the hood with a candle and pressing the parts together, he can see where they bind. (The binding location rubs the carbon of the smoke off. "File the bright spot" is the first thing you learn as a gunsmith. "File only a little" is the second.)

Once the parts fit by pressing, then the filing adjusts the fit. Sure, you can force the parts to fit with a high spot on the hood, but by carefully filing the high spots you (or your gunsmith) will

The 1911 is almost as easy to disassemble as the Glock, but the fitting required to install a match barrel is much more involved.

get contact across the whole hood face. The idea is to get a fit without slop or play, that goes together without needing force or binding.

Once the hood fits properly, the gunsmith checks the "carry up" of the fit. More commonly used as a term for revolver action, I use it to describe how high the barrel goes in the slide before stopping. A barrel that stops too soon will not have enough locking lug engagement to properly contain the round when fired. Early unlocking is bad for the brass, bad for the pistol, and will sooner or later cause you problems.

How high is high enough? The barrel front seat must come up to the top of the slide and be flush. If it stops early, the problem is in one of two places: muzzle or chamber. If the muzzle is too fat, it is binding on the slide seat and flexing the barrel. The check for muzzle bind is to press the barrel as hard as possible up into its locked position n the slide and watch for springback. If the barrel springs back, it is being flexed from the muzzle and needs a bit of polishing. If it doesn't spring back, the barrel is too thick just in front of the chamber and must be polished down. Luckily, this is a rare problem.

The gunsmith then checks cam lug fit. He'll assemble the Glock without the recoil spring assembly or striker assembly and watch the timing of the lug and its fit when the action closes. In many Glock barrel replacements, I've never seen a problem with cam lug fit. The dimensions aren't too important that is, making them larger doesn't improve accuracy – so the replacement barrel makers simply duplicate the factory cam lug dimensions.

The first thing the gunsmith checks is to see that the foot of the lug isn't too large. If the bottom of the cam foot sticks down too far, it will act to cam to barrel up too high in the slide on closing. If you have it the problem will not be subtle. When you have it the slide will stop before fully closing. The solution is to file the bottom of the cam foot until the barrel doesn't bind when closing. (Filed just enough, as taking too much off prevents the barrel from camming up high enough to be fully locked to the slide when closed.)

Once the barrel locks up to the slide, the gunsmith will then assemble the pistol with the recoil spring assembly and "play with" the Glock for a few minutes. He'll cycle it repeatedly, watching and feeling the action. He'll note if the barrel binds in cycling, if it is rubbing hard on top of the chamber. Does the slide close fully when hand-cycled and then allowed to close the last step on its own?

Any binding found at this point, or rubbing of the chamber top on the inside of the slide, is dealt with by some judicious filing and stoning. Once the action cycles smoothly and shows no signs of rubbing or binding, then

Why bother with a custom barrel? A Colt Light Weight Commander shot this group with a Bar-Sto barrel. A Glock could, too.

the gunsmith will test-fire your Glock. A new barrel often shoots to a slightly different point of impact than the old barrel did (something to keep in mind if you plan to swap barrels between competitions). The gunsmith may or may not adjust your sights.

Conversations with a Barrel Maker

In the course of working on this book, I talked with several barrel makers and managed to pry a lot of information out of them. The most indepth talks were with Irv Stone III of Bar-Sto barrels.

For those who are new to the aftermarket barrel business, Bar-Sto is the oldest match handgun barrel maker around. Irv's father was making replacement stainless Match barrels for the 1911 even before the formation of IPSC. It was, however, IPSC that made Bar-Sto a household word. In the old Bullseye days, you could have accuracy or you could have reliability in a pistol. But IPSC shooters were a stubborn lot and insisted on having both. For many years, one of the ingredients that you could almost always count on finding on a competition IPSC gun was a Bar-Sto barrel. Most of my match guns have Bar-Sto barrels. Others make barrels just as good, but when I started there was only Bar-Sto so most of my guns have them.

The conversations with Irv turned up a number of gems. The first is that for all their hardness, Glock barrels are actually soft. We're talking engineering/machinist standards here. Only a persnikety engineer or machinist could consider a material like steel as being "soft." Glock barrels are formed by the cold hammer forging method. The alloy used must be soft enough to be hammered into shape. The forged barrels are then finish-machined to final dimensions. Glock barrels are then Tenifer treated, as are the slides and other parts. Tenifer creates a very hard surface but doesn't affect the hardness of the interior of the treated part.

As a result, you have a relatively soft body (called the "substrate") and a hard surface. Think of a chocolate

bar with a gooey interior. If you apply enough force to the skin, it will crack. As long as the surface isn't broken, the candy remains intact. As soon as the covering cracks, the substrate, which offers no strength, allows the cracked portion to move.

"So what?" you ask. "My barrel isn't a cherry cordial." No, but in the words of Galileo as he left his trial, "It still moves." When you fire a round, your barrel expands with the pressure. The chamber expands, and the barrel expands behind the travelling bullet.

As long as the barrel is not expanded more than, or faster than, the tensile limits of the barrel steel, it will contract back to the original dimensions as if nothing happened. The high value of the "Elastic Limit" of steel is one of the attributes that make it so valuable in modern construction and manufacturing. If the tensile limits of the surface are exceeded, the substrate cannot offer much in the way of support. A barrel composed of a steel slightly

softer than the Tenifer-treated steel, but hard all the way through, supports its surface. If a momentary force exceeds the limits of the surface, the supporting substrate simply takes up more of the load.

At a high enough load (or overload, in the case of someone's too-enthusiastic ammunition loading efforts) all barrels will expire. However, the hard-soft combination of the Glock seems to allow them to break at a slightly lower pressure (a pressure that's still greatly over the accepted limits). Glock barrels demonstrate a type of failure other barrels don't.

When a case fails, the gases jet out of the ruptured case. Pressure that had been contained now is free. When the gas encounters an obstacle, the forces involved are now of a different nature. Where the previous exposure to the gases had been a pressure, now the gas impacts the surface. The elastic limit of steel to impact is generally lower than a gradually (even by combustion standards) applied force. A hard object can break under impact when struck with less force than a more gradually applied load.

I have seen 1911 barrels that survived a case blowout with no damage. The hard and tough-through nature of the steel allows it to shrug off such impacts. The steel or aluminum frame can also survive the impact. A Glock seems to react differently. The hard-surfaced but softer core barrel has a bit

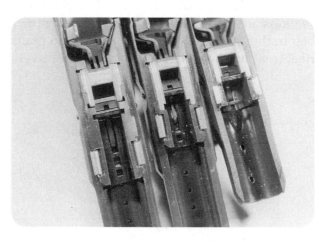

Different models and calibers require different barrels. When you order a barrel, be sure to specify exactly what you have and what you want.

less ability to deal with the impact of the jetting gases. The polymer frame has even less. So, a 10mm 1911 with a blown case might need new grips and a new magazine. A blown Glock will need a new frame. (I've personally seen both, and I own the Colt.) A 1911 faced with over-pressure ammunition gradually (or not so gradually) peens the locking lugs or cracks the barrel. A Glock seems to fracture at the chamber end.

Now, before you go out in a panic and send all your pistols to the smelter, we're talking a very small number of cases at very high pressures. As an example, the normal operating pressure of the .45 ACP case is under 20,000 psi. The normal 9mm/.38 Super pressure is 34,000 psi. For many years, competition shooters have been running their .38 super 1911s at pressures in the 45-50,000 level without any failures.

How high a pressure do you have to run things before the gun fails? I don't know. The factories won't tell us, and no one will lend me the testing equipment and guns to find out. The tensile strength of steel is variously (depending on the alloy) listing in the 130,000-plus psi range. Do not confuse tensile strength limits with operating strength limits. A barrel worked at 35,000 psi will operate for a million cycles without damage. A barrel run at 100,000 psi can quit in a few hundred.

You've got lots of safety margin in any pistol, provided you follow accepted reloading guidelines or use factory ammunition. As a guide to how picky custom barrel makers can be, you need to know something about the regular method of making barrels.

The customary method for making barrels is to start with a bar stock or forging and drill it and ream it smooth. Then the outside is machined to the rough dimensions of the finished product.

Either before or after the machining to final dimensions, the bore is rifled. Some are rifled by pulling a cutter called a broach through them. Others are rifled by pushing a rifled bore cross section-shaped carbide tip called a button through them. Once finished, the barrel is then heat treated to make it hard and tough.

At Bar-Sto, the barrel sections are heat treated before they are machined. Heat treating can subtly warp a part, diminishing a barrel's accuracy potential. By heat-treating first, Bar-Sto barrels are not then warped after they are shaped and can be counted on to be tough and straight.

After going to all that work, Irv can be justly proud of how tough and accurate his barrels are. Glock doesn't have to make any excuses, and the Bar-Sto method is not open to them. They have to make a hundred thousand barrels a year or more. They'd need four plants full of barrel machining production lines if they wanted to make barrels the Bar-Sto way.

Further Research

To find out more about Glock barrels and why they are particularly sensitive to lead bullets, go to Taylor Freelance and pick up a copy of the second edition of *The Glock in Competition*. There you will find the testing, measurements and results of serious inquiry. Why don't I just tell you here? Because I respect the intellectual property right of other authors, that's why. And the book is well worth the investment, even if you have no plans to shoot competitively. ♦

CHAPTER 26

The Glock in Competition

Generally speaking, any competition in which you can use any other self-loading pistol is a competition in which you could use a Glock. However, leaving it at that would make for a short and uninteresting chapter.

Any competition in which you need durability, reliability, ease of shooting and ease of use would be a competition suited to the Glock. You might have noticed I left out accuracy. I did so not because the Glock isn't accurate, but because of habit and custom. Not mine, but of those who shoot accuracy-only competitions. The two main forms of accuracy-only competition are Bullseye and PPC, and while both are stodgy, the first is nearly petrified. Bullseye has been an organized event since the end of the nineteenth century, when the organizing body was known as the United States Revolver Association.

Those who shoot Bullseye are stubbornly traditional. They often choose to use a .22 pistol made by a particular company that has been out of business for over 30 years. They are often slow to accept new technology, although the red-dot sights were quickly accepted. It will be a slow acceptance of Glocks in the Bullseye community. For the rest, the pace has been much faster.

Practical Competitions

The biggest events that Glocks are in are the Glock Sports Shooting Federations, the United States Practical Shooting Association and the International Defensive Pistol Association. Later we'll cover PPC, Pins, Steel, and others. The best book devoted solely to competition shooting with the Glock is the second edition of *The Glock in Competition: a Shooters How to Guide*, published by Taylor Freelance. In it you can find details of equipment restrictions and course parameters. To get the information otherwise, you'd

Bullseye shooters demand this level of accuracy. This group was shot at 25 yards from a Ransom rest.

One way to get adjustable sights on a target gun is to add a rib.

have to join all the various shooting associations and pore through their rule books. That may be fun, then again it may not be. Better to start smart and efficient, and here and in the Taylor book you can do that.

GSSF

The GSSF was founded by Glock and is the only shooting sport limited to a single brand of firearm. (If you want to shoot a GSSF match, show up with a Glock or be turned away.) The stages are simple compared to some of the other matches, but simple does not mean easy. Simple does mean a high volume of shooting, and it isn't uncommon for GSSF matches to have a much higher attendance than other handgun matches in a geographic area.

To shoot a GSSF Match, you need a Glock or Glocks, eye and ear protection, factory ammunition, and a membership in the GSSF, as well as some sort of case or holster to transport your Glock to, and around, the range. The three stages of a GSSF match are: "Plates," "5 to Glock" and "Glock M."

Glock Basics

The GSSF stages have certain things in common, things that other shooting competitions do not necessarily do. First of all, you will not be working from a holster during a GSSF match. All stages start from the low ready position. In Low Ready, you have both hands on the Glock, holding it down at a 45-degree angle in front of you. You can use a holster, but only to store and transport your Glock from one stage to another. On the command to "load and make ready" you unholster, insert a magazine loaded with 10 rounds and chamber a round. You are allowed to then change magazines and insert another fully-charged-to-10 magazine, for a total of eleven rounds in

the Glock. Magazines that can hold more may not be loaded past 11 rounds.

Second, you won't be reloading against the clock. If you've expended the 11 rounds in the gun and haven't solved your problem, you simply have to take the penalties you've got coming (generally, 10 seconds per missed plate or shot on target).

Third, you won't be moving with a loaded Glock. All stages are fired from a single position, and you won't have to deal with barricades, obstacles, hard cover or no-shoot targets.

All scoring is time plus earned time penalties. The target is the NRA D-1, otherwise known as the Bianchi target. Tombstone shaped, it has a set of impressed scoring circles on

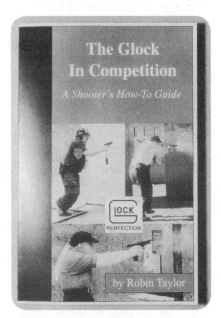

Robin Taylor literally wrote the book on Glock competitions. Want to shoot with a Glock and do well? Get the book.

SANDBAGGING AND GRANDBAGGING

Many of you already know what "sandbagging" is. If a certain competition has a classification system, sandbagging is holding back in one's performance on the classification portion so as to "earn" a rank lesser than ones abilities. If the cutoff for "A" class (as an example) is 80 percent of some standard, the sandbagger will carefully and deliberately shoot a classification course so as to post a 75-79 percent score. As a "B" shooter, he can then go to a big match, shoot to the fullest extent of his ability and "win" B Class. Done often enough, they will eventually be dragged up into A Class, but by that time their actual ability may be at the Master level.

I might point out that shooting is not the only sport or competition with this situation. Anything that is timed or scored and has different levels of performance suffers the same problem. Drag racing is one example, where exceeding a certain performance level can actually cause your overall score to suffer.

Sandbagging can cause all kinds of hard feelings. Shooters who make "mistakes" in classification stages (a typical IPSC club match will have one stage for classification among the three, four or five stages for the match score) but who perform up to their known level in all the other stages are viewed with suspicion (and usually referred to as "that sandbagging *&%#@!"). In the example given, a B Class shooter who wins B Class at a big match with a score that is 87 percent of the match winner (where 80 percent was the threshold for A Class) but who shot a 78 percent on the classification stage is widely viewed as a sandbagger exposed. Sometimes he is not, as everyone has good days where they shoot 'way over their head and still keep it all together. But, if it happens repeatedly, the powers that be can sit down and summarily promote a shooter to the next skill level.

Grandbagging, on the other hand, is an entirely different proposition. Here, the competitor practices the classification stage over and over until he can perform it (and usually it alone) above his actual skill level. One example is the standard exercise El Presidente. In it, the competitor stands with his back to three targets, hands raised in the surrender position. On the start, he turns, draws, fire two rounds on each target (at ten yards), reloads and fires two rounds each again.

In the old days, if you could perform an "El Prez", with all hits in under 10 seconds you were really good. If you could do it with all A hits under 10 seconds on demand you were an IPSC demigod. With repeated practice (and a mound of empty brass to show for it) even a B class shooter can get his time under seven seconds using today's equipment and loads.

But, having gotten a classification above his actual skill, what are the rewards? Unlike the sandbagger, a grandbagger won't go to the prize table earlier than he otherwise would have. The grandbagger gets status. There aren't that many Master shooters in IPSC. Even fewer make Grand Master. Having a card with M or GM on it is a status few can show. And since the monetary rewards in competitive shooting are few, status is a big deal. In IDPA the rewards are even less, but there are those who work hard to get classified in all four equipment categories. As for the coveted Four-Division Master card, few will ever earn it.

Avoid sandbaggers, and don't make fun of grandbaggers. After all, who doesn't want to be recognized for their shooting skill? Just so long as they actually earned it.

For many competitions, a holster is needed.

it. Hits in the center ("X") and next ("A") rings count as "zero time" shots. That is, they do not cause extra time to be added to your run. The next ring out is the "plus two" ring,

and here hits add two seconds to your run time. Hits on the rest of the cardboard cause five seconds to added to your run, while a complete miss calls for ten seconds added.

Your match score is the total time of your entries in the three stages in an equipment category.

You must use factory ammunition in your Glock. The use of reloads void the warranty, and are not allowed in GSSF competition. You will need eye and ear protection.

Plates

Simplicity, really. A rack of six falling plates at 10 yards. From the start, use your 11 rounds (if needed) to down the six plates as quickly as possible. You run the plates four times, each a separate timed run. If you don't miss, you can fire a mere 24 rounds. If you need extras, you've got

11 rounds for six plates. (A hint: you won't be winning if you're making up fast misses with extra shots.) Due to the small variances in plate size, spacing and rack height, every match you go to can have slightly different plates. Running out of ammo and leaving a plate standing costs you ten seconds per plate. Shoot fast, but don't miss.

5 to Glock

Five D-1 targets, one each at 5, 10, 15, 20 and 25 yards. The spread puts them in a cone, with the tip of the cone centered on the 25-yard target. From the start, you bring your Glock up and fire two shots at each target in any order. The eleventh round? That is to facilitate magazine changes and allow for the rare event of a malfunction. You can't use it to make up for an obvious miss. Three runs and then total the score/time.

Glock M

M features four D-1 targets, two at 10 yards and two at 20. Arrayed in between them are three poppers. The string is simple. On the start, raise your Glock and fire two rounds at each target and gun down one of the steel. If you need extra shots to drop the steel, use them (you've got 11, remember?) but don't use the extras to make up for obvious misses on the paper targets. Three runs, three steel poppers, and then total the score. Leave a popper up and it costs you 10 seconds. And no, you can't use an

In USPSA/IPSC and IDPA, you'll be moving to engage the targets.

Practical shooters love falling steel. Poppers and plates abound at some clubs and in some matches.

A G-29 has its own category is GSSF but not in other matches.

You'll never see this at a GSSF match. There are even more targets hidden behind the screens.

extra round from a following string to erase the standing popper penalty.

A cleanly run GSSF match require 81 rounds. If you miss a lot, the most you can shoot is 103 rounds.

But the fun at a GSSF Match doesn't stop there. Once you've entered and shot it in one category, you can go back and re-enter (assuming there is time and an open entry slot) and shoot the match again in another category. (You can't re-enter the same category.) There are many, depending on the host club and the number or ranges they have, and your skills and equipment. Besides the full sized gun, there is the Subcompact and MajorSub. Want to know how your times stack up using a super-compact G-36 and its .45 recoil, compared to your full-sized G-17 and its 9mm recoil? Get back to the registration desk and sign up.

Your skill will also determine where you can enter. Amateurs and Pro shooters are kept apart. The Pro shooters are those who have spent enough time at the business of shooting to have skills much nigher than the rest. A shooter who has a Master card in IDPA would be bumped to Pro from Amateur, as would a USPSA Master or Grand Master. Those on shooting teams sponsored by the Police Department they work for or Military shooting teams, are also Pros. Win too many guns as an Amateur at a GSSF match, and you're going

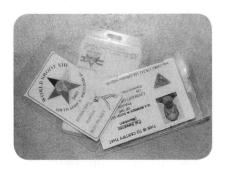

If you shoot many matches and join many organizations, you'll collect a box full of cards, ID, classifications, match cards and other what-nots.

to be bumped to Pro. The current number is three, but GSSF has sole discretion in setting the figure, so don't be surprised if it changes.

Many clubs holding their annual GSSF match have side events. Instead of the six plates of "Plates" they might have a plate rack with eight or nine plates in it. Or an array of poppers. Or anything that is fun to shoot but stays within the spirit of the GSSF match. And usually, the side events do not have an entry limit on them. Want to shoot the plates in a side match 20 times,and see if you can get your run under X seconds? Pay the man and get in line. It is easily possible to go to a GSSF match, meet hundreds of other Glock shooters, and turn a couple of hundred rounds of ammo into empty brass.

And the prizes at a GSSF match are many: Glocks. You can go to a match and win a new Glock. Again, if you win too many times you'll be bumped up from the ordinary shooters pool to the professional shooters pool, where you'll have to duke it out with the other pro

shooters for more Glocks as prizes. And as each event is sponsored by Glock, there will be a factory-trained armorer on hand to take care of the free upgrades to older Glocks, and (dare I say it?) tend to malfunctioning Glocks.

USPSA

The USPSA is the US branch of the International Practical Shooting Association. The idea, when IPSC was formed in the 1970s, was to come up with a form of competition that was closer in structure to what a "real life" encounter might be – closer at least than Bullseye or PPC, which had been the two types of handgun competition for decades prior to the organization of IPSC. Since the 1970s there has been a great deal of discussion as to just how relevant this, or any, form of competition may be to "real life."

In the USPSA, you will be doing all the things that a GSSF match isn't. You'll draw from a holster (unless a stage start has you picking the pistol up off a table, for instance) you'll move from one firing position to another, and you'll likely have to reload against the clock. In an IPSC (many competitors use USPSA and IPSC interchangeably when discussing the shooting, even though the National and International bodies differ slightly in some aspects) match every stage is different, and every match is different. There will be similarities simply due to the limits of range size and target design. After all, if you come to a window to shoot through it, there are only so many ways a stage designer can arrange three (or two, or four, etc.) targets on the other side. But you will not find stage designs carved in stone.

Moving, reloading, every stage different. Welcome to practical shooting.

You even have to deal with doors in practical shooting.

A USPSA match will also have two power levels and four equipment Divisions in which Glocks qualify. The two power levels are Major and Minor. Basically, 9mm is held to Minor except in Open Division, and all the others are Major. The power is measured by chronographing your ammo, and multiplying the bullet weight in grains times the velocity in feet per second. To make Minor, a load has to exceed 125,000. It is a pretty wimpy 9mm load that doesn't make Minor. (A 125-grain bullet at 1,000 fps.) A Major load is one that makes 165,000.

One additional limit for power comes into play when you consider equipment, and that is that 9mm isn't allowed to be declared (or loaded to) Major except in Open. In all other Divisions it is restricted to Minor. Why worry about what your ammunition can do? Because unlike a GSSF match, USPSA/IPSC shooting allows reloaded ammunition. In the interests of economy, and getting as much practice as possible, many competitors use only reloaded ammunition. At some club matches, and all matches at higher levels (State, Area, National, World) the Match Director will have a chronograph station where all shooters must report. There your ammo will be tested. Declare Major and fail to make the threshold, and you'll be scored Minor.

Why does it matter? The scoring rings on the targets are scored differently for Major and Minor. The quick rundown is this: Major is scored five, four and two points, while the same rings for Minor are scored five, three and one point. A "C" or a "D" hit with a Minor load takes more points away from your maximum possible than the same hit with Major would. Since your stage score, or Factor, is your points fired divided by the time you spent shooting, the deductions from the points total hurt your overall score.

The calculations of the stages scores for the Match Overall in IPSC can be positively byzantine, a sore spot with some competitors. Basically, the faster you shoot and the more points you score, the better you do.

Windows, changing light – you're expected to adjust to the problem.

Three-Gun competition shooters like the Glock for their durability. If your rifle hits your pistol when you're running, you know for sure your Glock will work.

The International IPSC target. Can't see the scoring rings? You're not supposed to until you score the hits.

The equipment Divisions the Glock can qualify for are Open, Limited, Limited 10 and Production. (No Glock can qualify in the Revolver category, even some exotic ones I've seen on the internet.)

Open

Open is just what you'd think. You can have extended (out to 170mm overall length) high-capacity magazines, compensators, a red dot sight and whatever other modifications you feel the need for. The end result is a large and sometimes heavy pistol that is extremely loud, holds around 27 rounds, and runs the courses faster than anything else. With the change in Major allowing 9mm, you can easily drop a comped 9mm barrel into your Glock, use tough, new brass, mount a scope, and shoot Open. If you want to switch back, it is easy enough to unbolt the various parts and convert your Glock back to a stock gun. You could even invest in a new slide, and keep the comped barrel in it all the time, and simply swap uppers and the scope to go back and forth.

Bolt-on mounts don't require modifications to your Glock.

The best Glock for Open? It should start as a 9mm, and can be based on a G-17, G-34, or even a .40 or 10mm. Since you'll be making wholesale changes (changes beyond the scope of this book) what you start with doesn't matter a lot.

You'll also need to be an experienced reloader, to craft ammunition that makes Major, shoots accurately and reliably, and doesn't break your pistol. And you'll need to invest in two or three hi-cap extended magazines at $150 each.

An Open gun (wild and expensive) and the shooter or a ladder at World Shoot XIII.

With this Glock and a 28-shot magazine, you're ready for Open.

Limited

Limited is only partly limited. You can't have a compensator. You can't have a red-dot sight. Your high-capacity magazine can't be longer than 140mm, and you have to be running a .40 caliber or larger pistol to declare Major. No, you can't shoot 9x19 Major (or 9x21) in Limited. But you can shoot 9x19 as a Minor caliber pistol.

I hadn't noticed it until it had been happening for a while, but it turns out that at the club level at least, there are always a few people shooting Limited Minor. Why? Cost and recoil. For the cost of surplus or reloaded 9mm, they can get in a lot more shooting than the same money spent on .40, 10mm or .45 ammo. And 9mm is softer in recoil, so their more shooting means less work and jolting. A 9mm Limited gun can hold as many as 22 or 23 rounds, and that's a lot of shooting before a reload.

For those who didn't want to get into reloading, shooting 9mm Minor had a brief moment in the sun. Surplus imported 9mm ammunition was selling at wholesale for less than $125 per thousand rounds until the war started and the Chinese decided they were going to buy the world's supply of copper. If you can reload your own 9mm, you could get the cost down, but each thousand rounds represents a couple of hours of handle pulling on a reloading press. For the amount of shooting it takes to recoup the investment in reloading equipment, a bunch of our shooters simply stuck with surplus factory 9mm. With much of the surplus now gone, and ammunition prices sky-high, shooting Limited Minor with a 9mm is still the lowest-cost option.

You can do anything to a Limited gun you want, as long as you don't put a comp

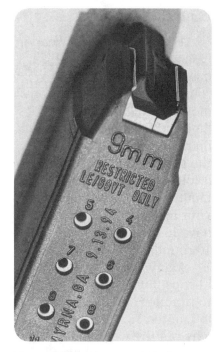

You need hi-cap magazines for some competitions, and you can do just fine with the old 10-shots in others. Use whatever works, is cheap, and is available.

or dot on it. You can adjust the trigger, change the sights, modify the grips, add a guide rod made out of the latest exotic material, etc., etc.

The perfect base to start a Limited pistol on would be a G-34 for Minor and a G-35 for Major. (You can also use a G-17/G-22, or one of the 10mm or .45s, but most shooters go with a 9mm or .40.) Add extended baseplates to your hi-cap magazines, and you're ready to cruise. While Limited is a bit less expensive than Open, it can still be pricey. The 140mm hi-cap mags can run over $100 each, and you'll need three or four. Reloading 40 to Major is easier than making Major with a 9x21, but not nearly as easy as making it in a .45 is.

Using this Glock without changing to a solid barrel will put you in Open.

Limited-10

When the Assault Weapon Law went into effect in 1994, magazines larger than 10 rounds couldn't be made any more. Recognizing what that limit did to the firearms retail market, the USPSA created the Limited 10 category. It follows all the rules of Limited, but you cannot load your magazines (even if you have hi-caps) with more than 10 rounds.

Many shooters who have hi-caps buy 10-shot mags to practice and compete in Limited 10. After all, why put the wear and tear on the expensive hi-caps? Many new shooters start in Limited 10. Some go out in search of hi-cap magazines so they can shoot Limited, but many never do. And many who shoot Limited 10 don't even do in search of other accessories, shooting a box-stock Glock.

What with the sunsetting of the law, Limited Ten is still in place. There are a few states where hi-cap magazines aren't allowed, so those poor wretched residents must stick with "Lim-10." Since the law has sunset there has been a great deal of discussion over just what to so with Limited Ten. Drop it? Fold it into the new Single Stack Division? Allow it only in those States that prohibit hi-cap magazines? The discussions are likely to go on for some time.

The perfect Limited 10 pistol would be a G-35, since the .40 caliber can be used at Major, for higher scores, and used with 10-shot magazines. But you can do quite well with almost any Glock model that will hold at least 10 rounds. Limited 10 is one of the two categories that shooters who are looking for practice with their carry guns enter. The other is Production.

Ported Glocks will get you bumped into Open in many matches unless you install a non-ported barrel.

Production

Production is what many shooters feel Limited and Limited 10 should have been all along. The limits to Production are quite strict. In the beginning, in recognition that all we could get new were 10-shot magazines, it had a 10-shot limit. It still does, but not for the reason it began with. All Production pistols are scored Minor, regardless of caliber, to encourage participation by 9mm shooters. You can't have ports or comps, even if they are a factory option. And you can't do anything that isn't a factory option. You can change sights (to another factory sight) you can do internal work to improve reliability (on a Glock? What would you do?) or trigger pull. Other than swap factory options, you have to shoot the pistol just as it came out of the box.

Armando Valdes running his Glock at the USPSA Nationals.

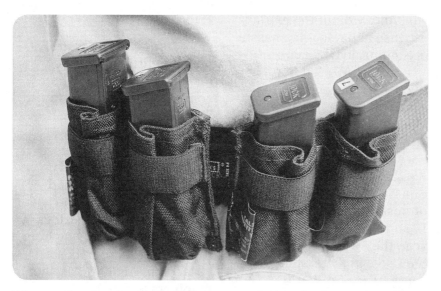

When you're shooting Limited Ten, you need a bunch of magazines. This California Competition Works pouch will keep you going throughout almost any stage.

If it's your carry gun and you want to shoot in competition, more power to you. If you want to be competitive, perhaps a different Glock may be in order.

A technical note that doesn't matter for Glock shooters: Production is limited to Double Action pistols. For USPSA equipment definitions, the Glock is a Double Action pistol. When you're shooting in Production, you won't have to worry about someone showing up with a $2000 custom 1911. They can't shoot production, even if their expensive (and tricked-out) 1911 pistol is a regular production item. Shoot Production with your Glock and you'll be shooting against other Glocks, and all the Rugers, SIGs, Berettas, S&W pistols and any other double action or Double Action Only pistols.

Production is the stomping grounds of the G-34. For accuracy, reliability, sight radius and recoil control, the G-34 is the gun to beat. Not to say you couldn't do great work with a G-17, G-19, or a 40, 10mm or .45 with downloaded ammunition.

Why still 10 shots, despite the law going away? Competitive shooters will go for any advantage, real or imagined. If the Division allowed magazines to be fully-loaded, shooters would feel compelled to go with the one that has the greatest capacity right out of the box: the Glock. Other 9mm pistols hold a round or two less, and for some that would be seen as an advantage. Why use a Beretta

There are 11 targets in there. All you have to do is find them and shoot them faster than the rest of the shooters in the match.

Get that Glock out of the attaché case and deal with the targets. Practical shooting stages are always different.

92, with 15 rounds, when a Glock holds 17? To avoid giving an advantage (real or imagined) to one pistol, the powers-that-be have held to the ten-shot capacity.

International Matches

One Division that gets no respect in the US is Modified. In Modified, the pistol can have anything an Open gun can have (except that it must be .40 or larger to score Major) but there is one catch: it has to fit the IPSC box. Modified guns thus require a bit more gunsmithing trickery to squirm into the box and still have comps and dots. Popular in Italy, Germany, the Eastern European and former Soviet countries, and the Philippines, hardly anyone shoots it here in the US. If you bolt a compact red dot scope to a comped Glock, you have a basic and quite serviceable Modified gun. And without the extra expense and reloading hassle of running an Open gun.

At each World Shoot, the rest of the world fields a respectable number of Modified shooters and Modified Teams. The USA does not.

At the 2002 USPSA Factory Gun Nationals, Glocks were profusely evident in Limited 10 and Production. Later that year, they were also all over the range in Pietersburg, South Africa for World Shoot XIII, in Standard and Production. (Standard is what the world body calls Limited) My friend David Sevigny won Production at the World Championships using a G-34 and Triton factory ammo.

Why no Modified in the US? I can only speculate, and there I think it is because it falls squarely between two trends: Open and Limited.

IDPA

After nearly 20 years of competition, IPSC had evolved to the point where some felt it had gone astray. Specifically, the emphasis on compensators and red dot sights (this was before Limited, Limited-10 and Production Divisions had been approved) and the use of high-capacity magazines were viewed as straying from the holy writ. From its start as a competition for six-shot revolvers, eight-shot 1911s and 14-shot Browning Hi-Powers, IPSC had become a game played with 28 round magazines. The pistols, with their compensators and red dot sights couldn't possibly be carried concealed except under a trench coat or in an attache case.

So the originators of IDPA put some very restrictive limits on equipment. They also insisted on things like concealed carry starts on stages, penalties for insufficient or incorrect use of cover, an 18-round ceiling on course design, and magazine limitations. The four Divisions are: Custom Defense Pistol, Enhanced Service Pistol, Stock Service Pistol, and Revolver. (Again, right off the bat we can eliminate the possible use of a Glock in Revolver.)

CDP is the customary stomping grounds of the 1911 pistol in .45 ACP. Stomping as in kicking butt in scores. You could use a Glock 21 in CDP, but you'd be competing against the pistols (and their practiced owners) of $2,000+

Dave Sevigny, shooting an indoor IDPA match. Yes, it's dark in there, and yes, you can see the muzzle flash. For the gun folks, it is a G-34. For the photographers, it was ISO 1600, 1/25 second exposure at f/5.0. Dark.

Dress should be comfortable and secure. This should be good for USPSA and, with a jacket or vest, for IDPA.

pistols. You can do it, but it will be like Michigan in July: tough sledding.

ESP is for the 1911s in other calibers. Here, a Glock in any caliber but .45 would work. However, be warned: if

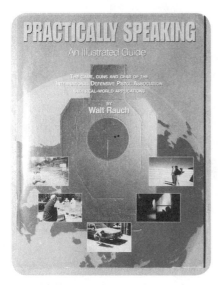

Walt Rauch has been a lot of places and done a lot of things. It's a good idea to pay attention to what he has to say.

you thought things were tough in CDP, they're even tougher in ESP. Those $2,000+ .45's? Well now they're $2,000+ 1911s in 9mm or .38 Super. They are game-winning tools in light-recoiling calibers, tuned by gunsmiths with decades of experience at making match-winning guns.

The one category of the four IDPA equipment Divisions that Glocks can compete and compete well in is Standard Service Pistol. The IDPA, instead if saying what you can't do, as IPSC does, has a list of approved modifications. If it isn't on the list, you can't do it. Basically, they want you shooting with a box-stock pistol. (No complaints there from Glock shooters.) 9mm only, 10 shots in a magazine, concealed carry or likely to be concealable holster, and you are good to go. The competition will be stiff, but only because of the skill level, and not because of the equipment disparity.

Like IPSC, you will draw to start a stage, move from shooting position to shooting position, reloading as you need to. The scoring is different from, and simpler than, the IPSC scoring system, consisting as in a GSSF match of time penalties added to the time of your run, for a simple time total as a score. What IDPA adds to the mix, besides the movement, are penalties for tactical errors. IDPA has penalties such as "Failure to Do Right" (applied to tactical errors or attempts to "game" the match for an advantage)

The kind of gun the IPSC box was intended to prevent.

and penalties for not getting yourself behind cover. The idea is to reinforce good tactical habits, and not allow the competition excesses of IPSC.

If you are in the position of carrying a handgun during the day, both USPSA/IPSC and IDPA offer good and relevant practice. they differ in what they offer, and it is up to you to get the benefit, but they are more alike than they are different, despite the sometimes heated debate that rages between them.

While IPSC recognizes Open, IDPA does not. Neither differentiates between Full size guns and compacts, as GSSF does. If you want an introduction to IDPA, one of the founders, Walt Rauch, has a book that can get you started. While *Practically Speaking, an Illustrated Guide* may appear slim, it is packed with information. One of the most valuable sections is the IDPA classification course. Unlike USPSA/IPSC, which has a host of classification courses (it can take six months of hard work to get classified in IPSC) IDPA has The Course. Ninety rounds later, your totaled time puts you into a performance classification. If you want to practice The Course so as to improve your classification, then it is all in print.

Other Competitions

If what you want is fun, and are not as concerned with the relevance (however defined) of the shooting competition to real life, then there are other games to be had.

PPC

Designed in the early 1930s as the training and qualification course for the newly-armed FBI, PPC evolved through the decades into a precisely-defined match. Starting as a relevant improvement in practical handgun shooting, it was quickly cast in stone as holy writ, and has changed little since then. What it amounts to is the precision of Bullseye shooting, with the positions shooting of IPSC, with the six-shot limit between reloads that the revolver origins required.

While you will draw, and reload against the clock, the time limits are so generous that the speed of your draw and the speed of your reloads do not matter to your end result. As an example, the Indoor PPC course (the indoor and outdoor courses differ in distance, rounds fired and time limits) has one stage that requires 24 rounds and three reloads (one magazine to start, and three new ones,

each six rounds). The time limit for the stage is two minutes and 45 seconds. It doesn't matter how slow your draw, or the following three reloads are. Even if they all-told take you 20 seconds (slow indeed!) you still have 2:25 to shoot 24 rounds, or a fraction more than six seconds each. You could disassemble, clean and reassemble your Glock in the middle of all this and still post a decent score.

The center you're trying to hit can be as small (indoors) as a playing card, so you'll need the most accurate ammunition your Glock likes. In many parts of the country (for example, where it gets really cold in the winter) indoor PPC leagues are quite popular. In recognition of the fact that most police departments now carry pistols instead of revolvers, almost every one you can go to will have a pistol category, sometimes two or three. ("Service" "Target" "Carry"

"Off-duty" are some of the categories I've seen.)

Indoor ranges can be quirky in their range rules. Some allow only jacketed bullets to cut down on lead exposure. Others allow only lead, to save wear and tear on the backstop. Indoor ranges with a rubber curtain in front of the backstop prohibit hollowpoint bullets, for they act like cookie cutters on the rubber matting. If you're going to go to an indoor match, ask what restrictions they have if any. Or load enough to shoot the match several times over, once with jacketed, once with lead, etc.

Time for a little bit of personal sputtering. The organizing body of PPC matches is the NRA. While they have done great things for the defense of firearms rights, on the subject of

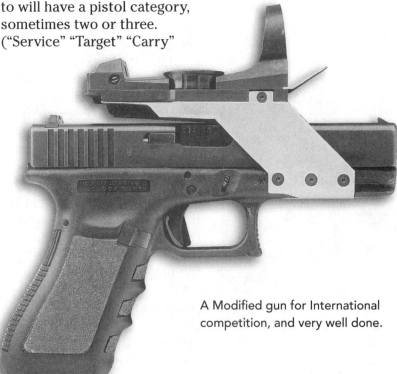

A Modified gun for International competition, and very well done.

PPC competition the NRA is schizophrenic. Due to its origins as a police training course, the NRA does not allow non-law enforcement people to shoot in sanctioned PPC matches. (Their reasoning, not my speculation.) What this means is that if you are an NRA member who isn't a police officer, you can't shoot in an NRA-sanctioned PPC match that your membership dues help sponsor. However, a police officer can, even if he isn't an NRA member.

The good news is that most local leagues don't give a hoot about the NRA prohibition and will let you shoot. As long as you stay safe and follow the rules, you're cool as far as they're concerned. But if you want to shoot in a bigger match than a local league, ask before you send in your entry fee. They may have to tell you no. End of rant.

PPC does not have a power factor, and does not recognize Open. Due to the mandated reloads every six rounds, the capacity or size of your magazines doesn't matter. Rather than subject your hi-cap magazines to the wear and tear of falling onto a concrete floor (indoors, remember?) invest in a clutch of ten-shot mags. And put your name on the baseplates.

Bowling Pins

Bowling pin shooting is as ritualized as PPC or Bullseye, but has an entirely different emphasis. The target is, no surprise, a bowling pin. The

The goal of all pin shooters: the tables at Second Chance.

standard distance is 25 feet. There are two table setting distances, one for 9mm and the other for all the other calibers/categories. The 9mm pins (usually nine of them, called "Nine Pin") are set one foot from the back edge of the table. The other categories (almost always five pins,

called "Five Pin" or "The Main Event", sometimes eight pins, called "Spacegun Optional", or ten in "Auto Optional") have the pins set three feet from the back edge.

Your job? Knock the pins off the table (not merely tip them over) faster than anyone else does. A good table will

The 9-Pin setup, with one already gone. You'd swear you can't miss when they're that close together. (And you'd be wrong.)

You have to knock the pins off, not just over.

If you don't want to go milling or drilling on your Glock but want to shot in Open, a bolt-on mount can serve you well.

have a steel top or be entirely constructed of steel. Tables of clubs just getting started may be plywood over a timber frame. Low misses soon make a mess of the tabletop, requiring more power to broom pins off the top.

The nine pin setting doesn't require more power than a 9mm has. You can use other calibers, but the recoil of the 10mm and .45 slows down your shooting. A .40 with slightly reduced loads could be quite competitive in nine pin.

The five pin setting requires power. You can't push a pin set three feet from the back edge off the table with a 9mm load. Even if you were to exceed all common sense and load your 9mm ammo beyond the +P+ power levels that some ammo makers offer to their Law Enforcement customers, it wouldn't be enough. Even a hot load in a .40 has a tough time of it. The five pin event is the bailiwick of the 10mm and .45.

Remember the Major/ Minor discussion we had back in the IPSC part of this chapter? Where it took 165,000 to make Major? The generally accepted useful minimum (the pins keep score in this regard, not the Match Director and his chronograph) for shooting pins is 195,000. Some competitors insist on even more power, going up to 210, 215 or even 220. (It is customary to drop the last three digits.)

Depending on the number of tables the host club has, the number of shooters they expect, and how much shooting they want to do, a host club can have multiple equipment divisions in these categories. For instance, in five pin it is customary to have at least Stock and Pin Gun categories. Stock is stock, and Pin Guns are allowed a compensator. Then there

Noise, pins, smoke, action!

Even small clubs can have a pin range. It doesn't take much room, just a welder and some steel.

Competition takes a keen eye and fast reflexes. Women can do well in shooting.

Loot and glory.

is the Space Gun category, roughly equal to Open in GSSF or IPSC. Some clubs split nine pin into Pin and Spaceguns, as hardly anyone shoots nine pin Stock. And no one will differentiate between full size and compact, as GSSF does.

The Main Event is straightforward. You shoot six tables of five pins each, each timed to the impact of the last pin onto the ground. Your five best runs are totaled, and the sixth run is your tiebreaker. Faster is better, but if you miss the clock is still ticking. More power is better, until it starts to slow you down. And a pin still rolling on the table doesn't stop the clock. Five Pin has an eight-round magazine limit in the Main Event, no limit in Spacegun Optional.

Nine Pin, Spacegun Optional and Auto Optional are scored differently. You can enter as many times as you want (up to the limit the match organizer or your wallet dictates) and your fastest single run is your score for the match. There is no magazine limit for Nine Pin and Spacegun Optional. There is an eight-round limit for Auto Optional.

No holster work, no movement, reloading only if you miss. While pin shooting was invented in the era of, and for, 1911 pistols in .45, Glocks can run with the best of them.

Steel

In the steel category, we have two different approaches, exemplified by The Steel Challenge, where

At the Steel Challenge, the plates don't fall and the shooting is fast.

the steel doesn't fall, and the American Handgunner Shootoff, where it does.

The Steel Challenge

Started in the very early 1980s, The Steel Challenge was a course intended to get the most speed out of the shooters. The courses of fire are quite simple, really. For the most part they consist of five steel plates. Your job is to draw and hit them with one shot each, ending on the stop plate. Five runs on each stage, with your four best runs being counted. The fifth is simply discarded. (The stages have varied over the history of the match, with some added and others dropped. Some might require movement, but not much. Others might only have three runs scored.)

The plates are mostly 10- and 12-inch circles, with some stages using rectangles 18"x24" in size.

There is no power factor, but there is a caliber limit. You can't use a centerfire caliber smaller than 9mm Parabellum. If you elect to use loads that are too light to reliably cycle your pistol, too bad. Scoring is simple: If you mark the paint on the steel, you have hit/scored the plate. You generally don't move. If you have to reload, your times are suffering badly from all the missing. What you have to do is draw quickly, shoot fast and don't miss.

Your total time for seven stages is your match score. The fastest shooter wins. What the organizers of The Steel Challenge, held each year in California, do is to recognize all the categories of IPSC, IDPA and many other competitions. What they don't do is differentiate between full size and compact. If you want to shoot your G-26, you'll be shooting against G-17s and G-19s, with the exact category depending on what holster you use.

You see, the draw is critical in The Steel Challenge,

You need a fast holster at the Steel Challenge.

On some stages at the Steel Challenge, you can't believe how big the targets are. You still have to hit them faster than your competition does.

so the equipment divisions are more concerned with what holster you use than what pistol you have. So, while the same G-17 pistol could be used in many categories, the holster you use, and where you place it on your belt, would determine if you enter in USPSA Production or Limited, or IDPA Standard Service Pistol.

American Handgunner

Unlike The Steel Challenge, in The Shootoff, the steel falls. Or at least that's the plan. There is no power factor, as everyone has to knock over the same steel plates. If you use a load that is too light, that's your problem that you should have taken care of before going to Colorado. (Generally all the steel will fall nicely to a 135 PF.) How much or little you use to accomplish the job is your problem, provided you don't damage the steel.

The format is simple. You and the shooter you are competing against on that particular run stand facing identical plate racks. In between the racks are a pair of poppers that will overlap when they fall. On the start signal, draw and knock down your plates, then knock over the popper on your side before the other guy does the same with his plates. First one down wins. Leave a plate standing, or finish late, and you lose.

Every squad is composed of competitors in the same equipment division. Let's say you are shooting a G-17. You are a Stock Auto shooter, and everyone in your squad will be in the same class, let's say you shoot in "B." The (however many there are) shooters in "Stock Auto B" squad will face each other over the 15 stages. The computer arranges the names in a different order for each stage, and there will be a printout waiting for you on each stage. You shoot the plates against your opponent for the winner of two out of the three bouts. The winner advances, and the loser sits down.

The last two shooters left on each stage shoot for a best three out of five series to determine the stage winner. Your stage score will be the number of bouts you win. Your match score will be the total of your bout wins from all the stages. Each stage, you start against a different member of your squad. If you win, you keep shooting and keep racking up bout wins. If you lose, you sit down and then start over on the next stage.

The shooting is intense and you can use up a large amount of ammunition. Let's say you're using 10-shot magazines to save wear and tear on your hi-cap mags. And, let's be as pessimistic as possible. For 15 stages, you lose every time you step to the line. That's two bouts each stage, empty your magazine on each run, and then sit down. You will still shoot at least 300 rounds in the match! If you win only a few bouts, you could easily add another hundred or two to the shooting total.

Win your category by going to the end on a good number of the stages, and you could get in nearly a thousand

Glocks can win at the American Handgunner Shootoff.

In the finals, all the category winners shoot off against each other.

The final plates in each run are overlapping poppers. Yours has to be underneath (first down) to win.

Since there is no spot-to-spot movement, "handicapped" is a relative term.

rounds of shooting! (The winners in big squads like Stock Auto B, C & D can shoot well over a thousand rounds.)

Once the main match is over, and the category winners have been decided, those category winners than face off against other category winners (Stock A Auto vs. Stock B Auto, etc.), winnowing the shooters down and combining categories until there is one man left standing. Whew.

One thing you must know: you don't get your brass back. There are a lot of competitors to run through. The shooters do all the scoring and resetting of targets. There isn't time to collect your brass, so the Shoot-off is not the place to be shooting 10mm or .357 SIG. What do most use use? The 1911 guys shoot .38 Super, .40 or .45. For the Glock shooters, there are three choices: 9mm, .40 or .45. If you don't have big hands, that limits it to 9mm or .40.

Benefits of Competition

The tangible rewards of shooting competition are not great. Oh, the "big dogs" can turn a match win into more business for their teaching schedule, or bring more students to their school. But money to finance a shooting career? Not. While the lucky few who make the PGA Tour can often finance their competition with the money they get, shooting can't. (I've even heard of promising golfers who didn't have the seed money to go on Tour being financed by syndicates of wealthy golfers who expect a return on their investment. If you consistently make the cut, you can pay them back quickly.)

For the most part, matches pay the competitors

Squads are made by category, so these Open shooters don't feast on Stock gun shooters.

Everyone faces identical racks to those of their competition. Down yours first and you'll keep shooting.

At large shoots, elaborate props are expected. This is a real jet aircraft, brought in for the World Shoot.

In USPSA Limited, Limited 10 and Production, and IDPA SSP, Glocks do very well.

with trophies or plaques (known as "glory") or cash, or products from the sponsors or guns (known as "loot"). Most matches are glory matches, some are loot, and a few are loot and glory matches. And the bragging rights are good only in the shooting community. (Just try telling someone at a cocktail party that you were the best OSS in Nine-Pin at a recent Bowling Pin match, and you'll catch them eyeing the exits.)

Women can do well in shooting.

Even if you don't win anything, you are better for the experience. The practice a match represents is good for you, giving you feedback on your skills, letting you know your limits, and getting you comfortable once again with shooting. If you carry a gun, then regular practice improves your chances of prevailing should you need it. (Any practice is better than none. Here is not the place to go into which competition is

"better" than another.)

Competition does more for you besides giving you practice, testing your skills and equipment, and giving you the possibility of winning loot and glory. If you let it. My wife, when she tried shooting, remarked afterwards that it was "the least sexist environment I'd ever been in." No surprise there. Competition shooters are accustomed to judging, and being judged on, their performance – in public, and with witnesses no less. And how they handle stress and disappointment is something everyone notes.

Bluster, bluffing, posturing and ego don't improve your scores. They don't make penalties go away. They don't improve your performance in subsequent stages or matches. As Mike Karbon, the fellow who taught me a lot about the firearms business and gear, once said, "The target never lies." If you missed, it is because you missed. Blaming the gear only gets people thinking unkindly thoughts

The range can be the least sexist environment you've ever experienced.

is dealt with by shrugging and saying something like: "I thought I'd gotten it." Not by railing against the injustice of it all, or throwing your gear around in a fit of pique. (As a matter of fact, too much of that can earn you an Unsportsmanlike Conduct penalty, and you may even be disqualified from the match.)

Shooting is not a high-mass, big-muscle sport like football. You need only respectable eyesight and good eye-hand coordination to do well. To do better requires grit, determination and practice. As a result, it isn't unusual for women to do well in shooting. If you are a *muy macho* man, accustomed to loud talk, condescending attitudes toward women, and being the best at everything, your ego may not survive the first match in which you

about you. Oh, shooters will joke about their bad luck on that stage, and how they should have done the other one. But a missed popper

shoot. A good woman shooter may very well beat you. (Even an average women, if you haven't practiced lately.) Since there aren't any "Ladies Tees" as in golf, she beat you heads up, on the same course and on the same day. You can't complain that "her advantage" let her beat you, as I've heard some golfers grumble about.

Having been bested, your choices in the shooting games are three: improve your shooting, improve your attitude, or improve both. If you chose to ignore the possibility of improvement as a course of action, don't be surprised if you have other shooters at a match making fun of you behind your back. They aren't being mean; they just can't resist it. If you show no signs of changing, they may even start to make fun of you to your face.

In shooting, there are no "secret techniques" no shortcuts that the better competitors hold as their advantage over the rest. If you don't know how to go about shooting a stage in the best way, ask someone. The best shooter in your squad will be happy to tell you what order to shoot, or which prop to engage first. And they won't mislead you (unless they've overestimated your skill) into a poor score. Competition shooters are a remarkably open lot, who want everyone to do well and have fun.

I won't go so far as to say that competition shooting builds character, but it sure can reveal it. ◆

Just when you thought it was bad enough being beaten by women shooters, along come the kids. With parental supervision, kids can also compete. And if you don't want to get beaten, I'd suggest you practice.

CHAPTER 27

Glockin' with a Stock

ven by the early 1990s there were rumors of a Glock Carbine. (It didn't take long for the rumors to surface, and there were already 9mm carbines on the market. But when you have a hot new product, people are going to ask about future plans and improvements.)

The select-fire G-18 offered one end of the desired spectrum of handgun use, lots of firepower. At the other end is the use of a handgun with a shoulder stock for more accurate or long range

shooting. Apparently the Mauser company sold literal boatloads of shoulder-stocked 1896 "Broomhandle" Mausers to China, where the appetite for them was insatiable. It was more compact than a rifle, lighter, and it held more rounds and was a semiautomatic when all military rifles were bolt actions.

Its shortcomings were equally obvious: lack of power, a certain fragility, lack of compactness when stored, even with a stock that was a holster, and slow to use from storage/holster. I'm sure back then that the intent on the

part of the Mauser company was to offer a product with much the same utility as of the half-century later M1 Carbine, a light, handy firearm that could be used by military personnel whose job involved other things, and for whom a full size rifle was sometimes an obstacle. I'm also sure that at least in China the 1896 carbine was hardly ever used for that. Instead it became a badge of office, a display of authority and status.

Nowadays in the military use the name has changed but the idea is the same: something for nothing. The modern impulse at the official level is called a "Personal Defense Weapon" and handguns are summarily not considered PDWs. (I didn't say it made sense, just that it was the "in" thing.) The PDW and a pistol caliber carbine occupy different niches in the non-military firearms market. The whole idea of the PDW is to get something for nothing. A PDW is supposed to be easier to shoot and hit with and to be almost as compact as a pistol. It is supposed to offer almost as much ballistic

A rare, expensive and highly-controlled (in the legal sense) firearm: a Beretta M-93 machine pistol.

performance as a rifle, and yet not be difficult to operate. A pistol-caliber carbine is just a rifle with low-cost and light-recoiling ammo. Ammo that doesn't do anything more in the carbine than it would in the handgun does except be a bit easier to shoot accurately and effectively.

Compared to a well-designed submachinegun, or a shorty carbine of the M-16 variant, a pistol carbine isn't any more compact, offers no more power, and doesn't do a thing that the others do. However, for a police agency or competition shooters, a pistol-caliber carbine makes a lot of sense. For the police, a Glock carbine could use the same magazines and ammunition, and training for the handgun would carry over to the carbine. Noise, recoil and the ability to hit the target would all be for the better. Indeed, for some unfortunate departments, getting a Glock Carbine might be the only way to get a shoulder-stocked firearm in a squad car. Some Chiefs are very touchy about allowing the officers under their command to have rifles, shotguns or submachineguns on patrol. They commonly allow only Supervisors or the SWAT team to have the "big guns" and not the patrol officers. Having a Glock Carbine would be a way to get those officers longer-range or more accurate firepower. (And if the department in question issues Glock 9mm pistols for example, there should not be any problem in getting the Carbines for issue in 10mm,

The Colt 9mm and the M1 carbine both fit the bill as carbines, but only the 9mm can be used on steel. And at $1500 to $2000 for one, you have to do a lot of shooting with cheap 9mm ammo to get back your investment. In USPSA/IPSC and IDPA, you'll be moving to engage the targets.

for more power and reach.)

For the competition shooters, a pistol caliber carbine could be quite useful. Many indoor ranges don't allow true rifle calibers to be shot. The extreme power can be very hard on the backstop, and the oppressive noise can be hard on the staff. For low cost, low recoil practice, a pistol caliber carbine can be very useful. And there are competitions starting just for the PCC. Some USPSA/IPSC clubs are allowing entries for PCC shooters in their regular handgun matches. After all, in performance it is just a handgun, so there is no worry about damage to the targets. (The standard steel target, the pepper popper, cannot stand up to rifle shooting. Each shot craters the face or drills a hole clean through. Continued use with rifles makes cratered or holed poppers hazardous when subsequently used with handguns or shotguns with birdshot.)

And things would be wonderful for Glock shooters if Glock made such a carbine. But they don't. More than 15 years of rumors, and not a thing. (Wouldn't it be just like Glock to introduce the Carbine after the second edition of this book has gone to press?) But never fear, the capitalist marketplace can correct that shortcoming. The people at Mech-Tech Systems Inc. have come to your rescue. Their first effort at making a carbine conversion unit was aimed at the 1911 market. The idea was to take care of the really rabid fans first, then go to the slightly more patient market of Glock shooters.

The Mech-Tech Carbine Conversion Unit (CCU)

The Mech-Tech is an upper assembly with attached shoulder stock, containing everything you need save the frame and magazine.

The Mech-Tech and a Glock frame, aligned for assembly.　　The Mech-Tech with an EO Tech Holosight installed.

Why attach the stock to the conversion unit, instead of making it mate up with the frame? To keep customers out of trouble, that's why. If the stock attached to the frame, and if you installed the stock to the frame without also installing the 16" barreled upper, you'd be in violation of Federal Law. It would then be a Short Barreled Rifle,

If you want something controllable, something with a stock is what you want. The problem is, both of these are very expensive.

and it comes under the same Federal legal category as a machinegun.

On our hypothetical carbine, installed with the 16" barrel and the stock, would be fine. Installing the 16" barrel without the stock would be fine. But, stock and short barrel – it's Leavenworth time! (One of my late uncles was a guard at Leavenworth when he was in the Army. Trust me, you don't want to end up there.)

So to save you potential embarrassment or worse, Mech-Tech designed their system with the stock attached to the conversion. Doing it that way also saves you the embarrassment of getting to the range with part of and not all of the conversion. Well, almost, but more on that later.

From front to back, the Mech-Tech CCU has a muzzle brake, the 16-and-a-fraction-inch barrel, the housing with sight base, bolt and recoil springs, and shoulder stock. In use, you install your Glock frame into the unit, without the factory slide assembly. Since the Glock frame is the

serial numbered part, the Bureau of Alcohol, Tobacco and Firearms doesn't consider the CCU a firearm. Some States might. (California, New Jersey and Illinois come to mind as likely candidates. Check the laws where you live. If they preclude using a Mech Tech CCU, perhaps you should start getting active to have the law changed. Or comparing housing prices in other, friendlier states.) Definitely check to make sure your state doesn't think the CCU is a firearm before getting one mailed to you.

The CCU comes with a sight base for a red dot or optical scope of some kind. You can also get the optional iron sights for those who simply must shoot without assistance.

Calibers and Compatibility

The CCU is offered for 1911 fans in six calibers. So far, the Glock version is available in five: 9mm, .40, .357, 10mm and .45. You can use your mid-size CCU with Glock models G-17, G-20, G-21, G-22, G-31, G-34, G-35. You have to specify which frame you have, the

The stock is on the conversion to keep it out of potential trouble.

large (G-20 and G-21) or the medium (G-17, G-22, G-31, G-34 or G-35) but the caliber of yours within a frame size doesn't matter. Mech Tech also offers a compact-frame CCU, used with the compact G-19. G-23 and G-32.

The bigger frames won't work on te compact-frame CCU. You will have to specify which caliber you want your CCU in. This is where it can get tricky, so be sure of what you want before you call and order, to save confusion. You can use either a 9mm or a .40 CCU on either a 9mm or .40 Glock frame, provided you have the correct magazines. So, you can shoot a 9mm CCU using your G-22 frame, but you need G-17 magazines to do so.

The same goes for the 10mm and .45, you need the correct magazines for the caliber you plan to shoot.

Most shooters will simply get the caliber CCU that matches their Glock, because those are the magazines they have.

Installation

Pretty simple. First, disassemble your Glock. Before you go wrestling things together, spend some time comparing the CCU to your

Many clubs and competitors are starting to use pistol caliber carbines in practical shooting. It doesn't take any more room than a handgun stage, and they don't hurt the steel targets.

As with handguns, USPSA competition with pistol-caliber carbines is fast and requires movement.

Mech-Tech made their conversion first for the 1911 and later for the Glock.

frame. Lock the CCU bolt back and turn it over. Notice how the Glock rails line up with the clearance slots on the CCU? Once you've got the relationship clear in your mind, find the adapter bridge in the packing material. (You did check to make sure everything was there before you tossed the box, right?) You need the bridge.

Why? The CCU is a blowback mechanism. The bolt slides straight back and forth within the receiver. The Glock, on the other hand, is a locked mechanism. The barrel tilts down at the rear to unlock. The frame and magazine are designed to feed a cartridge into the barrel in its tilted down position, but to fire it in its locked position. The Mech Tech barrel does not tilt. The job of the bridge is to get the round over the gap between the magazine and feed ramp, and up to where the Mech Tech barrel sits. With it, the CCU feeds just

fine. Without it, things are not so fine.

You might ask why Mech Tech can't put their barrel down where the Glock barrel is during feeding. Because it would be tilted and would shoot many feet high. The forward part of the Glock frame is proportioned to hold the barrel level in firing, not in feeding. The CCU barrel can't be tilted in cycling, there is too much weight involved. So, the CCU barrel stays up, and the bridge fills the gap.

Place the bridge on the feed ramp of your frame. Be sure the CCU bolt is locked open. Hold the frame upright and then hold the CCU over it. Lift the frame up into the clearance slots, and once it stops, push forward. You'll be compressing the rubber buffer as you push, and when you hear the click as the Glock assembly lever locks into place on the CCU, you're done. (You may have to push hard. I did.) If you are not keen on balancing

the parts, you can lock the CCU in a padded vise by its barrel, and then install the Glock frame on it while it is immobile.

Disassembly is equally simple. Lock the bolt back. Grab the Glock frame and pull the locking latches down. Pull the frame to the rear, and when it reaches the clearance slots on the CCU, pull it down out of the CCU. If you drop the bridge, pick it up and keep track of it.

On the 1911 units, some accessories can interfere with the installation of the CCU. Oversized safeties, slide stops and ambidextrous gear can be a problem. Since Glocks don't have any of that stuff, you shouldn't have a problem.

Testing

How did the CCU work? The sample was a 9mm (I happened to have lots more 9mm ammo on hand for testing than other calibers) and it worked flawlessly with full metal jacketed ammo. Installed on my G-22 frame it fed fine (with 9mm magazines, remember) and I was easily able to keep all my shots on the club 10" gong at 100 yards with it. I mounted various red dot sights on it but found the fastest was the EoTech Holosight. You could, if you wanted, install an optic that magnified the image, or install the optional iron sights if you wanted to or had to, to meet a competition requirement.

Once installed, I used it in our club's Pistol Caliber Carbine competition, and found it was quite

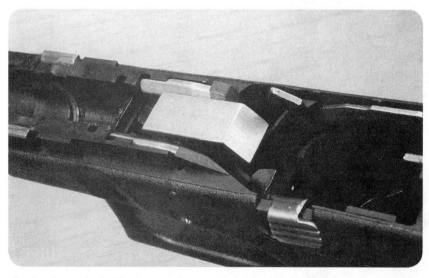

The bridge, which fills the gap between where the magazine presents the round and where the barrel actually is.

Compress the rubber buffer to lock the frame into the conversion unit.

The frame installed and ready for a sight. The silver bar on top is the scope mount.

On the first test-firing, we didn't bother with a scope. The conversion worked 100 percent with FMJ ammo.

competitive. I usually shoot those matches with a Colt 9mm, so it took a bit of getting used to, reloading by stuffing the next magazine right into my shooting hand instead of forward, as with the Colt. But, within a couple of stages I was doing just fine.

The longer barrel of the CCU adds velocity. To compare the effect of the 16.25" barrel of the CCU, I took the CCU, my Colt 9mm with its 10.5" barrel, and a 9mm handgun to the range and ran some ammo over the chronograph.

The CCU instructions recommend the use of +P ammunition, to keep the mechanism working properly and not short-stroking. I found the unit worked fine with everything but the softest powderpuff ammo. All the 9mm ammo that made USPSA/IPSC Minor power level worked the CCU just fine. It was less reliable with hollowpoint ammo, but that isn't a big deal. The idea is to have fun and get practice with inexpensive ammo, and for that hardball is just the ticket.

Not all loads increased their velocities by a significant amount. The velocity increase, if any, depends on the powder used. A fast-burning power will have all its energy used up before reaching the end of a 10" barrel, and an extra six inches of barrel may not add much if any velocity. Load the same bullet over a suitable charge of slow-burning powder, however, and you can get significant increases in velocity. To coin a phrase, your mileage may vary.   ◆

A rack full of pistol-caliber carbines at a match. This is from one squad!

Average price of the guns in this rack that aren't Mech-Tech conversion kits: $1600!

CHAPTER 28

Rimfire Glockin'

The only way to get good at shooting your Glock is to shoot. The more you do, the better you get.

The only drawback to practicing is cost. Ammo can be frighteningly expensive. If you're running a G-17, then the cost of 9mm "surplus" ammo used to be quite reasonable. However, if you're shooting a Glock chambered in 10mm or .357, the cost of ammo can bring tears to your eyes.

There is a solution. Every year, the ammunition manufacturers create "billions and billions" of rounds that solve your problem. The

round in question? The lowly .22 Long Rifle. Even "surplus" 9mm costs money. At a cost of $120 per thousand rounds (current reasonable retail price; things may change by the time you read this), 9mm costs $6 per box of 50 rounds. If you shop around, you can find .22LR on sale at one of the big box discount stores for $1 a box of 50 rounds. Even if you spend $1.50 for that box, and score surplus 9mm ammo dirt cheap at $5 a box, the $3.50 difference can add up.

You will probably never see a Glock rimfire pistol. The import points system is too great a hurdle, as the Glock

rimfire would have the dual problem of gaining no points for being so small, and losing points from being a blowback pistol. Could Glock do it? Sure, by making the whole thing here in the United States. (Don't hold your breath.)

Advantage Arms makes a rimfire conversion kit that simply replaces the upper assembly of your Glock. They offer five models, one to fit all Glocks from the G-17/G-22 as well as the big-frame 10mm/45s and the compacts. At a minimum. of $3.50 per box difference in price, you won't have to shoot a thousand rounds to pay for

It doesn't matter how cheaply you can reload 9mm, .40 or .45, you can't shoot it as cheaply as you can the .22 Long Rifle.

The Advantage Arms .22 conversion kit comes in its own carry case.

Inside the case are the conversion unit, cleaning rod and supplies, and a 10-round magazine.

To switch your Glock to a .22, simply dry-fire and remove the slide assembly. All you'll need next is the assembled frame.

The law enforcement model of the Advantage Arms conversion comes with the new Glock adjustable sight.

the conversion. And once it's paid for, the rest is gravy.

The Advantage Arms conversion is a complete upper assembly. The slide is machined from aluminum, so it will be light enough for the relatively wimpy .22 LR to blow it back and cycle the pistol. To change, simply check your Glock to make sure it is unloaded, dry fire it and remove the upper from the receiver. Then slide the Advantage Arms conversion on as if it were simply another Glock slide assembly. One small detail to be aware of is that the Advantage Arms conversion has an ejector that is hooked on the barrel,

and does not use the ejector buil into your Glock. If the Advantage ejector isn't properly assembled onto the barrel, the conversion will not work. It probably won't fit. Advantage Arms even went so far as to include a firing pin safety in the conversion slide, so just like your centerfire Glock upper, the Advantage Arms-equipped pistol will not fire if dropped.

The magazine for the Advantage is also a neat bit of engineering. Rather than re-invent the rimfire magazine, they simply used an existing design and encased it in a plastic housing to fit the Glock magazine well. As a

result, you have a fat plastic magazine that only holds 10 rounds. (I can't imagine the hassle of trying to come up with a magazine that not only held more than 10 rounds of rimmed rimfire cartridges, but also did not extend below the frame.) And they are still $25 each, even six years after the first book, a reasonable price to feed your shooting habit with cheap ammo.

The magazine feeds well, and Advantage has gone to the trouble of testing it with many different types of ammo. The ones they recommend, and with which it works best, are CCI MiniMags, Remington Golden bullets, Remington

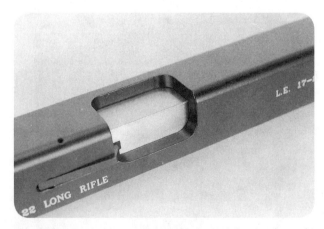

The Advantage Arms conversion barrel, being a blowback, doesn't lock to the slide.

The conversion has its own ejector and doesn't rely on the one already in your Glock.

Once installed, the conversion has the same size as a standard Glock, but its aluminum slide makes it a bit lighter overall.

The Advantage Arms conversion magazine is a magazine tube in an adapter to fit the Glock's magazine well. It comes with a modified Glock magazine loader to make charging the .22 magazine easier.

Thunderbolt. Many other brands of 40-grain high velocity .22LR ammo work well too. Since I had lots of Remington Golden ammo on hand, that was what I used in it for an afternoon to testing. Five hundred rounds later, I was out of ammo, every clump of dirt on the range had been dealt a devastating blow, I had a bunch of empty rimfire brass to pick up, and the conversion had not failed at all.

Also, the magazines lock open when empty. So many rimfire pistols do not, and most conversion units will not lock open when empty.

Accuracy? Well, besides being more accurate in the plinking sessions than the Glock had been with centerfire ammo, I don't know. The purpose of a conversion kit is not to try and shoot Bullseye with it, but to provide inexpensive practice. Oh, it is plenty accurate enough for even club-level target shooting, but that isn't why I'd have one.

On disassembly, I ran into a problem, and then read the instructions. (Even gunsmiths sometimes skip the instructions, even those who advise others to read them first.) Since the slide does not move the barrel, pulling back the slide to disassemble the conversion kit doesn't work. Here's the drill: After you check to make sure it is unloaded, dry fire to release the firing pin. Then press the barrel back slightly to release the locking lever. You can do it by pressing the muzzle against

a surface, like the shooting bench with a towel over it.

Once the barrel is back, you can press the slide lock latch down to then remove the slide. Once you do it a couple of times you'll get the hang of it.

Depending on where you get yours and the options you get, the Advantage Arms conversion kit can be yours for right around $200-$225. The list price is $249, and since it isn't a firearm you can order it

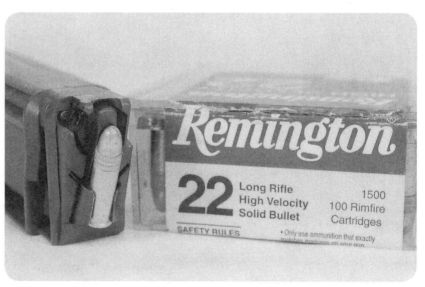

While other ammo also works, I started out with Remington; it never failed, so I didn't feel any need to switch.

by mail, or over the internet. At a minimum savings of $3.50 per box of ammo, or $70 per thousand rounds, you will get the investment back in 3,000 rounds of .22LR. How long will that take? It took me less than a week.

Sharp-eyed readers might note the Advantage Arms conversion does not use a locking block bridge, while the carbine conversion from Mech-Tech does, and ask why not? The carbine conversion fires a centerfire cartridge and uses standard Glock magazines. The barrel can't tilt, so the bridge covers the gap between the magazine and chamber. The Advantage Arms conversion uses its own magazines, and the magazine is held in the frame so as to feed directly into the chamber of the rimfire barrel.

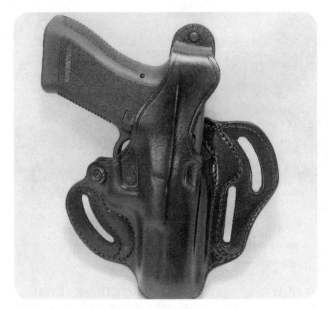

Once assembled, the Advantage Arms conversion works just like a "real" Glock – and even fits holsters like one.

Cleaning is simple, as all the parts are easy to get to and scrub. Rimfire ammo is notorious for being grubby, and the magazine has a drain hole. If it starts to malfunction from being dirty, slosh it in warm soapy water. Use a rod or pencil to cycle the spring and follower up and down, pumping water through the drain hole. Follow with a hot water rinse and dry. Oil lightly to prevent rust.

You will have to work hard to wear out one of these.   ◆

CHAPTER 29

Let There Be Light

The invention or discovery of fire was a huge leap forward. Not only did fire create heat for warmth but it cooked food, and it provided illumination to drive off predators during the night. It was just so inconvenient. Even when contained within a lantern, fire didn't provide much light, it was hard to direct, and the heat created a great risk of setting other things on fire.

Electricity changed all that. We now have compact and very bright illumination to guide us through the night. And Glocks, at least the third generation ones, have a rail where you can bolt that light. Many other makers are trying to catch up, using bolt-on rails and changing the machining patterns of their receivers. Glock just changed the mould and then started cranking out new frames. (As mentioned in the G-22 chapter, there are some guns that have feeding problems with lights on, but that is why you practice. If yours has that problem, upgrade to the new 11-coil

springs and make it feed with the light on.)

The Streamlight M3

The Streamlight company makes a light, the M3, that fits right onto a Glock 3rd gen frame. Installing it is simplicity. The crossbar is spring loaded and presses out of the way on the bevelled edge of the Glock frame. When it reaches the cross slot, it snaps in place, locking the light on. If you want to remove it, pull down on both sides

of the bar (something Glock owners should be familiar with) and slide the light forward and off.

The switch is on the rear of the light, just in front of the trigger guard when the light is on. The rocker switch moves both ways, and by pressing it in one direction you have temporary on. As long as you hold the switch, the light is on. As soon as you let go, it switches off. Press the lever in the opposite direction and it clicks on and stays on. Which one you select depends on the

The Streamlight M-3 on a G-19 with Dawson extension: 24 rounds of nighttime 9mm.

The M-3 fits on the light rail, and the cross bar locks it in place.

nature of your need. As one example, if you're searching a warehouse with your trusty canine companion, leave it on. Rover will be making enough noise that you won't be able to hide your location. If you are doing a stealthy search, and doing everything you can to keep from disclosing your position, you'd do a quick blink-on/blink-off when you needed to see what was in a hole or behind an object.

Blinking also extends the battery life, which with any modern flashlight is probably only an hour of run time. The Streamlight puts out 80 to 90 lumens (translation: brighter than you'd believe from such a small light) and runs for an hour on a pair of lithium 3-volt batteries.

Sure Fire Lights

If you have an older Glock, without the light rail, don't despair. A bright and compact light such as the Sure Fire Nitrolon G2, or their brand new Nitrolon G2Z combatlight will provide an amazing amount of illumination. What you have to do is use both hands, with one holding the light and the other holding your Glock, like the Harries technique taught at Gunsite. Reach under with your left, holding the light, and place the backs of your hands together. Use your thumb to press the switch.

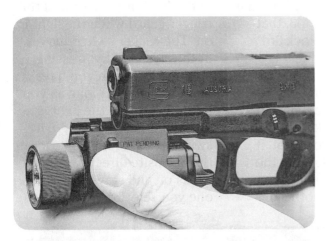

Just slide it back. . .

. . .until it locks in place.

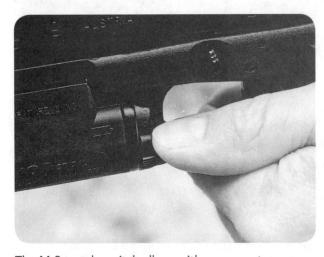

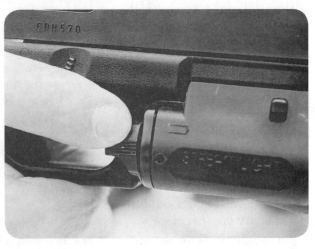

The M-3 toggle switch allows either momentary on. . .   . . .or constant on.

The SureFire lights, even the small ones like this G2 and 2Z, are plenty bright.

The Sure Fire lights have a cap button with a difference. If you screw the cap all the way in it will turn on and stay on. Unscrew the cap a bit, and then use the button as a blink-on/blink-off switch.

The Harris Technique: using the thumb to press the switch.

The Lasermax is not only compact (and red or green) but has its own rail, so installing it doesn't prevent you from installing other lights you might already have.

Using a pair of the same 3-volt lithiums as the Streamlight, the Sure Fire puts out a beam of light that you have got see to believe. Using a new reflector technology, the Sure Fire doesn't put out a beam like other lights, with crescent-moon shaped light bars and dark bars. It puts out a solid, even cone of light. Rated at "only" 65 lumens, the Sure Fire light is much brighter to the eye than other, brighter-rated, lights, and the light is solid across its field. You can get more power in the same size as the G2, up to hundreds of lumens.

For those who want to set fire to their neighbor's house, Sure Fire makes a light rated for 2500 lumens. Yes, 2500 – more light output than your car headlights, I think.

Again, the batteries on the regular lights last only an hour, but batteries are cheap, and for the light you get, who cares?

Modern lights are so bright that you can count on the startle/blink reflex. In dark or near-dark conditions, the light is so bright that if you shine it in someone's eyes without warning, he will involuntarily turn away and close his eyes. He can't help it.

Lasers

I have to admit it: I just don't get lasers. For the time and effort spent finding the laser, I can find the sights, hit the target, and then be looking for the unfortunate target's buddies. But people love lasers. If lasers are your bag, then look into Lasermax. They offer their latest in both red and green lasers, and the units are so compact they offer something I haven't seen elsewhere yet: a rail on the laser. The laser is so compact that it is sort of a rail spacer, and you can mount a light below it if you want.

So you can have light or laser or both, depending on your needs or desires. Without a light the laser is so compact it will go unnoticed, but you still won't be able to fit it into a holster. At least not unless the holster is a web-fabricated tactical thigh rig, with room to spare. ◆

CHAPTER 30

More Custom Glocks and Competitors

The old adage "imitation is the sincerest form of flattery" gives a nod to the profit imperative. If you see your competition beating you, taking your market share, you can either come in with something that leapfrogs their product or sit back and watch your customer base erode.

It took a while, but Glock found themselves faced with competition. The first was the S&W Sigma. Later came the Springfield XD, the S&W M&P, and now the Ruger SR9.

While a G-21 is bigger than a G-22, the Bar-Sto longslide is longer yet.

Of course it has a Bar-Sto barrel in it, and it's tightly fitted and not binding.

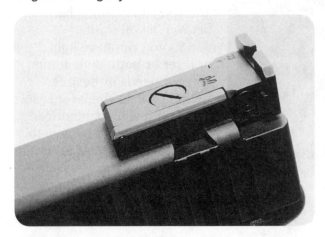

On the back, an adjustable LPA rear sight.

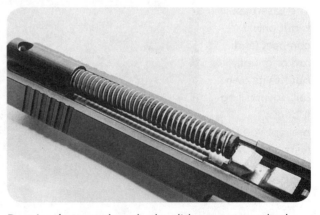

Despite the extra length, the slide uses a standard Glock recoil spring assembly.

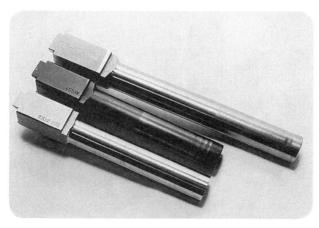

The Bar-Sto match barrel is a full six inches long.

Compared to a G-22, you can see how the scaled-up G-21 slide is larger.

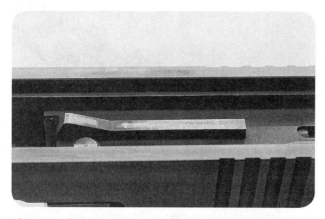

The cartridge pickup rail. On the Glocks in .45, the rail should look like this, with an angle in it. If yours doesn't, have Glock upgrade it.

Glock recoil spring assemblies are marked. The 5600 on the right is for a G-21. The 5579 on the left is for a G-22.

The Bar-Sto gun fed everything from my reloads to my stash of Black Talon (*left*), Super Vel (*center*) and WinClean (*right*).

Bar-Sto makes barrels for all the Glocks, in all the calibers, and they're all fully supported and tightly chambered.

The longslide is a big gun, and you need a big hand for it. I wear a #10 government glove, and as you can see I have to stretch to grab it.

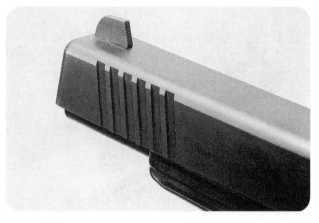

The front sight is a bit tall, but combineed with the adjustable rear it makes aiming easy.

If you use a CMPi aluminum mag extension you'll add a couple of rounds to the .45.

The Caspian slide is machined for lighter weight, just as the factory .45 slides are.

As a total custom gun, the CCF Raceframe is not just a Glock, but a Glock in metal. And you can have your own Glock worked over by master gunsmiths, as the Glock is now seen as more than just an industrial tool, but a work and life necessity that is worthy of their attention.

Sigma

The S&W Sigma appeared in the mid 1990s, and if you took the slide off you would be led to believe that you could interchange parts between the Sigma and a G-17 or G-22. Not

The *cognoscenti* may "diss" it, but S&W has sold a lot of Sigmas.

The Springfield XD is another contender for the crown of "King of Polymer" but it has yet to threaten Glock's dominance.

quite, but close – so close that Glock took S&W to court, but they finally settled.

Unloved, the Sigma has a singular reputation at the S&W factory: it has, by far, the lowest return rate of any product they have ever made.

Were it possible to obtain the information, I'd be curious to see if the S&W Sigma return rate mirrors that of the Glock return rate. As the information is proprietary, and closely-held, I suspect we'll never know. Offered in 9mm and 40,

the Sigma is a low-cost line of S&W, and they have not only sold truckloads of them here, but have sold many on contract to overseas police and military organizations.

XD

Made in Croatia, and imported by Springfield (with some design improvements Springfield insisted on) the XD is a hot competitor of the Glock in practical shooting circles. One aspect of the XD that makes it less comfortable as a carry gun is the rail location. The slide of the XD has a pair of support/cover rails that run its length, and make it feel not quite so flat as the Glock. However, it too has an enviable reputation for reliable function, and offers something that the Glock does not: a grip safety. The XD seems to be a mainly USA-market pistol, as I have not read of any large military or police contracts overseas.

S&W M&P

Coming out 20 years after the first Glocks, the M&P offers a few things that Glock does not and cannot without a radical change. First, you need not dry-fire the M&P to disassemble it. Also, you can change the size and shape of the grip by swapping out one of the backstraps for another. From small to medium to large, you can change your M&P grip size. Also, the M&P uses through-hardened slide, barrel and cam block, so you need not worry over

The S&W M&P offers options Glock does not and may well make inroads in Glock's market share. But they have a long way to go.

much about a catastrophic failure (i.e., breaking your frame). Last, the design of the frame includes an internal skeleton that the trigger and cam block are pinned to on assembly, so the trigger pull has less of the "spongy" feel that the more flexible Glock frame delivers.

Ruger SR9

Ruger has not been known for sleek, good-looking pistols, at least not until now. The SR9 offers a two-sided backstrap (no inserts to lose), a magazine disconnector and a thumb safety, all in a striker-fired pistol. And, as with the M&P, you need not dry-fire it to disassemble it. For now it is available in one size and caliber: full-size, 9mm, but it offers 17 rounds in each magazine. Considering the market segment, and the price point, they'll be flying off the shelves and Glock will have to work harder. But then competition is good for us, the customer.

CCF Raceframes

Ever find yourselves thinking "My Glock is great, but I'd rather have metal than plastic." Well, daydream no more. CCF Raceframes makes a Glock clone frame of steel or aluminum. The original plans also included a titanium frame, but the cost of titanium on the world metals market has gotten absurdly high. So much so that it is economically unwise to even try and offer Ti frames

(regardless of the design or company) simply because you have no way of knowing what you'll have to charge for the frames you make. The CCF Glock frame is available in the standard G-17/G-22 size, in stainless steel or aluminum. It also has an exchangeable

backstrap so you can alter the contour from Glock to 1911 grip angle.

An aluminum frame is about four ounces heavier than a standard Glock, while the stainless steel is a portly 17 ounces heavier. However, if you want a competition

Ruger's SR9 offers perhaps the biggest challenge to Glock. The Ruger has features Glocks don't, including a thumb safety, and will hit the stores at a lower retail price.

gun and not a carry gun, the steel frame makes the 9mm cartridge feel like a .22LR in a standard Glock frame.

Ray Harms, the guy behind the CCF frames, is a long-time custom gunsmith, and he put extra touches into the CCF frames. The area behind the trigger guard is "lifted" a common and expensive custom touch on 1911 competition pistols. The trigger guard is rounded, the mag well opened, the mag button area scalloped, and there is a picatinny rail out front for your lights, lasers, etc.

Don't bother showing up at a GSSF match with a CCF frame, as it is not Glock. But all your Glock parts will fit onto the CCF frame. If you are a Glock-certified armorer, it is an easy thing to simply order up enough parts to finish assembly. However, if you want more, you can get a custom slide from Caspian. You can have any caliber (within the limits of the G-17/ G-22 frame) cocking serration options, sight cuts, etc. A match barrel from someone else will complete the ensemble, and only a small number of parts in it will have come from Glock itself. I can even see guys at a gun club competing with Glock clones, not only on the range, but also in assembly, seeing who has the fewest actual Glock parts in their pistols.

One of the really cool parts of being a gun writer is the opportunity to test a custom gun. Or a bunch. The custom Glock I had a chance to test is the personal gun of Irv Stone III of Bar-Sto. As you can imagine, it has some really cool features, but surprisingly it has some box-stock ones, too. Why? Because some things on the Glock don't need changing, even from the point of view of the picky American competition shooter.

First, it is a long-slide. The slide is nine inches long, machined from bar stock by Caspian Arms. The

Available in stainless steel or aluminum, the CCF frame makes an attractive option for those who simply must have a metal Glock.

slide has vertical cocking serrations on the rear, with forward serrations that are tilted, in the style of so many 1911 slides. It takes all the standard parts of a Glock G-21 slide, except for the barrel. Thus, you can fit the regular extractor, recoil spring and the rest from a G-21. The barrel is a Bar-Sto, of course, and measures six inches. It is what Glock would have made, had they made a G-21L.

The rear sight is an LPA adjustable, basically a Bo-Mar clone. It has been slightly machined into the slide, thus the front sight is taller than normal, coming in at .315" tall. Irv has a lightened firing pin and a 3.5-lb. connector installed, so the trigger pull is a crisp (for a Glock) and light pull.

The curious thing is, it is a third generation frame with light rail. It has the upgraded trigger parts, but the trigger bar is coated with a dull black finish. If I had not known what the correct shape of the firing pin safety cam was, I'd have thought old parts got into a upgraded Glock.

The Bar-Sto barrel fits the slide just as you would expect, tightly but without binding. And for those who love the "push test" (pressing the chamber down when the action is locked, to see if there is any flex) the barrel sits rock solid when the slide is forward. The chamber is tight enough to prevent excess brass expansion on firing, but loose enough to work a hundred percent.

Bar-Sto is in the high desert of California, and every place Irv has to shoot is dusty, so he is keenly aware of proper chamber dimensions for reliable function. And, a lot of his customers are Marines from the 29 Palms Marine base in town, so he would get feedback if he were getting it wrong. The bore is cut-rifled, and handles lead bullets without a care.

The frame is standard, without any modifications in size, shape or surface texture. Why? Irv has hands large enough to not need a frame reduction. And, he still has the standard parts, so he can return this G-21 to is original configuration in less than a minute.

What can you use something like this for? Hunting would be one application. The longer barrel would give a bit more velocity, and with a heavier recoil spring installed you could use .45 ACP+P ammo or even .45 Super ammo and go slay your buck. Or better yet, go running through the woods of Tennessee chasing big wild pigs. In competition, it would make a soft-shooting Limited Ten gun for USPSA/IPSC, and if you had a supply of hi-cap mags you could shoot it in Limited. I'm afraid it wouldn't pass in IDPA or GSSF matches, but loaded down in power it would be a really trick falling plate gun.

And how does it shoot? As you'd expect. It is soft in recoil, and as far as accuracy is concerned you can hardly fault it. Our club has a set of gongs on the hundred yard range, and it was no problem to ring them with every hit shooting offhand. In all, I put several hundred rounds through Irv's Glock, and it never failed once.

Sending it back was a sad day, but if I really feel the need, I know where to get one made. Caspian makes the slide, Irv makes the barrels, all the internals are standard factory parts. If you find the barrel doesn't quite fit, Irv can fit it for a small charge. And if it does, then anyone who can take their Glock apart for cleaning can assemble an upper just like this. Or like this and in 10mm, which would be a real hunting powerhouse.

What if the 10mm/.45 framed Glock is just too big? You can duplicate this gun in 9mm, .357 or .40. It's just that Glock has already done it for 9mm and .40, so you wouldn't need to go the full custom parts route. That is, provided you can lay hands on a Glock longslide and barrel. They don't grow on trees. ♦

CHAPTER 31

The Glock Armorer's School

here are two Glock armorer's schools: a one-day school and an advanced, three-day school. Truth be told, if you have any mechanical aptitude at all, and a short-term memory that lasts longer than a few minutes, you can learn everything you need in order to keep your Glock going before lunch. The rest of the time in the one-day armorer's course is to bring the utterly new up to speed and to cover issues that only an armorer for a police department might have to cover.

The three-day class covers everything you'd need in order to work at the Smyrna assembly facility, and handle any problem that might come up. It requires memorization of parts names and demonstrating knowledge of the interchangeability of parts across models. In both classes you'll do timed drills ("Get that Glock apart in 30 seconds....") and recite the names and functions of the various parts. You'll learn all there is to learn about keeping a Glock running and repairing one that isn't. And it is a surprisingly small body of knowledge, for those of us used to the voluminous notes required for a 1911.

Glock manages to pad their armorer's manual, 2002 edition (that's the newest one available) to 72 pages by using large type, lots of white space, and lists of all the parts you can order. If I did the same thing with a 1911 armorer's manual, I couldn't see getting it all in in less than a three-volume set. If I did the Glock armorer's manual in the usual format (like this book) it would take 20 pages.

How do you get in? In the old days, anyone who wanted to could get in. Now you must work as an armorer at a police department that issues or authorizes Glocks, or you must work at a gunshop that sells Glocks. As a mere Glock owner you can't get into the class, but some ferreting out of class location and polite asking might get you in if the class isn't filled, or if someone drops out. If you can't get in, carefully reading the owner's

When you take the armorer's course, you'll get the manual and instruction.

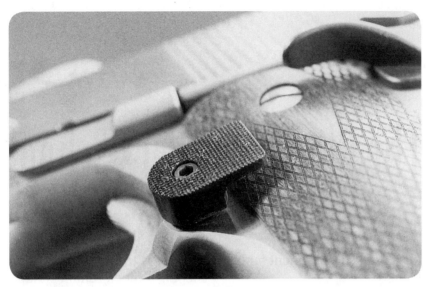

One thing you won't need or get in the Glock course is how to do wild custom things like this 1911 mag button.

manual will give you most everything you need.

Serial Numbers

The first Glock began at serial number AA000. When the first thousand had been made, ending with AA999, the number was changed to AB000. Things went on from there. Once the count had reached ZZ999, (676,000 pistols) the serial numbers were bumped up to AAA000.

European serial number customs are not like those here in the USA. There is a long continental tradition of four-digit serial numbers with letter prefixes or suffixes. The Michigan State Police used to contact us on a regular basis about this or that German Luger we'd bought or sold. Invariably, someone in the previous eighty or ninety years had reported their Luger stolen. The report usually got summarized down

to "Luger, #1234." So, when we reported the transaction of Luger, 9mm 1934 DMW, 4" barrel, g1234, their computer would generate a hit, and we'd get a postcard. So when Glock started off with a two-letter/three-digit serial number it was no great surprise. Imagine their dilemma when they found they were soon going to run out of numbers.

In addition to the AAA000 serial numbers, pistols imported into the USA have a "US" suffix. The suffix doesn't increase the number of serial numbers available to Glock, unless they start using suffixes for other countries, too. The "three and three" serial number plan gets Glock a potential 17 million possible combinations. Twice that, if you then allow duplicate with the "US" suffix. (AAA001US and AAA001 are different, thus doubling the potential.) I think if Glock gets to the point of having used up 34 million serial numbers, they'll be able to think of something.

Special orders also call for special serial numbers. The Miami Police department, like others, gets a special prefix, and to keep them separate from the rest, a four-digit serial number. However, in some future situation, I can see problems with reporting stolen Glocks. "Is that serial number MIA123US, or is it MIA0123US?"

The serial number is important to know not just because wherever you live must use it to fill out the paperwork for ownership. Glock uses it to track

As an armorer, you can upgrade magazines as well as pistols.

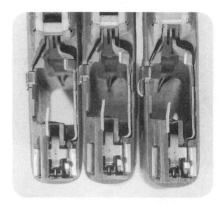

Which ejector goes with which model? You'll memorize that one during the advanced course.

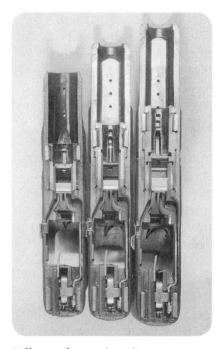

Different frames but the same assembly, disassembly and upgrades.

You can buy the sight pusher and learn how to use it. It isn't that expensive, and it's easy to learn how to use it.

The mystery of connectors, springs and trigger pull will be revealed to you.

production lots. An example is the "E" series recall. (Not really a recall, but if you ask and it needs it, they'll replace your frame.) Not all Glocks made in the E series were affected. Apparently not even all those made between the target dates were affected, either. The only way to find out if your Glock was affected by the production change is to call Glock (866-225-4095) and ask.

Knowing the serial number also lets you track if your Glock was part of the trigger upgrade, and if you have an old or new extractor/ breechface angle.

Or you could just ignore all that and hand your Glock over to the armorer at a GSSF match.

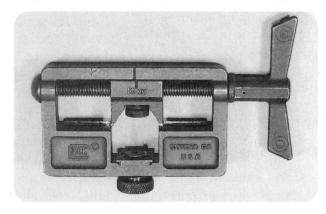

Springs and Parts

The process of the discovery and refinement of spring steel is lost to the mists of time, but the modern use of it is well known. Spring steel is simply iron with a certain amount of carbon in its composition. The varying levels of carbon can further be modified by the heating and cooling cycle used in the steels manufacturing or fabrication as a part. The modern alloy alchemist can create for you a steel for just about any use you would want or need. One thing that is hard to overcome is the tendency of steel to lose its flexibility, or, in shooter's parlance, "take a set."

But unlike earlier steels used for springs, modern spring alloys are a long time taking any kind of a set. The weakest spring in your Glock is the magazine spring. It has the hardest job, gets the least attention, and is most likely to be neglected. But it is easy to determine if your spring is tired. Have you started to get malfunctions at the end of a magazine? Is your Glock not locking open when it is empty? Get a new magazine spring. As discussed in the magazine chapter, magazine springs are easy to get, easy to change, and easy to forget. Get spares. Don't lose them.

What of the rest of the springs in your Glock?

All told, each Glock has six springs in the frame: the recoil spring, the firing pin spring, the slide stop lever spring, the disassembly catch spring, the trigger spring and the magazine catch spring. In reverse order:

Magazine Catch Spring

A simple section of spring wire, the magazine catch spring has an easy job. You can't wear one out and you will probably only need one if you lose the current one on disassembly. Let's do a thought experiment: Assume for the moment that the magazine catch spring is only good for 10,000 flexions. (An absurdly low figure. I'd bet on it going past 100,000.) Flexed once for the magazine to go in, and once for the magazine to exit the frame. Five thousand magazine insertions, at 17 rounds each, gets you 85,000 rounds. If you shoot ammo that only costs you $50 per thousand, that's $4,250 in ammo costs. Not bad, for a dime spring.

And, as I said, if it is more likely to go to 100,000, then add another zero to each figure. At a cost of less than a dollar, keeping a spare is prudent, but don't ever expect to use it. At the newer, more-realistic price of $150/K for ammunition, you'll have shot over $12,000 worth of ammo before that spring even thinks of quitting.

If it does break or you lose it, you'll have to hold the magazine catch in place with a fingertip or duct tape in order to keep using your Glock.

Trigger Spring

Ah, now we're on to something. As above, 10,000 flexions of the magazine catch spring leads to 85,000

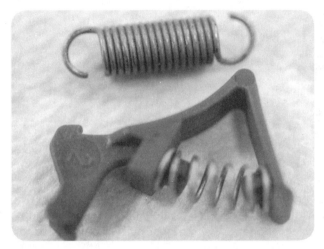

One of the subjects in a Glock armorer's course is trigger parts and their compatibility. The regular spring (*top*) can be replaced with a New York Trigger (*bottom*) but not in all combinations.

flexions of the trigger spring or more, due to dry-firing for disassembly and cleaning. A spare trigger spring is a good thing to have on hand. Is it likely to wear out? Not really, but it might break. After all, if Glock makes springs (or gets them from a subcontractor) that only break under hard use in one case in a few thousand, do you want to be that one?

You'll also need a new spring if you're heavy-handed in cleaning. It is easy enough to wrestle the spring out without damaging it, but some people are capable of breaking rocks. So a spare is a good idea. If you break this spring, your Glock is dead in the water. You'd have to be an enterprising and resourceful gunsmith (and not just a parts-swapping armorer) to modify some other spring to takes it place.

Trigger springs other than the New York Triggers have been known to break. Keep a spare or three. I do.

Disassembly Catch Spring

You know who has spares of these? Glock armorer's

course graduates, that's who. No one else needs them. The thing never breaks, it doesn't come out easily so it is seldom lost, and I've never heard of someone who needed one. Mine is still in my parts kit. If this one breaks, the disassembly catch rides in the down position and your slide rides too far forward when it chambers a round. It may not fire if it goes too far forward. (Good thing the spring never breaks.)

As a field expedient in case of this spring breaking, use pieces of duct tape to hold the disassembly catch in the up position. Ugly, but it works.

Slide Stop Lever Spring

The slide stop lever spring is attached to the slide stop lever, and if it breaks you'll need to replace the whole lever. Luckily, it hardly ever breaks. If it does break, the slide stop will bounce up and down under recoil and might possibly lock the slide open. Again, duct tape is the solution. Tape it down until you can replace it, and realize that your slide won't lock open when the magazine is empty.

Firing Pin Spring

The firing pin spring launches the firing pin forward once the trigger bar lets go of the firing pin tail. A broken spring is a bad thing here, as it means you have a polymer and steel paperweight. You should have a spare in your parts kit, even though a failure to fire caused by the firing pin assembly is more likely to be a ground-up spacer sleeve or firing pin tunnel liner.

Recoil Spring

This is the big one and the one everyone fusses over. "When to replace the spring" is the question that seems to consume many shooters. With the original design, you could measure the free length of the spring and replace it when it has been compressed to some shorter (and essentially arbitrary) length. Me, I replace the factory springs after 5,000 or 10,000 rounds. When using a replacement ISMi spring, I haven't replaced any yet. Testing with a recoil spring in a 1911 showed that after tens of thousands of rounds the spring had not appreciably shortened, so I gave up testing. Since the Glock doesn't seem to work its springs any harder, I don't see any point in replacing otherwise suitable springs with new ones.

The big question other shooters have is "What weight spring should I use?" There seems to be an idea that a lighter spring will cause the pistol to cycle faster, or that a heavier spring will reduce wear or preclude malfunctions with bad ammo or a dirty Glock. They are a combination of competition nuance and range myth. Some shooters read about the winning IPSC shooters using lighter springs in their guns for "faster shooting" and assume the spring is the cause. Actually, the spring is the reaction.

The best shooters use spring weight to time the recoil stroke of the pistol (usually 1911s, but more Glocks are appearing on the line) for them. The idea is to adjust the snap of the pistols cycle force and time in their hand so the sights line up just as the gun settles down from recoil. The timing is a very delicate affair, and can be thrown off by changing loads. (It can be a different bullet, different powder, different velocity, and sometimes it seems like a different phase of the moon has an effect.) Changing the spring makes a difference only for the best shooters, and only in a very small amount. The best comparison I can make would be to a race car. If you can't

take an Indy car through the turns any faster than 150 mph without losing control and putting it into the wall, what difference does it make that a particular brand of tire lets the pro driver take the turns at 220 instead of 210? At 155 mph, you will still be in the wall with either brand.

As for heavier springs precluding malfunctions, remember what pistol we're dealing with here. A Glock isn't going to malfunction. And when it does, the recoil spring you're using isn't going to make any difference.

Shock Buffs

I'm an old-timer. I learned on the Browning pistols, and was brought up as a shooter as a worshiper of John Moses. I'm still not sure about full-length guide rods in a 1911, and every now and then the feel of a polymer frame just send shivers up my spine.

Here's perhaps the most useful tool I encountered in the Glock armorer's school. This is a cruciform engagement inspection plate. It lets you see how much of the striker tail the cruciform actually contacts. Of course, you could make one with a regular plate and some spray paint.

A shock buffer will take the bang out of recoil.

For the longest time I resisted the use of shock buffs. The theory is that by using a sacrifical buffer to soak up the impact, you extend the life of the frame. My problem with the theory is that 1911 frames (for the longest time, the only one I was concerned about) work for hundreds of thousands of rounds without a buffer. And some guns didn't like buffers, chewing them up or occasionally locking open before they were empty.

What changed my mind was the feel. Some pistols felt much softer in recoil when there was a shock buff in place, much softer than you'd otherwise think. For those pistols that chewed them up (causing the shredded plastic to create function problems) or that locked open, I don't use buffs. For the rest, I do. In the Glocks tested, I used Mag Cinch buffers and had no problems. And as with the 1911 testing I did, some guns would feel significantly softer in recoil than others, using the same buff and the same ammo. I can only surmise that some very small difference in the dimensions of the pistols involved and the shock buff

Depending on how far you are from resupply, you may want to take along a pouch with spare parts and cleaning supplies.

installed lets one pistol react more favorably to the buff than another would.

In summary, the number of parts you might need for your Glock is small, and they're more likely to need replacement due to loss than to wear.

And if you can get a slot into the armorer's school, do it. Even if you never need the knowledge and can't get any of the goodies due to not being in a police department or working at a gun shop, you'll still have a good time.   ♦

Appendix: Suppliers

Advantage Arms, Inc.
25163 West Avenue Stanford
Valencia, CA. 91355
661-257-2290
www.advantagearms.com

Arredondo
1913 Fernridge Dr.
San Dimas, CA. 91773
909-596-9597
www.arredondoaccesories.com

Jerry Barnhart
Tactical Shooting Technology
P.O. Box 426
Oxford, MI. 48371
248-628-6301
http://ic.net/~burner

Bar-sto Precision Machine
73377 Sullivan Rd.
P.O. Box 1838
Twentynine Palms, CA. 92277
760-367-2747
www.barsto.com

Brownells
200 S. Front St.
Montezuma, IA. 50171
641-623-5401
www.brownells.com

California Competition Works
P.O. Box 4821
Culver City, CA. 90231
Fax: 310-839-4256

Caspian Arms Ltd.
P.O. Box 465
Hardwick, VT. 05843
802-472-6454
www.caspianarms.com

CPMi
352 Coogan Way
El Cajon, CA. 92020
619-579-9963

Dawson Precision, Inc.
3585 CR 272
Suite 300
Leander, TX. 78641
512-260-2011
www.competitionshooters.com

Dillon Precision
8009 E. Dillons Way
Scottsdale, AZ. 85260
480-948-8009
www.dillonprecision.com

EGW
4050 Skyron Dr.
Doylestown, PA. 18901
215-348-9892
www.egw-guns.com

EO Tech/Holosight
3600 Green Ct
Suite 400
Ann Arbor, MI. 48105
734-741-8868
www.eotech-inc.com

Fobus USA
1300 B3 Industrial Dr.
Southampton, PA. 18966
215-355-2621
www.fobusholster.com

Galco International Ltd.
2019 Quail Ave.
Phoenix, AZ. 85027
623-434-7070
www.usgalco.com

Grams Engineering
2435 Norse Ave.
Costa Meas, CA. 92627
www.GramsEng.com

Glock USA & GSSF
600 Highlands Parkway
Smyrna, GA. 30082
770-432-1202
www.gssf.com

Handgunner Shootoff
Paul Miller, San Juan Range
19878 Dave Wood Road
Montrose, CO. 81401
970-249-4227
www.sanjuanrange.com

Heinie Specialty Products
301 Oak St.
Quincy, IL. 62301-2500
309-543-4535
309-543-2521 Fax
www.heinie.com

IDPA
P.O. Box 639
Berryville, AR. 72616
870-545-3886
www.idpa.com

ISMI
P.O. Box 204
Carthage, IN. 46115
765-565-6108
www.ismi-gunsprings.com

KKM Precision
26 Affonso Dr #101
Carson city, NV. 89706
775-246-5444
www.kkmprecision.com

LaPrade (Scherer magazines)
Rt 10 240 A-1
Tazewell, TN. 37879
Fax: 423-733-2073

**London Bridge Trading
Company**
3509 Virginia Beach Blvd.
Virginia Beach, VA. 23452
757-498-0207
www.londonbridgetrading.com

Mas Ayoob - LFI
P.O. Box 122
Concord, NH. 03301
603-224-6814
www.ayoob.com

Dave Manson Reamers
8200 Embury Rd.
Grand Blanc, MI. 48439
810-953-0732
www.mansonreamers.com

Mech-Tech systems, Inc.
P.O. Box 5517
Kalispell, MT. 59903
888-844-8317
www.mechtechsys.com

Ransom Intl Corp.
1027 Spirie Dr.
Prescott, AZ. 86302
928-778-7899
www.ransom-intl.com

Rauch & Co, LTD
P.O. Box 510
Lafayette Hill, PA. 194440
610-825-4245

The Robar Companies
21438 N. 7th Avenue
Suite B
Phoenix, AZ. 85027
602-581-2648
www.robarguns.com

Shooting Systems
205 Lange Dr.
P.O. Box 245
Washington, MO. 63090
800-325-3049
www.shootingsystems.com

Starline
1300 West Henry St.
P.O. Box 833
Sedalia, MO. 65301
800-280-6660
www.starlinebrass.com

The Steel Challenge
818-897-5965
www.isishootists.com

Streamlight
1030 West Germantown Pike
Norristown, PA. 19403
610-631-0600
www.streamlight.com

STI
114 Halmar Cove
Georgetown, TX. 78628
512-819-0656
www.sti-guns.com

Sure Fire
18300 Mt. Baldy Circle
Fountain Valley, CA. 92708-
6122
714-545-9444
www.surefire.com

Taylor Freelance
8196 Quinault Rd.
Blaine, WA. 98230
360-371-2228
www.taylorfreelance.com

Trijicon
49385 Shafer Ave.
Wixom, MI. 48393
800-338-0563
www.trijicon.com

Triton Ammunition
P.O. Box 50
Wappingers Falls, NY. 12590
800-861-3362
www.tritonammo.com

**United States Practical
Shooting Association**
P.O. Box 811
Sedro Wooley, WA. 98284
360-855-2245
www.uspsa.org

The Wilderness
5130 North 19th Ave
Suite 7
Phoenix, AZ. 85015
602-242-4945
www.thewilderness.com

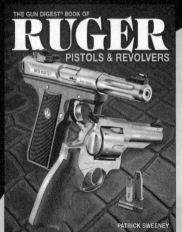
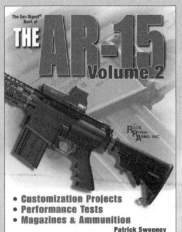
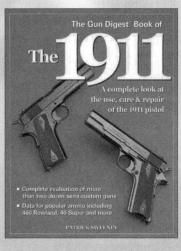

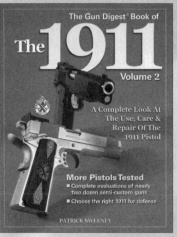